THE QUESTION
OF THE COMMONS

The Question of the Commons

THE CULTURE AND ECOLOGY OF COMMUNAL RESOURCES

Bonnie J. McCay

James M. Acheson

editors

THE UNIVERSITY OF ARIZONA PRESS

Tucson

THE UNIVERSITY OF ARIZONA PRESS

Copyright © 1987
The Arizona Board of Regents
All Rights Reserved

This book was set in 10½/13 Linotron-202 Palatino.
Manufactured in the U.S.A.

Library of Congress Cataloging-in-Publication Data

The Question of the commons : the culture and ecology of communal
   resources / Bonnie J. McCay, James M. Acheson, editors.
      p. cm. — (Arizona studies in human ecology)
   Bibliography: p.
   Includes index.
   ISBN 0-8165-0972-7 (alk. paper)
      1. Human ecology—Case studies.   2. Natural resources, Communal-
-Case studies.   I. McCay, Bonnie J.   II. Acheson, James M.
III. Series.
   GF49.Q47 1987
   333.7′2—dc 19   87-19833
                                                              CIP

British Library Cataloguing in Publication data are available.

Contents

II.   SPECIFYING THE COMMONS

III.   THE STATE AND THE COMMONS

About the Authors

E. N. Anderson, Jr. has done fieldwork in Hong Kong, Malaysia, and British Columbia, primarily in fisheries development and fishing communities. His interests include food production and consumption, nutrition, ethnobiology, and cognitive anthropology. Among his publications are *The Floating World of Castle Peak Bay, Mountains and Water*, and *Fishing in Troubled Waters*, the last two coauthored with Marja L. Anderson. He has been a professor of anthropology at the University of California, Riverside, since 1966.

Dan Bauer, a member of the Department of Anthropology and Sociology at Lafayette College, became interested in relationships between self-interest and communal institutions while a Peace Corps volunteer in Peru. His research among the Tigray of Ethiopia and the Chinatec of Oaxaca, Mexico, concentrates on local-level economic and political relations, particularly as they relate to land tenure. Among his publications is *Household and Society in Ethiopia*. He received his Ph.D. in social anthropology at the University of Rochester.

Fikret Berkes has been the director of the Institute of Urban and Environmental Studies at Brock University, St. Catharines, Ontario, since 1980. His educational background combines marine ecology with postdoctorate training in anthropology. He has published some thirty journal articles and book chapters on the interaction of human societies with their living resources and on related topics, and has participated in a number of international debates on common property resource management.

Robert A. Brightman's professional interests include structural anthropology, anthropological linguistics, ecological anthropology, hunter-gatherer societies, ethnohistory, and native North America. He has conducted research among Rock Cree in northwestern Manitoba, Houma and Chitimacha in Louisiana, and Potawatomi in Wisconsin and Michigan. His publications include *As My Informants Tell Me: George Nelson on Cree and Northern Ojibwa Religion and Legend* (coauthored with Jennifer Brown). He has been assistant professor of anthropology at the University of Wisconsin, Madison, since 1983.

JAMES CARRIER first did fieldwork on Ponam Island, Manus Province, in 1978. He has made detailed studies of Ponam fishing practices, marine tenure, and islanders' attitudes toward the natural world around them. He was senior lecturer and head of the Department of Anthropology and Sociology of the University of Papua New Guinea until 1986.

E. PAUL DURRENBERGER has done fieldwork among Lisu and Shan in Thailand, Icelandic farmers, and, with Gísli Pálsson, commercial Icelandic fishermen. His research and publications have been on peasant economics, law, religion, cognitive anthropology, and maritime anthropology. Among his publications is *Chayanov, Peasants, and Economic Anthropology*. He received his Ph.D. from the University of Illinois, Urbana, in 1971 and has been a professor of anthropology at the University of Iowa since 1972.

JAMES W. FERNANDEZ, professor of anthropology, was at Princeton University from 1975 to 1986 and is now at the University of Chicago. He received his Ph.D. in anthropology at Northwestern University under Melville Herskovits and received the Herskovits Prize of the African Studies Association in 1983 for his book *Bwiti: An Ethnography of the Religious Imagination in Africa*. His field research has been in sub-Saharan Africa and in Spain, and he is the author of numerous articles in professional journals and coeditor of two special issues of the *American Ethnologist* on cognitive and symbolic anthropology.

RAYMOND HAMES received his doctoral degree from the University of California, Santa Barbara, in 1978 and began teaching at the University of Nebraska-Lincoln in 1980. He has done fieldwork among the Yanomamo and Yekwana peoples of Venezuela and in Paraguay on topics in evolutionary and behavioral ecology and economic anthropology. He is co-editor of *Adaptive Response of Native Amazonians* (1983).

ELINOR OSTROM, codirector of the Workshop in Political Theory and Policy Analysis, has been a professor of Political Science at Indiana University since 1965. Her research interests are the problems of common-property resources (particularly water resources), the problems of organizing multilevel governmental systems for effective urban service delivery, and the effects of institutional arrangements on processes of development in the Third World.

GÍSLI PÁLSSON, an associate professor of anthropology at the University of Iceland, has done fieldwork in Iceland and the Cape Verde Islands. Most of his work has focused on maritime anthropology and the ethnography of communication. His publications include studies of territoriality among Icelandic fishermen and numerous articles on fishing coauthored with E. Paul Durrenberger. He received his Ph.D. in social anthropology from the University of Manchester in 1982.

PAULINE E. PETERS has held a joint appointment at Harvard University as assistant professor in the Department of Anthropology and institute associate at the Harvard Institute for International Development since 1982. She was educated at the University of Wales (Cardiff), the London School of Economics, and Boston University, where she received her Ph.D. in 1983. Her research interests include issues of agrarian change, political and economic transformations, and policy and practice in directed change with particular reference to central and southern Africa.

EVELYN PINKERTON, a Research Associate with the School of Community and Regional Planning, University of British Columbia, has taught anthropology there, and participated with other faculty in a major research project on the B.C. fishing industry. She has authored some dozen articles on natural resource management, the northwest coast fishery, and local communities' relationships to resource management. She organized a workshop on comanagement in May 1986, and her current interests include class conflict and development in a B.C. fishing-logging village.

ANTHONY STOCKS, an associate professor at Idaho State University, received his Ph.D. in anthropology at the University of Florida in 1978. His research, primarily in the upper Amazon of Peru, centers on human ecology, the Upper Amazon Indians, and social uses of anthropology. Among his publications is *Los Nativos Invisibles*.

LAWRENCE TAYLOR grew up in the clamming territory of Suffolk County, Long Island, and received his Ph.D. in Anthropology from the State University of New York at Stony Brook. He has been an associate professor of Anthropology at Lafayette College since 1978. His publications include *Dutchmen on the Bay* (an ethnohistorical study of Dutch immigrant oystermen on Long Island) and articles on his fieldwork in Donegal, Ireland, and on maritime and other topics in Europe and America.

RALPH E. TOWNSEND, a native of Eastport, Maine, has had a long interest in New England Fisheries. He received his Ph.D. from the University of Wisconsin in 1983 and has been an assistant professor of economics at the University of Maine since 1980. His research interests include the regulation and economics of fisheries.

PATRICIA J. VONDAL received her Ph.D. in Anthropology from Rutgers University in 1984. From 1981 to 1983 she conducted research on a successful, locally developed, regional poultry industry in South Kalimantan, Indonesia, and examined its relevance for rural development. In 1986–87 she was an American Association for the Advancement of Science fellow in the U.S. Department of State, Agency for International Development, Washington, D.C.

JAMES WILSON, chairman of the Scientific and Statistical Committee of the New England Fisheries Council, has been a professor of economics and marine resources at the University of Maine, Orono, since 1968. He helped prepare the U.S. arguments for the World Court arbitration of the Georges Bank/Gulf of Maine maritime boundary problem with Canada and initiated and helped develop a fisheries display auction in Portland. His academic work has emphasized observation and transactions cost analysis. He received his Ph.D. in economics from the University of Wisconsin in 1971.

Preface

THE SECOND HALF OF THE TWENTIETH CENTURY may someday be recalled as the time that we became painfully aware of the social and ecological costs of industrialization, rising populations, and unsound resource management. Industrialized nations routinely report problems of acid rain, ocean pollution, soil erosion, fisheries failures, and the seepage of toxic wastes. The Third World is plagued by soil erosion, deforestation, and the depletion and extinction of wildlife. Costs of environmental damage in the Third World are too often realized immediately in the loss of human health and life. In the wealthy industrialized nations, people increasingly suspect that they too are not immune.

Problems such as those outlined above are explicable as tragic outcomes of common property tenure (Hardin 1968). Garrett Hardin's phrase "tragedy of the commons" is one of several born in the liberal reawakening and "greening" of America in the 1960s and early 1970s and whose metaphorical and political power still resonates. Others include "blaming the victim," "small is beautiful," and "Spaceship Earth."

According to the theory popularized by Hardin, all resources owned in common—air, oceans, fish, grasslands, and so on—are or eventually will be overexploited. When resources such as trees, clean water, even the right to bear children, are "free" or open to everyone, costs arising from their use and abuse can be passed on to others. The rational individual has the incentive to take as much as possible before someone else does. No one is motivated to take responsibility for the resources. Because they belong to everyone, no one protects them. The causes of overpopulation, environmental degradation, resource depletion—even poverty, crime, and other social evils—may be found in freedom and equality.

Hardin's most important message was that we cannot rely on normal market forces nor on people's best intentions to save their environments and themselves. Problems such as overpopulation, water pollution, and deforestation have formal characteristics—their "common property" nature—that motivate people to behave in ways that are in neither society's best interests nor, ultimately, their own. In the 1960s and early 1970s, when environmentalists, social reformers, conservationists, and others were trying to gain more government support to redress social and environmental problems, the only thinkable solution to commons dilemmas was government intervention. In the 1980s, in tune with a more conservative political cast to public policy in America, Canada, and other nations, the same problems and the same theory trigger discussion of another solution: privatization.

Scholars in many disciplines, ranging from economics and psychology to biology, have explored the dilemma of the commons and debated its solutions. Anthropologists, too—in their studies of subsistence economics, cultural ecology, property rights, law, and social evolution—have addressed the issue of common property, bringing with them a rich tradition of inquiry into the relations between human groups and natural resources. This book contains seventeen original essays: fourteen by anthropologists, one by a biologist, one by a political scientist, and one by two economists. They depict and analyze cultural and situational variation in human relationships to natural resources and contribute to an anthropology and human ecology of the commons.

We cast our net widely in this effort to "capture" and make anthropological sense out of the commons. The subjects of the case studies in this volume include fishermen of Malaysia, the Pacific Northwest, Maine, New Jersey, Ireland, and Papua New Guinea; native hunters and fishermen of northern Canada and the Amazon; pastoralists of southern Africa; and mixed farmers of Ethiopia, Switzerland, Japan, Spain, and Borneo.

The case studies and introductory essay review and evaluate the theory of the tragedy of the commons. The explanatory simplicity of the tragedy of the commons is seductive—perhaps dangerously and disarmingly so—to social scientists in search of embracing, elegant theories that seem to offer some of the legitimacy of the "harder" social sciences such as economics and game theory. Moreover, the theory of the commons and the questions and ideas derived from it and from its critics touch upon, reawaken, and contribute to classical concerns in the social sciences, concerns that go beyond natural resource management and environmental problems. Foremost among these is the relationship between individual behavior and social welfare, a question well known to Locke, Hobbes, Adam Smith, and others and reiterated in recent concerns about relationships between individual and system interests in the social sciences and in biology.

A focus on common property and the institutions and meanings of "the commons" also brings us to other questions of sociocultural, economic, and ecological anthropology. What do "the commons," "communal activity," and "communal tenure" mean for different groups of people? How are the meanings of these symbols, social institutions, and human realities expressed, solidified, and transformed in the course of human negotiation and conflict? How do they relate to other symbols, institutions, and patterns of behavior and resource use? How do property rights and land use change in response to shifting demographic, ecological, and sociopolitical conditions? How can we know whether human behaviors, customs, rules and regulations, and beliefs and ideologies have conservationist functions, manifest or latent, and whether they represent "adaptations" for that purpose? Each of these concerns is reflected in one or more of the essays.

We held two symposia and one workshop to create the book. We had long been interested in the common-property paradigm from our work in fisheries as well as our theoretical concerns about ecological anthropology, adaptation, and economic organization. We looked for others who shared our interests and wanted to explore them further. To this end we organized a symposium at the International Congress of Anthropological and Ethnological Sciences in Quebec City, August 1983, and one at the Annual Meeting of the Society for Applied Anthropology in Toronto, March 1984. Meanwhile, we solicited papers from other scholars. With support from the Maine and New Jersey Sea Grant Programs, we organized a workshop, held in Maine in July 1984, to discuss the papers and the topics of the volume as part of the editing process. Afterward we continued to work closely with the authors to produce the book.

We appreciate the financial support for the meetings, the workshop, and the book given to us by the Maine-New Hampshire Sea

Grant Program; the Center for Marine Studies, University of Maine; the National Sea Grant Office, NOAA, U.S. Department of Commerce; and the New Jersey Sea Grant Program in two grants—NA83AA-D-0034 and NJSG-87-152. We are particularly indebted to Robert Abel of the New Jersey Sea Grant Program and Ron Dearborn and Robert Wall of the Main-New Hampshire Sea Grant Program. Special thanks go to Charles Bishop, Harvey Feit, Peter Fricke, Michael Orbach, M. Estellie Smith, and John Gatewood for their invaluable contributions to the workshop and symposia, to George Grant for apt use of a red pen, and to Robert Netting for his editorial guidance. To Ann Acheson and Richard Merritt we are indebted for their good humor and supreme patience as well as editing, and we thank June Needham, Nadya Silva, and other members of our department staffs for their forbearance and help. Above all we thank the authors. The book is the realization of a common endeavor.

Bonnie J. McCay
James M. Acheson

1 Human Ecology of the Commons

Bonnie J. McCay and James M. Acheson

IN 1968 THE BIOLOGIST AND HUMAN ECOLOGIST Garrett Hardin vaulted a theory that he called "the tragedy of the commons" from its place in textbooks, obscure nineteenth-century tracts, and the memos of colonial officers and modern management agencies to its current position as "the dominant framework within which social scientists portray environmental and resource issues" (Godwin and Shepard 1979: 265). The theory is powerful and controversial. It poses irreconcilable contradictions between individual and system interests. It locates the source of the problem in "common property," broadly understood to mean free and unregulated access to scarce resources.

This collection of original essays is an anthropological and ecological approach to the theory, the controversies surrounding it, and the phenomenon of "the commons." The chapters are grouped into three sections. The first, "Conservation and the Commons," brings ethnographic, ecological, and historical studies of hunter-gatherers and fishermen in the subarctic, the Amazon, Papua New Guinea, and the United States to bear on the topics of what conservation is, how it can be measured, and how it is related to common and other property rights. Chapters in the second section, "Specifying the Commons," address issues of community and the commons, sharing recognition that common property is a social institution. Included in this section are studies of farming, pastoral, and marine communal institutions in Indonesia, Ireland, Spain, Ethiopia, and Botswana, and the United States. The last section, "The State and the Commons," includes an economic analysis of public policy concerning fisheries management and three chapters that explore interrelationships among government agencies, local communities, and user groups in commercial fisheries of Malaysia, Iceland, and Canada.

1

THE TRAGEDY OF THE COMMONS

The idea that common property causes trouble is an old and persistent part of Western culture. Aristotle recognized it two thousand years ago: "that which is common to the greatest number has the least care bestowed upon it" (cited in Cass and Edney 1978: 372). This theory of the commons has played a strong role in longstanding debates over the enclosure of the Old World commons, rationales for the imposition of new forms of land tenure in the colonized world, and attempts to explain disasters such as rapid soil erosion and deforestation and the Sahelian famine of the early 1970s (see, for example, Picardi and Seifert 1977). The theory is general enough to have been applied even to the African slave trade (Thomas and Bean 1974), urban mugger-victim relationships (Neher 1978), and rice harvesting institutions in Java (Sturgess and Wijaya 1983). As the paradigm for "social dilemmas" involving discrepancies between "micromotives" and "macrobehavior" (Schelling 1978), it has been the subject of experiments by psychologists (Dawes 1980), particularly in the game theory form known as the "prisoner's dilemma." It is fundamental to scientific resource management in fisheries, forestry, soil conservation, rangelands, and other fields, and plays a quiet but strong role in social policy.

The Calf, the Child, and the Commons

Hardin's (1968) intent is to show how the freedom to have children leads to overpopulation. He bases his argument on an obscure early-nineteenth-century tract by William Lloyd (1833) who was engaged in the reigning debate about the political economy of population, labor, and the Poor Laws. Hardin's exposition closely follows that source, which he acknowledges and includes in a collection of essays (Hardin and Baden 1977). We shall also rely on the original to explain the theory of the tragedy of the commons.

Lloyd offered an analogy between the pastoral commons of old England and the labor market, and between a calf and a human child, the one armed with "a set of teeth and the ability to graze," the other with a "pair of hands competent to labor" (Lloyd 1977: 11). Rights to enter both the pastoral commons and the labor market are freely obtainable—common rights—and thus pastures are inevitably overstocked and their resources depleted, and labor markets are oversaturated, causing the low wages and miseries of the laboring classes.

Neither resowing the field nor raising the wages of labor would solve those problems because, given the freedom to put animals on the pasture and to bear children, overstocking and overpopulation will only recur. This analysis supported Malthus's pessimistic view of population problems: improved living conditions would merely prompt the production of more children who would soon saturate the commons again and reproduce the conditions of poverty.

Lloyd identified what is now called the problem of "externalities" (see Cheung 1970) as central to the commons dilemma. People are unlikely to restrain their own behavior when the immediate benefits of their actions are their own but the costs are passed on to society as a whole (or other specific groups), and any longer-term or external benefits that might accrue from an individual's self-instigated "moral preventive checks" are undiscernible. Lloyd posed the problem of overpopulation in these terms:

> It is idle to imagine, that, among laborers who have only the sale of their labor on which to depend for their maintenance, such abstinence can ever generally prevail; and this for the simple reason, that, against it, there are the natural passions which prompt to marriage, and the substantial benefits derivable from marriage while, in favor of it, to oppose these, there is no adequate individual benefit to be derived from abstinence. . . . His individual act could produce no sensible effect on the market of labor. (Lloyd 1977: 12–13)

More familiar to most readers is Hardin's version of the same argument. It combines Lloyd's image of the old English commons with the language of marginal utility from economics. A herdsman puts his animals on a pasture that he uses in common with other herdsmen. Even though there are signs that the condition of the pasture will worsen with additional stocking, it is only rational for each herdsman to add more animals to his herd because he gains the full benefits of each additional animal while sharing the costs of overgrazing (the externalities) with the other herdsmen. The positive utility to the individual herdsman of adding an extra animal is +1; the negative utility is but a fraction of −1. When resources are limited, the rational decisions of each individual add up to an irrational dilemma for the group. Freedom becomes tragic:

> The rational herdsman concludes that the only sensible course for him to pursue is to add another animal to his herd. And another; and another . . . but this is the conclusion reached by each and every rational herdsman sharing a commons. Therein lies the tragedy. Each man is locked into a system that compels him to increase his herd without limit—in a world that is limited. . . . Freedom in a commons brings ruin for all. (Hardin 1968: 1244)

Economics, Politics, and the Commons

Economists interested in fisheries and other natural resources have honed the fine points of the ideas behind Lloyd's and Hardin's concept of the tragedy of the commons. They have also observed that there are limits to this process: there is an equilibrium point at which the individual's marginal gain from adding one more animal to his herd is no longer greater than the marginal costs. However, this point is far beyond that of "maximum sustained yield" or the sustainable productivity of the system; it may be even beyond the point of maximum profitability (Gordon 1954, Scott 1955; Townsend and Wilson this volume).

Overcapitalization results. In an open-access system, when there is any profit at all to be made, new entrants are likely to be attracted despite evidence of decline in the productivity of the resource (Crutchfield and Pontecorvo 1969). Typically, far more "firms" and tools of production are employed in the exploitation of common property resources than are needed to harvest them efficiently. Overcapitalized firms are capable of harvesting resources at a rapid rate. Given their competition, they usually do just that. Overcapitalization also makes the job of resource managers difficult. Those "excess" producers are trying to make a living. They interact with politicians and resource managers to protect their interests, often by trying to prevent drastic changes in the system (Crutchfield 1979; for case studies in this volume see Pinkerton, and Durrenberger and Pálsson; for a similar analysis of interactions between American Indian herders and the Bureau of Indian Affairs see Johnson and Libecap 1980).

The tragedy is both environmental and economic. It is in no one's long-term interest. It is nonetheless inevitable unless something is done to intervene in the workings of the commons or to transform common property into private property. It is assumed that the users will not change the system themselves.

The popularity of the model may be related to its ability to generate both liberal and conservative political solutions. The idea of the tragedy of the commons became an influential way to argue that government must take a stronger role in dealing with problems of population, society, and the environment. A seemingly contradictory message—that government should leave this role to individuals and the private sector by encouraging privatization—is also carried by the metaphor and the theories that lie behind it (see DeGregori 1974).

Privatization and the Commons

In Lloyd's early-nineteenth-century terms, privatized rights create "a degree of isolation, by which the consequences, whether good or evil, flowing from the actions of individuals, can be more fully appropriated to the authors of them" (1977: 13). In modern terms, privatization internalizes costs and benefits, reduces uncertainty, and thereby increases individual responsibility for the environment and rational use of its resources (Demsetz 1967; Furobotn and Pejovich 1972). In common-property situations the market fails to do its job; privatization restores the working of Adam Smith's "invisible hand" of the marketplace.

From the economists' perspective, private property is more efficient than and therefore preferable to common property (but see Bromley 1982a, who argues that two sets of property rights cannot be compared this way since property rights themselves, through their effects on markets and prices, determine what is efficient). Most of the policy options proposed to resolve problems attributed to common property rights involve either giving some degree of exclusive rights over resources or developing "property-mimicking" ways of restricting and allocating access to resources (Townsend and Wilson this volume). In 1833 Lloyd offered a similar and similarly controversial way to solve the overpopulation problem:

> Since the earth can never maintain all who can offer themselves for maintenance, it is better that its produce should be divided into shares of a definite magnitude, sufficient each for the comfortable maintenance of a family, whence the number of families to be maintained would be determined from the number of such shares, than that all, who can possibly enter, should be first admitted, and then the magnitude of each share be determined from the number of admissions. (Lloyd 1977: 14)

CRITICAL PERSPECTIVES

Hardin's tragedy of the commons is a model and as such is abstract and simplified. The case studies in this book explore the historical, social, economic, and cultural contexts of the behavior of people involved in common property and communal activity. Even Lloyd (1977), lecturing in 1833, had a notion of the social and historical context of the overpopulation problem that he sought to explain by using the commons model. In the past, he observed, the "field for the employment of labor did not consist of one vast common as at present, but rather of many little commons distinct from each other" (1977: 13–14). Although there were enough poor people to keep wages down—and hence reduce the rewards of controlled reproduction—"much more must this be the case, when, by the change of circumstances, all barriers have been broken down, and the communication is free throughout England, Scotland, and Ireland" (1977:14). Accordingly, the fact that the labor market was "common property" is an inadequate explanation of the miserable wages received by the poor in the British Isles. Lloyd's notes on historical context suggest that capitalism and industrialization established the conditions for a tragedy of the commons.

One cannot properly generalize from the tragedy-of-the-commons model without incorporating contextual factors (Vayda 1986), such as, for example, the presence or absence of rules about uses of the commons, alternatives to exploitation of common resources, ways of monitoring and controlling the behavior of others in a commons, and so forth. Ignoring these contextual factors, many of which are assumptions built into the model, leads to the mistake of assuming that because people are engaged in common-property activity, they are involved in a tragedy of the commons.

Unfortunately, many of those using the tragedy-of-the-commons model have failed to recognize its assumptions and verify their applicability to the case at hand. Among those assumptions are that common property is always of the open-access variety; that the users are selfish, unrestricted by social norms of the community, and trying to maximize short-term gains; that the users have perfect information; and that the resource is being used so intensively that overexploitation and depletion are possible.

The individualistic bias of most commons models leads to underestimates of the ability of people to cooperate in commons situations (Runge 1981; Kimber 1981) and contributes to the tendency to avoid social, historical, and institutional analysis (see Bromley 1982). The model of the tragedy of the commons fails to recognize the social nature of property institutions, even though Western law, like the customs and law of many non-Western groups (Bohannan 1963; Hoebel 1954: 48), clearly conceives of property in social terms: "property rights do not refer to relations between men and things, but, rather, *to the sanctioned behavioral relations among men that arise from the existence of things and pertain to their use*" (Furobotn and Pejovich 1972: 1139, italics in original).

Moreover, as most authors in this volume assume, property rights are thoroughly embedded in historically specific social contexts whose meanings vary. Malinowski saw this many years ago (1926). The ownership of large canoes used for fishing by Trobriand islanders had been described as a simple version of communism: "the canoe appears to be owned jointly by a group and used indiscriminately by the whole community" (Malinowski 1926: 18). However, Malinowski found that common property, with joint owners, included not only equal rights of use but also complex and variable systems of rights, duties, functions, and obligations. The Trobriand institution also balanced individual and collective interests held to be irreconcilable in common property situations:

> "On a close inquiry we discover in this pursuit a definite system of division of functions and a rigid system of mutual obligations, into which *a sense of duty and the recognition of the need of co-operation enter side by side with a realization of self-interest, privileges and benefits.*

Ownership, therefore, can be defined neither by such words as 'communism' nor 'individualism', nor by reference to 'joint-stock company' system or 'personal enterprise', but by the concrete facts and conditions of use. It is the sum of duties, privileges, and mutualities which bind the joint owners to the object and to each other." (Malinowski 1926: 20–21; emphasis added)

Like communism in Trobriand canoe ownership, private property in fishing (Carrier, this volume) or other endeavors can be woefully misinterpreted. Once we pay attention to the "concrete facts and conditions of use" emphasized by Malinowski, private property too is seen to be a complex set of social duties, privileges, and mutualities (Bromley 1982; Dowling 1975), not a necessary and "natural" evolutionary response to resource scarcity (compare Demsetz 1967 and other property rights theorists, who see the transition to private property as an inevitable and natural response to resource scarcity).

The thesis of the tragedy of the commons fails to distinguish between common property as a theoretical condition in which there are no relevant institutions (open access) and common property as a social institution (the commons). The assumption that common property is the same thing as open-access is historically inaccurate. It also leads to arguments that restrictions on access are the only effective means of resolving commons problems, arguments that, when implemented, have led to tragedies of people dispossessed of their livelihoods by the enclosure of common lands (Ciriacy-Wantrup and Bishop 1975; see Hoskins and Stamp 1963). In true common property situations, rights of access or use are shared equally *and* are exclusive to a defined group of people. "Common property is not 'everybody's property' " (Ciriacy-Wantrup and Bishop 1975: 715), although it may be perceived and acted upon that way in specific circumstances. *Common property* should refer to an exclusive as well as inclusive notion of the commonwealth involved. It should refer to specified sets of use-rights (Anderson; Durrenberger and Pálsson, this volume). Specification implies some degree of legal or customary agreement and hence social concern and perhaps conflict about the use of common resources. Even the open-access version of common property may be specified (McCay, this volume). Designated common rights may be general and public or specific and contingent upon other rights, part of "the web of use-rights" (Thompson 1975) underlying the moral economy of human communities.

Another problem is the tendency to restrict solutions to the commons dilemma to the intervention of external authority on the one hand and privatization of property rights on the other, thereby ignoring the existence and potentials of other solutions, including user-group or local-community management of common property resources (Demsetz 1967; Anderson and Hill 1977; Ostrom 1977), a major focus of this volume. This tendency is promoted by another faulty assumption: that private property protects resources from abuse and waste, and common property does not. The literature on pastoralists, farmers, and others throughout the world shows that resource conservation is not ensured by the private-property status of resources (Gilles and Jamtgaard 1982). The development of "sod-busting" legislation at federal and local levels in the United States to protect landholders from dust blown over by tillage on neighboring marginal lands (Ebenreck 1984) is but one social response among many to the fact that private landholders can be no more socially and ecologically responsible than common property users of natural resources. More generally, it is important to specify what "common" and "private" mean and to understand conflicts over those meanings in particular situations and times.

The thesis of the tragedy of the commons also reduces the causes of environmental decay and economic loss to the nature of property rights instead of acknowledging the role of more complex features of socioeconomic systems. In their summary of the economic model of natural resource problems, Moloney and Pearse (1979) state: "The problem is clearly rooted in the nature of property rights. . . ." (1979: 860). Hardin takes this reductionist stance further: "It is not capitalism but the system of the commons that fails to furnish the adequate incentive" (Hardin 1977a: 6). This view is controversial. It can be argued that the common-property status of resources is neither a necessary nor a sufficient explanation of resource depletion and economic impoverishment. Problems blamed on common property rights, such as depletion of resources and impoverishment of communities, may be more closely related to capitalism and other manifestations of a colonialized and industrialized world than to common property per se (Franke and Chasin 1980; Emmerson 1980). The decline of the commons in England,

Europe, and elsewhere has had little to do with problems intrinsic to common property rights (Cox 1985; Fernandez, Peters, Taylor, this volume). Moreover, the effect of how users discount the future on the rationale for conservation behavior is largely independent of property rights (Clark 1973, Fife 1977). These and other critical points are made by the authors throughout the book in the context of their analyses of ethnographic and historical information on the commons in diverse times, places, and cultures.

The authors also address interpretative problems stemming from the criticisms themselves. One is the tendency to romanticize human communities and their abilities to apply wisdom and foresight in their relationships with their resources and each other. The authors in Part I, "Conservation and the Commons," correct that tendency by bringing empirical, theoretically informed research to the topics of the conditions under which resource conservation takes place, what conservation is, and how it can be measured.

Second, economists, social psychologists, and political scientists who have criticized the tragedy of the commons and related "prisoner's dilemma" models emphasize interdependence, communication, and cooperation as facts of the human condition that can lead to less inexorably tragic outcomes. The messages and findings are important, but the social facts involved require further specification and location in history, culture, and society. The authors of chapters in Part II, "Specifying the Commons," address that requirement.

Last, reactions to the Hardin scenario tend to polarize local communities and governments. They often claim ecological and social wisdom for the former without investigating the latter or the necessary interplay between the two levels of human organization and experience. Chapters in Part III, "The State and the Commons," redress that problem.

CONSERVATION AND THE COMMONS

The chapters in the first part of the book are concerned with the behavior and ideology of fishermen and hunters in relation to resource conservation. Wild fish and game are classic examples of open-access resources because of the practical difficulties involved in claiming and enforcing exclusive property rights to them or to their habitats. However, as Acheson and Carrier in particular show, it is sometimes possible to develop strong notions of territorial rights, even to the extent of outright private ownership claims, to valued fishing grounds, species, or techniques (see Berkes 1985 for a review of exclusive tenure systems in subsistence, artisanal, and commercial fisheries).

If open access is *the* problem, then restricting access to a defined body of people who inhabit or lay claim to a particular territory should lessen or solve the problem. Territoriality can be simply a redefinition of the boundaries of the commons, the carving out of smaller commonses within a larger domain. Within smaller territories—whether they be the vast ranges claimed by groups of pastoralists, the pastures, bogs, and wastelands that lie on the perimeter of village fields, or the fiefs claimed by groups of fishermen—access can still be open, albeit to a smaller group of people, and use of common resources unregulated. Pollnac (1984), using the notion of T.U.R.F. ("territorial use rights in fisheries" [Panayotou 1983]), has developed further refinements in the analysis of variations in territoriality, including the permeability of boundaries.

The importance of territoriality is that it can be the basis for the development of more restrictive common property institutions: rules and regulations about the distribution, use, and transfer of rights in the commons. If we can keep others out, it makes sense for us to do something about our own behavior. This point is made several times in this section. Hames, for example, sees territoriality as essential in a theory of conservation, and Stocks recounts the attempts of Amazonian Indians to keep outsiders from fishing a lake believed to be endangered by commercial fishing. Acheson shows that it is only in strongly defended territories that Maine lobstermen have successfully enacted informal and formal regulations on the numbers of traps used and other sources of fishing pressure on the stocks, and have achieved measurable economic and biological benefits. Brightman notes the post-fur-trade linkages between the existence of viable hunting territories and intentional conservation measures; he also emphasizes the problem that plagued Algonquians and other subarctic tribes experimenting with conservation in the subarctic: trespass by socially distant or antagonistic groups. The development of the fur trade, like the colonial trade and extraction empires of Africa (Peters, this volume) and other manifestations of the expansion of a world system made erasure of local sociopolitical and ecological boundaries a larger challenge to man-environmental relationships than property rights per se (Cronon 1983: 14).

Studies of Conservation

How do we know whether people are conserving? Hames argues that this question has never been clearly answered for any one group. This is because researchers have ignored the need for both behavioral data on patterns of resource use and acquisition and the creation of theoretically informed hypotheses about conservation versus efficiency. The same could be said of studies about fishermen, pastoralists, and others involved in essentially predator-prey relationships with renewable quarries. In basing our views on a few published case studies and arguments we may have been unfair to our audiences and the people we have studied to the extent that we have mythologized their ability to be "real" ecologists and "real" resource managers, at least as long as they and their cultures are isolated or protected from commercialization, acculturation, and government intervention.

Hames, Stocks, Berkes, and Acheson help correct the mythologizing tendency by providing carefully designed ethnographic and human ecological analyses of small-scale, informal, and subsistence systems of resource management and use. Their conclusions about whether conservation and the commons are mutually exclusive are mixed. Hames, who looks for evidence of conservation in open-access resource exploitation in the Amazon by using hypotheses from optimal foraging theory, tentatively concludes that Amazonian Indian hunters are not conservationists; they instead strive for efficiency in the procurement of protein. Native Amazonians respond to decline in the game available or increases in the costs of getting it just as participants in the classic common property fishery do: by trying harder and going farther. Stocks suggests that the Amazonian *varzea* lake dwellers he studied are conservationists in some ways, only weakly so in others, and are resource or ecological community managers in other ways. He broadens the definition of resource management to include not only bridles on the level of exploitation (conservation) but also resource enhancement, and he distinguishes among three types of resource management: the economizing sort implied in optimal foraging theory, the "rational social agreement, enforced by the coercive power of a strong state" that is the focus of common property theory, and customs that have latent management effects.

Another approach to the question of how conservation is related to tenure is to examine both more and less open resource exploitation situations for evidence of conservation. Acheson's revised study of lobstering territories in coastal Maine presents economic and biological evidence for the conservation and economic advantages of territoriality. His findings support the tragedy-of-the-commons argument about the economic and conservation value of more exclusive property rights, but in so doing show the ability of common-property resource users to develop ways of managing the commons, including territoriality or restricted entry, independent of government intervention.

Berkes finds evidence for wise resource management among Cree fishermen of James Bay, even though what they do and why and how they do it do not fit the standard notions of fishery science on how to manage. The Cree are involved in resource management, although in fishing (unlike beaver trapping and goose hunting) there is no real territoriality and few explicit regulations or practices that are in accord with professional fishery managers' notions of what is involved in management. In other words, access seems open and resources are apparently exploited freely, the ideal conditions for a tragedy of the commons. However, biological evidence for an impending tragedy of common property fish stocks within the range of the Cree community studied is restricted to one small area near the main settlement. Ecological data on other fish stocks, combined with observations about Cree fishing practices, suggest that conservation, measured by the effects of human behavior on wild stocks, can exist in a commons.

In his study of subarctic fish population biology and Cree adaptations Berkes indicates the biological factors and processes that should be identified, measured, and tested to attain scientifically meaningful insights about resource management. He shows that the Cree behaviors that he casts as "adaptive" can be understood only through fine-grained analysis of the structure, dynamics, and interactions of fish stocks. The definition of a particular management problem is also critically sensitive to ecological questions such as whether the stability of a natural resource is based on high or low productivity, slow or fast growth rates, or low or high ratios of production to biomass (measures of rates of renewability).

Misplaced Credit and Blame

Recognition that native and isolated peoples have developed systems that restrict access to and use of marine and terrestrial resources once thought to be unmanaged has led to renewed interest in the use of these traditional systems as the framework for ecologically sound economic development and socially acceptable resource management (Johannes 1981; Morauta et al. 1982; Ruddle and Akimichi 1984; Ruddle and Johannes 1985; Klee 1980). However, as Brightman, Berkes, and Carrier suggest, applying Western notions of conservation and man/environment relationships to the interpretation of non-Western systems, past and present, can lead to serious errors. It may be ethnocentric to assume that, where property rights are exclusive (to villages, clans, chiefs, or individuals), conservation is either the intent or the happy side effect. Many of the sea-tenure systems found in Indonesia and Papua New Guinea, for example, are better interpreted as the outcome of conflict over scarce resources (Polunin 1984). Similarly, as Brightman shows, signs of respect for animals are not necessarily signs of conservation. At issue are interpretations of data and discrepancies between Western, scientific, and other models of reality.

Brightman's review of early documents on Algonquian Indians in subarctic Canada takes issue with the idea that the European fur trade caused a breakdown in aboriginal systems of conservation and that this breakdown in turn caused overharvesting and severe shortages of game. He shows that boreal Algonquian religious ideas, particularly the notion that game animals killed by hunters spontaneously regenerate after death, probably encouraged indiscriminate killing more than conservation. Moreover, Brightman argues that a critical idea necessary for a Western form of conservation was probably absent in the pre- and early-contact days. This is the idea that people can influence the future availability and abundance of resources by selectively harvesting them in the present (see Townsend and Wilson, this volume, for doubts about the applicability of this idea in fisheries management).

Berkes notes that many Canadian Inuit as well as Cree Indians continue to hold that it is arrogant to assume that human beings can enhance future productivity by manipulating animals through tagging experiments, selective harvesting, and so on. He suggests that the lack of the respect and humility implied by such manipulation is an important drawback to Western conservation science. Carrier, too, emphasizes native ideology in contrast with Western scientific thinking in his chapter on the meaning of exclusive marine tenure among Ponam Islanders of Papua New Guinea. Melanesian peoples appear to share with boreal and subarctic Canadian Indians and Inuit a strong conviction that spiritual beings and animals or fish themselves are the active agents, whereas people are passive. Accordingly, it makes little sense for Ponams to use their exclusive ownership rights in waters and fishing techniques to increase fish stocks in the future by regulating harvests in the present. Rather, these rights are used to fulfill the social imperative to be generous with what one owns—a function quite different from that imagined by those who assume that territoriality or private property rights, combined with extensive knowledge of the environment, are solutions to tragedies of the commons. In this case, resource conservation is beside the point of exclusive property rights.

What is required, and offered, in these and other chapters in the volume is careful examination of the ways people understand and relate to their environments and of the ways ownership—common or exclusive—works in specific cultural and ecological settings.

SPECIFYING THE COMMONS

Social Action and the Commons

In her discussion of Hardin's thesis, M. E. Smith (1984) cites an encyclopedia definition of the classical counterpart of tragedy—comedy: "the drama of humans as social rather than private

beings, a drama of social actions having a frankly corrective purpose." The perspective taken by most authors in this book better
fits this definition of comedy than one of tragedy. Their case studies and theoretical discussions emphasize social action in relationship to the ecology and economics of common resources. The
chapters in the second part of the volume, by Ostrom, Peters, Mc-
Cay, Vondal, Taylor, Fernandez, and Bauer, address issues of community and the commons and share recognition that common
property, like other kinds of property, is a social institution.

Community and the Commons

One of the problems with Lloyd's and Hardin's use of the pastoral commons to explain the tragedy of the commons is that they
ignored the historical existence of regulations of the commons in
medieval and post-medieval England, the supposed source of
their parable. In this parable "each herdsman (entrepreneur) acts
essentially alone for his own good without regard for the good of
others; *there is no community*" (Fife 1977: 76, emphasis added). But
there was community, and communities often dealt with conflicts
and ecological problems associated with their common lands by
creating and enforcing rules about their use, as shown in studies
of comparable systems in Switzerland and Japan (Ostrom), Ethiopia (Bauer), Indonesia (Vondal), and Spain (Fernandez).

Ecological Cases for the Commons

Property-rights theorists, like ecological anthropologists, look
at the evolution of property rights and assume, contrary to the
Hardin model, that resource users may respond to changes in the
costs and benefits of their activities by changing the system (Demsetz 1967; Anderson and Hill 1977). They ask why some resources
are common property and others are not and what causes changes
in property. They answer the question by analyzing "transaction
costs," the costs of appropriating and defending different kinds of
property rights (Demsetz 1967). For example, Anderson and Hill
(1977) explore changing claims to land, cattle, and water in the
history of the American West in relation to changes in resource,
market, and legal conditions that affected the marginal costs and

benefits of "property rights definition and enforcement activities." The introduction of cheap barbed wire, for example, lowered the costs of claiming private rights to land and cattle, helping to stimulate enclosure of much of the open-range.

Given their shared grounding in microeconomics (see Rapport and Turner 1977), it is not surprising that the property-rights approach is similar to that of anthropologists and ecologists (for example, Dyson-Hudson and Smith 1978) who argue that the characteristics and value of resources in relation to the costs of defending them from others can predict territoriality. This approach is found in the early work of Julian Steward (1955), who argued for causal relationships between the abundance and reliability of natural resources and the presence and absence of exclusive property claims among the Indians of the Great Basin Plateau. It is similar in logic to Netting's (1982) explanation for the persistence of the commons in communities that acknowledge private property rights for many things:

> Resources that are needed by all but whose productivity is diffuse rather than concentrated, low or unpredictable in yield, and low in unit value tend to be kept as communal property with relatively equal, although not unrestricted, access by group members. Smaller, easier divisible, and more highly productive areas may be owned and inherited by individuals (Netting 1982: 471).

Case studies by Vondal, Bauer, Fernandez, and Peters in this volume as well as those analyzed by Ostrom (including Netting's study of common and private property in the Swiss Alps) reflect this ecological/economic logic for the commons in agrarian communities. Seasonally inundated swamplands and wet meadows, mountains, semi-arid and high-altitude grasslands, and so on are often treated as communal property. Among the reasons are the high costs of delimiting and defending boundaries in some environments or for some resources in relation to the benefits of claiming exclusive property. From another perspective, there may be advantages to maintaining access rights to a wide variety of microhabitats in risky and uncertain environments. Peters, for example, notes that herders in Botswana, even the wealthier ones who have a stake in privatization of lands and water sources, prefer to maintain some of the rangelands as common property despite government attempts to codify land tenure differently. This may be partly because of their need to be mobile in response to unpredictable semi-arid environments. This need and this situation have surely played roles in pastoralists' resistance to schemes that would draw boundaries and fix individuals or groups to specific territories (Livingstone 1977; Sandford 1983; see Gilles and Jamtgaard 1982 for other cases for the commons). Finally, communal tenure can help communities attract more people when natural and political disasters result in population loss (Bauer).

Changes in Property Rights

An ecological and social-action approach to the commons and changes in property rights counters the unilineal view of the evolution of property rights embedded in Western culture and in Hardin's scenario, here expressed in the words of the eighteenth-century jurist Blackstone:

> The earth and all things therein were the general property of mankind from the immediate gift of the Creator. . . . Thus the ground was in common, and no part was the permanent property of any man in particular; . . . when mankind increased in number, it became necessary to entertain conceptions of more permanent dominion, and to appropriate to individuals not the immediate use only, but the very substance of the thing to be used. (cited by Maine 1884: 244–45)

Contrary to the assumption of commons theorists that increased pressure on a scarce and common resource will lead in the long run to government management or privatization, the outcome of conflict or attempts to better manage resources can be a social agreement that some resources are common property. For example, common-field agriculture and related communal institutions of agrarian Europe, Africa, and Southeast Asia are less accurately viewed as relics of a romanticized village community than as historically specific ways of managing land and labor under certain socioeconomic and ecological conditions, including resource scarcity and the local conflicts it generated (Netting 1982).

In many parts of the world, forms of marine tenure other than open access suffered attrition due to the effects of modernization and the imposition of "the western tradition of coastal marine resources open to all citizens" (Johannes 1977: 121), just as complex forms of African land tenure were transformed and weakened by the imposition of Western rule and Western notions of both private and common property (Peters). However, the specification of natural resources as common property, even in the open-access sense of the term, is more complex. It can reflect not only relationships between local communities and their environments (Netting 1982), but also the outcome of competition between claims and claimants (Peters).

McCay points to the role of capitalist development and its dependence on freedoms of navigation, trade, and fishing in the process that led to specification of the open seas as open-access common property in the international law of the sea. She suggests another historical and social source for the law of open-access commons as it is expressed in eastern seaboard U.S. fisheries: social and political reaction to the Old World experience of enclosed commons—wild game and inland fishes—reserved for the powerful and the wealthy. Resource management involved blatant social discrimination in England and many other parts of the Old World. Decisions about the law of the commons in the New World consciously recognized this inequity and sought to make things different. Common property in fish, game, and even grazing lands in the United States came about through conflict and the determination of what things in society should be alienable and what things should not (Bromley 1982: 842). The debate continues (see Libecap 1981; Young 1982).

Common property—in the sense of communal use-rights to extensive resources—is logical under certain conditions of production and environment. Just as important is the fact that common property can come about through the claims of a community to free and equal access to resources that could otherwise become the property of only a privileged few. On the other hand, common property can favor the interests of those with power and wealth. It thus has multiple and sometimes conflicting meanings and values, as McCay shows in relation to issues of fishery regulations in the U.S. and Peters describes in relation to land tenure issues in Botswana.

Common property in the context of historical U.S. coastal fisheries and shellfisheries refers to "public ownership" (*res communes*) within accepted governmental boundaries, be they national or local. Although public ownership often carries with it a notion of public or sovereign stewardship, it may in effect amount to the same as *res nullius*, as recognized in the Spanish aphorism "That which is everybody's is nobody's" (Fernandez). Yet this too must be interpreted in part as the result of social and political conflict and the interplay of competing claims and claimants to the commons.

Fernandez's chapter on the Asturian region of Spain depicts one expression of the medieval European common-fields system, whereby even arable lands are treated as communal property, allocated to individuals for some purposes and thrown open for communal cattle grazing after the harvest. A similar system exists in Ethiopia (Bauer). It is arguable that the common-field version of the commons, highly specialized and framed by local regulations, is a form of intensification of production through its economic uses of labor, plow teams, and other resources and its mixture of crops and cattle on the same land. It fits certain ecological, demographic, and political conditions (McCloskey 1975; Guillet 1981), including relatively low population density or low rates of population growth, fragile soils or other agronomic conditions, and strong feudal and colonial rule.

As those conditions change, so may the system of property rights and land tenure. Contrary to the assumption of Hardin's model that legal and political changes must be imposed to correct problems of the commons, an ecological/economic perspective sees legal and political means of enclosing the commons as secondary to changes in land use and social relationships initiated by the commoners (Netting 1982). Well-documented cases of enclosure of rangelands and common fields and pastures in Europe, India, Africa, and elsewhere show that government enclosure and land tenure reform acts followed changes initiated by resource users. They were responding to commercial and technical forces that, in the language of property-rights analysts, changed the transaction costs of defining and enforcing property rights (Behnke 1985: 11; Anderson and Hill 1977). As Peters shows, the process of enclosure may entail native reinterpretations of the customary tenure system (see also Behnke 1985), as well as the imposition of Western concepts and imperatives.

No inevitable, unidirectional tendency exists for common property to be replaced by private property. Resources once held as private property can become common property: the herds of wild horses in the American West represent an obvious case (Anderson and Hill 1977). Property-rights systems also may shift back and forth in long cycles (as suggested by Friedman [1975] for the *gumlao/gumsa* changes in social structure and property rights among the Kachin of Upper Burma [Leach 1954]), in short cycles (Bauer), and even in seasonal cycles (Vondal).

Bauer shows the place of common-field communal tenure within a larger system that shifts from inclusive to exclusive forms of land tenure and associated kin and political relations. The Ethiopian villagers he studied respond to assessments of ecological as well as sociopolitical change by deliberately changing their tenure system. They opt for a common-field system as an incorporative system, a means of attracting labor and people to a new or revived village. As population density increases within the village, a deliberate decision is made to switch the tenure system to one based on inheritance. Tenure becomes more exclusive, more privatized, and differences between social classes and between insiders and outsiders more marked. Decisions to revert to communal tenure are made in the same way.

Vondal describes an unusual variant of common property in an agrarian society: swamplands in a rice-growing and duck-farming area of the island of Borneo, Indonesia. While wet rice agriculture is a paradigm of agricultural intensification and private property, villagers of the province of Kalimantan maintain common rights in the permanent swamplands. Every year the swampwaters rise during the wet season, and private property rights are submerged under common ones. Maintaining communal rights to the resources of the swamplands—with a set of informal understandings about their use—allows a high degree of diversity in production strategies (including subsistence and commercial fishing, trading, rice growing, and duck and duck-egg farming). This has made it possible for most villagers to engage in highly profitable duck and duck-egg farming, despite variations in private property holdings. Communal rights to the swamplands thus support both diversification and intensification of production. However, the interests of the larger-scale duck farmers threaten the regime and, interestingly, support maintenance of the common-property nature of the swamplands.

Specifying Community

Peters reviews the work of many of the economists, social psychologists, and political scientists who have criticized the thesis of the tragedy of the commons and the related "prisoner's dilemma" model for their failure to recognize interdependence, communication, and cooperation. She goes on to argue that the social facts in a commons dilemma and in any situation of tension between individual and group interests require further specification and location in history and culture. Like Taylor (this volume) she is concerned about the tendency of critics of Hardin's thesis to assume that "community"—which is not present in Hardin's model—implies solidarity, homogeneity, and collective action. It can, as it did in the Botswana case she describes, involve conflicts between users over access to the commons and over the very definition of property rights and law. Commons dilemmas must be explained in terms of the dynamics of conflict and competition between different social groups located in history and social systems rather than between the rational economizing individual—unspecified—and the group—also unspecified.

The tragedy-of-the-commons thesis, like other interpretative models, is rooted in history and political experience. The tendency to misspecify relationships between different types of tenure is found in the Western model of the commons, imported to Africa and other parts of the colonized world where it played its part in creating both communal or tribal tenure and efforts to privatize tenure. The Western model, of which the Hardin thesis is only a recent manifestation, is tenacious. It holds that common property is for the most part undesirable, although in some settings the colonial authorities effectively created common property to meet their needs (Bates 1983b). Common property is also viewed as amorphous, diffuse, ephemeral, and unspecified in comparison with private property, and this view, when it is successful in the political and legal process, plays a role in the enclosure of the commons. Historical and ethnographic research, on the other hand, demonstrates the specificity and complexity of communal property-rights

systems in southern Africa (Peters), including the existence of multiple and overlapping rights combining group and individual
claims that contrast sharply with the Western view of the tribal
common lands as the subject of undifferentiated, public use-rights.

Collective Choice and the Commons

Ostrom's chapter on communal regulations in Swiss and Japanese villages builds upon the work of Mancur Olson (1965) and
others in public or collective choice theory (see also Buchanan and
Tullock 1962; Sproule-Jones 1982; Ostrom and Ostrom 1977; Ostrom 1977; Bates 1983a). From this perspective, the commons dilemma is a parable of the problem of social order, the problem of
tensions or contradictions between private interests and the public
good that is central to all social science (Bates 1983a: 19). This approach, like that of institutional economics (Bromley 1982), differs
from the economic model of the commons in emphasizing (1) the
importance of group attributes and institutional arrangements in
relation to the structure of incentives and utilities for individual
decision making; and (2) the likelihood of a broader set of possible
outcomes, including user-group institutional solutions, in a commons dilemma.

Ostrom finds evidence for user-group solutions in the cases of a
Swiss village and a set of Japanese villages that have both private
and communal resources and a long history of regulating the commons. She criticizes the notion that a certain form of land use will be
accompanied by a certain set of communal regulations, and she
addresses the important question of how to predict the initiation,
survival, and performance of a variety of institutions for collective
action (see also Ostrom 1985a,b). She suggests that small-scale communities are more likely to have the formal conditions required for
successful and enduring collective management of the commons.
Among these are the visibility of common resources and behavior
toward them; feedback on the effects of regulations; widespread
understanding and acceptance of rules and their rationales; the
values expressed in these rules (that is, equitable treatment of all
and protection of the environment); and the backing of values by
socialization, standards, and strict enforcement. Many of these
conclusions are similar to those developed from the experimental

work of social psychologists on the commons dilemma (Dawes 1980; Edney 1981; Cass and Edney 1978). Sentiments and "community" are not enough.

Cultural and Symbolic Underpinnings of the Commons

Fernandez considers the loss of the commons in Spain. The tragedy of the commons is not only one of destruction by self-interested exploitation. It is a tragedy of rural impoverishment and agrarian crisis caused by the loss of common rights. It also is the loss of something valuable to human relationships, even where, as in Asturias, enclosure and privatization had less wrenching social and economic consequences than elsewhere in the Old World. But the commons is not entirely lost; periodically, it reasserts itself.

The problem of the commons is one of how society creates superordinate allegiance to something—the commons or the communal—that transcends people's immediate and everyday sense of reality. Traditional cooperative institutions of the Asturian countryside created such an allegiance. Fernandez expands the meaning of the commons to include human activity in common—for work and play, for production and reproduction. Most of the customs and institutions he describes have disappeared because of changes in the economics of rural production and the formalization of responsibilities of the state and municipalities for public goods and common resources. These traditions remain almost solely as folklore but are still able to evoke allegiance to common as opposed to separate interests.

Fernandez argues that the power of communal institutions derives less from their roles in coordinating individual (or household) interests to optimize benefits for all (the solution hoped for in "prisoners' dilemma" games) than in their roles as metaphors for reciprocity in human experience. When do people participate in cooperative and collective action? When this type of action offers them the possibility of regenerating themselves or reproducing their culture, and does so with the promise of payoffs that are long-term and enduring, transcending the human life cycle. Why do people defect from collective action? Changes in the scale of society, observed by Ostrom, play a role. Abuses in the systems, uncertainty about who will participate and in relation to whose commons, the secularization of authority and the mechanization and truncation of understandings of life also play a part. Just as significant may be an ontological shift, accompanied by and expressed in rural exodus, toward the urban experience and relationships of contractual obligation.

The "call to the commons" represents nostalgia for the imagined conviviality and diffuse solidarity of the past, the lost village community that has figured so much in Western culture and historiography. It represents a challenge to the present, as seen in its role in revolutionary movements on the larger scene in Spain and elsewhere and in its periodic revival in contemporary village affairs.

Tragic Choices

Hardin, Lloyd, and the economists who have worked with the theory of the commons do not completely ignore the social implications of the privatization solution, that is, the "tragedy of the commoners" (Ciriacy-Wantrup and Bishop 1975) that ensues when some individuals, firms, or families are excluded from shares of valuable resources. This outcome is acknowledged, but it is typically reduced to an unfortunate but necessary consequence of the need to bring individual and system interests closer together: "Injustice is preferable to total ruin" (Hardin 1977b: 28).

Beyond recognizing that privatization and other solutions to the commons dilemma have social problems of their own, we must consider what others have addressed: the "tragic choices" that must be made in resolving commons dilemmas (Calabresi and Bobbitt 1978). These go beyond who benefits and who loses to who shall decide, who takes responsibility, and how the decisions will be made. They are tragic not only in their distribution effects but also because in their deliberation they lay bare the structure of society that exists under its claims to justice and equal rights (Edney 1981).

The situation described by Taylor is one in which the commons, agrarian and marine, has long been enclosed and privatized. Even the fishing grounds are privately owned. The spirit of conviviality and cooperation that Fernandez associates with activities in common is expressed in Teelin, Ireland, in illegal fishing upon a common to which the villagers have no legal claim. The event that is the subject of Taylor's chapter centers on the question of whether the local community of fishermen should buy rights to the fishery through a cooperative.

Taylor asks whether an egalitarian community, defined as a community by its dependent and antagonistic relationships to outside authorities and powers, can develop its own ownership and management system. A major problem for such a community is that of authority: Can a man in such a community be a bailiff over his fellows? The men of Teelin, Ireland, evidently thought not. It is "natural" for the fishermen of Teelin to regulate access to salmon by taking turns in using haul-seines. This system follows the community's notions of reciprocal relations among kin and neighbors, and no institutionalized authority is required to enforce the system. But it was seen as "unnatural" for them to become involved in corporate relationships that involved the authority to regulate and enforce regulations within the community: "the river would run red with blood."

The anthropological challenge is not to choose between *communitas* and self-interest but to build interpretations of people's relationships to common resources on the fact that "actual communities act differently, not only from one another but internally with respect to various resources" (Taylor). One dimension on which communities differ is that of the locus and nature of authority. Differences in this and other features of social organization, as well as conceptions of what is "natural," may help explain why the Irish fishermen Taylor studied and the Indonesian Borneo villagers Vondal describes have not developed communal management institutions, whereas Ethiopian (Bauer), historic Asturian (Fernandez), and Swiss Alps and Japanese village (Ostrom) farmers have.

Tragedies of the commons may occur when revealing the structure of social organization is deemed too threatening or when issues of authority cannot be resolved. Moreover, the tragic choice may be that some things should remain in common despite the ecological and economic problems that may ensue. This choice may be made (1) because an open-access situation suits the interests of the more powerful group in a society (see Vondal for a telling instance), (2) because those most likely to be hurt by a dif-

ferent allocation scheme are able to exercise their power legitimately or illegitimately (McCay), or (3) because the commons and
communal activity are more meaningful as metaphors for reciprocity (Fernandez) that help individuals transcend their self-interests
and narrow lives and by so doing help resolve the contradiction
between individual interests and the collective good.

THE STATE AND THE COMMONS

Today all local human communities are encapsulated within (Bailey
1969) or fully integrated into larger sociopolitical systems. For example, the Cree Indians studied by Berkes have exclusive fishing
rights through the James Bay treaty with the government, and territoriality in Maine lobstering is informal because it is not sanctioned by state or national governments, which uphold the law of
open access. But there are always local systems of resource use and
property rights. In some cases they may be sanctioned and enforced by the state; in others they are different from or opposed to
those of the state. More important than touting the purported values of local versus government property rights or management is
understanding their interactions, the goal of the last section of the
volume.

Durrenberger and Pálsson, Pinkerton, and Anderson write
most explicitly of centralized government intervention in commons situations. Their subjects are contemporary, technologically
developed commercial fisheries in Iceland, Canada, and Malaysia,
and their foci are relationships between local communities or user
groups and the agents and agencies of the state. Townsend and
Wilson emphasize the economic and policy aspects of those relationships.

Privatization, Stinting, and Comanagement

Townsend and Wilson are economists who explain the logic of
privatization as a solution to commons dilemmas. Privatization or
property-mimicking regulation is often better than Hardin's prescription of coercive governmental intervention because of inefficiencies found in government management measures that preserve

open access while controlling, for example, the level of harvest or extraction (Crutchfield and Pontecorvo 1969). Townsend and Wilson are skeptical about the state's use of this policy in modern fisheries.

Management systems that are based on the idea that property rights must be changed but that are forced to simulate such through licensing and effort-limitation programs tend to be self-defeating. The user groups have "disharmonious incentives," that is, they capitalize even more, cheat, and misreport (see also Durrenberger and Pálsson, and Pinkerton). In turn, managers continue to promulgate rules that encourage the use of inefficient technology, creating a situation little different from open-access management. In addition, these management systems may be based on faulty science. The idea that the regulation of present behavior can influence the future availability and abundance of resources is the foundation of modern natural resource management. In fisheries this idea is based on a model that may inaccurately represent the population dynamics of many marine fishes, given the interdependence of species in indeterministic systems. Townsend and Wilson describe an alternative model of fish population dynamics that, in turn, leads to arguments for drastically different measures of fisheries management that are based on the behaviors and institutions that already exist among fishermen and their markets. Townsend and Wilson also show that prices are as important as property rights to the workings of the system. Management may be misdirected if it fails to do something about imperfect market relationships and competition from imports that affect prices and hence influence the timing of switching by fishermen from depleted to abundant prey species.

Though often simplistically juxtaposed to private property, common property rights, like all property rights, are highly variable and can include limitations that prevent tragedies of the commons. Moloney and Pearse (1979) outline a range of common property rights involved in state management of fishery, forest, oil and gas, and other resources, from the open-access, unregulated sort implied in Hardin's analysis, to regulated but still open-access commons, and to even more restrictive systems. The last category includes specifying a limit on the number of users (and defining who they shall be) and "stinting," which constrains how much of the resource shall be taken by each user. Stinting is an old English term for certain restrictions on the village commons. It is the closest to privatization, which it may become when and if stinted rights are fully commoditized, subject to buying, selling, and accumulation as capital within a market system.

Pinkerton extends the set of common property rights, focusing on rights that may be informal in the sense that they may be claimed or exercised by groups of users who do not hold state-legitimized authority over the use and allocation of resources. Among those rights is that of controlling the behavior of outsiders to the community, a right essential to systems of territoriality and to all efforts to establish systems of communal resource use and management. The studies of Brightman, Pinkerton, Acheson, and others in this volume discuss the role of the loss of that right, that is, "the tragedy of incursion," in creating tragedies of the commons.

Another right is the making of enforceable decisions about the use and allocation of a resource. In private-property arrangements it is often accepted that the owner has that right, subject to rules of the community (such as zoning regulations). In many situations the state by definition "owns" common property resources and the right to make decisions about them, but communities of users claim—informally, illegally, or formally—the right to participate in decision making or to comanage resources (see Pinkerton, McCay, Acheson, Anderson, Durrenberger and Pálsson, Fernandez, Taylor).

The State and Other Causes of Tragedies of the Commons

In Iceland, Canada, and Malaysia, as in the United States, ocean fisheries are treated as open-access resources within the boundaries of national sovereignty. In all three case studies, tragedies of the commons are evident as is the fact that open access is only one of a larger set of causes of those tragedies. Durrenberger and Pálsson locate one source of the tragedy of the commons in the process of capitalist economic development of Iceland's fisheries, and another in the cognitive framework and social relations of production created in that process. Anderson shows that national government usurpation of the right to specify—to determine rules of access and use concerning—the marine commons of west Malaysia, plus the higher national priority of political control and the lower priority of fisheries development and management, contributed to severe overfishing. In Canada, Pinkerton shows that provincial and federal fishery agencies helped cause tragedies of the commons in salmon fishing by failing to back up schemes to limit entry to certain fisheries with incentives to forestall escalated investment in redundant capital. Instead, government policies favored increased investments in both white and Indian fisheries. The problems and interest groups generated in the process created political pressures that worked against wise resource management.

Why Intervention Fails

One way to interpret the tragedy of the commons is as a problem of the locus of and loss of control. In the west Malaysian case both the fishermen and the government lost control, the former through usurpation by the government and the latter through the course of its own decisions, which ruled out any possibilities for effective action. Although Anderson argues for more power or control at the local level, he recognizes that localized control over the commons in west Malaysia might not have worked out much better. Fishermen reacted to the introduction of highly efficient trawlers, known to be capable of depleting inshore and nearshore fish stocks, with violent attempts to drive them out—a form of territoriality. The near wars that ensued can be interpreted as steps in the process of working out a way of managing the inshore and nearshore commons; but, Anderson cautions, one or two "strong men" could have emerged as virtual owners of the fishing grounds with or without interests in protecting the fish and shellfish. The critical message, however, is that everything that the government did (and failed to do) closed off all possible avenues for the fishermen to work things out and replaced them with next to nothing.

Anderson's guiding questions are why state intervention in a commons dilemma failed, and what might be done in the future and in other contexts in the Third World to reduce the likelihood of failure. He is pessimistic. There are few signs that unstable, authoritarian governments will be replaced by more stable and more democratic ones in the Third World. It is politically too risky for such governments to allow user groups or local communities to specify the commons, to work out, for better or worse, ways to deal with overfishing and conflicts over access to resources. Even cooperatives, which are often promoted as suitable vehicles for economic development *and* commons management, are likely to be co-opted for political purposes. In addition, if the resource base in question is of low national priority (for cultural and economic reasons), the state is unlikely to take action to avert depletion.

The problem of government decision making addressed by Anderson is not special to Malaysia. "Muddling through" (Lindblom 1959), while muddling, is a well-accepted interpretation of how the policy process in most modern societies takes place, and is grounded not only in political structures but also in the limitations and characteristics of human decision making. However, ways can be found to help people, even governments, draw upon the power they have to make better judgments in coping with problems (Anderson). One of these is to bring local people with expertise into the policy process, as in the comanagement proposal described by Pinkerton.

Comanagement and Property Rights

Pinkerton focuses on the bundle of informal property rights—those not legitimized by the state—that are claimed by coastal communities and on the successful effort of the Nimpkish (Kwakiutl) Indian band and others in British Columbia to exercise one of the most critical of those rights: control over interception of migratory fish stocks by others. In this case, the state, through its fishery management and development policies, has caused or worsened the twin tragedies of resource depletion and over-capitalization. State management policies have also had discernibly negative impacts on some sectors of the fishing industry as well as on some coastal communities.

Indian communities are trying to hold the problem of resource decline in check and in so doing must reassert their power, their rights to specify the commons. The term *comanagement* signifies their political claim to the right to share management power and responsibility with the state. It is an attempt to formalize a *de facto* situation of mutual dependence and interaction in resource management. It has also become a challenge to the legitimacy of the state, especially in the context of widespread loss of confidence in it as the steward of common property resources. The state has so far responded by allowing, under severe political pressure, only the informal exercise of local rights to manage fisheries.

Social Dramas and Sociopolitical Change

The literature on resource use and management pays scant attention to social dramas over rights to common property resources. As in so many cases of citizen activism (Krauss 1983), the incidents and the structures and relationships they create are ephemeral and relatively small-scale. They are not always successful. Yet the changes they create within people—who become critical analysts of social and political structures and who recognize their own potentials for action—and within communities and even broader frameworks of power and authority can be enduring and even revolutionary (see Rudé 1980).

Pinkerton presents the Area 27 Closure incident at Alert Bay in 1977 as one such social drama: an event that revealed the structure of power and rights in salmon fishery management, including the ability of people in local communities to act. That action is significant to standard theories of the commons and collective action (see, for example, Olson 1965). The fact that it did occur must lead us to question their assumption that self-interested individuals and heterogeneous, even fragmented communities are unlikely to muster the collective will to deal with commons dilemmas.

Grassroots and Effective
Common Property Management

Both Anderson and Pinkerton question the effectiveness of management that is monopolized by the state and has little input from "the grassroots." Fishery management in Iceland is unusual in the extent to which the grassroots level is continuously involved in problem definition and resolution at the national level of policy making. Durrenberger and Pálsson show how grassroots politics frames, influences, and determines most administrative and legislative decisions concerning the fisheries of Iceland. Included in the Icelandic decision-making process are hard choices familiar to other commons situations, that is, between the need to protect and allocate access to a limited good and the sentiment that access should be open and equal to all citizens; between "common sense" and science; between a rationality defined solely in terms of economics and one that accepts the role of the social context in determining the optimal and rational; between the need to control overcapitalization and the commitment to full employment and equality of access.

One reason for the evident success of fishery management in Iceland is the centrality of a common-property productive activity—fishing—to Iceland's economy. There are fewer competing objectives and priorities in Iceland than in larger and more complex nations. Nations such as Canada and the United States are hampered in their ability to manage natural resources wisely by the many different and sometimes competing objectives of the state—for example, the conflict between concerns in U.S./Canada international relations and the management of local salmon stocks. Therefore, there may be more of a case in those nations or in countries such as Malaysia than in Iceland for restoring some power to manage the commons to user groups and local communities.

The Icelandic management process is open and flexible, able to respond to and incorporate the interests of diverse actors and groups, in sharp contrast to the systems portrayed by Anderson and Pinkerton and those with which we are familiar in the United States. Comanagement is a social reality in Iceland; it does not need a special label, nor need it be based on either homogeneity on the part of the users or total accord between users and managers. Accordingly, the state is trusted in Iceland. The boat quota system being considered in the 1980s will privatize rights to catch fish in a property-mimicking way. It is controversial because of realistic worries about its effects on the structure of the industry. But if it is accepted it will be partly because the state is trusted to be impartial in the assignment of quotas, a trust that enables the continuation of the ideology of equal, or equitable, access and the effective management of a limited good.

Contrary to the limiting assumptions of the thesis of the tragedy-of-the-commons thesis, common property encompasses a wide variety of institutional arrangements that delimit access and impose restrictions on use, including tribal property, the communal lands of peasant communities, informally and formally managed common-property activities such as fishing, hunting and trapping, oil and gas exploitation; grazing allotments on federal rangelands; and others. By equating common property with open access, the tragedy-of-the-commons approach ignores important social institutions and their roles in managing the commons. Moreover, its policy solutions—government intervention or privatization—can weaken or demolish existing institutions and worsen or even create tragedies of the commons. The authors of the chapters that follow help us to understand the commons and common-property institutions as part of the more general task of discovering, as Berkes (this volume) writes, "the conditions under which the 'tragedy' occurs and those under which it does not."

Part *I*

CONSERVATION AND THE COMMONS

2 The Lobster Fiefs Revisited

ECONOMIC AND ECOLOGICAL EFFECTS OF TERRITORIALITY IN THE MAINE LOBSTER INDUSTRY

James M. Acheson

FISHERIES HAVE A PERSISTENT and in some cases disastrous tendency toward overexploitation. The most widely accepted cause is the common property or open-access nature of legal rights in the marine environment (Christy and Scott 1965; Gordon 1954: 132). In the absence of private ownership, fishermen have no incentives to curtail fishing activities in response to declines in catches or increases in costs, because no property right guarantees that fish not taken today will be available in larger quantity or at greater weight in the future. What one fisherman does not catch today goes to other fishermen (Crutchfield 1973: 116–17).

Accordingly, the fishing industry of the United States, as elsewhere, has had serious and long-term difficulties, exacerbated until the late 1970s by intense competition with foreign fishing fleets. In the New England area, cod, haddock, and hake have become far less plentiful than they were in the past, and the once-flourishing sardine (herring) industry has been greatly reduced.

The lobster fishery in Maine is unusual in the United States. Informal norms about territoriality and hence exclusive ownership exist. Territorial arrangements have substantial economic and ecological effects with implications for Maine lobster-fishing management and for fisheries management as a whole. Lobster catches have been relatively stable since the 1940s, varying from 16 to 21.7 million pounds a year (Townsend and Briggs 1982: 10). However, catches and incomes are not uniform. Fishermen in some areas earn higher incomes and have different effects on the biomass than those in other areas. Such differences can be explained in terms of variations in lobster-fishing rights.

FEATURES OF THE MAINE LOBSTER INDUSTRY

The American lobtser (*Homarus americanus*) is found in waters off the Atlantic Coast of North America from Newfoundland to the Carolinas. The state of Maine consistently produces far more lobsters than any other state in the United States. The study area along the central Maine coast is one of the most productive areas of all.

Throughout the 1970s there were approximately 9,000 lobstermen in Maine. About 2,300 were full-time fishermen; the rest were "part-timers" who earned most of their income ashore (Acheson *et al.* 1980b: 258). The techniques employed by lobstermen along the entire length of the Maine coast is about the same. Lobsters are caught in wooden traps or "pots" about three or four feet long made of oak frames covered with hardwood laths or vinyl-covered wire.[1] The traps are usually placed in the water in "strings," or long rows, so that a man can see from one buoy to another in the fog. On a good day (usually the calm morning hours), a lobsterman in this area might pull about two hundred traps. Typically lobstermen have about four hundred to six hundred traps each.

Most lobstermen fish alone from gasoline- or diesel-powered boats 28 to 32 feet long, equipped with depth sounders, hydraulic "pot" haulers, ship-to-shore radios, and compasses. A lobsterman's activities vary greatly from season to season. During January, February, and March, when lobsters can be caught only in relatively warm, deep water, three to ten miles offshore, lobstering is generally more dangerous and unprofitable. Bad weather and high winds increase trap losses and make the work more difficult. Some men stay ashore during this period to build lobster traps, and others use their boats for scalloping or shrimping. Those who persist in lobstering during the winter may pull their traps no more than six or seven times a month.

Spring (April 15 to June 15) and fall (August 15 to November 15) are unquestionably the busiest months of the year, when men have the largest number of traps in the water and pull them every chance they get. As the water warms in the spring, lobsters are available in shallower water closer to shore. During the three- or four-week molting season (roughly June 15 to August 15), traps are typically placed very close to shore, only feet away from breaking surf. During this period, catches are so small that men bring many of their traps ashore and do maintenance work on their boats. In the fall, lobstermen begin to move their equipment into deeper water again and lobsters can be caught in larger numbers.

Although all lobstermen move their traps according to this general pattern, they are not all equally effective as fishermen. Skill and willingness to work greatly affect catches and incomes. In some instances skilled fishermen catch more than twice as many lobsters as unskilled fishermen with the same number of traps in the same territory.

The state of Maine, which has jurisdiction out to three miles from shore, has passed some important conservation laws. A legal lobster must have a carapace length of more than 3 3/16 inches and less than 5 inches.[2] Regardless of size, breeding females are protected by a law requiring any lobsterman who catches an egg-bearing female to throw her back. He may also cut a notch in the tail flippers of "berried lobster." Notched-tail lobsters may never be taken. In addition, the state has a licensing requirement, and lobstermen must mark their traps and buoys with their license number and assigned colors. Despite the fact that only thirty-seven state Sea and Shore Fisheries wardens patrol some 2,500 miles of coast, these laws are almost universally obeyed. Violations can result in court action and suspension of fishing licenses, effectively barring lobstermen from the fishery.

There are few data on the effectiveness of these formal, state-wide measures. However, in other lobstering regions and in other fisheries, such restrictive conservation laws have been found to exacerbate economic inefficiency and to have questionable effects on fish population levels (Crutchfield and Pontecorvo 1969; De-Wolf 1974). Certainly the Maine laws do not begin to solve the problems inherent in managing a common property resource. They do not limit entry into the fishery and do little to restrict fishing effort. However, informal norms concerning territoriality limit both. In all lobstering areas there are barriers to entry. In some areas there are special local rules about the number of traps that may be fished or the length of fishing seasons.

TERRITORIALITY IN
THE MAINE LOBSTER INDUSTRY

From the legal view, anyone who has a license can go lobster fishing anywhere. In reality, far more is required. To go lobster fishing, one must be accepted by the men fishing out of a harbor. Once a new fisherman has gained admission to a "harbor gang" (Acheson 1979), he is ordinarily allowed to go fishing only in the traditional territory of that harbor. Interlopers are met with strong sanctions, sometimes merely verbal but more often involving the destruction of lobstering gear. This system is entirely the result of political competition among groups of lobstermen. It contains no "legal" elements.

As a rule, the area fished by any one harbor gang is quite small. In the summer, a man will rarely fish more than three or four miles from his home harbor, and even in winter, when men are fishing in deeper water, they are rarely more than ten miles from home. Territories fished by one harbor gang are rarely more than one hundred square miles; most are far smaller. This means that a lobsterman spends his working life crossing and recrossing one small body of water.

The dividing lines between most lobstering territories are relatively minor features that would be familiar only to men intimately acquainted with the area. Along the shore, a rock, ledge, cove, or perhaps a big pine tree may mark a boundary. Offshore boundaries are usually marked by reference to landmarks onshore or on islands.

To some extent, delineation of boundaries varies with distance from shore. Close to shore, boundaries are known to the yard. Farther offshore, boundaries are less definite. Thus in the middle of the winter, when men are fishing far from shore, there is a good deal of mixed fishing between two harbor gangs. In part, this pattern can be explained by the fact that it is more difficult to establish exact boundaries far from shore. More important is the relative competition for fishing bottom. In the winter, lobsters are available over a wider area and fewer men are fishing. In the summer, when more men are fishing shallow areas along shore, there is more competition and more interest in maintaining exact boundaries (Acheson 1972: 64).

Violation of territorial boundaries meets with no set response. An older, well-established man from a large family might infringe on the territorial rights of others almost indefinitely, whereas a new man or a part-timer would almost certainly have trouble very quickly. Sooner or later, however, someone—usually one man acting on his own—will sanction the interloper. First, the violator may be warned, usually by having his traps opened or by having two half-hitches tied around the spindle of his buoys. If he persists, some or all of his traps will be "cut off." That is, his traps will be pulled, the buoy, toggles, and warp cut off, and the trap pushed over in deep water where he has little chance of finding it.

Small-scale trap cutting is endemic all along the coast. There are, however, factors keeping trap cutting at a minimum. Most important is the knowledge that the destruction of traps will bring almost certain retaliation. About once a decade, small incidents escalate into "lobster wars" in which dozens of men attack each other's equipment in widespread forays, destroying large numbers of traps and even boats (Acheson 1979: 271).

All conflicts, regardless of how many men are involved, are kept very quiet. No matter how justified a man feels in cutting off another man's gear, he will rarely advertise his skill with the knife. Trap cutting is illegal and can lead to loss of license; silence also reduces the chances of retaliation by victims. Thus, when trap cutting occurs, people in coastal towns and state officials are apt to hear only vague rumors from the primary actors. Even the victims remain silent. Legal prosecution is usually unsuccessful, and there is a strong feeling among fishermen that the law should be kept at a distance. The result is what Bailey (1969: 144–47) calls an "encapsulated system"—one political system operating with its own set of rules within a larger system.

Two different types of lobster-fishing areas exist along the study area of the central Maine coast. I call them *nucleated* and *perimeter-defended* (see Hockett 1973: 69). The lobstermen do not have terms for the different territorial arrangements, although they are aware of the differences, which relate to the amount of mixed fishing allowed. In the western part of the study area (between Cape Newagan and Friendship; see Fig. 2.1), territorial arrangements are highly nucleated. That is, men from each harbor gang have a strong sense of territoriality close to the mouth of the harbor where they anchor their boats. This sense of ownership grows progressively weaker the farther one goes from the harbor mouth. On the periphery there is almost no sense of territoriality, and a good deal of mixed fishing takes place. A stranger trying to fish in an area close to a harbor nucleus would almost certainly meet with violent opposition from a number of men. However, the reaction would be much less violent if he were to invade an area fished by multiple harbor gangs, where the sense of ownership is weaker.

Farther east on the mainland, the territories are still nucleated, although lobstermen say that boundaries become "harder," meaning that there is less area where mixed fishing is allowed and that larger areas are fished exclusively by men of a single harbor gang.

The island areas of Penobscot Bay are, however, perimeter-defended territories. In the cases of Monhegan, Matinicus, Green Island, Little Green Island, and Metinic Island, boundaries are sharply drawn and defended to a yard. Definition of these areas is in terms of their outermost boundaries, and the feeling of ownership does not sharply decrease with distance from the island harbors where the men anchor their boats. There is very little mixed fishing. Even in winter when fishing offshore in deep water, men from perimeter-defended territories rarely venture into areas they do not claim for their exclusive use. Periodically, a man may furtively and guiltily put a few traps outside his own area where he thinks no one will notice, but there is a strong feeling that if one is going to keep others on their side of a boundary one should stay on one's own side.

In both types of territories, but most clearly in the perimeter-defended areas, claims over ocean areas are tied to formal ownership of land. Ownership of land on an island is held to mean ownership of fishing rights in nearby waters, despite the fact that legally the ocean areas are part of the public domain. On Matinicus, for example, no one is allowed to fish in the island's territory unless he owns land on the island. A major argument against selling land to "summer people" is that thereby an island family may lose its

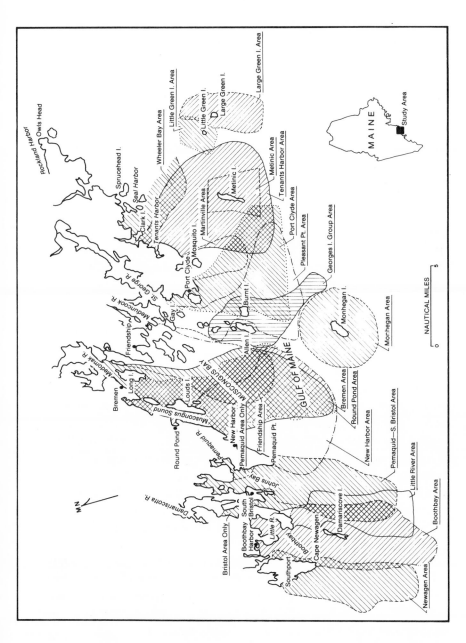

FIG. 2.1. *Lobster fishing territories along the central Maine coast, 1980.*

Rockland Harbor
Owls Head

Sprucehead I.
Seal Harbor
Clark I.
Tenants Harbor
Port Clyde
Mosquito I.
Gay I.
Burnt I.
Allen I.

St. George R.
Medunicook R.
Friendship R.
Friendship

Bremen
Long I.
Louds I.
Muscongus Sound
Round Pond
Pemaquid R.
New Harbor
Friendship Area
Pemaquid Pt.

Medomak R.

Damariscotta R.
Little R.
Johns Bay
South Bristol
Boothbay Harbor
Southport
Cape Newagen
Damariscove I.
Boothbay

Bristol Area Only
Boothbay
Pemaquid Area Only

MUSCONGUS BAY

GULF OF MAINE

Little Green I. Area
Little Green I.
Large Green I.
Large Green I. Area

Wheeler Bay Area

Martinville Area
Metinic I.
Metinic Area
Tenants Harbor Area
Port Clyde Area
Pleasant Pt. Area

Georges I. Group Area

Monhegan I.
Monhegan Area

Bremen Area
Round Pond Area
New Harbor Area
Pemaquid–S. Bristol Area
Little River Area
Boothbay Area
Newagen Area

MAINE
Study Area

NAUTICAL MILES
0   5

fishing rights. One man bought a very small island in the Muscle Ridge channel solely to gain fishing rights to adjacent waters. He does not live on the island and does nothing else with it except to use the surrounding ocean for lobster fishing.

In perimeter-defended areas, ownership rights to the waters are not merely usufructary. Even if the owner is not using his water territory, his fishing rights remain and may be rented out. In these areas, ownership rights are so strong that men who own whole islands rent out water areas to men from nearby mainland harbors. Most of the lobstermen fishing in the Metinic Island area, for example, rent fishing rights from the two families who are legal owners of the island. The family members cannot completely exploit the island's water area, and so they outfit several men from the mainland with boats and gear and allow them to go fishing in their preserve. Arrangements vary. In some cases the families take half the gross income of these renters as return on the capital equipment and as rent on the water area. These rental rights are inherited patrilineally as are land property rights.

A critical difference between nucleated and perimeter-defended territories concerns ease of entry. In nucleated areas it is relatively easy to gain acceptance to harbor gangs. If a man is a resident of the community and shows a willingness to abide by local fishing norms, he will eventually be accepted into the local harbor gang. Entry into these harbor gangs is, however, by no means open. Admission depends on a combination of factors. Violation of certain essential norms means certain rejection (Acheson 1979: 261).

It is much more difficult to gain admission to harbor gangs that maintain perimeter-defended territories. This is to be expected. There is no sense in maintaining sharply defined boundaries by violence against other harbor gangs if any newcomer can join one's own gang. Thus, men who strongly defend the perimeters of their territories also limit membership in their own harbor gangs to a much greater extent than do men fishing in nucleated areas. As will be seen below, this results in more fishing area per fisherman than in nucleated areas (Table 2.1).

.Entry to harbor gangs in perimeter-defended areas is essentially limited to men who belong to families owning the land and adjacent water areas, and to men who are accepted on a rental basis. The unoccupied islands (Green Island, Little Green Island, and Metinic) are each privately owned by one or two families, whose members reserve all fishing rights solely for themselves. It is virtually impossible for a newcomer to enter these harbor gangs, except in some instances as a renter. A few newcomers, however, have been able to establish themselves as fishermen on permanently occupied islands such as Matinicus and Monhegan.

Most fishermen have access to all of the fishing grounds within the area controlled by their own harbor gang. In a large number of instances, however, certain subareas of the territory are used exclusively by one man or a small number of men, and others are expected to stay out. For example, one zone around Isle au Haut is fished exclusively by the members of a family who used to live on the island but now reside in Stonington. Other members of the Stonington gang are expected to stay away from this harbor in recognition of the fact that this family still owns land along the shore.

Age, length of residence, and status within a harbor gang also influence access rights within a harbor gang's area. At a permanently occupied offshore island outside the study area, members of old established families have reserved some choice ledges and shoal areas for themselves and a few of their kin. Newcomers and some of the younger fishermen have to fish in less desirable locations within the harbor gang's territory. Fishermen can be restricted to tiny areas indeed. A college professor who has a cottage on the shore of an offshore island puts a few dozen traps in the bay adjacent to his own land, but he has been told there would be trouble if he tried to fish elsewhere in the island's area.

PROCESSES OF BOUNDARY MAINTENANCE AND CHANGE

Before 1920, all lobstering areas along the Maine coast were undoubtedly perimeter-defended areas. Most areas are now nucleated. The advent of nucleated territories is relatively recent, and the change from perimeter-defended to nucleated areas is by no means complete.

In the 1920s, lobstering was done only in the summer in very small territories held by small groups of men who defended them vigorously. In great part, this pattern was connected to the technology in use. Since lobstering was done from a sloop or dory, fishing in stormy winter waters was very difficult. Even in summer, the area that one could fish was limited, since one could learn the bottom only by hand lead line, and the travel radius was small. Since a man's income was dependent on a small area, he zealously maintained its boundaries. These small territories were typically held by a small group of kinsmen and were passed down to descendants. Fishing areas were usually adjacent to legally owned coastal property, where it was felt that the landowner had a right to the lobsters.

This pattern has persisted into the present 1980s, as we have seen, around the small, privately owned islands of Penobscot Bay, around the large, permanently occupied islands farther out to sea (that is, Matinicus and Monhegan), and to some extent near the mainland harbors in the eastern part of the study area. In the western part, this pattern has broken down. Small, perimeter-defended territories have been amalgamated into larger nucleated areas where most of the ocean area is fished by men from at least two harbors.

The breakdown of small, perimeter-defended territories followed technological change. As motors came into common use in the 1930s, the range a lobsterman could fish increased. In the 1950s the use of depthfinding equipment further increased the effective range of a lobsterman.

As we have seen, lobster-fishing technology is the same along the entire coast. Several different sets of factors caused the differential breakdown of the perimeter-defended territories (Acheson 1979). Two points bear repeating. First, boundary breakdown or maintenance is the result of conflict and political pressure. Second, the willingness to defend a boundary or invade another area depends on (1) the ability to form "political teams" (Bailey 1969), and (2) the existence of alternate income opportunities for the people involved.

Technological and political factors, operating in different geographical contexts, produced the differences in territories described. In the western part of the study area, where the coast is strongly convoluted and formed into deep bays, traditional open-ocean areas of communities have been under great pressure from men in towns farther up the rivers and bays. Before the advent of engines, men from bay communities such as Bremen and Muscongus had to restrict their fishing to the summer months when they could catch lobsters in the waters close to their home harbors. During the past few years, more and more men from bay communities have been purchasing larger boats capable of fishing in open ocean. Since the costs of a $35,000 boat cannot be covered by using it only during the summer, these men must fish year-round. This means that they must invade areas that were formerly the exclusive territories of towns such as New Harbor and Friendship on open ocean. Obviously, they are willing to sacrifice a great deal to get to open water. The alternative is to be bottled up in small traditional territories near their home harbors where they can fish only a few months a year.

For the men in the invaded areas, it is not worthwhile to repel the interlopers. It is true that invasion means that these men will have more competition in areas they once held exclusively. However, an attempt to stop the upriver men from their incursions would mean a full-scale "war," resulting in large financial losses. Even though there is some bitterness directed toward the men from bay communities, men from open-ocean harbor gangs feel it is better to mix than fight. Thus, the traditional perimeter-defended boundaries in areas at the mouths of estuaries have broken down, resulting in nucleated fishing territories. Around Muscongus Bay and the deeply indented bays of the Boothbay region, harbors on the ends of peninsulas are apt to have very small areas for exclusive use. The rest are fished jointly with men from harbors farther inland. The amount of mixing is especially great in winter, when men from more inland harbors must come outside. However, perimeter-defended areas have been maintained farther up these rivers and bays.

A combination of factors has allowed the small, perimeter-defended areas to be maintained around some of the islands in our study areas. First, distance alone has had a dampening effect on the incursions of the mainlanders. Moreover, mainland harbors in this part of the coast, for example, Pleasant Point, Tenant's Harbor, and Port Clyde, have both shoal water and deep water so that members of these harbor gangs can go fishing year-round without pushing into areas controlled by other men. (In this respect, these areas are unlike upriver ones such as Round Pond and Bremen.) Second, and more important, the mainland harbor gangs are composed of larger numbers of men who are not organized in ways that allow political effectiveness in the long run. Friendship, for example, has about ninety-five lobster boats owned by men who live in at least three towns and who have little in common besides occupation. The same is true of the other mainland harbors in the area. Their lack of organization prevents aggressive, long-term efforts that would result in changes in boundary lines.

"Owners" of island areas have long put up a spirited defense of their boundaries. Several factors have made them very effective. The islands are owned and controlled by a small number of nuclear households strongly linked by ties of agnatic kinship and the need for mutual aid. Their small numbers, kinship ties, and longstanding tradition of cooperation make it relatively easy to coordinate the defense of their lobstering area. The vehemence of their defense is bolstered by the fact that they have few alternative economic opportunities. Moreover, their long-term ownership of island property gives them special claim to the adjacent ocean areas. In Maine, virtue is attached to remaining in the same place for a long time. Thus, friends and enemies alike see these long-established island owners as preservers of a valued tradition or admired status quo. To a great degree, this is true of all the perimeter-defended areas. For these reasons and for the time being, there are several areas along the Maine coast where perimeter-defended areas remain—little fiefs carved out of the public domain.

PERIMETER-DEFENDED VERSUS NUCLEATED AREAS: DIFFERENTIAL EFFECTS ON THE ECONOMICS AND ECOLOGY OF MAINE LOBSTERING

Perimeter-defended territories are held by men who tend to form highly effective political groups that serve both to severely restrict entry into the fishery of these areas and to enable the enactment of local conservation measures. Both these factors have produced

TABLE 2.1

Square Miles per Boat in Nucleated and Perimeter-Defended Areas[a]

	HARBOR	NUMBER OF BOATS	TOTAL AREA (IN SQUARE NAUTICAL MILES)	SQUARE NAUTICAL MILES/BOAT
Nucleated areas	Port Clyde	39	30.4	0.78
	New Harbor	36	44.7	1.2
	Friendship	95	25.3	0.27
Perimeter-defended areas	Green Island	8	11	1.4
	Metinic (south end only)	7	10.8	1.5
	Monhegan	12	20	1.7

[a]Only the boats of full-time fishermen have been counted. Part-time (skiff) fishermen have been excluded. The number of boats, and not number of men, had been used since many boats carry more than one man. These data were obtained in 1975.

great differences in fishing effort between nucleated and perimeter-defended areas.

Differences in ease of entry into harbor gangs fishing the two different kinds of areas have produced substantial variation in the number of boats (and fishermen) per square mile. Data comparing three perimeter-defended areas with three adjacent nucleated areas show that men from perimeter-defended areas have far more fishing area per boat than those from nucleated areas (Table 2.1).

The difference between nucleated and perimeter-defended areas is even greater than these figures indicate. If the amount of productive fishing bottom and the amount of mixed fishing were taken into account,[3] the ratio of square nautical miles per boat would be lower than indicated in the nucleated areas.

Since there are fewer boats per square mile in perimeter-defended areas, and since men fishing in those areas use no more capital equipment per man than those in nucleated areas, there is a great difference in the amount of fishing effort in these types of territories. Thus, in perimeter-defended areas, a higher proportion of the lobsters reaching the minimum legal size remain uncaught and grow to larger sizes.

Another difference between the two types of areas is that conservation efforts are practiced in the perimeter-defended territories. The men fishing off Matinicus Island, for example, have voluntarily agreed to limit the number of traps they fish. Such trap limits have two benefits. First, they increase a fisherman's profits by lowering his production costs. A man with a small number of traps does not spend as much for trap stock, and usually pays less for bait, fuel, and boat depreciation as well. Second, a man with fewer traps keeps better track of them, pulls them more frequently, and loses fewer. This reduces lobster mortality, since lobsters in lost traps are apt to be permanently caught. Moreover, when traps are pulled frequently, molting lobsters which would otherwise have been eaten by their brethren are released and given a better chance of survival.[4]

Trap limits do not cut down the total catch. When trap limits are imposed, men dispense with the marginal traps—those not fishing well—and put the remainder to better use so that yield per trap is increased. Thus, with a trap limit, it may take men a little longer to catch the same volume of lobsters, but over the course of the annual cycle the same catch is harvested (see also DeWolf 1974).

From the early years of this century, the men of Monhegan Island, another perimeter-defended territory, have tried to conserve the lobster resource by imposing a closed season. The inhabitants of Monhegan persuaded the state legislature to pass a law forbidding fishing in Monhegan waters from June 25 to January 1. Thus, Monhegan lobstermen fish only in midwinter when the price for lobster is very high and when they have few other economic options. They put their traps "on the bank" in the summer when they have alternate employment in the tourist industry, leaving the defense of their territory to the state fish wardens. This closed season keeps anyone from setting traps during the critical months of July and August, when fishing for molting lobsters would result in very high mortality.

It is critical to note that one man cannot gain the benefits of a trap limit or closed season by unilaterally reducing the number of traps he fishes or the number of months he fishes. If he reduces his fishing effort (and others do not), he is obviously putting himself at a competitive disadvantage—the commons dilemma. But if everyone reduces effort simultaneously, each man will still catch his "fair share" of lobsters. Such conservation measures will work only in areas where everyone agrees to them. So far this has occurred only in perimeter-defended areas, where harbor gangs are organized to enforce strong controls over the actions of their members and to defend their areas. Voluntary controls are not characteristic of the relatively loosely organized harbor gangs fishing nucleated areas.

There is a persistent rumor along the coast that men fishing in areas such as Green Island, Monhegan, Matinicus, and other perimeter-defended areas earn larger incomes and catch larger lobsters than men fishing anywhere else along the coast. The reason, lobstermen explain, is that the islanders reserve private fishing areas for themselves and keep everyone else out. A preliminary study indicated that these rumors had substance to them (Acheson 1975; Wilson 1977.)

We hypothesized that differences in income and catches were due to the differences in effort and fishing practices discussed above. To verify this set of hypotheses, we gathered data on the relationships among type of territoriality (nucleated or perimeter-defended), income, catch size, fishing effort, estimated stock density, and other measures. Two studies were done. First, between June 1972 and May 1973, twenty-eight lobstermen were persuaded to supply detailed information on income and business expenses.[5]

Second, fourteen lobstermen from various harbors were asked to record data on their catches twice a month from March 1973 through January 1974. On every string of traps pulled, they recorded the date, location of the string, depth (in fathoms), number of "setover days" (number of days since the trap was last pulled and rebaited), and whether the string was in an area fished exclusively by men of one harbor or in an area of mixed fishing. On every trap pulled, they recorded another set of data: the carapace lengths of the legal-sized lobsters caught in that trap and the length of the proven breeding stock, that is, female lobsters carrying eggs or with notched tails. To facilitate the recording of these data, the men were provided with metric calipers and data sheets. About a fourth of the total information was obtained by University of Maine staff members who accompanied the fishermen. Data were obtained on 9,089 lobsters, of which 3,327 were caught in nucleated areas and 5,762 in perimeter-defended areas.

The lobstermen were chosen with a view toward controlling for several important variables. To control for ecological differences, all were picked from the same small study area. Seven men fished in nucleated areas, the other seven in perimeter-defended areas. All areas in this part of the study are adjacent to each other. In some cases, the men from nucleated areas were fishing only yards away from the men from perimeter-defended areas.

Moreover, the amount of capital used by the men studied is comparable. On this part of the coast, lobstermen use between 350 and 600 traps each. The exact number a particular man uses depends less on the type of area he fishes than on factors such as age, skill, and ambition. More men fishing the offshore islands have larger diesel-powered boats with radar. Not all boats on islands are large, though, and many men on the mainland have comparable investments in boats. In short, there is no obvious difference in the amount of capital employed by the men in nucleated areas and by those in perimeter-defended areas. To control for skills, all the men chosen were full-time fishermen with a reputation for marked success.

BENEFITS OF TERRITORIALITY

We obtained unmistakable evidence that reduced fishing effort in the perimeter-defended areas has both biological and economic benefits.

Biological Benefits

First, lobsters caught in the perimeter-defended areas are larger than those caught in nucleated areas. This is shown in the frequency distribution of lobsters caught (Fig. 2.2). Men catch a higher percentage of small lobsters in nucleated than in perimeter-defended areas, and a higher percentage of larger lobsters in perimeter-defended areas than in nucleated ones. For example, 8 percent of all lobsters caught in nucleated areas were 83 mm, but only 6.4 percent of those caught in perimeter-defended areas were. Additionally, 1.9 percent of the lobsters caught in perimeter-defended areas were 98 mm, whereas only 0.8 percent of those caught in the nucleated area were this big. Since a high proportion of the lobsters that molt into the legal-size range are immediately

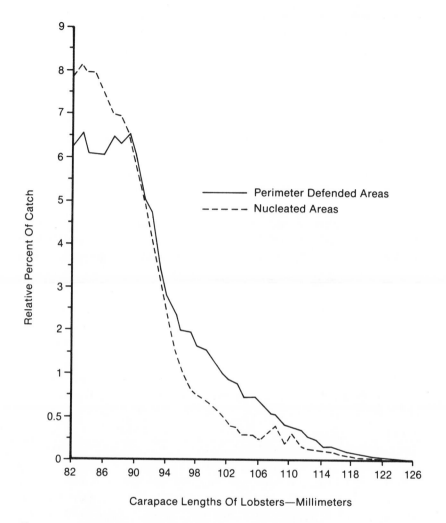

FIG. 2.2. *Distribution of catch by length: perimeter-defended and nucleated areas. Perimeter-defended: mean 89.98; N, 5762. Nucleated areas: mean 87.89; SD, 5.88; N, 3327. The curves were smoothed by using a 4-mm moving average. A t-test indicates there is less than a 0.005 chance of the two samples being drawn from the same population. Calculated value of the t equals 12.55.*

caught in nucleated areas, fewer survive to larger sizes compared to those in perimeter-defended areas. This is reflected in the fact that the mean carapace length of lobsters caught in the nucleated areas is shorter (87.8 mm) than that of those caught in the perimeter-defended areas (89.9 mm).[6]

This difference in size undoubtedly affects the numbers of eggs released in the water in these two types of areas and ultimately the long-term prospects for the lobster fishery itself. Only 6 percent of female lobsters become sexually mature under 90 mm (carapace length), but nearly all females are mature by 105 mm (Krouse 1973: 170–71). Thus, all but a very small proportion of female lobsters become sexually mature between 90 and 100 mm. The percentage of lobsters in this critical size range is higher in the perimeter-defended areas than in the nucleated ones, which means that a higher percentage of female lobsters in the perimeter-defended areas reach a size at which they can extrude eggs. The probability that a female will reach maturity in the perimeter-defended areas is 1.52, or nearly 50 percent higher than it is in the nucleated areas (Wilson 1977). In our sample, 2.7 percent of the lobsters caught in perimeter-defended areas were egg-bearing females, as opposed to only 1.2 percent in the nucleated areas.

Evidence suggests that the fishery benefits if a larger number of females are allowed to survive to breeding size. For example, Thomas (1973: 43–56) argues that the relationship between recruitment (of lobsters into the fishery) and egg production is positive (as eggs increase, recruits will increase) and will remain so in the foreseeable future. Since the number of eggs is a function of the number of females, it can be argued that lobstermen in perimeter-defended areas are doing more to maintain the biomass than those in nucleated areas. However, the men in the perimeter-defended areas are not gaining all the benefits of their activities. Lobster larvae float and travel via currents during one growth stage and then settle down to sedentary existence. The exact pattern of this movement is not known (Pontecorvo 1962: 245), but a lobster born by virtue of conservation practices at Monhegan or Metinic may well end up living its entire adult life in an area many miles away.

There is, however, evidence that the stock density of lobsters is higher in the perimeter-defended areas. This means that there are more lobsters on any given unit of bottom in a perimeter-defended

TABLE 2.2

Stock Density of Lobsters in Pounds/(Trap Haul × Setover Days) in Nucleated and Perimeter-Defended Areas[a]

			SEASON I[b]		SEASON II[c]		SEASON III[d]	
Perimeter-								
defended	A.	Exclusive	0.24409	(662)	0.26478	(2245)	0.47130	(2681)
areas	B.	Overlapping	—		0.25465	(31)	0.33414	(98)
Nucleated	C.	Exclusive	0.05353	(326)	0.11133	(313)	0.26735	(610)
areas	D.	Overlapping	—		0.13782	(400)	0.27949	(1483)

[a]The first number in each square is the lb/(trap haul times setover days); the number in parentheses represents the sample number of lobsters in each category. We did not begin to collect data on setover days until mid-April, so our information on Season I is slight.
[b]August 1 to December 31.
[c]January 1 to April 30.
[d]May 1 to July 31.

than a nucleated area. Stock density must be measured indirectly. Estimates can be obtained with figures on catch per unit of effort (CPUE).[7] This is measured in lobstering by dividing catch (lb.) by trap haul (TH) times setover days (SOD) (Thomas 1973: 38). By this measure, we see a significant difference between perimeter-defended and nucleated areas with regard to stock density (Table 2.2).

Three aspects of Table 2.2 call for comment. First, in seasons II and III, shown in lines A and D, there is a great difference in the CPUE of the exclusive territory of perimeter-defended areas and the overlapping parts of nucleated areas.[8] Second, within perimeter-defended areas, stock densities drop as one moves toward the boundaries of regions fished with men from other harbor gangs. And third, in the nucleated areas, on the other hand, the CPUE of the more exclusive areas, close to harbor mouths, is lower than that of the overlapping areas. This is probably because of greater fishing effort in the areas close to harbor mouths, which are easily accessible to part-timers and highschool boys with small skiffs.

Economic Benefits

Men in perimeter-defended areas catch more and bigger lobsters, and they catch them with less effort. Both facts translate

TABLE 2.3

Catch Characteristics by Area and Season

	SEASON I[a]		SEASON II[b]		SEASON III[c]	
	NUCLEATED	PERIMETER-DEFENDED	NUCLEATED	PERIMETER-DEFENDED	NUCLEATED	PERIMETER-DEFENDED
Number of lobsters caught	366	767	710	2268	2093	2779
Number of lobsters caught per trap hauled	0.61986	1.294	0.4788	0.9569	0.7609	1.038
Mean pounds of lobster caught per trap hauled	0.77288	1.644	0.5654	1.209	0.9113	1.295
Pounds per lobster	1.1648	1.253	1.181	1.319	1.197	1.238

[a]August 1 to December 31.
[b]January 1 to April 30.
[c]May to July 31.

directly into economic benefits. The evidence that the men from perimeter-defended areas trap more lobsters can be seen by comparing mean numbers of lobsters caught per trap in the two types of areas (see Table 2.3).

In every season, the number of lobsters caught per trap is larger in perimeter-defended areas than in nucleated areas. If a man from one of these areas pulls as many traps as a man from a nucleated area, he obviously catches a larger number of lobsters to market. Men from nucleated areas can earn more than men from the perimeter-defended areas, but to do so they must pull many more traps and greatly increase their effort. There is, of course, evidence that some of the men in perimeter-defended areas are cutting down on numbers of traps hauled. However, there is no evidence to suggest that such informal trap limits have so greatly cut down the number of traps of any single man that his income is jeopardized. Rather, such limits have stopped the escalation in numbers of traps.

Men from perimeter-defended areas catch larger lobsters than men in nucleated areas (see Fig. 2.2 and Table 2.3). At all times of year, the men from perimeter-defended areas catch more pounds per trap than men from nucleated areas. The fact that lobsters are sold by the pound helps the men from perimeter-defended areas obtain a higher economic return per trap. Moreover, larger lobsters which can be sold as "dinner lobsters" in high-priced restaurants bring a higher price per pound than the smaller lobsters or "culls." Since men from perimeter-defended areas catch a greater proportion of dinner lobsters, their income is boosted still higher. In this regard, one group of men who fish a perimeter-defended area has made arrangements with a dealer to receive 6 cents per pound more than the going price for all lobsters they catch. The dealer is willing to give it to them because of the large number of dinner lobsters they bring in.

The gross income earned by lobstermen from nucleated areas and that of those from perimeter-defended areas differs greatly. From October 1972 to March 1973, I interviewed eight lobstermen from perimeter-defended areas who made an average gross income of $22,929 from the lobster industry during the preceding year.[9] The average gross income of fishermen from nucleated areas was $16,499. The sample is small but the difference, $6,430, is surprisingly high.

Summary of Biological and Economic Effects of Territoriality

Perimeter-defended lobster territories are characterized by more restricted entry than are nucleated ones. There are fewer boats or fishermen per square mile and lower levels of fishing effort in the perimeter-defended areas. Fishing effort has also been controlled by various local conservation measures, such as limits on the number of traps allowed or local closed seasons. These measures do not affect total catch, but they tend to reduce total lobster mortality and increase the proportion of the more valuable large lobsters caught. Greater stock density in the perimeter-defended areas suggests that reduced effort has halted the process of overexploitation. Economic gains from the strategy of maintaining a strong defense of traditional boundaries are shown in higher mean numbers of lobsters per trap, more large and hence higher-priced lobsters, and higher gross incomes.

THE RELATIVE IMPORTANCE OF TERRITORIALITY

A large number of factors affect catches and thus influence the incomes of fishermen. The number of lobsters a fisherman obtains varies greatly depending on the season of the year, the number of traps employed, and his skill. Fishermen also believe that the type of trap influences catches, along with the bait used, the type of heads (funnel-shaped nets that allow easy entry and prevent escape), the type of bottom, and depth. Fishing skill, in large part, is a matter of understanding all of the factors influencing lobster behavior and knowing how to build the correct types of traps, get the correct type of bait, and position those traps in areas where there are concentrations of lobsters.

The question remains: How important is the system of territoriality in influencing catches in comparison with some of these other variables? In order to answer this question a larger-scale study was done between 1977 and 1979 in the Muscongus Bay region of Maine in which detailed information was recorded on almost ten thousand lobster traps pulled by eighteen cooperating fishermen from four adjacent towns. For every trap pulled, information was recorded on the size of the legal lobsters caught, trap construction, trap location and depth, bait used, and skill of the fisherman.

A regression analysis showed that a number of variables had statistically significant influences on catches (Acheson 1980a). Season was the most critical. There are more lobsters to be caught in the fall months just after a new group has molted and become legal size; as the year progresses, an increasing number of these newly legal lobsters are caught, leaving a smaller pool that can be legally taken. Next in importance was trap size. Larger traps with more retention chambers outfish smaller ones. The next most important variable was the fisherman's town, followed by variables indicating fishing skill and trap construction material, and ending with those on depth, material on the bottom, type of heads used in the traps, and some kinds of bait.

The town variable is critical for our purposes. Fishermen from each of the four towns in the study have their own fishing territories (all nucleated in this study). Its appearance in the middle of the list of variables that influence catches suggests that the area where men are fishing is of considerable importance. Moreover, there were considerable differences in catches between towns, even though all participants came from four adjacent nucleated territories on the same bay.[10] The fishermen from Bremen were catching more lobsters, all other factors controlled, than men from New Harbor, Pemaquid Harbor, and Friendship. Why town is an influential variable and whether territoriality is reflected in it is difficult to answer. In this case, there was an unusual concentration of lobsters in Bremen waters during the summer and fall for several years during the 1970s. Both fishermen and biologists recognize the possibility of such temporarily high concentrations of lobsters in certain locations, but the reasons are not known (Acheson 1981: 663–667). Two fishermen have even suggested that some of the differences in catches noted above between nucleated and perimeter-defended areas may be explained by unusual concentrations of lobsters rather than by differences in numbers of fishermen per unit area and conservation efforts. During our earlier study, there was one such unusual concentration of lobsters in one of the perimeter-defended areas. However, it cannot explain the higher catches per unit effort observed in all perimeter-defended areas.[11]

MANAGEMENT IMPLICATIONS OF TERRITORIALITY

The state of Maine has done little to take advantage of the fact that perimeter-defended areas are more productive. Moreover, the state has instituted none of the conservation measures men from these areas have adopted for themselves (e.g., trap limits and closed seasons). Officials felt that the administrative costs involved in establishing and maintaining small fishing areas would be prohibitive. In addition, since the existence of the territorial system is hidden from official eyes, the state's officers have little information on any possible beneficial effects.

Many serious fishermen, however, have long felt that legally formalizing territories would be beneficial. On more than one occasion, fishermen from perimeter-defended areas have asked me pointedly whether I thought it would be possible to petition the legislature to enact laws formalizing their traditional fishing areas and limiting the number of men allowed to fish in them. Conservation of the resource is one motive; but it should be noted that all these fishermen envisioned laws which would allow them to fish in "their" areas, while the costs of enforcing the boundaries would be passed on to the state wardens.

In the 1970s there was increasing pressure to pass laws concerning some of these conservation measures. In 1974 and 1975, a bill was proposed that would have limited the number of traps a fisherman could fish. This bill was defeated. A number of other proposed bills have been discussed but have never been enacted. In the early 1980s, however, the fishermen of Swan's Island proposed that a law be passed requiring fishermen to use a limited number of traps within the Swan's Island area, arguing that this would reduce the number of "ghost traps," lost or abandoned, that continue to kill lobsters. In 1984 the Maine Commission of Marine Resources agreed to enforce a five-hundred-trap limit within the Swan's Island area. The measure benefits the Swan's Island fishermen in two ways. First, it cuts their costs for gas, bait, and traps without sacrificing the competitive edge of skilled fishermen. One can catch as many lobsters with five hundred traps as one thousand; it merely takes a little longer. Second, the measure establishes the Swan's Island area as a legal entity and charges the state wardens with keeping out "outsiders," on the grounds that they use too many traps. There are also conservation benefits from a trap limit, but in the minds of the local fishermen these are apparently of secondary consideration. The "ghost trap" issue appears to be little more than a rationalization to legalize a profitable perimeter-defended area whose borders were becoming increasingly difficult to defend.

WHY NOT PRIVATE PROPERTY?

If property rights confer such benefits, why have sole ownership institutions not been developed (Scott 1955)? Why are territories held jointly by sizable groups of individuals?

In answering this question, we must speculate because private property rights have never developed at any place or time in the history of the industry. A clue is provided by the few instances in which some influential individuals are able to reserve spots for their own private use in the harbor gang's territory. None of these men, it should be noted, fishes only in his own exclusive "spots," nor do they obtain most of their income from lobsters caught in such spots. They always fish throughout the area held by their own harbor gang. The reason is clear: concentrations of lobsters are found in different places over the annual cycle and from year to year. A man confined to a small territory would not likely have adequate catches most of the time. A lobster-fishing territory, if it is to be viable, must contain several different microecological niches. In particular, it must contain shallow "shedder bottom" to permit fishing in the warm months, and deep water where lobsters are found in the colder months. Such zones can be miles apart.

Moreover, the "owners" of these "private spots" typically have a good deal of difficulty reserving them for their exclusive use. The same is true of the small, perimeter-defended territories. Successful defense of the boundaries of perimeter-defended areas often demands the coordinated efforts of a group of fishermen, and even then the cost can be quite high (Acheson 1979: 266ff.).

These observations suggest that it would be very difficult or impossible to divide the entire coast into small territories owned by single individuals. If a person is going to fish year-round or even most of the year, he needs access to a large and diverse area. The costs of defending such a territory would be prohibitive. Given the numbers of fishermen in the industry, if individuals were allowed to reserve for themselves even small zones of a few square miles of fishing grounds, hundreds of men would have to find other work. Anyone who attempted to set up a system of privately owned fishing zones would face strong opposition from the majority of men in the industry whose livelihoods would be threatened.

CONTROLLING THE COMMONS

One of the themes that runs through the literature on fishing communities and fisheries economics is the competitive, predatory behavior of individual fishing firms, their inability and unwillingness to conserve the marine resources on which they depend, and their tendency to overcapitalize. These factors are related to the fact that, by law, many marine areas and resources are open-access common property. Since oceans are owned by no one and may be exploited by everyone, no one has any interest in maintaining the resources. Why should one man reduce his fishing effort to conserve? The fish he does not catch today will be caught by someone else tomorrow. Under these conditions, a fisherman is only being rational when he expands the amount of capital equipment he owns and tries to catch all the fish he can as quickly as possible.

The result is what Hardin (1968: 1245–46) has called the "tragedy of the commons." Common property resources of all kinds—the air, waters, oceans, publicly-owned land—are subject to abuses and overexploitation that do not occur with privately owned resources. It is not only that common property resources are overexploited by a callous public; they are also subject to a kind of escalating abuse as people vie with each other to strip bare resources owned in common. As Hardin explains it, those exploiting a common property resource are locked into a system in which it is only "logical" that they increase their exploitation without limit. As far as fisheries are concerned, the tragedy takes the form of overexploitation, depletion of fish stocks, underutilization of capital resources, and where opportunity costs are low, acceptance of low incomes (Crutchfield 1964: 212).

At both the national and regional levels, attempts to regulate fisheries usually take the form of manipulating fishing seasons, fishing areas, and the type of fishing gear used. Although such regulations may limit fish mortality, economists have pointed out that they are probably ineffective and certainly make fishing more inefficient (Pontecorvo and Vartdal 1967; Crutchfield and Pontecorvo 1969; DeWolf 1974). Fishing quotas and seasons, for example, leave expensive boats tied to the dock much of the time and trained crews out of work. They also increase competition for new equipment and for a "share of the catch" when fishing is allowed. Several economists have strongly argued that a better management system would involve limiting entry into the fishery either by a licensing system (Pontecorvo 1967; Christy 1973) or by taxation (Pontecorvo and Vartdal 1967), which would cut production by increasing marginal costs.

The lobstermen of Maine have already created a system that produces all the benefits these economists have envisioned. Given what we know about the theory of common property resources, we can only deplore the breakdown of the traditional perimeter-defended areas. In perimeter-defended areas, access to the resource is highly controlled, and escalation of fishing effort has been prevented by the use of political power to enforce local conservation measures. Moreover, in these areas, fishermen are not caught in a self-defeating "competitive withdrawal" (Crutchfield and Pontecorvo 1969), but can cooperate to conserve the lobster stock and raise their income levels. In nucleated fishing areas, the traditional means of controlling escalating fishing effort are breaking down. The data we have on differences in average size of lobsters, size of catch, size of stock, and fishing incomes suggest that men fishing in nucleated areas are bearing the costs of increased participation in an industry that has many characteristics of an open-access common-property fishery.

NOTES

This chapter is a revised and updated version of "The Lobster Fiefs: Economic and Biological Effects of Territoriality in the Maine Lobster Industry," which originally appeared in *Human Ecology* 3(3):182–207 in 1975. Permission has been granted by Plenum Press to reprint the article. The research on which this paper is based was financed by the National

Marine Fisheries Service (Contract No. N-043-30-72) and the National Science Foundation (Grant No. AER 77 06018).

1. The laths and wire allow free circulation of water while retaining larger, legal-sized lobsters. The open end of the trap is fitted with a funnel-shaped nylon net which lets lobsters climb in easily but makes it difficult for them to get out. Along the central part of the coast, the study area, one or sometimes two traps are attached to a small styrofoam buoy with a "warp" (nylon or hemp rope). Distinctive sets of colors, registered with the state, mark the buoys belonging to each lobsterman. Fish remnants from nearby processing plants are used as bait.

2. It is standard practice to measure lobsters on the carapace, from the eye socket to the back of the body, where the carapace ends and the tail begins.

3. First, in nucleated areas, not all of the bottom is productive of lobsters. An estimated 25 percent of the area fished by Friendship and New Harbor men is mud bottom which rarely produces lobsters. Second, much of the area fished by men from nucleated harbors consists of zones of mixed fishing. Men from New Harbor, for example, fish over 44.7 square nautical miles of ocean. Only about 12.6 square nautical miles of that is fished exclusively by them. Men from Port Clyde fish some 30.4 square nautical miles, but 13.3 of them they share with men from other harbors. In contrast, all of the area "owned" by men in perimeter-defended territories produces lobsters at some time of the year, and no part of these territories is shared with men from other gangs.

4. State biologists are convinced that a large number of lobsters are killed by being caught in untended or lost traps. As of 1984 a "venting" bill is in effect, requiring vents, or extra exits, to ensure that most of the small, illegal-sized lobsters are able to escape from traps. Bills have been unsuccessfully introduced requiring fishermen to pull their traps every forty-eight hours.

5. Early in 1973 the U.S. Internal Revenue Service began to investigate the Maine lobstermen. A high proportion of the fishermen in Maine were audited by the IRS. Many were forced to pay additional tax money, and several were charged with criminal fraud. Late in the spring of 1973, the men had become so fearful and suspicious of anyone asking information about income that this part of the project had to be dropped. However, enough data, had been collected in the pre-

ceding months to allow us to come to tentative conclusions concerning the economic effects of territoriality.

6. The difference in the mean carapace length of lobsters caught in nucleated vs. perimeter-defended areas is very small. However, because females become mature between 90 and 100 mm, these slight differences in size are significant, since they mean that there is a higher proportion of mature females in the perimeter-defended areas.

7. In the past, attempts have been made to assess the density of lobster stock by using figures for catch in numbers of pounds, or pounds caught per trap. Neither is a valid index since neither takes into account the number of times a trap is pulled or the working time of the bait. Two areas producing 1 pound per trap do not have the same stock density if the traps in one are pulled twice as often as in the other.

8. Along the periphery of nucleated and perimeter-defended areas some mixed fishing is allowed. The term "overlapping" refers to lobsters caught in these areas, whereas "exclusive" refers to lobsters caught in areas where only men from a single harbor gang go fishing.

9. These are gross income figures earned from lobster fishing alone. Although net income figures would undoubtedly be more valuable, they are almost impossible to compute accurately since it is difficult to estimate depreciation on boats and equipment, and no records are kept on routine maintenance. In order to protect informants, income figures are not broken down by variables such as age or harbor gang.

10. No information from perimeter defended areas was collected in this study. Such information would likely show a greater influence of territoriality on catches there than in nucleated areas.

11. Men fishing in the perimeter-defended area where an unusual concentration of lobsters is believed to have occurred in the early 1970s claimed that there was nothing unusual. They said that fishing is always better than in nearby nucleated areas. The few reliable figures I have been able to get on income support their assertions. The island fishermen have consistently higher incomes than men from nearby nucleated harbors.

3 Common-Property Resource Management and Cree Indian Fisheries in Subarctic Canada

Fikret Berkes

ACCORDING TO CONVENTIONAL WISDOM, fish resources are common property and therefore tend to suffer from the tragedy of the commons. This concept originates in Hardin's (1968) tragedy-of-the-commons parable, initially formulated to describe the inevitable decline of a common grazing land on which each villager has a right to graze as many cattle as he wishes.

The parable can be easily reformulated for fisheries. Consider a bay or a lake with a certain finite capacity for biological production. There is a profitable fishery on this body of water, and each participating fisherman, as a rational being, seeks to maximize his gain. Each new boat he or his family adds to the fishing fleet brings a gain of almost +1. But as the number of boats and their fishing capacity keep on increasing, sooner or later the bay will be overfished, and there will be a social cost of −1. Since, however, the effects of overfishing will be shared by all fishermen, the loss incurred by the individual adding the boat is only a fraction of −1. Thus, each fisherman has an interest in increasing his fishing effort (more boats or simply bigger boats and/or better technology) because, rationally, this is the only sensible course to follow. Each and every fisherman sharing the resource reaches the same conclusion, and hence "the freedom in a commons brings ruin to all" (Hardin 1968).

The parable provides a deterministic or mechanistic model, verified by many empirical case studies in fisheries around the world. Its pessimistic predictions are often cited to emphasize the necessity of government-formulated regulations. In the field of fisheries management, the parable has attained the status of conventional wisdom, and it is used by some as if it were a scientific law.

Many researchers have cautioned, however, that common-property resource use need not always be associated with a tragedy in the way that the deterministic model predicts. Social controls of many kinds exist to govern common-property resource use. As Ciriacy-Wantrup and Bishop (1975) point out, common property (*res communes*) is different from unowned resources (*res nullius*): "common property, with the institutional regulation it implies, is capable of satisfactory performance in the management of natural resources." McCay (1978: 398–99) puts the matter in a nutshell: "The analytical model used by fisheries economists assumes that all fishermen behave as anarchic villains in a 'tragedy of the commons' (Hardin 1968) which leads inexorably to resource depletion and economic waste. . . . Participants are believed to lack self-regulating mechanisms and motivation . . . despite evidence that many communities of fishermen do have ways of altering the common-property and open-access nature of marine resources."

ASSUMPTIONS OF THE COMMONS MODEL

Stillman (1975) and O'Riordan (1976) observed that there are several hidden assumptions in the tragedy-of-the-commons model. For the tragedy to occur, three conditions must be fulfilled (adapted here from Stillman with additions and modifications): (1) The resource must be owned in common by a group of people (common property), and further, must be freely open to any user (open access). (2) The users must be selfish. Individuals must be able to pursue self-interest as opposed to collective good. While attaining private gain, users must be able to override social pressure from the community. There is a further assumption here that the users are maximizing their short-term gains without regard to the long-term viability of the fishery or the welfare of their community. (3) The resource must be used so intensively that the rate of exploitation exceeds the natural rate of replenishment of the resource, that is, the harvest exceeds sustainable yields.

Stillman (1975) argued that, given these premises, there is no

logically consistent solution to the tragedy. Within its assumptions, the parable is a tautology. Thus, all "attempts to solve the
tragedy within its parameters are doomed to failure." O'Riordan
(1976) observed that the fascination of the parable is its *insolubility*.
The real challenge of the tragedy is that the solution has to be
sought beyond the three premises.

The following case study describes a small-scale society that
has generated norms and institutions to manage natural resources. This case study will be used to test the assumptions of the
model of the tragedy of the commons, and the findings will be
placed in the context of fisheries management in the Canadian
North, and more generally, in small-scale fisheries throughout the
world.

THE STUDY AREA AND THE PEOPLE

The study area is eastern James Bay in the Canadian subarctic (Fig.
3.1). The Cree Indian village of Chisasibi (formerly Fort George,
population about 2,000) is located about 1,000 km north of
Montreal. Relatively isolated until the construction of a large hydroelectric project on La Grande River begun in 1972, the village has
had a road connection since the mid-1970s to the south and to the
east where dams LG-2, LG-3, and LG-4 are located. In exchange for
their claims on the land on which the dams were built, the Cree
signed a treaty with the government (the James Bay Agreement)
that specified and consolidated their land and resource use rights,
made provisions for regional self-government and economic development, and provided monetary compensation.

The eastern James Bay Cree are organized into eight bands,
including Chisasibi and its northern neighbor, Great Whale (Poste-
de-la-Baleine), and southern neighbor, Wemindji. In Chisasibi
there are two broad social groups: the terms *inlanders* and *coasters*
distinguish families who traditionally hunted in the interior and
along the James Bay coast, respectively. Within the band, hunting
groups traditionally consisted of several nuclear families, usually
ten to twenty people, spending most of the year together in bush
camps. Following the settlement of the Cree in permanent villages
in the 1960s, hunting groups consisting only of men have also

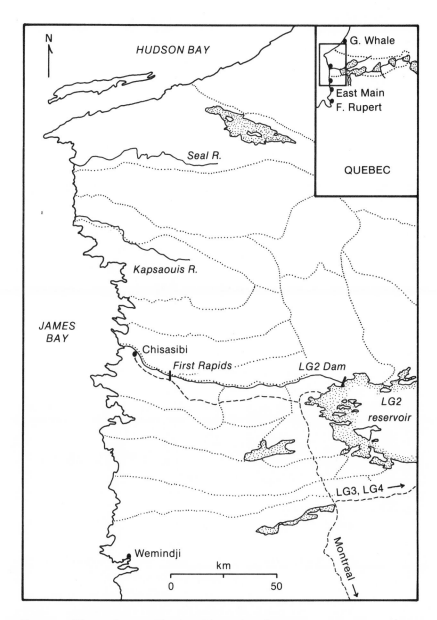

N

HUDSON BAY

G. Whale

East Main
F. Rupert

QUEBEC

Seal R.

Kapsaouis R.

JAMES
BAY

Chisasibi
First Rapids

LG2 Dam

LG2
reservoir

LG3, LG4 →

Montreal →

Wemindji

km

0   50

FIG. 3.1. *The study area. The dotted lines show beaver-
trapping territories.* Inset: *extent of Chisasibi
hunting/fishing/trapping areas.*

become common. The human ecology and native fisheries of the area have been investigated by Berkes in a series of substantive papers (Berkes 1977, 1979, 1981) and more specialized studies (Berkes 1982a,b, 1983; Berkes and Gonenc 1982).

The Land-Use System

As shown in Figure 3.1, there is a community hunting/fishing/trapping area with a reasonably well defined boundary. Under the James Bay Agreement, Chisasibi hunters and fishermen have exclusive use-rights to a part of this area (most of the western quarter), and for trapping purposes they have exclusive use-rights for the entire area.

The community hunting area is divided into some forty traplines (in Cree, *nituhuschii*, "my hunting land"), as partially shown in Figure 3.1. The beaver trapline system is a recent institution formalized under the provincial government in the 1950s. However, according to the hunters, the family-based land-tenure system on which it is based has existed for a long time. The trapline holder (*amiskuchimaaw*, "beaver boss") effectively controls more than just the beaver resource. Under the traditional common-property management system in Chisasibi, all persons wishing to hunt, fish, or trap are expected to inform the boss of the area involved. Such requests would rarely be turned down, but nevertheless this arrangement ensures that the boss controls access to his area and knows about all harvesting activities taking place on it. Information management is involved as well: specialized knowledge is needed to travel to an area and to know where to hunt after getting there.

In addition to beaver, the Canada goose is hunted on a territorial basis in Chisasibi (Berkes 1982b). Goose territories are only on the James Bay coast (elsewhere geese are not abundant), and they are controlled by the *paashchichaauchimaaw* ("goose-shooting boss"). The goose territory system is not formalized and mapped. It is more fluid than the government-sanctioned beaver trapline system but just as real within the traditional management sphere. In Chisasibi the two kinds of bosses are not necessarily the same people, and the boundaries of the two kinds of territories do not necessarily coincide.

Hunting bosses in Chisasibi often talk about their ownership of the land and animals. However, the word used, *nitipaaihtaan*, means "ownership to take care of" or "to control," and differs fundamentally from the term for ownership *nitipiwaawsiiun*, which is used for personal belongings, things that can be bought and sold.

The hunters say that the land and animals belong to God; the boss is given not really the animals but the *responsibility* for the distribution of the wealth of the land. The boss manages the harvesting activity for the benefit of the band society as a whole: he leads the hunt, supervises the sharing of food, making sure that no one goes hungry, and enforces customary laws with respect to harvesting activities. The boss inherits the hunting territory, usually from his father or from an uncle; he cannot sell or buy it. If he does not manage it for community benefit, he can be forced by social pressure to step down. This does not happen often. In Chisasibi, there was only one case in recent years. The beaver boss in question neglected to pull out his traps (usually done at the end of March), a fairly serious violation of trappers' customary law, and was subsequently forced to relinquish his authority.

The Chisasibi Cree land-use system is a good example of what Ciriacy-Wantrup and Bishop (1975) mean by common property as an institution, one that can work well for the management of natural resources in the absence of private property in the Euro-American sense. Hunting territories are *not* private property; they are communal property in which hunting bosses exercise leadership by mutual consent. It is a common-property system with traditional or neotraditional institutions partially backed by government legislation. Local-level management plays a more important role than government management. The land and the animals are *res communes,* not *res nullius:* everyone's property is not no one's property. This is not to say that the land-tenure system is completely free of troubles. It has been under pressure from (1) improvements in access, especially new roads in the interior; (2) increased population; (3) more efficient transportation and hunting technology; and (4) erosion of traditional knowledge and values (Berkes 1982a,b).

Territoriality is found in the harvest of some resources but not others. The two species hunted on a territorial basis in Chisasibi, beaver and Canada geese, are the most productive and predictable of all the species in the hunt. On the basis of catch per unit of effort, goose hunting is about twice as productive (11.5 kg/man-day or work) as fishing (mean of about 6 kg/man-day of work) (Berkes 1979). Feit's (1973) data from southern James Bay indicate that beaver are about as productive as geese in Chisasibi. In terms of predictability, beaver may be considered an almost stationary resource—unlike, for example, otter, which is very mobile and is not trapped on a territorial basis. Although migratory, Canada geese are a predictable resource because the same feeding areas are used year after year, and thus hunters are able to use the same set of hunting locations. Based on detailed knowledge of goose behavior, time-tested hunting techniques ensure a productive harvest, weather permitting (Berkes 1982b).

The presence of two overlapping and species-specific hunting-territory systems in Chisasibi based on the productivity and predictability of the resource may be offered as support of Dyson-Hudson and Smith's (1978) "economic defendability" theory of territoriality adapted from biological ecology. However, there must be at least one other precondition for the formation of territories: the demand for the resource must exceed the supply. Otherwise one would expect territories in the more productive fishing sites, such as the seine-fishing area at the foot of the First Rapids of La Grande River (the site of the LG-1 Dam to be built in the 1990s). At the First Rapids, Chisasibi families harvested 50 to 100 kg per day of work before construction began in 1979 (Berkes 1982a). This highly productive harvest is also highly predictable; any family can go to the First Rapids in August and come back with 50 to 100 kg of fish. This catch provides enough smoked fish to satisfy an average household's requirements over the fall and winter months. The supply of the resource itself is not seen by the Cree to be a limiting factor: fish are a staple resource, a back-up supply of food when other animals are scarce or absent.

THE FISHERY

General Description

There are no defended fishing territories, but this statement needs to be qualified. First, a family or person going fishing would normally notify the boss of that area, not as much to obtain permission as to politely acknowledge his authority. Second, individual fishermen have favorite fishing areas, and it is the specialized knowledge of the land and the very indented James Bay coastline that generally determines access to a particular fishing area. In practice, the only open-access area is in the estuary, within a radius of some 15 km of the old village site.

Until the 1970s and 1980s, inlanders as a group lacked knowledge of the coast and rarely participated in James Bay fisheries, whereas coasters lacked knowledge of the interior and almost never fished in inland lakes and rivers and rarely at the First Rapids. This situation has changed, and it has become fairly commonplace to find traditional coastal people fishing in lakes along the roads to LG-3 and LG-4 dams and to Matagami/Montreal.

Subsistence fishing tends to be a part-time cooperative activity in which almost every household participates. In the summer, it is a primary activity. In other seasons, it is a secondary activity that supplements harvests from hunting and/or trapping. As in hunting and trapping, the unit of production is usually the family, although it is not uncommon for two older men from different households to join forces and go fishing together. The main fishing technique on the James Bay coast and in the newly created reservoirs involves setting short (50 m) gillnets of various mesh sizes from 7-meter, outboard-equipped canoes. Smaller paddle canoes, sometimes outboard-equipped, are used in lakes and rivers in the interior. Other fishing equipment includes hand-drawn seines at the base of rapids for migratory fish, rods and reels, and traditional set lines for the larger, predatory fish.

The fish that comes out of a net normally belongs to the owner of the net. The food taken home is used by members of the household. However, considerable amounts also go to kin in other households, close neighbors, friends, and whoever expresses desire for some fish, in that order, as long as supplies last. Successful fishermen obtain prestige from giving away fish, but most of them also expect to be paid back in some way eventually. Even though Chisasibi is a relatively large village and has been disrupted by the construction of the hydroelectric project, exchange networks and reciprocal relations still exist. Families who do not exchange fish or other wild food often pay back with favors (e.g., use of a truck) or with cash. A negligible portion of the total community fish catch is sold through the local cooperative store.

The Cree fishery can hardly be characterized as a free-for-all. Fishing operations are orderly, and the techniques simple but precise. Although there are no rituals in the killing of fish as there are for such species as black bear and beaver, there is a code of ethics that essentially provides for respect for other fishermen and for the fish. For example, there are approved ways of killing animals quickly and without mess. There are rules against boastful behavior and against waste. One eats what one catches. This does not mean, however, that boastful behavior and waste are absent. Many hunters/fishermen admit to violating some of these rules—and to suffering a loss of hunting success for a time as a consequence. This belief is strong even among the younger hunters. It may be absent among many of the teenagers, the first television generation in Chisasibi, who are only marginally involved in the hunting economy and often not susceptible to social sanctions.

The use of "proper" fishing methods and practices is ensured by social pressure. For example, if more than one group is fishing at the First Rapids seining site, they take turns. One sweep of the net takes about five minutes, but it is usually necessary to wait thirty minutes between successive sweeps so that the fish will come into the cove again. With three groups present, each group would have to wait about ninety minutes for its turn. People are respectful of the others' turns. Over several years at this site I never observed anyone even attempting to fish out of turn. People frown upon and criticize those, for example, who do not provide sufficient berth for others' nets or who use gillnets with a mesh size smaller than usual. Even researchers came under social pressure when they used experimental nets that catch undersized fish (Berkes 1977).

Characteristics of Subarctic Fish Populations

To appreciate the ecologically sensible nature of the practices of Cree fishermen, one must consider certain properties of subarctic ecological systems and their fish populations. The conventional wisdom in ecology is that subarctic ecosystems are characterized by low species diversity, great population fluctuations or cycles, and generally low ecological stability. However, arctic and subarctic fish population assemblages in lakes have characteristics of ecologically mature communities: usually there is a large standing stock (biomass) of old and large-sized fish, analogous to trees in a tropical rain forest (Johnson 1976).

The reason for this is a matter of scientific controversy (Johnson 1976; Power 1978). The simplest explanation appears to be the one proposed by Power (1978). Growth of subarctic fish is relatively rapid until maturity; after maturity it slows down. Mortality rates decline rapidly through early life and stabilize at a low level through much of the life span. These growth and mortality patterns produce a population with many small, few intermediate-sized, and many large fish—hence the unusual bimodal length-frequency distributions often observed.

Berkes and Gonenc (1982) modeled a hypothetical whitefish population with assumptions consistent with findings in the James Bay area. The length-frequency distribution obtained corroborated Power's (1978) theory, and seems to be a realistic whitefish population model for the James Bay area, with relatively few intermediate-sized fish of 25–35 cm, and many large fish, with a mode at about 50–55 cm (Fig. 3.2).

Such a population would include more than ten reproductive year-classes of significant size. The presence of so many reproducing year-classes of fish in the population may be considered insurance against the variability of the physical environment which, in some years, results in complete reproductive failure.

Some authors have questioned the supposed "fragility" of northern ecosystems, pointing out that these systems have high ecological resilience, or ability to bounce back (Dunbar 1973). In the case of fish populations, the ability to bounce back probably has to do with adaptations of the sort outlined above. The significance of this for human ecology is that fish are indeed a staple resource, as subarctic hunters/fishermen well know, a resource that remains relatively unaffected by perturbations in the physical environment.

However, the presence of many old and large fish in an unfished northern lake gives a misleading impression of the actual biological productivity of the system. Since primary or plant productivity is generally low in the north, fish productivity is low as well. The potential yields of fish in estuarine and freshwater areas in James Bay may be on the order of 0.4 kg/ha/yr to the north of La

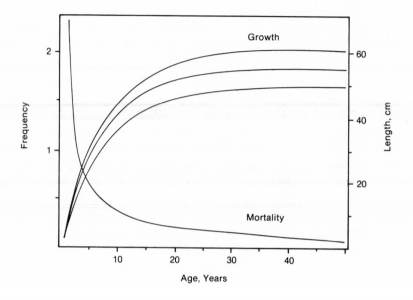

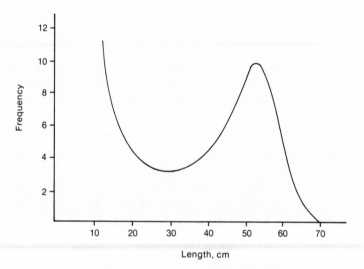

FIG. 3.2. *Growth and mortality curves of the whitefish population model (top panel), and the length-frequency structure of the population as calculated mathematically from the growth and mortality curves (bottom panel). Assumptions and calculations are given in Berkes and Gonenc (1982).*

Grande River and 0.6 to 1.0 kg/ha/yr to the south of it (Berkes 1981). (In temperate coastal areas and lagoons, common values are on the order of 50–100 kg/ha/yr.) The highest recorded actual yields in the area were from the estuary of La Grande River, averaging 0.9 kg/ha/yr in 1973–79. In the less intensively used Eastmain estuary the mean for the years 1975–79 was 0.3 kg/ha/yr.

In addition, most of the species in the harvest are slow-growing fish; they are recruited (or become available to the fishery) at a fairly late age. According to a survey of age-weight relationships, the Cree fishery for most species was based mainly on fish of about ten years of age (Berkes 1981). Some species, such as brook trout, grow faster and may be harvestable at four years or so, but others, such as sturgeon, may be harvestable only after twenty years or more.

A harvest based on ten-year-old fish implies that the turnover rate is low. If each age-class up to ten represented an equal biomass (a conservative oversimplification), only about one-tenth of the total biomass could be taken per year. Some studies in the Northwest Territories of Canada have postulated a production to biomass (P:B) ratio of 1:10 for the dominant lake stocks. The findings in James Bay area appear to be consistent with this ratio. That is, for a given body of water, only about one-tenth or less of the standing stock of fish can be harvested each year on a sustainable basis.

Ecologically Adaptive Practices
of Cree Fishermen

The management problem facing Cree fishermen is how to harvest the sparse production of a large area, where the stocks consist of old fish available in large and conveniently fishable units, but where the rate of renewability of the resource is very slow. There are a number of Cree practices that help solve the problem.

1. Fishermen tend to concentrate at a number of traditional fishing spots where the catch per unit of effort is known from experience to be high. An example of such a site is the First Rapids of La Grande River, where large numbers of cisco in prespawning aggregations can be obtained in August at the foot of the rapids. Since fishermen cannot afford—in terms of time—to fish when

they are not obtaining good returns compared to other subsistence alternatives, and have limited amounts of gear, they select situations in which fish are easy to catch. Thus, groups of fishermen concentrate, year after year, on the same prespawning aggregations, feeding or overwintering concentrations, and migrating or spawning populations, at specific times and places.

2.   Fishermen have extensive knowledge about the times and locations of appropriate concentrations of fish. Fishermen of the more traditional families who spend part of the year on the land know the most suitable fishing areas in every bay (or lake) within the family territory. Given great travel distances, extensive knowledge of the terrain is essential. This is particularly true on James Bay to the north and south of Chisasibi where the coast is shallow and extremely indented, and where the navigator needs to know the configuration of the coast at different phases of the tide.

3.   Fishing effort is deployed opportunistically, and fishermen cooperate to take advantage of good fishing locations. A family group may concentrate its spring fishing effort on feeding populations of whitefish in a coastal inlet. If initial catches are high, other groups will come until the fish are locally depleted (for the year). If initial catches are low, the group quickly relocates its camp and nets to areas in which fishing is better.

4.   The amount of fishing effort deployed is subject to compensating mechanisms. For example, if a fisherman missed the August First Rapids fishery or did not get a good catch, he might spend relatively more time and effort at the October La Grande estuary fishery or the November/December La Grande south channel ice-fishery. If the ice-fishery that year happened to be going well for the few who tried it, many would join in, so that in a good year there would be as many as fifty to sixty fishing groups (with one to two 50-m gillnets each), but in a bad year only two or three.

In summer, when there are no other subsistence alternatives, many people continue fishing even though the catch per unit of effort is low. The fishermen compensate for the low yields per net simply by setting more nets. A fishing group monitored by Berkes (1977) had an average of 2.7 net sets per day and were obtaining 4.4 kg per net set in June. In August the average yield dropped to 2.2 kg per net set, but the number of net sets went up to 4.3 per

TABLE 3.1

Fishing Effort and Catch per Net Check for One Fishing Group Near Chisasibi

	JUNE	AUGUST	OCTOBER	NOVEMBER
Total catch, kg	140	85	60	44
Number of net checks	32	39	14	8
Catch per net set, kg	4.4	2.2	4.3	5.5
Net checks per day	2.7	4.3	2.0	2.0

SOURCE: Berkes 1977

day, so that the total daily catch still remained around 10 kg. In October and November, when the catch per net set went back up to 4.3 kg and 5.5 kg, the number of net sets went back down to 2.0 per day (Table 3.1).

The concentration of fishing effort in space and time, the opportunistic nature of the fishery, the rapid communication of fishing success that permits the redistribution of the fishing effort, and the ability to compensate for year-to-year and seasonal variations may all be identified as adaptations to the subarctic environment.

The knowledge of the environment and the resource base is, of course, important for fishermen/hunters everywhere. The specialized knowledge required to get to some of the more distant harvesting areas and to fish successfully there results, indirectly, in territorial use of the fish resource. However, the lack of a rigid territorial system for fishing allows for more flexibility in the distribution of effort to optimize yields than would otherwise be possible. The mode of production requires cooperation rather than competition. The sharing of knowledge and catches functions as insurance in an environment in which fishing success is highly variable in space and time.

Management Significance of Cree Fishing Strategies

Coastal and estuarine fish stocks near Chisasibi are exploited every year mostly in the form of bursts of fishing effort at specific times and places. The more distant stocks (coastal or inland) are exploited once every few years. Accordingly, near Chisasibi,

TABLE 3.2

Catch per Unit of Fishing Effort, Near Chisasibi and Away, 1975–81

	MEAN HARVEST PER CHECK OF 50-M GILLNET	
	WEIGHT, KG	NUMBER OF FISH
Chisasibi, spring/summer	4.3	15
Chisasibi, fall/winter	5.5	21.5
South coast of James Bay	6.6	8.5
North coast of James Bay	9.2	12.5
Inland	11.7	7.3

SOURCE: Berkes 1979 and unpublished

catches consist of many fish of relatively small size. By contrast, in the more distant fisheries, catches consist of relatively small numbers of large-sized fish (Table 3.2).

The fishing strategy in the area within 15 km of Chisasibi was examined (Berkes 1977). It is a multispecies fishery. With every multispecies fishery, there is a basic management dilemma. In fisheries theory, the curves of yield against fishing effort and against mesh size are different for each species. It is impossible to harvest more than one species at the optimum level for each, hence the dilemma. In practice, in commercial fisheries the choice of fishing strategy usually represents a compromise to harvest as many of the valuable species as possible (see, for example, Gulland 1974).

Within the 15 km radius of the village, there are two desirable species, whitefish and cisco, and one undesirable species, longnose sucker. These three species make up 91 percent of the harvest (Berkes 1979). The gillnet mesh sizes commonly used on the coast near Chisasibi are 63.5 mm (2.5 in.), 76.2 mm (3 in.), 88.9 mm (3.5 in.) and 101.6 mm (4 in.). The smallest-mesh net selects for cisco, and the larger ones for whitefish (Berkes 1977).

The choice of 76.2-mm and larger nets is a strategy for catching whitefish. This strategy works well beyond the 15 km radius of the village where whitefish are relatively abundant. Within 15 km of the village, however, whitefish is relatively rare and cisco abundant. Here, the larger-mesh nets still catch more whitefish than cisco, but the total catches are small because of the escape of the smaller cisco through the mesh. In this area, Cree fishermen predominantly use the smaller-mesh nets, and it has been shown statistically that the use of this mesh size results in the doubling of the total catch per net check (Berkes 1977).

The Cree fishing strategy shows one way in which a multi-species fishery can be managed: by focusing on one species in one area, and focusing on a second in another area. However, this solution has the drawback of overfishing the whitefish within 15 km radius of the village through the removal of juveniles with the small-mesh net.

Cree fishermen also have some control over species composition, another aspect of resource management. Data on species composition in biological samples and in the Cree harvest are compared in Figure 3.3. Assuming that the biological samples represent the actual populations available for harvesting, it can be seen that the two desirable species are taken in higher proportions than are present, and the one undesirable species is taken in lower proportions than present. Although there are year-to-year variations, the evidence for selectivity is consistent over several years.

In the farther and less accessible fishing areas, larger-mesh gillnets are used: 114.3 mm (4.5 in.), 127 mm (5 in.) and 139.7 mm (5.5 in.). These nets are used on stocks that may be fished once every few years. Since the area used for fishing in a given year is much smaller than the total area available, fishing grounds may be rotated, analogous to the fallowing technique in farming. Rotational or pulse fishing an area only once every so many years appears to be a common feature of many northern native fisheries, including Inuit fisheries (see, for example, Johnson 1976). Short bursts of intensive fishing with a mesh size appropriate for the harvest of accumulated production of several years allows the fishermen to optimize their fishing time and effort. Instead of trying to harvest a sustainable yield every year of small individuals over a large area, fishermen who have the appropriate knowledge of fish distributions use pulse fishing to obtain a high catch per unit of effort consisting of large fish.

We devised a computer experiment to evaluate fishing strategies used by Cree fishermen (Berkes and Gonenc 1982). Given the known gillnet selectivity values, the known growth rates of whitefish and a length-frequency composition that approximates a whitefish population that has not been fished for many years, it

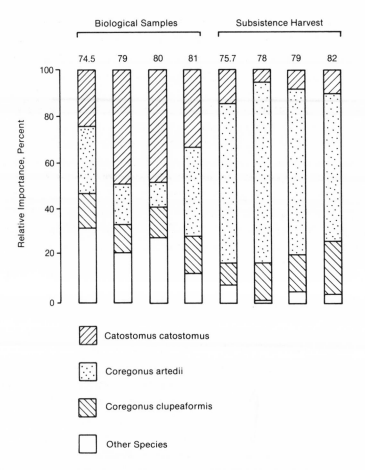

FIG. 3.3. *The species composition in biological samples and the subsistence harvest. The Cree fishery is shown to be selective for cisco* (Coregonus artedii) *and whitefish* (C. clupeaformis) *but against longnose suckers* (Catostomus catostomus). *Data from Berkes (1979) and Berkes (unpublished).*

can be shown that the most productive fishing may be conducted with the use of 127-mm and 139.7-mm mesh nets. The accumulated production of many years, in the form of ten-year-old and older fish of 40 to 60 cm, is available to these large mesh sizes as a large, exploitable biomass.

However, this strategy would not work well in areas fished

every year, that is, in the coastal fisheries near Chisasibi. If the characteristic age structure of these populations is ecologically adaptive, as assumed, the use of a mix of gillnet mesh sizes, as done in near-Chisasibi fisheries, makes more management sense than the use of any single mesh size alone. A mix of mesh sizes "thins out" the entire population, rather than selectively depleting large fish critical to reproduction in an environment in which reproductive success is highly variable from year to year.

Thus, (a) in pulse fishing, the Cree use of single mesh size (127 or 129.7 mm) gillnets is indeed appropriate for whitefish in remote areas, and (b) in more heavily exploited, nearby areas, the strategy of using a mix of gillnet mesh sizes (63.5 to 101.6 mm) to harvest more year-classes at a lower rate for each makes more ecological sense than the selective harvest of older year-classes at a high rate (Berkes and Gonenc 1982).

The Question of Conservation

Unlike some of the Pacific coast tribal groups, the James Bay Cree do not have biological management expertise, nor do they hire expert advisors. The impressively sophisticated fishing strategies outlined in the previous section are all part of their traditional practice. These practices constitute management, if management is defined as controlling how much fish is harvested, where, when, of what species, and of what sizes (Gulland 1974; 1).

The question that often comes up is whether the harvesters in traditional societies manage their resources consciously. As Hames (this volume) asks, Is what may be perceived as "conservation" in reality the outcome of exploitation strategies simply designed to be as efficient as possible? Hames argues further that the question of whether tribal peoples were conservationists has not been clearly answered for even one group. These questions are posed as if there is a universally agreed-upon and culture-free definition of conservation.

Brightman (this volume) concludes that the Cree of Manitoba adopted practices for the conservation of beaver only after they had extensive experience with beaver overharvesting. He points out that among this group the idea that hunting pressure could reduce populations was absent. They believed that the numbers of animals available to hunters were determined by factors unrelated to the numbers killed.

Brightman's case closely parallels the present case study. James Bay Cree fishermen also believe that fish is an inexhaustible resource, and that the numbers available are independent of the size of the previous harvest. To maintain productivity, it suffices to observe proper harvesting procedures and to maintain an essential humility toward nature and respect for the animals. This is a fundamentally different ideology from the Western preservation-conservation one of noninterference with nature (Livingston 1981) or the Western scientific concept of conservation with its emphasis on yield maximization based on population dynamics (see Livingston 1981 for the distinction between the two Western ideologies). We must recognize that different definitions or concepts of conservation already exist, and specify *our* definition when seeking to evaluate any set of resource exploitation strategies.

According to the IUCN/WWF/UNEP[1] World Conservation Strategy definition, conservation is the maintenance of essential ecological processes and life-support systems, the preservation of genetic diversity, and the sustainable utilization of species and ecosystems (Talbot 1980). Applying this definition to the Cree resource-use systems, we find no evidence that Cree practices violate essential ecological processes and life-support systems, and no evidence that they damage genetic diversity. There is only positive evidence that Cree practices preserve ecological processes, life-support systems, and genetic diversity.

Regarding the last part of the IUCN criteria, the key phrase is *sustainable utilization*. Has the Cree fishery been sustainable? With the exception of the whitefish within the area close to (less than 15 km from) Chisasibi, there is no evidence of overexploitation of any of the stocks. Comparison of the length-frequency distribution of coastal whitefish and cisco in James Bay in the 1970s with those sampled in the 1930s shows no significant differences (Berkes 1979). The number of year-classes in the whitefish and cisco populations indicated healthy stocks, especially in comparison to the commercially exploited stocks of these species in northern Canada, many of which show the truncated age-class structures which have been associated with stock failure.

The most important index of sustainability is "catch per unit of effort" (CPUE). In Chisasibi, the CPUE is very high by the standards of commercial gillnet fisheries (Berkes 1979). For example, the total average fishing effort at Chisasibi during the ice-free period was estimated at about 5,000 m of gillnets. The community catch was about 36 tons edible weight. In the Lake Winnipeg commercial fishery, for the same period, *each* fisherman set 7,300 m of gillnets and obtained 5 to 7 tons dressed weight (comparable to edible weight). This result shows a catch per unit of effort which is only about one-ninth of the Chisasibi fishery.

How is sustainable management possible in the absence of government regulations to conserve the stocks? It is widely assumed that subsistence harvesters have no impact on fish populations because there are too few of them to damage the stocks. This assumption may be rejected on the basis of the data indicating species selectivity, and on the basis of the presence of fishing strategies that make ecological sense. The sustainability of the Cree fishery cannot be explained simply on the basis of too few fishermen to overexploit the stocks.

The key to the management of a subsistence fishery such as that in Chisasibi may be that the harvest is linked to needs. A family group that needs 10 kg/day of fish appears in many cases to be able to obtain that amount regardless of the seasonal fluctuation of fishing success. However, beyond that amount, any excess catch ends up being given away; there is little incentive to accumulate a surplus. Thus, a subsistence fishery has a built-in self-limiting principle.

It should be emphasized that, in the James Bay area, Cree subsistence fishery is not subject to government regulation. Government regulations on fisheries elsewhere in the Canadian subarctic include restrictions on kinds of gear and mesh size, and prohibitions on fishing at certain times and places where fish are congregated and vulnerable to overexploitation.

By contrast, Cree fishermen use the most effective gear available to them and the mesh sizes that give the highest return in a given situation, and they concentrate their fishing efforts on aggregations of fish that are most efficiently exploitable. Cree practices violate nearly every conservation-oriented, indirect-effort control measure in the repertory of contemporary scientific fisheries management.

Furthermore, the Cree abhor catch-and-release practices currently fashionable in North American sport fishery management, disapprove of population surveys, and oppose tagging experiments. All of these violate the ethic against playing with animals. Indeed, many groups of northern Indians and, according to George Wenzel (personal communication), Canadian Inuit (Eskimo) think that animals will go away if you count them or otherwise show disrespect. In many of these groups, as with the Cree, it is the animals who are considered to be making the decisions; hunters are passive. Any management system claiming to maximize productivity by manipulating the animals is considered arrogant. Thus, not only does the Cree ideology differ from Western scientific management, but it also opposes it.

Judged against the IUCN criteria for conservation, the Cree fishery may be called an example of successful conservation. However, judged against the conventional Western scientific criteria, the Cree are not conservationists because, among other things, they do not know and do not seem to care about animal population numbers, they never throw back undersized fish, and they concentrate their efforts on vulnerable aggregations of fish.

Post-1950s scientific management based on maximum sustained yield (MSY) has led to the collapse of such major resources as the Peruvian anchovy, has generally resulted in the alteration of ecological balances among the key species in the system, and has rarely led to the "sustainable utilization of species and ecosystems" (see Larkin 1977 for an authoritative critique of MSY). Are conventional Western scientific criteria suitable for evaluating traditional fishery management?

If one considers the ethnocentricity of the claim that the conscious manipulation of living resources on the basis of population dynamics data constitutes *the* relevant criterion for conservation and management, one can turn the argument around. One can argue that in Western science the idea that the lack of respect for animals could reduce the harvest was absent, that there was a conviction that the numbers of animals available to fishermen/hunters were determined only by the application of a population-dynamics approach.

Perhaps the real contribution of a case study such as this one to the understanding of common-property resource management is its suggestion that the Western scientific approach may benefit from the injection of personal identification with and respect for the resource. If nothing else, some humility toward the resource would counterbalance the tendency for heavy-handed management in exploiting resources as a commodity and to the fullest possible degree.

TESTING THE ASSUMPTIONS OF THE COMMONS MODEL

The Cree fishery case study violates all three assumptions of the model of the tragedy of the commons. First, the resource is common property but not open access. The Chisasibi Cree control access to most of the major fish stocks readily available near the community, and their traditional control of the land is to a large extent supported by provincial and federal law through the James Bay Agreement. Furthermore, within the community harvesting area, the only area freely open to all is the estuary within a 15 km radius of the old village site. In the rest of the area, band members have harvesting rights but are expected to inform the boss of the area they are planning to visit and to respect his management authority. Access to much of the community territory requires specialized knowledge of the terrain, and this effectively limits access to those who have traditionally used that area.

Second, individual self-interest does not override the collective interest. Effective social mechanisms ensure adherence to rules which exist by virtue of mutual consent within the community. People who violate these rules suffer not only a loss of favor from the animals (important in the Cree ideology of hunting) but also social disgrace. This is no light matter, as seen in the case of the beaver boss who was forced to abandon his position because he neglected to remove his traps at the end of the trapping season.

Third, the resource is not used so intensively that the rate of exploitation exceeds the natural rate of increase. Except for one fish stock in the most accessible estuarine waters, the resource is used below its full productive capacity.[2] In eastern James Bay and the northern Quebec areas as a whole, the harvesting rate ranges from as low as 1 percent of the annual biological productivity of the area to as high as about 10 percent, but almost certainly not more (Berkes 1981).

The Cree fishery is not unique in violating some or all of the assumptions of Hardin's model. The tragedy of the commons is not inevitable in all fisheries. The task for the managers of common property resources is to find out the conditions under which the tragedy occurs and those under which it does not (see Berkes 1985).

IMPLICATIONS FOR MANAGEMENT OF SMALL-SCALE FISHERIES

Subsistence fisheries in the James Bay area have much in common with artisanal or small-scale fisheries elsewhere in the world. There are some ten million small-scale fishermen, who contribute nearly half of the total world fish catch used for direct human consumption. The rest is caught by large-scale fishing enterprises, which also account for almost the entire world catch for industrial reduction purposes (Thomson 1980). After more than three decades of fisheries development activity, small-scale fisheries persist and continue to be important (Panayotou 1982). There are good reasons to protect them from competition from large-scale fisheries: small-scale fisheries are more fuel-efficient and contribute more jobs per unit of investment than do large-scale fisheries (Thomson 1980).

Moreover, many small-scale fisheries have developed management systems that counter the assumptions of the common-property paradigm and solve the commons dilemma. They do this in a variety of ways that are, presumably, related to the variety of social and biophysical environments in which they operate. The decline of fisheries in many cases is not because of the absence or inadequacy of local-level management, but because open-access conditions were forcibly created and the rate of resource exploitation increased in the course of colonialism or other political and economic transformations (see, for example, Johannes 1978). Thus conservation may require the restoration of traditional institutions and practices. For example, in Oceania the traditional reef and lagoon tenure system has been legally recognized and restored for conservation purposes (Johannes 1978). More generally, there is increased interest in a "policy to give the artisanal fishing communities exclusive control over the fishing grounds around their villages" (Thomson 1980), as is done in the coastal fisheries of Japan (Asada *et al.* 1983).

Many fisheries managers, however, remain skeptical about local-level management. To understand why, we must look at similarities and differences between scientific and traditional management. What the Cree fisherman and the scientists have in common is that they both believe that the world is orderly and that it is important to have accurate information about the behavior, habits, and ecological requirements of the fish in order to have a successful fishery. This is where the similarity ends. There are fundamental differences about the means by which to achieve a sustainable harvest, and these are related to fundamental differences in ideology or world view.

Professional resource management is based heavily on scientific reasoning. Cree management, and perhaps most traditional management, is not (see Brightman and Carrier this volume). The Cree system of resource use combines maximizing harvest efficiency with rules of proper attitude and procedure. Depending on the definition of conservation used, it can be variously concluded that the Cree are or are not conservationists. Many investigators have questioned whether practices that have the *effect* of conservation were *designed* in the first place to do so (see Hames this volume). The present case study suggests that the question introduces an unfortunate dichotomy. The Cree are not practitioners of reductionist science. They find it difficult to separate the economic reasons (maximizing harvest efficiency) from the biological reasons (keeping harvest within sustainable levels) behind their practices. They try to maximize return per unit of effort *and* ensure future fishing success at the same time.

To achieve a more harmonious relationship between scientific managers and local fishermen, the bioeconomic paradigm will have to be revised to incorporate social and cultural considerations. There are signs that this is happening, including the fall into disfavor, if not disuse, of yield-maximization management techniques based on population analysis alone (see, for example, Larkin 1977). In science, paradigm change occurs when the practitioners find themselves unable to solve a growing number of problems. This is the case in fisheries science in the 1980s, despite the availability of more and better population data than ever before and the greatly increased mathematical sophistication of models.

The tragedy-of-the-commons paradigm, despite its success in explaining the decline of resources that have been flung open to cutthroat exploitation, is inadequate as the model for all fisheries.

Future fisheries management may do well to emulate fisheries-management techniques devised by fishermen and their communities, including the restoration of closed-access conditions and the supremacy of long-term societal interests over short-term individual interests while reducing the exploitation rate to tolerable levels. For fisheries managers, it should make more sense to regulate fisheries in ways consistent with the existing self-regulation of communities of fishermen, than to assume that fishermen will behave as "anarchic villains" caught up in the tragedy of the commons.

The Cree fishery is not alone in violating the assumptions of the commons paradigm. Local-level management exists in many fisheries, including commercial ones in the Western world and many artisanal fisheries elsewhere. Such management systems do not mesh comfortably with government regulations. Part of the reason must be that, unlike scientific management, traditional management is not usually predicated on a biological rationale. Thus, reconciling traditional systems with scientific management will depend to a large extent on the ability of the bioeconomic model of fishery management, which has been changing rapidly since the 1970s, to accommodate different views of man-environment relations and to incorporate social concerns. In practice, this would require a change in approach in common-property resource management, from regulating the fishery despite the fishermen, to regulating the fishery in a manner consistent with the existing self-regulatory mechanisms of communities of fishermen.

NOTES

I owe much to the fishermen and various organizations in the study area. I am indebted to many colleagues for the development of the ideas in this chapter, including Harvey Feit, Henry Regier, Terry Fenge, Marguerite MacKenzie, George Wenzel, Francis Henderson, Rob Brightman, and to the editors, Bonnie McCay and Jim Acheson, who encouraged me to develop the Cree case study further. The research was supported by the Social Sciences and Humanities Research Council of Canada.

1. IUCN/WWF/UNEP represents the joint effort of the International Union for the Conservation of Nature and Natural Resources, the World Wildlife Fund, and the United Nations Environment Programme.

2. The overall potential productivity of fish in the area has been estimated by various authors using the morphoedaphic-index (MEI) approach, based on nutrient availability and ecological recycling rates. It is a broad-brush limnological technique appropriate for use when stock-by-stock population data are very difficult or impossible to obtain, as in the case of the Canadian North with its thousands of lakes. A review of findings on fish-productivity potential may be found in Berkes 1981. Reasonably reliable records of the actual community fish harvests are available from questionnaire studies undertaken under the James Bay Agreement. These have been checked and verified against actual field data on harvests (Berkes 1983). From these two sets of fairly detailed data, it is possible to estimate the harvest in comparison with fishing potential.

4 Game Conservation or Efficient Hunting?

Raymond Hames

CULTURAL ECOLOGISTS OFTEN ARGUE that hunter-gatherers have developed a number of cultural institutions and practices designed to allow them to achieve equilibrium with their environments. The equilibrium is found in an evident lack of resource degradation in the home ranges of the groups in question (Sahlins 1968) and the apparent long-term stability of their populations (see, for example, Birdsell 1968). It results, in part, from conservation practices motivated by and reflected in, for example, reverence for animal life shown in religion, ritual, and mythology (Martin 1978; Nelson 1979, 1982), limited needs (Sahlins 1968), or game taboo systems (McDonald 1977) which deter overexploitation. Destruction of natural resources and severe environmental degradation—tragedies of the commons—are said to be characteristic of state systems in which desire for profit or personal aggrandizement motivate uncontrolled exploitation. When native peoples engage in similarly destructive behaviors and opt for short-term maximization, these actions are attributed to their linkages to state systems through trade or colonization (Leacock 1954).

The question of whether none, all, or some hunting peoples are conservationists has not been clearly answered for even one group. An adequate answer to this question requires behavioral data on patterns of resource use and acquisition. Although religious beliefs, for example, may motivate individuals to behave, conservation can be achieved only through their behavior and its material consequences. There have been few attempts to demonstrate the behavioral correlates and environmental impacts of cultural practices believed to have conservation functions. An exception is H. Feit's analysis (1973) of Waswanipi Cree hunting-ground rotation. However, even in this excellent work it is impossible to demonstrate

92

whether hunting-ground rotation is designed to maintain animal populations ("conservation") or to permit hunters to hunt as efficiently as possible.

Amazonian hunters and fishers may regulate their predatory impact on game populations in at least two related ways. The first, conservation, involves reducing the overall intensity of hunting, decreasing its intensity in different habitats or "patches," or tabooing the hunting of particular species or age and sex classes within species. This behavior requires short-term restraint for long-term benefits. The second, resource management, may be defined as activities that enhance the environment of game animals with the effect of increasing their abundance. Examples include burning scrublands in native North America and Australia to maintain forage for bison and kangaroo, respectively (Lewis 1982), and in Amazonia, the organic enrichment of lakes through dumping practices (Stocks 1983a,b and this volume). Management in this sense has not often been reported in Amazonia, perhaps because it has not been looked for and is more difficult to detect than conservation. I thus focus on conservation.

Using data on hunting and fishing among lowland Amazonian peoples, I deduce and test three pairs of predictions of hunters' responses to game depletion from two competing perspectives: conservation and short-term efficiency. At the end of the chapter I suggest some conditions under which conservation is likely to evolve. Any persuasive account of conservation as a human adaptation requires a theory that shows that conservation is by design (*sensu* Williams 1964b) and not a side-effect of some other process, specifies the conditions under which conservation will evolve, and predicts how individuals will systematically regulate their behavior to conserve resources.

RESPONSES TO GAME DEPLETION

Conservation Hypotheses

I pose three conservationist predictions about how hunters respond to game scarcity. The first is to decrease the overall rate of hunting as game density declines. This assumes that depletion is, in large part, a function of the intensity of hunting and that the relaxation of hunting effort allows game to rebound from depleted levels. This is the conservation version of a time-allocation model. The second, or patch-choice method, is similar but involves the diminution of hunting effort in patches of the environment (habitats) that have been severely depleted of game species. That is, hunters allocate less time to depleted patches and more to rich patches, allowing the former to recover. The third, or taboo method, involves total abstention from particular game species, or even particular age and sex classes within species, through cultural rules. McDonald (1977) argues that certain game species are tabooed in lowland South America to prevent overexploitation or local extinction.

Efficiency Hypotheses

These conservationist predictions can be compared to those of short-term optimization models about how foragers should respond to game depletion. Optimal foraging theory (Pyke *et al.* 1976) predicts that hunters will attempt to maximize their net rates of return while hunting. In the simplest of these models a hunter is assumed to be indifferent to the long-term effects of his hunting behavior and attempts to maintain the highest rate of return over the short term—that is, to hunt as efficiently as possible. In regard to time allocation, if game becomes depleted (indexed by decreasing hunting efficiency) an optimal forager will allocate more time to hunting—the exact opposite of the conservation hypothesis. The efficiency hypothesis assumes that the value of animal protein is relatively high and inelastic so that hunters will attempt to make up for decreased rates of return by increased hunting. This is not to suggest that a hunter is attempting to maintain a particular level of consumption (although there may be levels below which he does not want to fall), but rather that increased time allocated to hunting has greater utility than alternative uses of time (Winterhalder 1983).

The patch method relates to a concrete issue in optimal-foraging theory known as the marginal-value theorem (Charnov 1976a,b). This model predicts that a hunter will leave or ignore patches that have low rates of return and will spend time in patches that have higher rates of return, as long as the extra travel time to richer patches does not lower his overall rate of return. In doing so a hunter will maximize his hunting efficiency. Therefore, we should expect a positive correlation between the amount of time spent in a patch and the rate of return for that patch. Unfortunately, this prediction is identical to the one made for the patch-method version of the conservation hypothesis.

The tabooing method of conservation relates to the model of diet-breadth expansion and contraction in optimal-foraging theory. Hunters will start to take game species they previously ignored, due to their low rates of return, as they deplete highly preferred game species (those which have the highest rates of return upon encounter). By doing so, hunters will maximize their rates of return in the face of game depletion. The main difference between this prediction and the conservation model is that in the diet-breadth model high-ranked, depleted game species are *always* taken when they are encountered in the search, whereas in the conservation model they are *never* taken when encountered during a hunt.

To my knowledge, few Amazonian human ecologists have gone to the field to develop or test theories of conservation or optimal foraging (but see Hawkes *et al.* 1983). As a result, available data lacks the precision needed to evaluate conclusively the competing hypotheses. It can, however, be used for preliminary quantitative evaluations of the time-allocation and patch-choice hypotheses. Anecdotal and qualitative analysis must suffice for the taboo hypothesis.

Time-Allocation Hypotheses

The conservation prediction is that hunters will decrease hunting time allocation as game depletion increases. The optimization or efficiency prediction is that hunters will increase hunting time as game depletion increases. Vickers's (1980) longitudinal study of Siona-Secoya hunting contains the most appropriate evidence for evaluating these hypotheses. Vickers collected data on mean length of hunt and hunting efficiency in the village of Shushufindi during the first, second, and fourth years of its existence (Table 4.1). Assuming that hunting efficiency is a fair index of game depletion, we find that as hunting efficiency decreases (increasing game depletion) in the fourth year, hunting time increases. This

TABLE 4.1

Siona-Secoya Hunting Time and Efficiency

SETTLEMENT DURATION	TIME (HR/HUNT)	EFFICIENCY (KG/HR)
First and second years	7.56	2.48
Fourth year	8.48	1.40

SOURCE: Vickers 1980

suggests that the Siona-Secoya are not conserving game. Instead, game has a sufficiently high value to induce greater efforts toward its acquisition compared to alternative uses of time.

Comparative data collected by John Saffirio (Saffirio and Hames 1983) on Yanomama "forest" villages and "highway" villages on both hunting and fishing time allocation and efficiency provides another evaluation of the time-allocation hypotheses.[1] Highway villages are Yanomama villages that have been established along a portion of the Trans-Amazon system. During the construction of the highway, game was heavily depleted by highway workers who hunted with rifles and shotguns, and a great deal of game was evidently scared off by the disruptive influence of the highway itself. In addition, the fishing productivity of the area declined when streams that formerly crossed the land now occupied by the highway were diverted. Forest villages, by comparison, occupy relatively undisturbed forest and are located five days' distance from the highway. Table 4.2 shows that highway hunters hunt a third less efficiently than forest villagers and that they hunt more than twice as intensively as forest villagers. Table 4.2 also shows that highway villagers fish half as efficiently as forest villagers and allocate twenty percent more time to it than do forest villagers.

Both the Siona-Secoya and Yanomama examples directly contradict the conservation hypothesis. Hunters and fishers who have depleted game resources (or have had them depleted for them) hunt and fish more intensively. Protein resources are sufficiently valuable that hunters will allocate more time to their acquisition should their rates of efficiency fall as a result of game depletion.

A weaker test of the time-allocation hypotheses can be made through a comparison of hunting and fishing efficiency and time

TABLE 4.2

*Hunting and Fishing Time and Efficiency in Yanomama
Forest and Highway Villages*

	TIME (HR/DAY)	EFFICIENCY (KG/HR)
Hunting		
Forest	0.96	0.98
Highway	2.40	0.69
Fishing		
Forest	0.60	0.37
Highway	0.81	0.18

SOURCE: Saffirio and Hames 1983

allocation across a number of Amazonian societies. Again assuming that hunting and fishing efficiency is a fair index of game and fish depletion, we expect a positive correlation between time and efficiency if conservation is occurring and a negative correlation if short-term maximization is occurring. I was able to gather data on these variables for twelve societies (Table 4.3). The correlation between efficiency and time is negative (Pearson's $r = -0.67$) and significant ($p < 0.01$).[2]

TABLE 4.3

Hunting and Fishing Time and Efficiency in 10 Amazonian Societies

GROUP[a]	TIME (HR/DAY)	EFFICIENCY (KG/HR)	SOURCE
0. Machiguenga	2.18	0.16	Baksh in press
1. Waorani	1.34	2.43	Yost and Kelley 1983
2. Cocamilla	1.69	2.02	Stocks 1983
3. Ye'kwana	1.81	1.60	Hames 1979, 1980
4. Shipibo	1.20	1.23	Bergman 1980
5. Yanomama[b]	1.56	0.75	Saffirio and Hames 1983
6. Makuna	2.48	0.72	Arnhem 1976
7. Yanomama[c]	3.21	0.56	Saffirio and Hames 1983
8. Mamainde	1.91	0.52	Aspelin 1975
9. Yanomamo	3.00	0.49	Hames 1979
10. Wayana	2.54	0.47	La Pointe 1970
11. Bari	4.08	0.31	Beckerman 1983

[a]Number indicates a group's location on scattergram (Fig. 4.1)
[b]Forest village
[c]Highway village

Still more indirect evidence concerning conservation among Amazonian populations may be made by comparing hunting efficiency as determined by technological differences and time allocation. Comparisons of shotgun and bow hunting among the Ye'kwana and Yanomamö (Hames 1979) and among the Waorani (Yost and Kelley 1983) indicate that low hunting efficiency leads to more intensive hunting in each case. Although these are not tests of the conservation hypothesis they do again support the hypothesis that protein is valuable enough that hunters exert considerable effort should efficiency decline.

Patch Hypotheses

Data on patch hunting behavior is more difficult to obtain since few ethnographers have been interested in documenting hunting variability through space. Again, Vickers's longitudinal study of the Siona-Secoya is valuable (Vickers 1980; Hames and Vickers 1983). As noted above, Vickers (1980) shows that hunting efficiency for the Siona-Secoya dropped by nearly half after four years of inhabiting the same village site, indicating considerable game depletion. This was particularly true in hunting zones near the village. A comparison of the frequency of hunts to near, intermediate, and distant zones reveals that near-zone hunting decreased in frequency from the first and second to the fourth years whereas distant-zone hunting increased in frequency over the same period (Table 4.4). Thus, it appears that the conservation and the efficiency hypotheses are both supported.

Data on the intensity (hours over a 216-day sampling period) and the efficiency of hunting (kg/hr) in hunting zones exploited by

TABLE 4.4

Siona-Secoya Settlement Age and Hunting Frequency by Zone

Settlement age	Near zones $\bar{x} = 5$ km	Intermediate zones $\bar{x} = 11$ km	Distant zones $\bar{x} = 25$ km
First and second years	61	26	12
Fourth year	48	17	35

Source: Hames and Vickers 1983; Vickers 1980

TABLE 4.5

Yanomamö Hunting Time and Efficiency by Zone

Zone[a]	Time (hr)	Efficiency (kg/hr)
Iguapo	1137	0.79
Manguera	458	0.75
Cua	49	0.00
Makanahama	720	0.47
O'doiyenadu	854	0.42
Shanama'na	72	0.53
Wohokuha	53	0.28
Audaha emadi	105	0.30

Source: Hames 1980: 46, Table 1
Note: Correlation coefficient (Pearson's r) $r = 0.64$, $p < 0.025$
[a]Ranked by decreasing distance from village

the Yanomamö are shown in tables 4.5 and 4.6, respectively. For both groups the correlation (Pearson's r) between hunting-zone intensity and hunting-zone efficiency is positive and significant. Previously (Hames 1980), I argued that a number of time constraints (and gasoline constraints for the Ye'kwana) did not permit Ye'kwana or Yanomamö hunters to exploit richer and more distant hunting zones more intensively. In any event, data on the Siona-Secoya and Ye'kwana and Yanomamö tend to support both the conservation and efficiency hypotheses. It is obvious that another

TABLE 4.6

Ye'kwana Hunting Time by Zone

Zone[a]	Time (hr)	Efficiency (kg/hr)
Metacuni	302	5.43
Watamu	408	3.39
Sedukurawa	225	2.34
Manguera	39	0.00
Cua	399	0.96
Makanahama	140	1.01
O'doiyenadu	326	0.80
Shanama'na	330	2.07
Wohokuha	99	0.96
Audaha emadi	168	0.12

Source: Hames 1980: 46, Table 1
Note: Correlation coefficient (Pearson's r) $r = 0.50$, $p < 0.05$
[a]Ranked by decreasing distance from village

test, which distinguishes between the two hypotheses, must be devised.

Taboo and Diet-breadth Hypotheses

Almost by definition a taboo animal is conserved. Nevertheless, the important issue is whether the taboo is designed to conserve threatened species or whether conservation is a "fortuitous effect" (Williams 1966) of some other process (such as sumptuary laws). McDonald (1977) contends that native Amazonian game taboos function as a "primitive environmental protection agency" designed to conserve endangered species. Others insist that Amazonian game taboos are better understood for their social and ideological significance—from differentiating cultural groups and social statuses to serving as structural mediators of symbols in native ideological systems (see Kensinger and Kracke 1981).[3] Ross (1978), in contrast, implies that large Amazonian game species (tapir, deer, and capybara) with low natural densities and low rates of reproduction are those most frequently in danger of local extinction. As large game become depleted they are tabooed by small, nonexpanding Amazonian village populations to maximize hunting efficiency and/or minimize variance in protein intake. Throughout his paper Ross considers the costs (for example, pursuit of game into swamps and rivers and the price of trade shotguns and shells) and risks (for instance, pursuit of game near enemy villages) of taking taboo game animals, variables that are also critical in diet-breadth models. He states, "From the point of view of long-term adaptation, behavior of this kind, which promotes a sustained yield rather than encouraging maximal resource use, has far greater selective advantage." He adds, "A consequence—not necessarily a function—of some taboos might be to restore certain seriously reduced animal populations" (1978: 28). It is clear that Ross's model has much in common with an optimal-foraging model of game taboos (Kiltie 1980; but see Ross 1980: 544).[4]

The existence of game taboos on animals that, because of their large size, *appear* to be very profitable animals to hunt presents a formidable challenge to optimal-foraging theory and especially to the optimal-diet-breadth model. A basic prediction of the model is that, as high-ranked game become depleted, lower-ranked game that were formerly outside the diet breadth will enter into the new diet breadth, but high-ranked game will continue to be taken when they are encountered on a hunt regardless of how rare or depleted they become. From a diet-breadth perspective, one could simply assert that taboo animals are animals with low rates of return and outside of the optimal diet breadth, that is, they are tabooed because hunting them would lower hunting efficiency. Although I believe that this is essentially the correct answer to some game taboos (other animals, such as jaguars, may be tabooed because they are dangerous to hunt, and others, such as carrion eaters, because handling them may cause infection), it is a rather unconvincing statement because it does not, for example, clearly account for the taboo on tapir and capybara for the Achuara and the lack of such taboos for the Yenewana.

In the diet-breadth model the rank of a game species is determined by its net rate of return upon encounter. The rank of a species can vary as a result of hunting technology and what is sometimes called behavioral depression (Charnov *et al.* 1976). The blowgun provides a good example of how technology can affect the rank of a game species. Many observers (Butt-Colson 1973; Ross 1978; cf. Yost and Kelley 1983) have noted that the blowgun is usually incapable of killing, or killing easily, animals greater than about 20 kg. For blowgun hunters most big game such as capybara, tapir, and peccary would fall out of their diet breadth. A taboo against hunting them would allow them to hunt more efficiently by deterring them from pursuing game species which would lower their hunting efficiency.

Behavioral depression refers to changes in habits of game species that have been subjected to heavy predation. Charnov *et al.* (1976) point out that these animals can become nocturnal, more wary of predators, or move into habitats which make search, pursuit, and approach more difficult. Through behavioral depression it is entirely possible that an initially high-ranked game species can have its rank lowered sufficiently to move it out of the optimal diet breadth. This would occur when "handling time" (stalking, pursuit, and retrieval) has increased such that it is more efficient to ignore game formerly taken upon encounter and spend time searching for other game. However, if depleted game has taken refuge in certain habitats (patches), or has been wiped out every-where else but in a particular habitat, an optimal-patch-choice model (Charnov 1976; Charnov and Orians 1973) could be em-ployed to predict game taboos. In this case, handling time of a game animal could remain the same (or even decrease) yet the animal would be taboo.

A simple diet-breadth model assumes that game animals are randomly distributed in a homogeneous environment. On the other hand, a patch-choice model assumes a heterogeneous en-vironment in which certain patches (habitats) have different rates of return for a hunter because they have, for example, different mixes of game species. Therefore, in a "patchy" environment, hunters will search for game only in patches that have high rates of return. They will ignore patches with low rates of return (that is, a patch or patch type will be ignored if its marginal rate of return is less than that of the currently used set of patches). In a sense, a hunter will have an optimal-patch breadth—a restricted set of areas in which he will search for game. An effective way of signaling to a hunter that a particular patch is not worth the effort to hunt would be to place a taboo on an animal that is restricted or has become restricted to that patch. (One would not want to taboo entry into the patch because it could, for example, contain impor-tant plant resources.) It is perhaps significant that Ross notes that tapir and capybara are found in riverine environments where they escape from pursuing hunters by swimming and diving and that deer are found in swamps where pursuit is difficult; all three ani-mals are taboo. In swamps, huntable terrestrial biomass is low; moreover, low floristic diversity may mirror low aboreal game di-versity and density. Furthermore, from this perspective it is easy to see how technology could influence diet breadth through patch choice. Blowgun hunters are forced to hunt small game (less than 20 kg) that may be abundant in patches where large, commonly tabooed game is absent or rare.

CONSERVATION OR EFFICIENCY?

The quantitative evidence shown above evaluated on indica-tors of conservation is equivocal. Nevertheless, it casts doubt on the existence of conservation in lowland Amazonia. This is particularly true of the time-allocation studies: the data consistently indicate a negative correlation between hunting efficiency (as an index of game depletion) and time allocation. This relationship was found within a single village through time (Siona-Secoya), between two villages of the same culture over space (Yanomama highway and forest villages), and cross-culturally in Amazonia. It appears that native Amazonians regard protein as sufficiently valuable to intensify their efforts for it in the face of depletion. Furthermore, it indicates that they are pursuing a strategy of short-term maximization and that they are not, as yet, constrained by the possible long-term consequences of their actions.

It should be noted that the time-allocation hypotheses and patch-allocation hypotheses are not truly independent. One could argue that increases in overall time allocation are the result of trying to exploit more distant hunting zones while suffering lower rates of return in the process—because of added travel time—in order to conserve resources in near zones. This interpretation can be ruled out only by showing that distant zones have higher rates of return. Data on hunting efficiency and distance of hunting zone from the village for Ye'kwana and Yanomama hunters (Hames 1980: 46, 50) demonstrate positive correlations in each case (Ye'kwana $r = 0.92$, $p < 0.001$; Yanomamö $r = 0.72$; $p < 0.01$). Therefore, hunters increase their efficiency by hunting in distant zones.

Another problem in seeking indicators of conservation or efficiency was seen in the patch-time hypotheses in which conservation and efficiency predictions were identical. This problem has been noted and explored in detail by human socioecologists (Durham 1981: 226–228; Winterhalder 1981: 97; Smith 1983). One way to distinguish between these two predictions is to hypothesize that conservationists passing through game-depleted patches will not take game found there. Instead, they will go on until they reach undepleted patches. In contrast, efficiency maximizers will take everything they encounter. This test is possible because all Amazonian horticulturalists are central-place foragers and must move through near hunting zones to reach distant ones. My experience suggests that the efficiency hypothesis will hold: Ye'kwana and Yanomamö hunters will take game in near zones if they encounter it, even when they are passing through these zones in order to reach more distant hunting zones.

Although the role of wild-protein procurement in Amazonian

native adaptations is a contentious issue (Gross 1975; Ross 1978; Beckerman 1979; Chagnon and Hames 1979; Vickers 1980; Johnson 1982), I think it is fair to say that most human ecologists believe that gaining adequate dietary protein at a reasonable cost is a problem faced by all Amazonian populations. The issue is how people respond to decreases in consumption and/or increases in acquisition costs of high-protein foods. I have shown that native Amazonians intensify their hunting efforts and/or extend their hunting ranges. Identification of these responses does not rule out others, such as village relocation or fission, nor does it rule out complex interactions among variables. Nonetheless, attempts to relate informant-generated data on historic patterns of settlement relocation to problems of protein acquisition fail to yield significant results, even though informants cite other environmental problems (Gross 1983; Hames 1983).

Optimal-foraging theorists (Pyke *et al.* 1976; Krebs 1978) recognize that conservation can evolve as a means to maximize hunting efficiency. Simple optimal-foraging models assume that hunters are unconstrained by time limitations such that the goal of hunting is to maximize the net rate of return over the short term while foraging. However, if one assumes that the goal of hunting is to maximize efficiency over a period of, say, several years, hunters may accept lower rates of return (by ignoring rare, high-return game, for example) over the short term to maximize hunting efficiency over the long term. From this time perspective it should be clear that conservation and efficiency are not mutually exclusive and that the former is a means to the latter. The conditions under which conservation or long-term maximization could evolve are explored below.

CONDITIONS FOR THE DEVELOPMENT OF CONSERVATION

The important question is not whether Amazonian horticulturalists are conservationists but rather, what are the conditions under which conservation is likely to evolve? That is, we need a theory of conservation. Toward this end I would like to suggest three conditions that would have to exist in order for conservation to develop.

First, the local population would have to be territorial, that is, able to defend their resources against outsiders who might subvert their conservation plans. According to Dyson-Hudson and Smith's (1978) application of Brown's (1964) model of economic defendability, territoriality is most likely to evolve in groups that occupy areas characterized by relatively dense and predictable resources. In Amazonia, riverine areas—oxbow lakes in particular—may have fish resources that meet this condition. However, territoriality would not be necessary for conservation if a group had a home range that did not overlap with a neighbor's home range.

Second, local populations must have mechanisms for dealing with their own members who might decide to break conservation conventions. The spatial organization of village domestic structures characteristic of most of Amazonia (especially long houses, or *malocas*) would make cheating without detection very difficult, as would the perceived seriousness of supernatural sanction (for example, the Ye'kwana believe that killing an anaconda will cause the entire village to be destroyed by a flood) or even social sanctions meted out to those who break conservation rules.

Third, conservation implies that unregulated hunting and fishing or population growth places so much pressure on a group's resource base that increases in work effort and/or decline in the consumption of limiting resources will ultimately result in a crash of the group's population. However, the probability that conservation will develop to prevent a population crash depends on at least two factors: (1) availability of unoccupied areas for resettlement (that is, expansion), and (2) alternative sources of or substitutes for limiting resources (that is, economic or technological innovation). In Amazonia there is considerable evidence to indicate that population density in native areas is considerably less today than it was in pre-Columbian times (Denevan 1976). For example, the Yanomamö have a population density of approximately 0.20 persons/km (Hames 1983: 425), and many villages have the option to expand into unoccupied areas. This fact alone may account for the lack of evidence of game or fish conservation among Amazonian populations. As for economic innovation, Roosevelt (1980) has suggested that depletion of fish and game resources by a number of prehistoric riverine Amazonian populations led to increased reliance on the protein in maize as a substitute for animal protein.

It is risky to assume that native ideology about potential fish and game resources can offer any proof that strategies of conservation or short-term efficiency are being followed. Ideological factors are best regarded as approximate causes of behavior that dispose individuals to behave predictably under particular circumstances. In turn, determining whether the behavior generated by ideology is an adaptation designed to solve some problem set forth by the environment requires a different level of analysis—one that measures human impact on the environment and how that interaction ultimately affects human survival and reproduction. If researchers wish to convincingly demonstrate conservation they must enter the field with a theory of conservation from which hypotheses can be deduced and then tested with quantitative data.

NOTES

I would like to thank the following colleagues for reading this chapter and offering thoughtful suggestions: Kristen Hawkes, Bonnie McCay, Alan Osborn, Eric Smith, Tony Stocks, Dennis Werner, and Bruce Winterhalder. It is based on a paper presented at the 82nd Annual Meeting of the American Anthropological Association, Chicago, Illinois, November 16–20, 1983.

1. Both hunting and fishing provide animal protein for the diet. Since they are alternative means of solving the same adaptive problem they are analyzed separately (Tables 4.2 and 4.3) and jointly (Table 4.4), depending on available published data.

2. All critical values of Pearson's r used are one-tailed.

3. It should be noted that, following Ross (1978), I am dealing with blanket or general taboos that extend to all group members regardless of status or condition, rather than specific ones on consumption of game animals determined by an individual's status (male, female, old, young) or condition (pregnancy, illness) found in complex array in lowland Amazonia. It should also be noted that not everyone in the

Kensinger and Kracke (1981) volume regard social and ideological analyses of food taboo systems as necessarily competing with ecological explanations (e.g., Taylor 1981); for that matter, neither does Ross (1978: 1). See Johnson (1982) for discussion of levels of analysis in Amazonian research.

4. Kiltie (1980), in a comment on Ross's work, suggests that a model of diet-breadth contraction and expansion could account for Amazonian taboos. In reply, Ross (1980: 544) discounts the diet-breadth model by suggesting that increased search time needed to encounter large, depleted game would drop large game from the optimal diet breadth. Ross errs. In an optimal-diet-breadth model, search time is not charged to individual prey species because it is assumed that all game within a patch are searched for simultaneously. Thus search costs are equalized for all species. Ross also distinguishes between "maximal resource use" and "optimization" without clearly defining either concept.

5 Resource Management in an Amazon Varzea *Lake Ecosystem*

THE COCAMILLA CASE

Anthony Stocks

ONE IS BROUGHT TO REFLECT ON INDIAN PEOPLE of the Upper Amazon River and its tributaries as resource managers by comparing accounts of the region when it was first discovered (Werlich 1968; Sweet 1974)—a "rich realm of nature" in David Sweet's terms—with the known destruction of natural resources, species, and ecological communities in the nineteenth century and on to the present. Garrett Hardin (1968) sees tragedies like this as the result of a combination of freedom to exploit (common property rights) and population growth (increased demand).

Native Indian population growth could not, however, have caused the ecological destruction that began in the nineteenth century. All firsthand accounts stress large-scale depopulation of native groups in the first hundred years of contact (Denevan 1976; Dobyns 1966; Stocks 1983b). In the nineteenth century, populations were low compared to precontact times. Changes in the logic and mode of production, brought about by the penetration of European mercantile and industrial capitalism even into the Peruvian Amazon, are more likely causes. It is well known that capitalist systems produce for exchange and seek to accumulate surplus value, whereas precapitalist or subsistence systems produce more for use than exchange. The latter are more dependent upon local environments and sustained yields of natural resources; they are also less likely to encourage consumption beyond needs. Are they, then, more likely to prevent tragedies of the commons or to develop good systems of resource management?

The purpose of this chapter is to explore resource management in a noncapitalist mode of production. It can be argued that today—and for a long time past—there is only one mode of production, the capitalist one in which local or regional social and economic formations provide the varying means by which labor is linked to the system of production for exchange (Wallerstein 1974, 1979). Nevertheless, systems like that of the Cocamilla of the Upper Amazon, eastern Peru, are only imperfectly wedded to capitalism and in some important respects retain their identity as a domestic (subsistence) mode of production (Sahlins 1972). This is particularly true for fishing, which is mainly for subsistence and hence the focus of this study.

ON RATIONALITY AND RESOURCE MANAGEMENT

Resources and their allocation have been an underlying theme of theories of society since at least the seventeenth century. In *Leviathan* (1950; orig. 1651) Thomas Hobbes assumed a state of "Warre" as the natural condition of humans without a strong political ruler. In a state of war, all persons would attempt to appropriate for themselves the resources on which life depends. The desire to accumulate was assumed to be natural, and nothing but the selfish aims of others would prevent accumulation. Only the state with its power to "overawe" the individual could inhibit selfish instincts and their consequences. In a state of nature,

> there be no Propriety, no Dominion, no Mine and Thine distinct; but only that to be every mans, that he can get; and for so long as he can keep it. And thus much for the ill condition, which man by meer Nature is actually placed in; though with a possibility to come out of it, consisting partly in the Passions, partly in his reason. (Hobbes 1950: 106)

The role of reason lay in agreements between individuals to submit to a common rule. The political state is a rational social contract. There can be no management of resources without political rule, a claim recognizable in the tragedy-of-the-commons thesis three hundred years later.

John Locke (1939; orig. 1690) on the other hand posed a natural society that was self-regulating. The basis for tenure in material resources is the labor that each person invests in nature. Without labor, resources are maintained and recognized as part of the common stock. Each person naturally labors only for the things he can use, and there is thus no basis for wanton killing or hoarding.

Professional resource managers, educated in developed industrial societies, tend to take the Hobbesian position that rational social agreement, enforced by the coercive power of a strong state, is the only conceivable kind of management. However, anthropologists and others are coming to recognize that human ecological relationships may be governed by something besides sheer greed and chaos, or means/ends reasoning, backed by a coercive state: ritual behavior (Rappaport 1967; Harris 1966), birth control, kinship systems, and other sociocultural practices may serve to regulate human relations with their environments. Although these have rational dimensions, the relationships between human conscious and unconscious ideological structures and their behavior is neither simple nor readily understood (Harris 1974).

Moreover, theorists in evolutionary ecology underscore the importance of *all* aspects of species behavior in understanding adaptation, and the possibility that there may be natural "economizing" functions in both human and nonhuman predators that protect against the overexploitation of resources (see, for example, Charnov 1976a; E. Smith 1984). Natural selection works on all aspects of species behavior. Why expect human rationality alone to bear the burden of regulating relations between people and their resources?

A modern theory of resource management should recognize that relations between humans and their environments are complex, involving many aspects of sociocultural systems, and that a definition of resource management that stresses rationality with the coercive backing of the state as the only kind of management is shallow indeed.

TYPES OF RESOURCE MANAGEMENT

Management implies control. Resource management can be viewed as the systematic behaviors in human cultural and behavioral systems that have the effect of controlling natural resources in such a way as to meet human objectives. Obviously, resource managers have the choice of controlling resources in order to destroy them. This practice is not, however, generally included in the concept of management, which usually also includes a notion of the objective of sustainable yield. A theory of resource management should, at the least, examine biological, social, and cultural mechanisms that affect the protection and allocation of resources.

The kind of management most familiar to most people involves goal-directed, means/end rationality. People consciously recognize the condition of resources in their systems and make decisions about their use that are based on long-term and short-term benefits, economic rationality, and their understanding of the means by which they can obtain goals such as sustained yield. This I will call *rational management*. Along with Hobbes, we can see this kind of management as rooted in the social level of patterned behavior, because it is here that compromise and the subordination of the individual to the social group, based on reason, are found.

A second kind of management, which I call *optimal-foraging management*, depends on individual optimizing or economizing behaviors. Certain predatory behaviors in humans may be accounted for by "optimal foraging" theory (see Pyke *et al.* 1976 and Krebs and Davies 1978 for reviews of the biological theory and Winterhalder and Smith 1981 for its application to anthropological subjects). Although optimal-foraging behaviors may be rationalized in thought, they are not dependent on human consciousness, at least insofar as they are predictable by theories that can also be applied to nonhumans. They seem to be the result of natural selection, but it is not clear for any species what the means of transmission is. Such behaviors tend to maximize yields per unit of energy output of the predator on a short-term basis. Some optimal-foraging behaviors may have the *effect* of resource management but this is not, in theory, their goal, although one could argue that selection would favor behaviors that promoted both short- and long-term efficiencies.

Somewhere between behaviors that are explicable by optimization theories vaguely rooted in natural selection (or cultural selection) for efficiency and selfishness in the short term and behaviors that are consciously constructed with the aims of long-term, altruistic resource conservation lies another realm of resource management. I shall call this category *customary management*. It includes individual practices that have the effect of conserving or enhancing resources but are not evidently efficient or "economic." The conscious motives for the behaviors with this result are those that come into play whenever any tradition is followed. The behaviors present themselves to the individual and others in his group as expected and normal behaviors. They may not require information processing about the state of the environment or careful accounting of costs and benefits to be carried out. They are rooted in tradition and custom.

COCAMILLA RESOURCE MANAGEMENT

Optimal-Foraging Management

The marginal-value theorem in optimal-foraging theory predicts that most foraging time will be allocated to resource "patches" with the highest rate of returns, usually measured in energy "currency" (Charnov 1973, 1976a; Charnov and Orians 1973). Accordingly, organisms will switch to other patches when the rate of the return in the original declines relative to others available, and this may happen before the original patch is severely depleted even though the prevention of resource depletion is not the goal of the organism's behavior.

One area of Cocamilla behavior to which this theorem is relevant is out-migration from the community. The state of the lake resource is the subject of constant discussion among community members, and information pooling with visitors from other areas about the quality of fishing and hunting elsewhere is extremely common. Decisions to migrate may be considered as decisions to select another patch that promises a higher rate of return. Out-migration seems to have been high for a long time. The community of Achual Tipishca, where I lived from 1976 to 1978 and again in 1979 and 1981, has equilibrated at a population of about three hundred people for nearly one hundred years except during the *barbasco* boom of the 1950s. Since there is a high natural rate of population increase in the riverine communities of the Upper Amazon (Hearn

1977; Stocks 1983b), out-migration is a logical explanation for local community stability. In addition, there is considerable flux in personnel within the community; between 1976 and 1981 it was about 15 percent a year in Achual Tipishca.

Out-migration and changes in personnel may be due to individual calculations of resources in different patches. However, the mechanisms for migration are not this simple. The "pull factor" of higher rates of return on another lake or river rarely seems a sufficient condition for migration conditions. A related "push factor" based on the social structure and social relations within the community plays an important role, too. Low fishing yields, particularly during the winter high-water season, strain social relations within the patrilocal extended family. Sons-in-law are under great pressure to provide for wives' parents as well as their own. If the couple happens to live matrilocally against community custom the pressure to produce is even greater. A low-producer son-in-law may be accused of "stinginess," a powerful push factor among the Cocamilla, especially when there is information about better hunting and fishing elsewhere.

Optimal-foraging theory also distinguishes between two predation goals: energy maximization and time minimization (Schoener 1971). Time minimizers tend to forage only long enough to assure basic energy requirements, and it is assumed that such animals have alternative uses of their time. Humans practicing the domestic mode of production may fall into this class. If they do, it would indicate that in a subsistence economy people will not overexploit their environment, substantiating the argument that there are different resource-exploitation "logics" in different modes of production.

A test of this prediction was done among the Cocamilla. The time-minimization hypothesis leads to the prediction that, the more efficient fishing is, the less time people will spend doing it. I first calculated the month-by-month fishing hours and compared the results to a month-by-month analysis of fishing efficiencies, using data I had collected on fishing for the community as a whole (Stocks 1983a). The correlation was negative ($r = -0.15$) but statistically insignificant, based on 12 data points. Subsequently I reanalyzed the data on a weekly basis for two families who were entirely subsistence fishermen. The correlation between fishing intensity (hours spent) and fishing efficiency (yield per hour) is still negative ($r = -0.25$) and is significant with 49 data points at the 0.10 level. This can be compared with figures obtained from data on one net fisherman's annual fishing patterns in which the correlation between fishing intensity and fishing efficiency is $r = +0.05$. This person sells some fish commercially.

The analyses provide support, albeit weak, for the time-minimizing hypothesis and for its use as substantiation of the argument that people working under the domestic, primarily subsistence, mode of production are less likely than those working under a commercialized mode of production to overexploit natural resources.

Finally, fishermen in Achual Tipishca, the study community, show a strong tendency to fish areas of the lake more intensively where their efficiency is highest (Stocks 1983a), an indicator of patch selectivity. The fact that efficiencies change through the year in different parts of the lake and that fishing is adjusted accordingly reflects fine sensitivity to average returns of different parts of the lake. Parts with consistently low returns are fished only occasionally, apparently for the purpose of sampling.

Rational Management

The Cocamilla communities of the Huallage River in eastern Peru have the legal status of Native Communities under Peruvian law. This gives them rights with regard to their subsistence resources, provides them with land titles, and makes them legal corporate entities: all prerequisites for rational, community-level resource management.

The major stimulus for the five Cocamilla communities of the Huallage River in working to secure Native Community status was probably their long-term concern about deterioration of their lake and forest resources. A major concern in the community of Achual Tipishca was the fact that commercial fishermen from the district and provincial capitals were harvesting large quantities of fish from the lake. One of the first acts of the community once it gained Native Community status was to prohibit commercial fishing in the lake.

They did so not to reserve commercial fishing for themselves but because they were painfully aware of the relationships between commercial fishing and paucity of the fish needed for community subsistence. The facts are encoded in oral history. In the 1950s the community's population grew from around three hundred to nearly one thousand. The cause was the community's access to lands off the floodplain where *barbasco* could be raised. The source of population growth was mestizo entrepreneurs who moved into the community, bringing Cocamilla and other workers from other areas. *Barbasco* was being exported to the United States in large quantities.

As the population grew, the quality of fishing declined. As the quality of fishing declined, fishermen began using *barbasco* for its original purpose, fish poison. In normal times and with a much smaller population to feed, the Cocamilla devote only about 1 percent of fishing time to the use of fish poison, despite the fact that *barbasco* fishing is the most efficient means of getting fish short of large nets (Table 5.1). However, with large numbers of people and fewer fish, they poisoned the lake. The Cocamilla recall that the lake was *triste* during the *barbasco* boom. The community decided not to allow the use of *barbasco* in the lake, based on the rational observation that frequent use of the substance destroys the resource. This decision was reinforced by laws of the state and testifies to the concern of fishing communities as well as the government about resource management. However, fishing laws

TABLE 5.1

Comparative Efficiencies of Various Fishing Techniques

Technique	Intensity (hr)	Yield (kg)	Efficiency (kg/hr)
Commercial net	60.67	135.0	2.23
Casting net	28.25	88.0	3.12
Spear (gig)	134.72	154.5	1.15
Hook and line	254.90	196.0	0.77
Fish poison	52.90	94.5	1.79

NOTE: These data are from one family only, which was chosen because they fished purely for subsistence and used all five techniques. Both the casting net and the commercial net were borrowed and were not available to them during the entire year; thus, these figures cannot be used to determine their choices as to which technique to use except in the cases of spear, hook and line, and fish poison. This family used fish poison rather more frequently than most.

116 CONSERVATION AND THE COMMONS

are rarely enforced due to lack of personnel. Other forms of resource management are therefore necessary.

Another limitation on rational resource management is that
there are competing rationalities. The case cited above, in which
Native Community status was used to prohibit commercial fishing, rested upon a notion of the rights of native communities that
differs greatly from the national government's interpretation,
which is that the lakes and rivers are a national commons. In 1983
the natives' attempt to protect another lake's resources from commercial exploitation was defeated by armed forces from the National Guard, spurred by the Peruvian Ministry of Fishing (Arturo
Tapayuri, pers. comm.).

Customary Management

Cocamilla practices surrounding the disposal of household garbage, fecal material, and animal entrails appear to be examples of
customary management. They involve behaviors that have the effect of enhancing a resource but include neither community-level
decision making and coercion nor, at least on the surface, individual optimization.

Waste products in Achual Tipishca find their way directly to the
lake. The lake is the customary dump. As many as 44.5 metric tons
of waste organic materials are dumped into the lake each year by
the community (Stocks 1983a). This supplement to the lake food
chain supports fish that are harvested mainly during the high-
water season when fishing is poor in other parts of the lake. Dumping of wastes is done for reasons quite separate from the quality and
quantity of fish. Animal entrails are dumped into the lake rather
than given to the dogs because people feel that dogs are "ruined for
hunting" if fed entrails. It would be considered poor housekeeping
to deposit household garbage under the houses on shore rather
than in the lake. It would also be antisocial: the lakeshore is true
"community property," where women go daily to talk, wash
clothes, gather water, and dump their manioc and plantain peels
into the lake.

Beliefs and practices about "dying lakes" provide another example of customary management, with the effect of resource conservation. Dying lakes are old oxbow lakes in the floodplain that

have become choked with water hyacinths and other vegetation, deoxygenated, and partially silted in. They are known by the Cocamilla to harbor numbers of *paiche* (*Arapaim gigas*), a large relative of the codfish that breathes surface air. The *paiche* move between the river and the open lakes during the high-water season and seem to find adequate breeding conditions in the dying lakes, although the subject has been little studied by biologists.

Dying lakes are the subject of taboos. They are considered dangerous places, repositories of spirits that are thought to be those of dead shamans. Traditionally, dying lakes were rarely fished. When they were, elaborate ritual precautions were taken. We can hypothesize that the taboo had the effect of protecting a valued species of fish during its spawning season, as has been suggested for *Brycon* species and other important fish among the Ye'kwana of Venezuela (Hames, pers. comm.). The problem with testing a hypothesis such as this is that the behavior is so tightly encoded that it is almost impossible to find instances of use of the dying lakes that would enable collection of data such as average rates of return to compare with rates of return in other lacustrine or riverine environments. None of my informants fished in a dying lake at times when I was collecting empirical data. The Cocamilla seem to choose other sources of fish more often, even those that seem not much better. Lakes that are essentially ponds left in the floodplain, that dry up during the low-water season, are intensively exploited, despite the fact that it is as hard to fish them as it is to fish the dying lakes.

Food taboos suggest customary management, too (see also Ross 1978). The Cocamilla neither hunt nor eat dolphins (*Inia geoffrensis* and *Sotalia fluviatalis*), their greatest competitors for fish protein. Dolphins are surrounded by a startling array of folklore that centers on their alleged ability to transform themselves into humans, enter the village at night, and deceive wives when their husbands are out of the village. The name of the dolphin is *ipirawira* ("penis fish"), a name that focuses on their mammalian sexual parts and reminds people of their dangerous behavior.

One might think that if dolphins were killed the Cocamilla would enjoy more fish. Dolphins also destroy fishing nets, another reason for killing them. It is possible that hunting them is avoided because, being highly intelligent, dolphins tend to avoid fishing nets and are thus inefficient to hunt compared with alternatives (an optimal-foraging-strategy explanation). It is also possible that the Cocamilla see their relationship with dolphins as symbiotic instead of competitive (N. Smith 1981: 97–98), but if so, they do not express it.

The dolphin taboo, extremely widespread in the Amazon Basin, is very difficult to explain either in general or in the case of a specific community. But we can speculate on some of its effects. One is the possibility that by keeping a major predator population intact the Cocamilla and other fishing groups have helped prevent extreme fluctuations in fish populations lower in the food chain. This possibility is given some credence by findings in the Middle Amazon (Fittkau 1970, 1973) that the elimination of a major predator, the caiman, resulted in overall depression of resources at lower trophic levels. If this were so, behaviors and beliefs surrounding dolphins could be understood as a kind of risk management that has the effect of preserving the stability or reliability of the food resource, a worthy objective of resource management.

MULTIPLE DIMENSIONS OF RESOURCE MANAGEMENT

The Cocamilla are resource managers whose relationships to natural resources are part of an integrated set of cultural practices. No single theory can explain the range of Cocamilla behaviors that are either consciously directed toward or have the effect of resource management. Nonetheless, it is reasonable to assume that both biological and cultural evolution (Durham 1978) has shaped many of the institutions, beliefs, and practices of the Cocamilla in ways that seem to mitigate the effects of constant predation on the lake environment.

Several features of the Cocamilla situation seem to be important to their roles as resource managers. The community, at least until revision of the Native Communities law by the early 1980s, had more or less exclusive use of the lake resource and could obtain some legal and enforcement backing of its attempts to regulate how it is used. In addition, the Cocamilla have enough experience and perhaps the right kinds of theories to be conscious of the limited capacity of the lake to support exploitation for market exchange. As long as the human population does not exceed the carrying capacity of the lake, the optimal-foraging management tactics may work fairly well to keep exploitative pressures below the danger point. Time minimization helps keep fishermen from taking more than they need. Out-migration helps keep local population size down and may be keyed, directly or indirectly, to the status of the fish stocks and other local resources.

Such effects, benefiting individuals but also tending to preserve stability in the lake/river ecosystem, are redundant to some degree with the effects of other management strategies. Customary management tactics also have the effect of resource enhancement and long-term system maintenance. Rational resource management seems, on the surface, to be directed toward preserving long-term yields, but it may be suspect because of its openness to short-term changes in values that are influenced by political expediency, consumer needs, and a host of other immediate factors. This redundancy reflects the fact that most aspects of adaptation to environments are too important to survival to be left solely to the conscious intents of human beings. All culturally constructed systems—language is a conspicuous example—contain similar degrees of redundancy. Viewed thus, human adaptation to the physical environment appears as a long-term exchange of information. The messages given by humans are transmitted by their *total* behavioral repertoire.

Controls on local population size, exploitation strategies, and willingness to cooperate to conserve resources are all subject to change from increased involvement in commercial activities. A change in the mode of production may also decrease the practice and resource effects of customary management as it results in changes in social relationships and indigenous culture.

The tragedy of the commons, at least of the *varzea* lake commons, was not evident among the Cocamilla of the late 1970s and early 1980s. However, the situation is delicate because the Cocamilla are now involved in cash markets. The Cocamilla fairly successfully halted the effect of commercialization on the fishery resources of their lake, but the management of their forest resources is more problematic now. By the 1980s they had begun to sell hardwoods to the market. They seemed much less sensitive to the condition of forest resources than they are to lake resources.

Likewise, monocropping for market sale has become increasingly common with the result that land needs have expanded, land use is more intensive, and the forest has less and less time to regenerate. It seems obvious, though, that this situation is the result of an increasingly strong linkage of the Cocamilla to the capitalist mode of production.

ℵ

NOTES

The field research upon which this paper is based was done in 1976 to 1978 with support from the National Science Foundation, the Social Science Research Council, and a Fulbright-Hays Doctoral Dissertation fellowship and in 1981 with support from an Idaho State University Faculty Research grant.

6 Conservation and Resource Depletion

THE CASE OF THE BOREAL FOREST ALGONQUIANS

Robert A. Brightman

THE QUESTIONS OF WHETHER ABORIGINAL American Indian groups were engaged in hunting practices that conserved the game animals upon which they depended and about the role of the European fur trade in causing the depletion of many species of game reflect debates about tragedies of the commons (Hardin 1968). Can conservation exist without westernized notions of private property or without government regulations and the police power to enforce them? Are tragedies of the commons caused solely by the lack of restraints on rights to hunt, gather, harvest, use, or are there other factors that must be taken into account? Has the introduction of Western institutions, values, and laws destroyed existing communal or private property-based systems of resource management?

Although less celebrated than the famous "family hunting territory," boreal Algonquian conservation systems[1] are an important issue in Subarctic ethnology and ethnohistory. That mobility and other aspects of the hunting praxis may have latent management effects is readily agreed upon (see Paine 1973; Winterhalder 1981). This chapter focuses on *conscious* conservation practices intended to promote scheduled capture. I use documentary and ethnographic data to address three issues relating to conservation in northern Manitoba, an area occupied prehistorically and to the present by Cree-speaking people today self-identified as *asiniskawiðiniwak*, or "Rock Cree" (see Smith 1975). The first issue is whether management in the boreal forest and adjacent woodlands areas was aboriginal, as claimed by Martin (1978) and others (Bishop 1984; Feit 1973;

Vecsey 1980; Speck 1915), and as denied by Ray (1974, 1975) and Hickerson (1973). I suggest here that conscious management systems had a historic inception with the caveat that the problematic character of the sources makes any categorical answer a necessarily unreflective one.

The second issue concerns the cause of the observed depletions of fur-bearing animals and big game in many areas of the boreal forest south and west of Hudson's Bay by the early 1800s (Rogers and Black 1976; Ray 1974: 117–24; Bishop 1974: 245–49). This is also related to the question of the purported "breakdown" of aboriginal conservation, if such existed. There is abundant evidence from seventeenth- and eighteenth-century sources that most Crees and other boreal forest Algonquians were *not* practicing conservation, but instead killing more animals than they could use either domestically or commercially. During the 1740s, James Isham of the Hudson's Bay Company's facility at York Factory observed, "It's a little strange the Breed of these beaver does not diminish greatly considering the many thousands that is killed of a year" (1949: 143). Isham's remark was prophetic. I explore how the severe game shortages came about, rejecting the argument that the overkill was a predictable *sequitur* to fur-trade involvement. I emphasize instead Cree beliefs about animal population dynamics—"religion" in the conventional ethnographic idiom— as do other scholars (Martin 1978; Vecsey 1980; Feit 1973), but we differ substantially in our understanding of what those beliefs were and how they related to hunting and conservation behaviors.

In the third section, I take up questions about circumstances under which conservation systems may have developed and discuss the integration of technical and religious interpretations of conservation in the ethnoecological knowledge of contemporary Rock Cree in northern Manitoba.

ABORIGINAL CONSERVATION OR INDISCRIMINATE KILLING?

During the 1820s the Hudson's Bay Company introduced conservation measures—seasons, quotas, and selective trapping of female and juvenile animals—in areas south and west of Hudson

Bay. Although Ray (1975: 58) is probably correct in stating that these measures were alien to *most* subarctic Indians, the qualification is important. There are isolated references to Indian conservation well before the 1820s in both the boreal forest and Great Lakes areas. With the exception of Bishop (1984), no one has used these sources to motivate an argument for aboriginal conservation by Algonquians.

The earliest known reference to Algonquian management pertains to Crees on the south shore of Lake Superior in 1660 who selectively spared juvenile beavers (Radisson 1943: 226).[2] Lahontan (1905, 2: 481–83) wrote that the Ottawas in the late 1600s preserved beaver habitat and maintained breeding populations by sparing males and females at each lake or colony; these practices were concomitant with an allotment system of land tenure (see Rogers 1963: 33). Iroquoians were also practicing conservation at this time. In 1684 an Onondaga chief represented management as an institution among "all Indians" (Brotherston 1979: 56). In 1746 at York Factory, Crees were said to leave a male and female unmolested at each lodge (Drage 1968, 1: 149). Assuming a functional relationship between usufructory rights in lodges and management practices, other sources (Bacqueville de la Pothèrie 1931: 325; Hearne 1958: 153, 155) also suggest conservation by Crees trading at coastal forts on Hudson's Bay in the 1700s. Hearne, for example, described the estimation of beaver-lodge populations from placental scars on butchered females; Manitoba Rock Crees employ the same technique today. Finally, Harmon (1905: 237–38) ascribed both conservation and exclusively held hunting tracts to all boreal forest Indians east of the Rocky Mountains during the first two decades of the nineteenth century. Harmon clearly overgeneralized, but his remarks demonstrate the presence of both institutions among some of the Ojibwa and Cree groups with whom he traded.

The above findings must be placed in the context of a far greater body of evidence for the lack of conservation and intentional management and for a proclivity to kill animals indiscriminately in numbers beyond what were needed for exchange or domestic use (Martin 1978: 164–65; Bishop 1974: 291; Ray 1974: 117–23; Dobbs 1744: 39; Drage 1968, 2: 17; Graham 1969: 16, 154; Dunn 1845: 62; Isham 1949: 81; Robson 1965: 51; Ellis 1967: 85).

Samuel Hearne (1958) was a repeated eyewitness to the practice of killing all the animals possible, living on the delicacies, and then abandoning the meat to rot (pp. 25–26, 42, 48–59, 75–76, 87, 259). His descriptions apply directly to the Athapaskan-speaking Chipewyans, but he wrote that this killing "however wasteful it may appear . . . is a practice so common among all the Indian tribes as to be thought nothing of" (1958: 25). As Hearne wrote:

> They insisted on it, that killing plenty of deer and other game in one part of the country, could never make them scarcer in another. Indeed, they were so accustomed to kill everything that came within their reach, that few of them could pass by a small bird's nest, without slaying the young ones, or destroying the eggs. (1958: 75)

Less subject to Eurocentric bias are the reports of long-term and large-scale game shortages in many districts of the Hudson's Bay Company's Northern Department (Bishop 1974: 246; Ray 1974: 117–23). In the Nelson River District of northern Manitoba, overhunting and starvation in the early 1800s are documented. During the first decade the post journals make occasional references to starvation. By 1815 traders perceived both fur bearers and big game as on the decrease. There were nine cases of famine cannibalism between 1811 and 1815 (Hudson's Bay Company [HBC] B141/e/1). The district report for 1825 (HBC B141/e/2) was that the fur-bearing animals were exhausted, the game animals nearly so, and that the Indians were heavily dependent on the post for provisions and likely to starve in winter without them. That year, the 135 adult males in the district traded only an average of five beaver pelts each (HBC B239/H/1; see Simpson 1931: 14–15 for reports of no beaver at all in 1824). In 1827 Nelson House, the central post of the district, was closed to allow beaver and other species to recover.

There is also earlier evidence for indiscriminate and nonselective hunting in the woodlands and subarctic regions. During the seventeenth century in the St. Lawrence region, for example, Montagnais were reported as not conserving beaver: "When the Savages find a lodge of them, they kill all, great and small, male and female. There is a danger that they will finally exterminate the species in this region, as has happened among the Hurons" (LeJeune 1897: 57). Game depletions followed, as they followed comparable conditions in the west and south of Hudson's Bay in the early 1800s (Bishop 1975: Gadacz 1975).

Finally, evidence for indiscriminate hunting by Iroquoians in the Great Lakes area in the early period links this behavior to religious beliefs and raises the issue of knowledge and belief:

> [They] have this maxim for all kind of animals, whether they need them or not, that they must kill all they find, for fear, as they say, that if they do not take them the beasts would go and tell the others how they had been hunted and that then, in times of want, they would not find any more. (Dallion, on the Neutral, in LeClercq 1881, 1: 269)

It is clear that some groups were practicing conservation in the seventeenth and eighteenth centuries while others were not, and that whatever conservation systems may have been in place broke down by the late 1700s or early 1800s, when the Crees in the Northern Department had overhunted beaver and big game to the point that reliance on hare and fish, migration south onto the plains, and starvation became humiliating and tragic consequences.

Early references to conservation are not decisive evidence that purposive management existed independently of European contact and involvement of Indians in the fur trade. The earliest accounts noted above are of groups in the Great Lakes area, already involved in the trade as producers and middleman and thus perhaps motivated to harvest beaver on a sustained-yield basis. More detailed studies of particular regions and populations (for example, Hickerson 1967 [Rainy Lake Ojibwa]; Bishop 1974 [Osnaburgh and Lac Seul Ojibwa]; Morantz 1983 [East James Bay Cree]) give no reliable indication of conservation prior to 1821. In arguing against precontact conservation, at least in the areas south and west of Hudson's Bay, I also stress the relative abundance of evidence for overhunting as against conservation in the early literature, Radisson's statement that only the Cree were trapping selectively circa 1660, and the probability that pre–fur-trade boreal forest hunters with high mobility, low population densities, and relatively reliable game resources might not need to conserve animals. (This does not preclude the possibility that Crees were practicing conservation for reasons unrelated to practical considerations as we define them; see below).

Paradoxically, the fur trade provided conditions conducive both to the inception of conservation systems where none may have existed and to the destruction of existing or emergent systems. The new market for animals susceptible to management would provide incentives for the innovation of management practices or for the perpetuation/elaboration of existing ones. However, competition for animals and large-scale population movements could result in increased pressure on game and also in disregard for boundaries between regional bands. Without such boundaries, hunters and trappers would have no practical incentive to conserve since the animals they spared might be taken by others, the commons dilemma. Yet, as Bishop (1974, 1984) suggests, limited-access land tenure and conservation later reappeared as adjustments to depleted environments and dependence on trade goods.

This indeterminacy makes possible multiple alternative reconstructions of conservation in historical perspective. Management was and is practiced by boreal forest Algonquians in the nineteenth and twentieth centuries. These systems (a) could have existed prehistorically, been disrupted by historic economic and/or ecological circumstances, and subsequently resurfaced; or (b) could have emerged in response to the fur trade, undergone subsequent disruption, and then reappeared. For the areas south and west of Hudson's Bay, the weight of the evidence suggests that conservation was a postcontact innovation that did not develop on any scale prior to game depletions in the early 1800s and the Hudson's Bay Company's ensuing management policies.

GAME DEPLETION, TECHNOLOGY, AND THE FUR TRADE

It is clear that new technology enabled increased pressure on animals and that the fur trade provided incentives for harvesting greater numbers than in the past. It is less clear that these conditions lead inevitably to game shortages, unless we can endorse, following Innis (1970: 5), the discredited assumption that Indians had an expanding desire for trade goods. Yet, as has been persuasively demonstrated (Rich 1960; Ray 1974: 68, 141–42; Ray 1978), Crees and other Indians trading into Hudson's Bay and inland posts were decidedly non-European or "non-economic" in aspects of their trading behavior. Much of this behavior was consistent with the premises of Weber's substantive rationality as elucidated by Polanyi: "The substantive meaning implies neither choice nor insufficiency of means; man's livelihood may or may not involve the necessity of choice and, if choice there be, it need not be induced by the limiting effect of a 'scarcity' of the means" (1968: 140). The problem with conventional explanations of overkill by Indians centers on evidence that Cree consumer demand for trade goods remained relatively constant during the years of overhunting preceding the game depletions. It did not increase. It has also been assumed that competition between trading concerns led inexorably to the shortages (Ray 1974: 117), rather as though the avarice of the traders could be translated directly into increased predation by Indians. How then did the fur trade articulate with faunal depletion?

Competition between trading concerns tended to keep Cree purchasing power in excess of Cree consumer demand (cf. Ray 1978). Between 1763 and 1821 competition between trading companies resulted in a proliferation of inland posts, which reduced Cree time and labor costs. The relative costs of goods to the Indians also declined during this period of competition. Greater quantities of goods were given as gifts, and Crees continued the practice of taking debt at one post and trading furs at another (Ray 1974: 141–42).

While costs of trade goods declined, Cree demand for those goods was relatively inelastic. As Acheson (pers. comm.) suggests, Cree trading behavior corresponded to a backward-bending supply curve—when the price of fur went up, quantities supplied went down since Cree consumer demand remained relatively constant. Isham (Rich 1960: 49) recognized this in 1749: "The giving Indians a larger Price would occasion the Decrease of the Trade." Further insight comes from Graham's observations in 1768 at York Factory.

> And if the trading standard were enlarged in favor of the natives, would ruin it all; for I am certain that if the natives were to get any

> more for their furs, they would catch fewer, which I shall make plainly appear viz. One canoe brings down yearly to the fort [York Factory] one hundred made beaver in different kinds of furs, and trades with me seventy of the said beaver for real necessaries. The other thirty beaver shall so puzzle him to trade, that he often asks me what he shall buy, and when I make an answer, Trade some more powder, shot, tobacco, and hatchets, his answer is, I have traded sufficient to serve me and my family until I see you again next summer; so he will drink one half, and trade the others with me for baubles. (Graham 1969: 263)

So far were the Crees from disproportion between scarce means and multiple ends that they might not know what to trade for. This non-European relationship between supply and demand posed a formidable obstacle to the traders. Most of the evidence from the eighteenth century suggests that their continual exhortations to "not be Lassy, Keep close to trapping in the winter" (Isham 1949: 54) fell on unreceptive ears. Where population densities were low and where consumer goals could be met with one hundred "made beaver" (cf. Ray and Freeman 1978: 54) in furs and meat per "family" per year, it is probable that Crees *could* have provisioned themselves without hunting animals to below their reproductive capacities.

Demographic changes may have affected Cree hunting pressure on animals. Population densities may have increased substantially after 1763 when the Crees lost their middleman role in the trade between Hudson Bay and the interior. Many Crees probably took up permanent residence in the boreal forest as fur producers then. However, in the Nelson River District and many other areas, the Indian population was drastically reduced by a smallpox epidemic in 1780–1781, and it was very slow to recover. Paradoxically, the game depletions came about during a period of minimal population density relative to earlier estimates (Thompson 1962: 92).

It is, however, likely that technological changes, in combination with the fur trade, induced changes in the distribution of population and, in particular, a tendency to work the same area for a longer period of time. Under aboriginal conditions, killing animals in numbers sufficient to produce drastic game shortages is likely to have entailed what Indians considered disproportionate energy expenditures. Several references to Cree activity schedules in the 1700s suggest that industrious and unrelenting pressure on wildlife was far from characteristic, even when new technology was introduced, as for example: "while they have a sufficiency or abundance, they never have any thought to provide for the future; but lie in the tent and indulge their enormous appetites" (Graham 1969: 154). The least-effort principle, well-documented among hunters (Paine 1973; Sahlins 1972; see Hames and Stocks this volume), may have latent conservation effects. Nomadic hunters will move to a new activity area when they perceive energy costs as disproportionate to returns.[3]

Although aboriginal technology has been excessively discredited, it is clear that muskets, ice chisels, knives, axes, snare wire, steel traps, and castoreum significantly lowered costs of pursuit and capture and increased rates of capture. New technologies that reduce the costs may cause hunting groups to stay longer, with the effect of greater hunting pressure on the animals in the area. Contrary to the conventional assumption that Crees always dispersed into small groups in the winter months, there were cases in which whole regional bands attached to particular inland posts moved *en masse* to hunt in the same general area of their territory (HBC B/83/a; HBC B141/a/1).

More efficient technology and new incentives provided by the fur trade made game shortages possible but not inevitable. Game shortages came about not because Crees were killing more animals to obtain trade goods, but because they were reproducing under new technological conditions what was probably the aboriginal convention of killing as many animals as possible within the limits set by their assessments of costs and benefits. The potential for overhunting was already present. Steel traps, guns, and other tools made it easier. It was precisely in connection with the most efficient new hunting techniques that the major accounts of what Euro-Canadians defined as "waste" occurred (see Isham 1949: 81 and Graham 1969: 154 for caribou slaughters and shooting and spearing from canoes; Thompson 1962: 156 for effects of steel traps and castoreum bait on beaver soon after introduction west of Hudson Bay around 1797).

MAGICO-RELIGIOUS CONCEPTIONS AND OVERHUNTING

Martin (1978) and Vecsey (1980) argue that boreal forest Algonquians refrained from overkilling animals in precontact times because of a religious obligation to hunt selectively. Martin maintains that the rule was suspended in historic times after Indians defined animals as disease agents responsible for early epidemics. I agree with Martin that nominally "religious" ideas were relevant to the game shortages. However, the earlier references suggest that such ideas encouraged rather than proscribed indiscriminate hunting. Conservation requires some organization of land tenure such that practitioners realize the benefits of selective predation. Conservation also requires resource conditions sufficiently abundant that animals can be harvested selectively rather than indiscriminately for immediate consumption and trade. Less attention is paid to a third precondition that has materially conditioned hunters' decisions about how many animals to kill. Hunters have to be aware that they can influence the availability of animals in the future by harvesting selectively in the present. We are accustomed to regard such knowledge as patent but have perhaps prematurely generalized it to nomadic prehistoric and early historic Algonquians with low population densities, high mobility, and initially, few practical incentives to experiment with conservation.

The following passages are accounts by eighteenth-century observers of Cree concepts concerning the impact of hunting on animal populations:

> They have a maxim very prejudicial to this country which is that the more beasts they kill, the more they increase. (Robson 1965: 51)
> They make prodigious slaughter every season among the deer from an unaccountable notion that the more they destroy, the greater plenty will succeed. (Ellis 1967: 85)
> They kill animals out of wantoness, alleging the more they destroy the more plentiful they grow. (Graham 1969: 165–66)
> They kill all they can, having an incontrovertible maxim among them, which is "the more they kill, the more they have to

kill" and this opinion, although diametrically opposite to reason or common sense, is as pertinaciously held by them as his tenets are by the most bigotted enthusiast. (Umfreville 1790: 38)

Given the enthusiastic and sometimes reciprocal plagiarism of the time, these accounts may not all stand as independent attestations. It is, however, clear that a distinctively non-European ecological concept is being described.

These passages are early references to the boreal Algonquian idea that game animals killed by hunters spontaneously regenerate after death or reincarnate as fetal animals. Manitoba Crees in the 1980s call this process *akwanaham otoskana*, "[animal] covers its bones." Such events are taken for granted by some Cree trappers. I was told on a number of occasions that an adult, trapped animal was "the same one" that had been killed the previous winter. Modern Crees also state that ritual procedures for disposing of animal bones and blood prefigure and influence animal regeneration and reincarnation. This knowledge was present in the nineteenth and eighteenth centuries and probably derives from archaic strata of Algonquian culture.

In comparing Indian and Western ecological knowledge, Bishop (1981) discusses "respect," the complex of ritual attitudes toward animals supposed by Martin (1978) and others to have included a rule limiting kills to what was needed in the short term.

A key difference between the two systems was the absence in the former [Algonquian] of a more general concept of animal population dynamics. And just as it is possible to practice conservation without "respecting" game, so it is possible to respect animals and simultaneously and perhaps unawaredly hunt them to extinction if the motives and means for obtaining them are present. (Bishop 1981: 55)

There is abundant evidence (Thompson 1962) for animal ceremonialism in the eighteenth century, but none that indiscriminate killing was religiously proscribed or that management or avoidance of "waste" was religiously enjoined. The availability of animals to hunters and trappers was understood as subject to ritual influence, but the idea that hunting pressure could reduce species populations in the long term and on a large scale was absent.

Instead, when killed, butchered, consumed, and disposed of with "respect," animals were understood to regenerate or to be reborn in proportion to the numbers killed.

Although the question might be raised as to how professional hunters could have so ignorant a conception of animal population dynamics, a more reflective question is why Indians would over-kill animals if they defined themselves as capable of stabilizing game populations by selective hunting. Nelson (1982: 222), for example, states that "the finite nature of the resource population is easily understood" by contemporary Koyukon (Athapaskan) of the Alaskan Plateau and that such understanding is essential to a "conservation ethic." It is by many Crees in the 1980s. However, the conviction that hunters can reliably manipulate the quantities of animals subsequently available to them cannot, in the face of contrary evidence, uncritically be ascribed to prehistoric and early-contact-period Algonquians.

The absence of management and the practice of indiscriminate hunting could follow as conjoined aspects of the same premise. If hunters are unaware that animals can be managed, they may also be unaware that they can be hunted to depletion. It cannot be assumed that Crees and others involved in game depletions initially understood their own role as determinants. Rather than inhibiting overkill, religious definitions of the human-animal relationship encouraged it insofar as they premised an environment of primordial abundance in which game could not be destroyed but only temporarily displaced. Some contemporary Rock Crees reproduce this traditional understanding. Similarly, some Osnaburgh House Ojibwas stated in the 1960s that conservation was unnecessary because animals were "given" to hunters when they were needed (Bishop 1974: 36). These understandings are held also by subarctic Athapaskan groups (see Sharp 1979: 91; Jetté 1907: 604).

I thus disagree with Martin's (1978) explanation for overkill, but I endorse entirely his insistence that the ecological and religious knowledge of Indians is indispensable for interpretations of productive practice. Such knowledge is too frequently ignored, undervalued, or relegated to the hazily defined sphere of "ideological" rationalization. The inconsistency of such reductionism with more sophisticated ecological and/or Marxist writing has been amply discussed and demonstrated (cf. Friedman 1974; Ellen 1982).

THE EMERGENCE OF CONSERVATION AFTER 1821

As I have argued, conservation practices did not develop in or diffuse to most areas of the boreal forest until well after 1821. This is the more remarkable for the fact that at least some Algonquians recognized their role as effective agents in the destruction of the beaver—while locating the ultimate cause in decisions of supernatural beings. In 1797 two Cree or Ojibwa Indians of the Swan River District (Manitoba) told David Thompson that the creator being and the trickster-transformer intended to destroy the beaver, and introduced knowledge of castoreum bait to Indians for this purpose, with tragic results:

> We are now killing the Beaver without any labor, we are now rich, but shall soon be poor, for when the beaver are destroyed we have nothing to depend on to purchase what we want for our families, strangers now over run our country with their iron traps, and we, and they, shall soon be poor. (Thompson 1962: 204)

Tragedies of the Commons as Tragedies of Invasion

Thompson reflected on the spread of various Indian tribes into new lands, searching for beaver, and what we would now call the problem of the commons:

> The Nepissings, the Algonquians, and Iroquois Indians having exhausted their own countries, now spread themselves over these countries, and as they destroyed the beaver, moved fowards to the northward and westward; the Natives, the Nahathaways [Crees] did not in the least molest them; the Chippaways and other tribes made use of Traps of Steel and of the Castorum. . . . Every intelligent man saw the poverty that would follow the destruction of the Beaver, but there were no chiefs to control it; all was perfect liberty and equality. (1962: 205–6)

Why, given apparent understanding of what was happening, did not the Crees, Ojibwas, and others develop conservation rules, such as selective killing, to prevent the most severe game shortages? The commons situation is an obvious explanation, if it is recast as one of the loss of boundaries and the inability to control incursions by others. The Crees and the Ojibwas were in no position to benefit from any selective trapping they might choose to practice if Algonquians, Nippissings, and others were overrunning their lands with steel traps. The Crees and Ojibwas, in fact, interpreted these incursions as another worldly consequence of spiritual decisions.

The game shortages were less tragedies of the commons than tragedies of invasion. The scattered references to conservation practices in the 1600s and 1700s suggest no necessary barriers to the institutionalization of conservation. Within the regional band,[4] Algonquians negotiated effective compromises between exclusive rights to animals or land and the moral imperatives of generalized reciprocity. The Ojibwas described by Thompson spoke of "strangers" overrunning their land. It is precisely at the margins of the moral community rather than within it that trespass functioned to render conservation disadvantageous. As Bishop (1974: 214–15) and others have documented, this was also the case after 1821, when the Hudson's Bay Company imposed quotas, seasons, rotation, and other conservation measures, and the effects of these were often negated by trespass, almost invariably on the part of "strange Indians" from other districts and regional bands.

The conventional assumption that effective conservation presupposes exclusive tenure rights in delimited hunting tracts or territories needs to be qualified. If there is consensus as to conservation, there need be no consensus about exclusive tenure, and vice versa. The closest empirical approximation is the Ottawa allotment system described by Lahontan (1905, 2: 481–83) in which trapping groups settled on different areas of the village's territory every winter. Each group trapped selectively and benefited from the selectivity of the sector's previous occupants.

In most areas of the boreal forest south and west of Hudson's Bay, historical circumstances afforded neither the consensus as to conservation nor the freedom from incursion by outsiders that might have allowed management to function at a regional band level of organization, without partitioning of the band territory into tracts in which hunting groups or local bands possessed exclusive rights. Accordingly, when conservation emerged, it was as a functional concomitant of hunting territories, which in turn have been explained variously, that is, in relation to a shift from big game to marketable fur-bearing animals (Leacock 1954), adaptations to changing environments favoring exploitation of more sedentary game (Bishop 1970, 1974), and the allegedly post-1821 introduction of the tract system by Hudson's Bay Company personnel (Ray 1974: 195–204).

The Cree did not, however, immediately respond this way. Many Crees, most in several northern districts, reacted to the game shortages of the early nineteenth century neither by trying to fight the invaders nor by experimenting with conservation, but rather with the characteristic hunters' expedient of movement out of the depleted areas. In the years following 1821, so many Crees moved south into the parklands and plains that officials feared there would be insufficient numbers left to prosecute the fur trade (Ray 1975). In addition, the Cree resisted conservation measures introduced by Europeans after 1821. It was not until around 1850 that measures introduced by the Hudson's Bay Company became common in many areas. Given a perspective in which events such as diminishing animal populations and incursions by outsiders are governed by spirit agencies, it is doubtful that either warfare or conservation appeared practical. An effective conservation system presupposes both knowledge of practical techniques and conviction that (a) indiscriminate hunting causes faunal depletion, and (b) controlled or selective predation will result in a reliable supply of game, none of which appear to have existed on any scale prior to around 1850.[5]

Sense, Interest, and Cultural Change

Crees made practical decisions about how many animals to kill in terms of symbols, or socially constituted signs whose premises were relatively arbitrary (Friedrich 1979) in relation to changing material circumstance. Sahlins (1981: 68–70) distinguishes "sense" and "interest" as conjoined aspects of the signs in whose terms objects and events are socially valuated. The "sense" or "value" in Saussurean terms is the conventional, socially-shared meaning of a sign, reciprocally determined and differentiated by the meanings of other signs (Saussure 1966; Benveniste 1966: 91–96). The actors' experience of the sign as "interest," on the other hand, derives from the position of the valuated object in relation to purposive activity. In novel contexts of activity, disparities between "sense" and "interest," or between the "interests" of different parties, may develop. The circumstances of practical activity may no longer conform to the conventional values by which they are acted upon.

The capacity of slain animals to renew themselves by regeneration or reincarnation is, and was, one aspect of the "sense" or sign value of *pisiskiw*, "mammal," in Cree culture. Cree productive behavior during the early fur-trade period reproduced and presupposed this conventional valuation of animals, but under novel ecological conditions in which muskets, ice chisels, steel traps, and castoreum were placing unprecedented pressures on animal populations. Animals took on additional instrumental "interests" through their new value in trade. Nothing in the new technology or "interests" themselves would have made their lethal consequences patent to the Crees. They may or may not have been aware that more animals were being killed but, as I have indicated above, the connection between intensified predation and game shortages was not likely to have been self-evident.

In the late eighteenth and early nineteenth centuries, however, it must rapidly have become obvious that something was wrong: animals were not regenerating in proportion to the numbers killed. This disparity between convention and experience would eventually act back on Cree valuations of animals and hunting, leading to their adoption of conservation techniques. By the mid-nineteenth century, Crees south and west of Hudson's Bay developed or borrowed and experimented with conservation techniques, and sustained-yield harvest systems for beaver, muskrat, and marten were institutionalized in many areas.

A variety of other preconditions may have existed for the inception of conservation, including freedom from trespass, increased sedentism associated with a primary reliance on hare and fish, sufficient abundance to permit scheduled capture, dependence on Euro-Canadian trade goods purchasable with furs, and perception of fur-bearing animals as scarce resources. As Bishop (personal communication) points out, there was considerable microhistorical and microecological variation with respect to these preconditions. Conservation emerged at different times in different areas and undoubtedly under different circumstances. Even so, it was necessary that Crees redefine animals as manageable.

The documentary records are quiet about this redefinition and the reciprocal interplay between religious reformulation and practical experimentation that must have prompted it. In speculating about it, we should beware of assuming that "practical" and "religious" categories of knowledge are always isomorphic or that disparities must be resolved Bishop (pers. comm.). There may, for example, have long existed an unresolved contradiction between the doctrine of infinite renewal and recognition that hunters could exterminate animals locally. Among some contemporary Rock Crees, this contradiction is engaged by the understanding that humans can decimate animal populations only if the animals or *acāhk* beings ("spirits") *permit* hunting and trapping to have that effect. It is, in any event, clear that Crees encountered in the game shortages a contradiction of cosmic proportions: despite conventional ritual treatment, animals were not renewing themselves but were disappearing. And some Crees recognized overhunting as at least a proximate cause for the depletions. For example, the 1814 District Report for Nelson River stated: "natives say beaver not to be found, its skin having been most sought after by traders for many years past, nearly exhausted, reason they give for not killing more of them" (HBC B141/e/1).

It remains to be specified whether the conservation techniques that appeared in the wake of the game shortages were developed independently by Indians or inspired by Hudson's Bay Company policies. These policies are detailed in the post-1821 correspondence of the period (Fleming 1940 and summarized by Ray 1975). It is clear that traders saw hunting tracts and conservation as functionally linked policies for rationalizing the trade. The post managers introduced bans on summer furs and on trade in castoreum and steel traps, premiums on muskrat and marten to divert pressure from beaver, relocations of posts to less depleted areas, beaver quotas, bans on trapping during breeding seasons, bans on pregnant and/or juvenile animals, and rotation among sectors of regional or local band areas.

As noted above, Crees and other groups initially circumvented the Company's conservation policies when and how they could. How their acceptance and the hypothesized redefinition required came about is uncertain. The religious interpretation of conservation by some contemporary Rock Crees (see Feit 1973 on Waswanipi) and cultural transformations among other boreal Algonquians lead to conjecture that the game shortages motivated a reinterpretation of indiscriminate or "wasteful" hunting and trapping as offensive to animals and to the spirit entities regulating each species. The beings are understood to regulate the regeneration, movements, and distribution of animals as well as human access to them. Many Crees state explicitly that *misimōswa* ("Great Moose"), *mistamisk* ("Great Beaver"), *misipisiw* ("Great Lynx"), and other beings interfere with the harvests of hunters who trap unselectively or waste the products of animals.

From this point of view, the game shortages may have been reinterpreted *a posteriori* as punishments for overhunting and waste. Precisely this reinterpretation occurred among Labrador Naskapi when in 1914 the main herd of barren-land caribou failed to migrate south along its usual route. The famine that ensued was attributed to the anger of the caribou spirit at prior waste and overhunting (Strong 1929: 284–85; cf. Speck 1935).

CONTEMPORARY CONSERVATION PRACTICES

Conservation in one or another form is practiced by many Rock Cree trappers and hunters in northwestern Manitoba, although underutilization and the alleged inefficiency of younger trappers (as assessed by their seniors) have made it technically superfluous in some areas. It usually includes more than observing provincial government rules about seasons and quotas. The verb *iskōh-* refers to the act of sparing animals that might easily be taken in order to preserve them for future harvesting, or in the case of more mobile animals that may not be retrievable later, it refers to the religious proscription of excessive overkilling. In contrast, the verb *cāhkītā-* refers to the practice of overhunting an area until it is depleted of game. Methods of implementing *iskōh-* vary. Hunters may simply not fire on game if they have no immediate need for meat or hides; I observed three instances in which woodland caribou were spared for this reason. The term can also denote conformity to seasons and quotas, and it includes such practices as removing traps from a lodge before a beaver colony is trapped out and selectively sparing juvenile or pregnant animals by holding fire or setting snares in runways at some distance from the beaver lodge. Of sectors of traplines that are rotated, it is said that the land is *kīyām-īwa-*, "resting."

Different trappers use different techniques, and not all practice conservation. Some who do not conserve say that it is unnecessary because animals will be reborn. Failure to conserve beaver and marten has led to depletion on particular traplines or trapline sectors; the nonconservers are usually invited to trap with less prodigal relatives until their lands recover. Among trappers who do conserve, some have an essentially Western scientific understanding of sustained-yield game management. Others have inherited creative syntheses of Algonquian and Western conceptions. They define failure to trap and hunt selectively as exemplifying precisely the religiously proscribed act of *cāhkītā-*, "overhunting," or *mīstin-*, "waste," that is punished by the game spirits or the animals themselves. The depletion of animals on a trapline is understood by these men and women less as an objective decrease in the numbers of animals present than as a limitation on their visibility to the trapper and on his/her access to them. This redefinition of conservation as a religious obligation undoubtedly reaches back into the 1800s, and exemplifies the conjoined processes of cultural reproduction and transformation (Braudel 1980: 25–54; Sahlins 1981: 67–72).

RELIGION AND ECOLOGY

My representation of prehistoric and early-contact-period Algonquians as "indiscriminate" hunters does not express or imply criticism or disparagement. Indians, like other human beings, have on occasion induced ecological crises through the unintended consequences of their productive activities. A signal difference between the Algonquians and the architects of ecological tragedies in industrialized states is that the former brought disaster only upon themselves. Moral evaluation of terms like "overkill" and "waste" from a Western perspective is both extraneous and objectionable. To be relevant, such concepts require historically contextualized Algonquian definition (see Bishop 1981: 55; Krech 1981: 96–97).

A discussion of how religious concepts influence subsistence strategies and decisions inscribes itself in the ongoing dialogue between what Keesing (1981) has labeled "adaptationist" and "ideational" perspectives on the organization of sociocultural systems. In the existing ethnological division of labor, ecologists and Marxists focus primarily on production, whereas ritual and myth are franchised to the symbolists and structuralists. Rather than partitioning "production" and "religion" as ethnographic categories between materialist and semiotic spheres of determination, we should examine both in their structural and behavioral dimensions. Lévi-Strauss wrote that "observation never reveals the isolated performance of one type of wheel-work or the other; we can only witness the results of their mutual adjustment" (1973: 11). Knowledge of religious premises may be as critical as knowledge of population density or species biomass to the understanding of how subsistence and resource-management decisions are made, how they were made in the past, and how they reproduce and transform themselves through time. Far from devaluing the effects of technological and environmental circumstances, the perspective outlined here takes their meaningful encompassment as critical for reasoned ecological analysis since it is as sign values and not objective qualities that these circumstances are experienced and acted upon.

ᘉᘓ

NOTES

This chapter is based on research supported by the Canadian Ethnology Service, the Smithsonian Institution, and the American Philosophical Society, and by a postdoctoral fellowship at the D'Arcy McNickle Center for the History of the American Indian. For knowledge of Cree management systems, past and present, I am endebted to Johnny Bighetty, Charles Hart, Cornelius Colomb, Jeremy and Caroline Caribou, Jean-Baptiste Merasty, Solomon Colomb, Luc and Caroline Dumas, and many other patient and generous individuals. For comments on various versions, I am indebted to James Acheson, Karen Art, Fikret Berkes, Charles Bishop, Harvey Feit, Raymond Fogelson, Eric Hamp, Jenny Kiratli, Bonnie Mc-Cay, Robert Netting, Marshall Sahlins, Michael Silverstein, and Ann Straus. I appreciate also permission from the Public Archives of Manitoba to cite material from the Hudson's Bay Company Archives. Finally, my thanks to Bonnie McCay for a superb and probably formidable editing job.

1. Descriptions of boreal Algonquian conservation practices in the present century are provided by Cooper (1939: 69), Burgesse (1945: 12–15), Davidson (1926: 86), Jenkins (1939: 13), Landes (1937: 89–95), and Lips (1947: 388, 435).

2. See Bishop (1984) for an interpretation of Radisson's remarks as evidence for prehistoric and early-contact conservation and exclusive land tenure.

3. Decreasing ecological efficiency was, of course, only one among several reasons for moving camp; Rock Cree consultants seldom mentioned it (cf. Woodburn 1972 on the Hadza).

4. The regional band was a complex of interrelated extended families, often with fluctuating or alternating personnel, who exploited a loosely defined territory and were oriented to the same fishing and trading centers in summer.

5. An important desideratum of this analysis concerns the factuality and adaptiveness, under prehistoric technoeconomic circumstances, of the cosmological doctrine that game resources are inexhaustible. Given a highly nomadic regime, indiscriminate hunting may have functioned to increase species growth rates and enhance reproduction by keeping populations well below "carrying capacity," or population levels at which, if the population is density-dependent, growth rates and reproductive success or fecundity decline. This doctrine may, therefore, have objective consequences, from a Western point of view. It is clear that excessive killing *per se* did not subject the Crees and other boreal Algonquians to ultimate biological destruction. Whether such behavior was necessarily *more adaptive*, either in terms of survival and reproduction or in maximizing energy capture, than more selective killing is subject to question.

7 Marine Tenure and Conservation in Papua New Guinea

PROBLEMS IN INTERPRETATION

James G. Carrier

FROM TIME TO TIME in the 1970s and early 1980s the government of Papua New Guinea seized on the idea of expanding and commercializing traditional, largely inshore fishing. The goal was to improve the country's balance of trade by reducing the import of tinned mackerel while increasing employment and income in rural areas. Unlike the case in many areas of the Third World, in Papua New Guinea small-scale fishing was not much more than a subsistence activity associated at most with small, local barter markets. One concern was that if the government fostered commercialization of the traditional fisheries, it would have tremendous impact on them, about which little was known, and would create conditions for increased levels of exploitation of marine resources about which, again, very little was known.

As of 1984 little commercialization had taken place. Although it might seem that the government was wise not to act in such a state of ignorance, there were reasons to be optimistic that the environmental impact of fisheries development would be slight. Because of their long traditions of fishing, Melanesian maritime peoples had an intimate acquaintance with their marine environment and hence could be expected to know how to monitor and manage the fish stocks. Moreover, they would be motivated to manage fish stocks because these were the sources of their livelihood. Perhaps most important, the foundation of marine resource conservation—systems of limited entry and conservation—seemed to exist in Oceania and Papua New Guinea in the form of traditional systems of marine tenure (Johannes 1978, 1981, 1982).

In Papua New Guinea, as in many other areas of the developing world, there has been a great deal of interest in "traditional" systems of resource management and conservation and their possible roles as models or bases for management and conservation systems in the context of political and economic development (Morauta *et al.* 1982). Systems of marine tenure that involve exclusive property rights to areas of rivers, reefs, and seas, as well as (less commonly) rights to species and particular capture techniques, are found throughout Oceania and Melanesia.[1] They have been interpreted as having the intended or unintended functions of conserving seafood stocks. Of particular interest is the extent to which intervillage fishing rights—recognized and defended boundaries between fishing grounds claimed by different villages—and intravillage fishing rights—the case to be reported on here—represent forms of what fisheries biologists and economists refer to as limited entry, the single most important prescription for presenting tragedies of the commons: "Where fishermen can limit access to a fishing ground, it is in their best interests to fish in moderation so as to foster good future yields. Where access to the fishing grounds is unlimited, however, fishermen can exert little control over total catch rates" (Johannes 1982: 241). Village "ownership" of fishing grounds may be used not only to restrict access to members of the village and those who gain permission from the village or a chief, but also as the basis for enactment of regulations that are tailored to fit local environmental and social conditions (Johannes 1982: 241–42).

It is recognized that traditional intervillage fishing rights and other indigenous forms of marine tenure do not guarantee sound management and conservation of fish stocks. They may be ineffective in relation to migratory stocks (Haines 1982) and in subsistence and cash economies in which needs or profit desires of "owners" may exceed the capacity for sustained yield (Haines 1982; Johannes 1982: 243). Moreover, with commercialization their conservation functions may be overshadowed by boundary disputes (Johannes 1982: 243–44). However, there is still a great deal of optimism that, with further ethnographic and biological research on the nature of traditional marine tenure systems in Papua New Guinea, they will prove to offer the basis for local-level management and conservation.

This optimism rests on limited evidence and questionable assumptions. Although a connection between exclusive systems of marine tenure and conservation may exist in some areas of

Polynesia and Micronesia, at least one researcher has observed the lack of substantial evidence for conscious conservation practices in maritime Papua New Guinea and Irian Jaya (Polunin 1984).

The notion that traditional marine tenure systems are linked to the conservation of fish stocks in Oceania is partly supported by the assumption that since native people are intimately familiar with the ecological systems they exploit and upon which they have depended, they have learned the necessity and techniques of conservation (see Waiko and Jiregari 1982 for similar reasoning in relation to agricultural systems of Papua New Guinea). A broad objection to this perspective has been raised by Bulmer (1982), whose overview of the human ecology of Papua New Guinea suggests that circumstance, not intent, accounted for "the most important conservational forces of the past" (1982: 64); that the conservational functions of "jealously guarded rights restricting access to certain highly localized resources" were rarely for the benefit of any more than a man and his heirs (1982: 63); and that the "record of the past suggests that traditional Papua New Guinea societies scored more points for adaptation, innovation, and development of new resources than they did for conservation" (1982: 63).

The purpose of this chapter is to point out the danger of presuming intended or unintended conservation when one finds a case of limited entry or exclusive marine tenure. Optimism about local-level marine resource management in developing Papua New Guinea rests on unexamined assumptions about the way people understand their environment and the way ownership works. I examine those assumptions and the workings of intra-village fishing rights as they pertain to Ponam, one of the islands off the northern coast of Papua New Guinea (Carrier 1981, 1982; Carrier and Carrier 1983).

PONAM GEOGRAPHY, ECONOMY, AND SOCIAL ORGANIZATION

Ponam Island is an infertile sand cay lying about three miles off the north-central coast of Manus Island in Manus Province, Papua New Guinea. The island is about two miles long and seldom more than about three hundred yards wide, running roughly northwest to southeast. It is surrounded by an extensive shallow lagoon about twelve miles long and varying from one-quarter mile to one and one-half miles wide. At the time of fieldwork, around 1980, there were about five hundred Ponam Islanders. About three hundred of them lived on the island, while the rest lived elsewhere in Papua New Guinea as wage laborers and their dependents.

Traditionally Ponams specialized in fishing and trading their catch for foodstuffs and other necessities with mainland Manus agriculturalists. Following colonial penetration in the first decade of this century the trade deteriorated, and since World War II islanders have been unable to support themselves in this way (Schwartz 1963). They supplemented fishing and trading with wage labor. By the 1970s migrant Ponams, well educated and frequently in high-level civil-service posts, were remitting substantial amounts of money home to the island. Residents produced little but fish, coconuts, and a few pigs; they acquired almost everything they needed to survive through trade and commerce, and were increasingly dependent on remittances from migrants.[2]

However, at the time of fieldwork, around 1980, fishing was still the primary local source of food and wealth and was carried out by both men and women. Ponams practiced or remembered a wide variety of fishing and other marine exploitation techniques used both inside and outside the lagoon (Carrier 1982). The most common techniques were angling in the lagoon or in the shallow waters over coral formations outside the barrier reef, speargun fishing, fishing with nets inside the lagoon, and reef gleaning. Net fishing and angling were used primarily by men, reef gleaning by women, and speargun fishing by both men and women.

Since the beginning of this century the island was one political unit, subdivided socially and territorially in complex ways associated with what I call *moieties* (although not associated with marriage) and a system of double unilineal descent involving matriclans, totemic groups which did not affect the ownership of productive resources; and patriclans, divided in patrilineages (which may be further subdivided), which had as their main function the ownership of productive resources and techniques.

The patriclans formed the agnatic core of cognatic groups that descend from focal ancestors. These cognatic groups were important in ceremonial exchanges which occurred frequently on Ponam and through which much wealth passed. To some degree, the ability of the cognatic groups to perform creditably in exchange depended on their social repute and on their ability to generate obligations toward them by nonmembers and to discharge previous obligations. Likewise, the ability of individual Ponams to perform creditably in exchange depended on repute and the ability to generate and discharge social obligations. This discussion is not tangential to the subject of this chapter, because the meaning and uses of "ownership" in marine resources and fishing techniques were framed by ceremonial and other exchange. The patrilineal groups that "owned" marine property and their leaders used that property to generate and discharge obligations and so to maintain their repute and social credit and thus their place in exchange.

PONAM MARINE TENURE

Although marine tenure concerns the ownership of reef and sea and things pertaining to them, it is important to note that in Melanesia "ownership" has not been of the sort commonly found in industrial societies of the West, where resources may be owned outright by individuals or corporations who are free to use or dispose of them as they see fit. One significant aspect of Melanesian ownership is that property in natural resources was owned not by individuals but by clans, lineages, or other kinship-based groups. Fishing equipment of all sorts was personal property on Ponam. However, those areas of reef and sea and those species and fishing techniques that were owned were the property of patrilineal descent groups, usually no more than three or four active, resident adult males (see Carrier and Carrier 1983). Usually one or two leaders of a patrilineal group held executive power over the property. Their ownership was that of trustees for the group, relatively free to manage the property in conventional ways but likely to face strong challenges if they attempted anything new, and even stronger challenges if they tried to sell the group's property.

Descriptions of the marine tenure system and its relationships with social organization on Ponam and in the larger Manus region are provided more fully elsewhere (Carrier 1981). This brief and general account suggests the complexities of marine tenure on Ponam. Marine holdings reflected islanders' ecological differentiation of their reef and sea and the major social and political divisions of the island. The boundaries of the marine holdings of different patrilineal groups generally coincided with the boundaries of important ecological zones within the shallow lagoon and its protective reef edge, but the pattern of holdings varied between the north and south halves of the island's waters on the one hand, and the east and west halves on the other, reflecting fundamental historical divisions within Ponam society (Fig. 7.1).

Although land property on Ponam was close to our notion of *fee simple* private property—in which the owner also has exclusive access to the products of the land and control over what is done to it—marine ownership was very different. The patrilineages and clans that owned segments of reefs and the sea did not necessarily hold exclusive rights to capture all the fish that might be found in their property. There were countervailing rights (a) to some species (tuna, mullet, kinds of anchovies); and (b) to certain fishing techniques (particularly collective ones) that were held as distinct property by patrilineages. Rights to capture a school of tuna or to use a particular netting technique (almost always in particular waters or defined paths through the lagoon) might be exercised by one patrilineage in sea or reef areas owned by another patrilineage. In addition, the Melanesian land-tenure principle that a person who improves the land by clearing and planting it acquires usufruct rights thereby (Crocombe 1971: 305) allowed for countervailing property claims to bottom-fishing rights in the case of the construction of stone traps (*papai*) that lie along the north barrier reef. Although an individual building one of these had to obtain permission of the waters owners, once it was built it passed automatically to the builders' patrilineal descendants, who did not need to ask permission of the waters owners again.

The world of exclusive property rights on Ponam was the world of men; women had rights close to our notion of common property. Women had generally free access to all individual (as opposed to collective) fishing techniques and waters inside the lagoon, and one collective net fishing technique was free to all women in all waters at all times. In addition, most fishing techniques that could be done

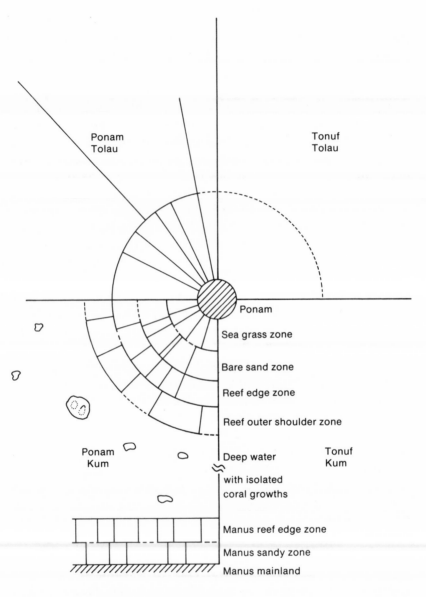

Ponam
Tolau

Tonuf
Tolau

Ponam

Sea grass zone

Bare sand zone

Reef edge zone

Reef outer shoulder zone

Ponam
Kum

Deep water

Tonuf
Kum

with isolated
coral growths

Manus reef edge zone

Manus sandy zone

Manus mainland

KEY: _____ = boundary between holdings
.... = boundary between ecological zones, not between holdings

FIG. 7.1. *General pattern of Ponam sea holdings, in relation to ecological zone boundaries.*

by individuals alone and were demersal (*hire has*) rather than benthic (*lo has*) could be used in any waters at any time, with a few limiting conditions.

Apart from the existence of countervailing rights, ownership of reef and sea areas, fish species, and techniques differed from land tenure and our notions of private ownership in other ways. Gaining the permission of an owner did not involve any sort of payment or share of the catch. Islanders considered this sort of permission as part of the routine of friendly relations and could grant standing permission to some kin. Moreover, the ability of patrilineages to exercise their ownership of marine areas, species, and techniques by refusing permission to others—that is, by limiting entry or access to others—was contingent upon the *realpolitik* of the situation. For example, one clan owned the right of angling with live bait over shallow coral formations in the Seeadler deeps, using hooks of mollusc shell, and residual rights to all sorts of angling (*jai*). When steel hooks were introduced, they gave permission to others to use them. In the 1930s they tried to withdraw that permission but other islanders violated the edict, eventually forcing the clan to give up its claims to angling rights.

CONSERVATION AND PONAM PROPERTY RIGHTS

There is little evidence that the elaborate and overlapping systems of marine tenure of Ponam were used for explicit conservation purposes. For one thing, ownership did not appear to include the right to close a fishing ground for conservation or other purposes.

There was one reported exception. In the northern waters of Ponam, at a time when one clan (rather than patrilineage) controlled the reef, the clan's ownership was similar to some Polynesian and Micronesian systems in that they had the right to close all or part of the reef to the catching of all or certain kinds of reef creatures. As a practical matter this seems to have been important only for *sa'ul* for shell money and trochus for sale. The clan's exercise of the right appears to have been more for appropriation of labor and wealth than for conservation: the clan organized mass gathering expeditions, involving other islanders as well, and claimed a large percentage of the produce. In any case, the clan's right disappeared after World War II, when rising prices for trochus stimulated a rebellion on the part of other islanders and dissolved the clan's control over the reef, returning control to patrilineages.

The rest of this chapter is concerned with why the Ponams did not use—or did not often use—their system of property rights to husband the resources on which they depended. I will attempt to show that the island's society did not satisfy the twin assumptions that familiarity with the environs leads to a Western-style ecological understanding and that exclusive marine tenure leads property owners to husband marine resources. I will do this first by comparing Ponam ecological theory with one version of Western ecological theory and second by investigating the social nature of Ponam marine tenure.

ETHNOECOLOGY: PONAM AND WESTERN

From the age of three or four years, Ponams spent a large amount of time on or in the sea closely observing the fish that they had to catch if they were to eat their next meal. As might be expected, they learned a great deal about the fish and shellfish they sought. However, ecological models, like all models, require not just facts but the organization of facts in particular ways. Models develop in response to particular problems, questions, and ways of thinking. Accordingly, Ponams did not organize the facts that they knew about marine life into the same models that westerners have produced.

The Western model that I have in mind is that which lies behind ecological management. It is not necessarily the same as the scientific model used in fisheries management, which tends to focus on single species rather than ecological relationships among species. However, the two come from similar scientific orientations. In the Western model, each species is more or less unique: it occupies a niche defined by what it does and how it is uniquely adapted to its environs. Second, each species forms a part of the environment of others within an ecological community or system. Thus, the reduction or elimination of the population of one species will affect others directly or indirectly—most evidently by its effect on prey or predators. This is of course Darwin's conception of the web of life connecting seemingly separate parts of the environment. Third, in some influential conceptions, the web of life is viewed as a functionally integrated whole. The whole and its integrity and balance are threatened by loss of any one component. Although this perspective is increasingly challenged by ecologists and evolutionary biologists (see Vayda and McCay 1975), it remains an important rationale for conservationists in their attempt to protect endangered species. The extinction of a species is undesirable because each one makes a unique contribution to the environment. Loss of a species upsets the environment and has unfortunate and permanent results. This argument is held to be correct in principle.

Finally, the Western model tends to see human action as the principal agency of ecological disruption. Many environmental studies and arguments are concerned with the impact of human action on the environment. Again, there are counter perspectives but the model persists in influencing policy and thinking, in this case notably in fisheries management, where more attention is given to "fishing mortality" than to other aspects of the environment or fish stocks.

Underlying the model is an assumption that life on earth is self-contained and materialist. Explanations of the behavior of species and of the environment itself must refer only to interspecies relationships, the attributes of species and populations, and the material environment (for example, energy flows and material cycles). No external agencies are conceived of, all living things are part of the grand interaction, and no living thing is excluded from consideration.

The Ponam ecological model was strikingly different in its specifics and in underlying assumptions about life on earth. Whereas the Western model stresses and relies on the uniqueness of species, for Ponams this concept was unimportant except as recognized differences pertained to a pragmatic conception of fish and shellfish as things to be caught, eaten, or traded. Knowledge of fish centered on where and how to catch them and whether or not to bother, eminently reasonable concerns in a fishing community. The orientation to marine life was in terms of the islanders' requirements for physical and social survival rather than in terms of the various relationships which may exist within the realm of marine life itself.

Consequently, Ponams saw each sort of fish existing more or less independently rather than as being related to each other as part of a functionally integrated whole. The observed fact that two different sorts of things live in the same neighborhood did not necessarily lead to interest in their relationships. Islanders were knowledgeable about the interactions of some species but not very interested in them. For example, some Ponams observed that dugongs and sea turtles were less common than when they were younger and that sea grasses had spread within the Ponam lagoon (it is worth noting that other Ponams disagreed). But generally they were uninterested in making any connection between the two sets of knowledge, much less in speculating about how the interplay between turtles and dugongs and sea grasses affected the amounts and kinds of fish found in the lagoon. In contrast, government biologists who came to Ponam to try to persuade islanders to give up hunting and killing dugongs and sea turtles argued that the elimination of these animals would reduce grazing pressure on the sea grasses in the Ponam lagoon. A reduction in grazing would result in both the spread and the changed composition of sea grasses, with consequent disruption of the fish populations and presumably undesirable consequences for a fishing community like Ponam.[3]

Although it is hazardous to speculate, the example of people, coconuts, and palms might have seemed similar to the Ponams. Ponams regularly gathered ripe coconuts from the ground and green ones from the trees. This did not, as far as the islanders were concerned, have any noteworthy effect on the palms, and as long as a few nuts were left to sprout, the groves would continue. Why then should a few turtles and dugongs have any effect on the sea grasses, much less indirect effects on the fish?

In addition to the islanders' view that species are relatively isolated from and independent of each other, their model differed in terms of the role of humans in relation to the environment. Any conscious conservation system requires some appreciation of the effects of human actions on natural resources and the environment. Ponams saw this as negligible in most cases. One reason

may have been what Bulmer (1982: 64) calls "circumstantial"—
they had never been able to make a noticeable difference in their
marine environment given limitations on population and technology in the past. However, this was not entirely the case, and in
any event the Ponam conception of human agency as relatively
unimportant reflected a fundamentally different conception of
how things work. Contrary to the materialist view of a self-order-
ing and self-sustaining natural environment, Ponams held that the
ordering and operation of the world was dictated by God. God
and, as we shall see, fish themselves were the critical agents of
change in natural resources.

Ponams were first exposed to mission influence in 1916. They
converted to Catholicism in the 1920s and became syncretic Chris-
tians. Like most Papua New Guineans they wholeheartedly em-
braced their own interpretation of Christianity, including the idea
of divine creation. They did not adopt the Enlightenment view
that God was merely the ultimate cause of things, that His involvement ended once creation was complete. Rather, God acted
continually in the world. In some respects, Ponams saw God as an
ultimate ancestor. Just as ancestors monitored and judged the behavior of their descendants and allotted reward and punishment
accordingly (Fortune 1935), so did God for all people. Ponams did
not totally deny the impact of human agency on the course of
things, since the divine and the human were not mutually exclusive, but they emphasized God's role over their own. As part of
their religious orientation, Ponams believed that substantial
changes in the marine environment such as the extinction of species were not necessarily undesirable, though they may be inconvenient in practice.

Because humans had so little impact on the environment, conservation was not really possible. The costs of conservation, which
usually involved giving up something, could not possibly be balanced by any real benefit. The case of sea turtles, which the government urged Ponams to conserve, illustrates this point of view.
Sea turtles were extremely important in Ponam life; essential to
weddings and other feasts, hunted regularly, and enjoyed as a
regular part of the diet. Ponams objected to the government's plan
because giving up the hunting and consumption of sea turtles
would have been very costly and would, they felt, bring nothing

in return. If sea turtles were going to die out, as the government said, it would be because God wanted them to. A halt on hunting sea turtles would not change God's mind but would be very costly to the Ponams.

Ponams had detailed knowledge of their environment, but because of their different interests, beliefs, and orientations, they construed it differently than Westerners do. Observing the same environment, Ponams came to different conclusions. They would agree that each species is unique, but were not impressed by this uniqueness, being more concerned with commonalities. Second, though they recognized that species could affect each other, they thought this was relatively unimportant, and certainly did not view species as part of an interrelated whole. Third, they did not assume as a matter of principle that environmental change is undesirable. Fourth, they saw divine rather than human action as the salient source of environmental change. Unlike Westeners, they did not see life on earth as self-contained and materialist. Rather, any attempt to explain the environment which did not refer to supernatural, spiritual forces would have struck Ponams as silly.

At another level of ecological knowledge is the relationship between the intensity of exploitation and levels of yield, in this case, between fishing effort and catches. Western understanding is that this is variable but predictable: beyond a certain point, greater fishing effort will reduce the supply of fish and breeding stocks so much that yield will decrease. At the functional level, concerned with what happens as fishermen vary the level or amount of fishing, the Ponams' model of the effort-yield relationship resembled the Western model. At the causal level—concerned with why this happens—it did not.

Islanders were quite aware that areas could be overfished. They said that this had happened on some of the small islands off the northeast Manus coast. There, much closer than Ponam to the provincial capital and hence market of Lorengau, rapacious fishermen of the northeasterly islands were said to have fished their lagoons so much that it became much more difficult to catch fish than before. The Ponam model was similar to the Western one at this functional level, and so was the functional remedy. Ponams said that if people from these overfished areas wanted to increase their catches, they had to fish less.

The cause of overfishing, however, differs between the two models. The Western model holds that catch decreases largely because the population of fish is decreased. Ponams hold that catch decreases because fish become wary. Fish learn that a baited hook or a swimmer with a speargun is dangerous. They flee when these things appear, just as they learn that certain areas of the lagoon are dangerous and so move elsewhere. Fish, many Ponams explained, are like people: confronted with danger, they move. They also learn: if they slip the hook once they are not likely to be attracted to one again. Thus, at this more pragmatic level of knowledge, fish themselves are the agents of ecological change and the cause of decreased catches. Islanders used this theory to account for the presence of Japanese and Korean fishing vessels in Papua New Guinea waters: the vessels were following fish that had fled waters closer to Japan and Korea.

The difference in theories of causality should not be dismissed as a mere academic matter or as showing a colorful but wrongheaded village theory that distracts us from islanders' valid practical understanding of the relationship between fishing activity and catch size, and hence the logic of conservation. Rather, it should sensitize us to the possibility that Ponams saw the environment and their place in it in a way fundamentally different from that of Westeners and to different effect.

Moreover, one should not confuse Ponam agreement with the functional remedies prescribed by a Western theory of ecology and resource management with the likelihood that they will apply those remedies in all cases. Just because islanders agree that it is possible to overfish (because the fish learn and move away), it does not follow that they see any given case of falling catch as the result of overfishing.

A brief example will illustrate the point that the explanations and remedies the Ponams may apply to instances of falling catches can be nonsensical in terms of Western science. In the last century the island of Sori, to the west of Ponam, had extensive beds of *Ibricaria punctata*, the shell used for the manufacture of shell money, in its lagoon and reef. The shells were intensively harvested. At the beginning of this century the Sori beds failed. Around the same time Ponams found extensive beds of *Ibricaria punctata* in their own waters. About mid-century the Ponam beds began to fail, too.

Although Ponams could agree with the abstract proposition that too much shell gathering would lead to failure of the beds, most who talked about these instances of failure saw the cause in a very different light: in both cases it was a matter of social disrespect and supernatural or ancestral retribution. Growing disrespect among Sori Islanders for the group that controlled the production of shell money led God or perhaps the ancestors to move the beds to Ponam. After World War II similarly growing disrespect led to the dissipation of the Ponam beds. Islanders were unsure about where God had relocated the beds. This case shows that even though islanders held some conceptions of the environment whose functional aspects meshed with Western understanding, the fundamental way they viewed the environment was alien to Western thought. One cannot focus on a few similarities of practice and ignore the alien cultural superstructure. The Ponam superstructure disposed islanders to draw practical conclusions about particular cases in ways which are often at variance with Western understanding.

THE SOCIAL CONTEXT OF PONAM MARINE TENURE

The previous section suggests that, although Ponams had an intimate knowledge of their environment, their understanding of it differed enough from Western ecological models that we should doubt their ability or interest in undertaking the sort of fisheries management that some ecologists feel limited entry and traditional systems of marine tenure make possible. One of the links connecting exclusive marine tenure and sound management practice is weakened. In this section I will examine the second link: the assumption that marine property owners are motivated to conserve (or to maximize long-term income over short-term gains) by the privileges, rights, and control implied by their ownership.

The marine property I will discuss is fishing-technique ownership, especially the right to participate in collective net fishing. In Ponam, technique ownership was more significant than waters or reef ownership and was easier to study. Moreover, the values and practices concerning ownership and the behavior of the owners were similar in all forms of marine tenure: waters, technique, and species.

With the exception of one variety used only by women, all cooperative net-fishing techniques were owned and used only by men. The common forms involved the use of several pairs of wood-framed, hand-held nets, about twelve feet by eighteen feet. In some methods crews of net handlers arranged pairs of nets in a straight-line barrier, and other Ponams paddled canoes toward the barrier nets, making noise and herding the fish as they moved. In others, the net handlers arranged several pairs of nets in a circle and walked the nets through shallow lagoon waters, collapsing the circle and trapping fish in the nets as they went. In either case, the fish belonged to the pair of nets that caught them. Distribution was another matter.

Ownership in a collective net technique involved the technique as a whole and the right to participate in it by bringing a pair of nets. Patrilineal groups owned rights to participate, and all the patrilineal groups that held those rights usually collectively owned the technique. Nonowners could participate only by providing equipment or labor with the permission of owners. Owners collectively decided whether to grant participation rights to other patrilineal groups and whether to mount special fishing expeditions, for example, at the behest of an islander who desired a large quantity of fish for use in ceremonial exchange. For each expedition, one person served as the net-right leader.

Distribution of the catch took place where the patrilineage owning the net right had its men's house. It included a hot fish meal for participants in the fishery. The rest of the fish was apportioned in equal shares to each person who contributed to the expedition, one share each to crewmen and owners of equipment (canoe, nets) and of the net right (see Carrier and Carrier 1983 for further analysis of the distribution). Ownership was rarely, however, used for the accumulation of more than one share of the catch. Most owners also served as crew, and the rules and practice worked against anyone receiving more than one share of a net's catch, even though net-right owners were doubly entitled, as crewmen and as right owners. People did not, in other words, use their ownership to maximize their income as they might, for example, by letting one right owner use one's canoe and another use one's nets, while going as a crew member with a third right owner. Those who because of their property rights could have secured a disproportionate share of the catch for themselves in fact failed to do so.

This practice is in accord with a distinction Gregory (1982) draws between Western societies, oriented to the circulation of commodities (and the personal accumulation of wealth), and Melanesian societies, oriented to the circulation of gifts. Gregory notes that in Western societies people attempt to increase their net "incomings" as much as possible, while in Melanesian societies, as in Ponam collective net fishing, they try to make their "outgoings" as high as possible. Generosity is what makes this possible and what lies behind the net-right owners' behavior in foregoing extra shares of the catch to which they may be entitled, and in some cases foregoing *any* share of the catch.

When asked why they allotted themselves no share of the catch, Ponam net-right owners said that the catch was smaller than they would have liked, and thus their share would be at the expense of others who had participated in the expedition. In other words, they made the sacrifice to acquire a reputation for generosity. The reason to gain that reputation was, they said, that in future expeditions they would have no trouble attracting a crew and thus no trouble getting fish.

Seen in the context of Ponam's scarcity of able-bodied male labor because of high migration rates, the sacrifice appears economically rational. However, there were other ways to get fish than leading a net and hence depending on a crew: angling, spear fishing, and going as crew on someone else's net were more rewarding (Carrier and Carrier 1983). In addition, the idea that present sacrifice leads to future reward falls to the ground, as Ponams themselves admitted, because realistic expectations of the future were that later expeditions also would not catch enough fish to reward everyone adequately. The net-right owner admittedly envisioned a future of more self-sacrifice rather than future material benefits from present abstention.

Accordingly, Ponam collective-net-fishing practice is not in accord with the assumption essential to the Western economic model that owners (a) seek to benefit materially from their property; and (b) therefore are motivated to conserve resources they own in order to maximize their long-term income. What do Ponam owners seek to gain? Pressed further in the line of questioning above, islanders argued that the motive for generosity in the distribution of fish caught with one's net rights was to establish or maintain one's name or repute and the name or repute of the patrilineage that owned the net right. This was a matter of honor on Ponam. It was also essential to the ability to generate credits and repay debts, crucial to participation by individuals and cognatic descent groups in ceremonial exchange and other transactions (see below).

The point of ownership on Ponam, then, was not to accumulate fish—this could be done in ways that did not involve ownership— but to be as generous as possible with one's own and one's lineage's property. This motivation is reflected in Johannes' (1982: 245) observation that in some of the Manus villages he visited, "the right to give away fish was the most highly valued aspect of . . . fishing rights," echoing Malinowski's much earlier statement (1918: 90) that among Trobriand fishermen "the privilege of giving is highly valued." It is important also that the measure of generosity on Ponam did not rest on the amount given. Rather, it lay in the relationship between what was owned and what was given away. Irrespective of absolute catch sizes, within the normal range of catch sizes the net-right owner who gave away all of his share of a small catch was considered more generous than the owner who gave away only part of his larger share.

Repute and social credit had an economic aspect, but in a restricted sense. At most, having them meant that in the future a Ponam would be given fish if others caught fish and he did not. This was not maximizing wealth. Certainly, Ponams agreed, it is nice to know that you will not go hungry when others have fish. However, as a practical matter this was unimportant, for a person of repute was also industrious and hence rarely likely to be without fish. In any event, as I noted above, being a net-right holder was one of the less rewarding ways of getting fish. On Ponam, then, repute was not used to gain advantage in the competition for land, labor, and capital and so converted into significant wealth. It could not be used—or at least was not used—to lay claims to enough advantage or wealth to create noticeable social or economic inequality.

Repute and social credit were important for two reasons, one fairly specific to Ponam itself, the other applicable to almost all Melanesian societies. The specific reason concerned ceremonial exchange. For Ponam, unlike most Melanesian societies, these exchanges were highly remunerative for villagers because much of the money and goods that migrants sent back to the village were sent as contributions to these exchanges. Those with repute and credit were fully able to participate and so to receive a full share of the remittances, an important economic resource for the island. Credit created through generosity with marine property allowed both cognative descent groups and individuals to participate and benefit more than would otherwise be the case.[4]

On Ponam, and in other Melanesian villages, the repute gained through generosity was necessary not only for participation in ceremonial exchange but also in day-to-day life. Gift transactions dominating the very social relationships which Western bureaucratic rationality excludes were central to daily life. Western commodity-exchange systems are dominated by formal structures that allow people to convert wealth into the necessities of life without much regard for personal relationships. If a westerner wants, say, a loaf of bread, he or she knows that there are stores that operate at predictable times, and whether or not the would-be purchaser of bread is known, liked, or disliked by the clerk or store owner is immaterial. Stores sell bread to people who have the money. In such a situation it is possible for people to focus on the accumulation of wealth, for its conversion into consumables proceeds relatively smoothly and unproblematically.

However, if you were a Ponam who wanted a bag of rice, for example, you faced a very different and uncertain situation. Stores were not predictably open nor were tradesmen predictably inclined to sell to you. If the owner was not happy with you, he could quite easily say that he was tired or sick or had work to do or did not have the item you wanted, could not make change, or provide any other reason for not selling you want you want. He must be willing to sell that bag of rice, and his willingness was influenced by what he and others thought of you. In the more complex realms of island life such as building a house, making a canoe, or organizing a ceremonial exchange payment, the larger number of people involved made the uncertainty even greater. No one was obliged to cooperate, and all were jealous guardians of their prerogative to decline or drag their feet.

The use of property rights for the accumulation of wealth *per se* makes little sense in this context, for the conversion of wealth into consumables or services does not proceed as smoothly, predictably, and unproblematically as it does in Western commodity-exchange systems. Instead, the creation and maintenance of repute and social credit are essential to ensure the cooperation of others. The fisherman who was generous with his catch, the waters owner who granted requests by others to fish in his or her territory, the right holder who forewent his own share of the catch— these people were in a sense securing through their generosity the future compliance of fellow Ponams, their willingness to be a bit more cooperative so that life would be that much less uncertain, that much less taken up with cajoling reluctant store owners to find the key and sell a bag of rice, reluctant neighbors to find a broom and help clean a village street, reluctant kin to put off gathering coconuts until tomorrow and help participate in exchange today.

Exclusive ownership created the right to exercise discretion in allowing others to use property. This right created both the possibility of refusal and the conditions for generosity. The power of refusal or generosity applied not only to the ownership of productive techniques but also to the ownership of the reef and the sea. The owner was under substantial internal and external pressure to be generous. Accordingly, owners were constrained from exercising their discretionary powers of ownership by their desire to earn repute and by other islanders' expectations of open-handedness. A refusal to permit others to use property was a sign of a rupture of social relations that carried the risk of further souring the relationships between the people involved while making future cooperation much less likely (see Carrier 1980).

It was especially difficult for an owner to refuse permission to use or share in the use of rights to waters, fishing techniques, and species when the request came from a large body of islanders or the island as a whole. Such a request was rare and probably more often tacit than explicit. One instance occurred during a government Department of Primary Industries project to encourage the development of small-scale village fisheries in the late 1970s. Ponam, along with four other Manus villages, received government grants and low-cost loans to purchase diesel-powered freezers. Participating villages were to freeze their catch for sale to the department's fisheries station in Lorengau, on Manus Island. The project failed for a number of reasons (see Carrier n.d.), but while it was operating, Ponams were doing a great deal of angling at night with pressure lamps. This technique required permission of the waters owners. Owners willingly gave their permission. It is unlikely that they would have dared to refuse however much their ownership formally entitled them to do so. The fishing was being undertaken, as Ponams saw it, to benefit the island as a whole. A reluctant owner would have alienated *all* the neighbors.

On Ponam, the social context of the system of marine tenure operated to encourage maximal exploitation rather than the husbanding of marine resources. Not only did islanders expect waters and technique owners to be generous with fish and permission to use rights, but owners themselves wanted to be generous, concerned as they were to secure repute and social credit. Decisions that might have alleviated pressure on marine resources by limiting access to waters, species, or techniques of capture would have been nonsensical within the social context of Ponam since they would have meant the loss of repute and social credit and the alienation of fellow Ponams.

OWNERSHIP AND CONSERVATION

The variability of cultural conceptions of the environment is an important question for ecologists and resource managers. A society that has an intimate acquaintance with its environment may have a great deal to teach us about flora and fauna, as Johannes (1981) has so clearly shown, and may thereby illuminate our own science. However, the organization of this knowledge and the cultural assumptions that underlie it may be less accessible to scientists. As Bulmer has written, "the underlying beliefs about the nature of the universe and the powers at work in it are hard, if not impossible, to relate to modern conservationist principles" (1982: 69). Ponams and marine scientists may observe the same facts when they look at the island's marine environment but they are likely to organize and act upon those facts differently in light of their different practical concerns, cultural traditions, and experiences.

What is required for a conservationist cultural orientation? Jochim (1981) has suggested a system of territoriality and ownership of resources; environmental predictability, which allows planning; and conditions that encourage the continued and close monitoring of resources. Leach (1972), echoing Malinowski's theory concerning relationships between levels of risk and the emergence of magic, suggests that a conservationist orientation is most likely to exist in societies that are operating very close to the limit of what they can extract from their environment. In her use of these ideas to analyze a number of societies in Oceania, Chapman (1985) found some support for the hypotheses of Leach and Jochim, but also suggested that a number of other factors, both social and historical and including the existence of a pronounced social hierarchy, are associated with a conservationist view of the environment.

It is possible that, of the factors listed above, the Ponams had only territoriality and resource ownership. Ponam Island, like most areas in Melanesia, had neither the environmental stress nor the pronounced social hierarchy that appears to be associated with a more conservationist perspective. Planning and monitoring may have been made difficult by their lack of means of keeping accurate records of fishing activity and catch size. They were neither motivated nor equipped to observe the sorts of long-term changes that concern ecologists. Moreover, the short-term changes they observed may have been readily explained by recourse to the actions of God and fish rather than the direct interaction between men and fish.

Ownership of marine property rights in Ponam was, like ownership in any case, hedged by values and practices that shape what it is that owners can and want to do. On Ponam these values and practices appear neither to have motivated waters owners to conserve stocks nor to have permitted them to do so. Instead, because of the way that ownership was linked to esteem, owners were motivated and expected to allow and even encourage fishing. This does not mean that they were not economically rational. They converted their property into what was clearly a valued good, repute, which in turn could be used to make life easier and more enjoyable. Because of the way repute was generated, however, the scarce resource was not fish but ownership itself, for this is what made it possible to be generous. And this quantity the Ponams conserved assiduously, making sure that others did not encroach on their ownership and stoutly maintaining their right not to be generous. The importance of ownership itself may help account for the fact that the Ponam system of marine tenure was so complex. This rationality did not, however, lead owners to act to conserve fish stocks since these were in and of themselves not the significant element in the generation of repute and social credit.

It is risky to assume that the conception of exclusive property found in non-Western cultures is similar to the Western notion of private property, much less that people in other societies will seek to use their property rights in the same way as Western commercial property owners. If we cannot assume that conceptions of the environment and of the nature and uses of property resemble what is found in the West, the logic of the tragedy-of-the-commons model—that creation of exclusive property will lead to conservation where open access or common property leads to resource over-exploitation—may not apply. We cannot assume that limited entry in Melanesian fishing societies plays a role in the conservation of marine resources.

This chapter has shown the problematic nature of assuming that ecological knowledge and the existence of an exclusive property-rights system are signs of the existence of or potential for the husbanding of natural resources. What is required is careful examination of the ways people understand their environments and the ways that ownership works in specific cultural and ecological settings.

It is uncertain whether the system of tenure and the values and practices of ownership that I have described would survive the pressures that commercial fishing could be expected to generate. Ponams had their doubts, too. They speculated that any shift to commercial exploitation would be on an individual rather than a collective basis. Moreover, they suggested that in such a situation their system of marine tenure and the social context associated with it would undergo qualitative change to the extent that it would no longer be recognizable as a Ponam system. If their assessment proves correct, it will support the conclusions I have reached in this chapter: Ponam marine tenure and the values and practices associated with it would be of little help in limiting exploitation and protecting marine stocks.

ᵔᒌ

NOTES

This chapter is based on sixteen months' fieldwork on Ponam Island, Manus Province, between November 1978 and December 1983. Research was supported in part by the University of Papua New Guinea Research Committee. The chapter has benefited from discussions with N. Polunin of the University of Papua New Guinea, Department of Biology, and R. Johannes of the Commonwealth Scientific and Industrial Research Organisation Division of Fisheries and Oceanography at North Beach, Western Australia, and from the advice and encouragement of B. Hudson, formerly of the Papua New Guinea Department of the Environment and Conservation, Wildlife Division. As well, I am grateful to Margaret Chapman of the University of Queensland, Department of Geography, for the opportunity to see some of her work while it was still in manuscript form. Finally, I thank the governments of Papua New Guinea and Manus Province for their permission to carry out this research, and the people of Ponam Island for their patience and good humor.

1. Marine tenure systems were and are common in Papua New Guinea. They are less well documented in the anthropological literature on societies of the southern, Papuan region of the country than elsewhere, although river tenure is reported there for the Mekeo (Belshaw 1951: 10) and for the Orokaiva (Crocombe and Hogbin 1963: 37–38). Villagers have reported a loose form of intervillage tenure around the mouth of the Fly River in the southwest (Olewale and Sedu 1982: 253) and a similar report refers to intravillage marine tenure in Tatana Village, Port Moresby (Gaigo 1982). Marine tenure is reported for the Trobriand Islands (Malinowski 1918: 88), in Milne Bay to the east of the New Guinea mainland, and among the Tanga (Bell 1947: 312), Mandok (Pompanio 1983: 123–25), Maenge (Panoff 1970: 190), and Ponam (Carrier 1981) of the Bismarck Archipelago, as well as in societies down the

Solomon Islands chain to the southeast of the Bismarcks (e.g., Allan 1957: 50–51; Ivens 1930: 258). Although there seem to be no reports of marine tenure on the northern, New Guinea coast of Papua New Guinea, there is evidence for it along the north coast and coastal islands of what is now Irian Jaya (Feuilleteau de Bruyn 1920; Galis 1955, 1970; van der Sande 1907: all cited in Polunin 1984). This evidence is sparse because of the haphazard distribution of anthropological research and even more because of lack of systematic ethnographic interest in Melanesian sea tenure.

2. I have chosen to use the past tense in my depiction of Ponam Island and its people rather than to follow the tradition of the ethnographic present. Partly this is a stylistic attempt to dispel the air of reified traditional permanence that still hangs over much of the ethnographic literature on Melanesia, and partly this is in recognition of the fact that Ponam has undergone profound change in this century and even in the last twenty years, and that islanders are quite capable of changing their minds and their society again soon. My use of the past tense does not indicate that I am describing beliefs and practices which I know to have changed or disappeared. I am describing the state of a living society as it existed and was described to me during fieldwork. Although the potential confusion or misinterpretation is regrettable, I believe it is preferable to the pitfalls of the ethnographic present.

3. I make no assertion that this is a scientifically correct analysis of the ecological relationships among dugong, sea turtles, sea grasses, and fishes in lagoons. Empirical support for this argument is only partial (see Heinsohn *et al.* 1977). Rather, I have presented the environmentalist argument as it was described to me and to Ponam Islanders. My thanks to R. Johannes for bringing this matter to my attention.

4. There were two conceptually distinct but practically intertwined sorts of participation in Ponam ceremonial exchanges. One was the participation of cognatic descent groups whose apical ancestors were the siblings of the forebears of the focal parties to the exchange. These groups did not figure directly in fishing. However, each partriline that held marine property was itself the agnatic core of such a cognatic descent group, and generosity with the property belonging to the patriline established credit for the cognatic descent group of which it was a part. This credit allowed the cognatic group to participate and benefit more than would be the case otherwise.

The second and simpler sort was participation by individuals. Those who were generous with the marine property they controlled or with the fish they were entitled to distribute were able to establish credit on which they could draw when the proceeds of ceremonial exchanges were distributed. In each case, then, generosity produced benefit in ceremonial exchanges and the significant amounts of wealth which flowed through them.

Part *II*

SPECIFYING THE COMMONS

8 Embedded Systems and Rooted Models

THE GRAZING LANDS OF BOTSWANA AND THE COMMONS DEBATE

Pauline E. Peters

IN SUB-SAHARAN AFRICA, relations between rights to land and patterns of land use and land management are matters of central concern and active debate. In the decades since political independence, many governments have introduced new forms of land tenure. These new policies often continue changes initiated under colonial rule and have given rise to systems of land tenure that are highly variable among and within countries.

Current attempts to understand the variability of land tenure prolong a debate concerning the nature of indigenous forms of landholding and land rights that has been a staple of African scholarship since the early years of this century. Key issues are the nature of "overlapping" rights, the relationship between entitlements of individuals and lands held in common, the appropriateness of the descriptive label *communal,* the relation between usufruct and ownership, and the connection between the nature of land rights on the one hand and issues of scarcity, responsibility, and land management on the other.

The urgency in the debate over these issues arises from a congeries of problems: demands upon the land's ability to feed expanding human and animal populations, accelerating land degradation in many arable and grazing areas, and increasing conflicts over access to land. These problems have been exacerbated by competition between incompatible uses, alienation of land by the politically powerful, and appropriation of land by governments for large-scale irrigation, water, and energy projects.

One of the paradigms that has been most influential in discussions concerning grazing land in Africa is the tragedy of the commons, a thesis first projected by Garrett Hardin (1968). This interpretative framework (in various guises) has been taken up with enthusiasm by numerous researchers, governments, and international agencies. Overall, the enthusiasm has been misplaced and has evoked criticism of the paradigm's premises and application.

Taking the case of Botswana's grazing land, this chapter posits an intellectual line of descent from colonial models of preferred land tenure to those, including tragedy-of-the-commons models, that inform land policy in Botswana since 1975. It traces historical processes that explain both the family resemblance between the colonial and post-colonial schema of explanation-cum-prescription in matters of land tenure, and the series of changes taking place with respect to the patterns of use and rights in the grazing areas. This analysis is founded on two propositions: first, that the commons system is by its very nature a sociocultural system embedded in historically specific time and space; and second, that analytical modes are rooted in historical experience.

THE CASE OF BOTSWANA: GRAZING LAND POLICY AND A POSITED TRAGEDY OF THE COMMONS

Government White Paper No. 2 of 1975 introduced a new national policy for Botswana's tribal grazing land. It was a response to urgent concern that the national cattle herd was growing at a rate that promised to outstrip the carrying capacity of the range. Given current models of land management, the outcome was feared to be devastation of available pastures.[1] The proposed remedy was based on the explicit assumption that "unless livestock numbers are somehow tied to specific grazing areas, no one has an incentive to control grazing" (Republic of Botswana 1975: 1). Consequently, it was proposed that existing "communal" lands be zoned into communal, commercial, and reserved land. Land in the commercial zones was to be leased to individual owners of large herds for use as ranches; the "traditional" grazing system was to continue in the communal areas with, however, provision for establishing group ranches ("livestock management groups of small owners") if local users agreed. The reserved areas were to be set aside for future use, but in practice this category remained on paper only.

The process of rezoning land and fixing herds and owners to particular areas has proved difficult. In some districts the policy has been resisted or rejected. Even the owners of large herds have been less enthusiastic about taking up leases or ranches than had been anticipated, and many of even the wealthiest cattleowners have been unwilling to assume the high financial and management costs entailed. The statement of the White Paper that "all that is needed is some fencing and some piping of water" seems very sanguine in retrospect. In fact, a 1982 report (Carl Bro International 1982: 4.88) concludes that for most small herd owners the assumptions underlying the policy are inappropriate. As of the end of 1985, it is unclear whether the policy will be redirected in light of the accumulating evidence.

It is the logic of the argument underlying the policy that needs examination. The thesis is simply stated: the primary cause of overgrazing and range deterioration is unrestrained growth in the size of herds. Behind this is a traditional system of grazing on communal lands that is held to be "a free for all" (Republic of Botswana 1975: 5). The parallel between this thesis and the thesis known as the tragedy of the commons is quite clear (Ramatlabama Ranch Management Centre 1981). Compare, for example, the following two statements:

> The tragedy of the commons develops in this way. Picture a pasture open to all. It is to be expected that each herdsman will try to keep as many cattle as possible on the commons. (Hardin 1968)

> Under our communal grazing system it is in no individual's interest to limit the number of his animals. (President Khama, White Paper on the Tribal Grazing Land Policy, 1975)

This diagnosis of the problem leads, with what seems an inescapable logic, to a simple prescription for its cure: "stockowners should be given complete control over the areas where their animals graze. They will then have an interest in looking after their grazing" (Republic of Botswana 1975: 18). Because the root of the problem is located in the commons' similarity to "a fund anyone can rifle" (Hardin 1968), the solution for Botswana is to make it impossible for individual cattle owners to ignore the effects their use has on their pastures. By making them responsible for their own land, they will be forced to assess the costs and benefits of its use.

Despite this disarming simplicity, both diagnosis and prescription of Botswana's rangelands must be challenged. Literature on those lands presents what appears to be a paradox. On the one hand, it is posited that the failure to prevent overgrazing and to halt the degradation of the range is caused by haphazard patterns of range use in which individual herders are not limited to, and hence not responsible for, a particular section of range. On the other are descriptions of the emergence of *de facto* control of grazing land, which is the consequence of the private ownership of boreholes, introduced in the 1930s but enormously accelerated in the 1960s and 1970s, in the communal grazing areas. The first problem is said to require some means of tying individuals to demarcated areas, whereas the second raises the issue of how to prevent certain individuals from effectively appropriating for their exclusive use areas that are legally communal. The literature tends to be divided between these two foci.

The paradox is only apparent. It is precisely in the *relation* between the two prevailing patterns that the paradox is resolved, but the specification of that relation is difficult. The confusing mix of part commons, part open access, part illegitimate private control can, I think, be explained as the outcome of two processes that have been taking place since the 1930s. They contradict each other and, not surprisingly, are producing tensions and conflicts. These two processes—the increased movements of some cattle herders across formerly discrete grazing territories (*dinaga*) and the increasing fixity of some herds to the permanent water sources provided by boreholes—with the consequent problems of overuse and unequal access, cannot be explained by the thesis of the tragedy of the commons.

A model based on the dualism permeating Western thought (individual vs. society, private vs. communal, self-interest vs. altruism, ideal vs. actual) fails to provide the analytical tools necessary to understand the paradoxes and conflicts in Botswana's grazing areas. Rather, the interpretative framework has to incorporate historical process, political and economic structures, social organization, and systems of meaning. Of particular importance is the reciprocal determination, or dialectical relation, between social practice and structure of meaning.

MODELS OF THE COMMONS

The linkage made in the grazing land policy of Botswana between an anticipated tragedy of the commons and the consequent need to create new property rights reflects a dominant perspective in the social scientific literature on common property. However, it is not without critics. Debates rage over the nature of a commons, the relation between individual behavior and group action, and the appropriate models of analysis. The most commonly cited problems are the absence of a historical and institutional analysis and, in particular, the confusion of commons systems with open-access regimes, the individualistic bias of interpretative models, and the tendency—inherent in dualistic models—to misspecify the relation between individual property rights and other systems of rights to resources.

A number of authors have noted that discussion of commons systems has been muddled by a failure to distinguish a commons, "in which a number of owners are co-equal in their rights to use the resource" (Ciriacy-Wantrup and Bishop 1975:714), from an open-access system, in which there are no features of exclusion (see Godwin and Shepard 1979). Hardin's (1968) claim that "freedom in a commons brings ruin to all" assumes no restrictions or limitations on use—his commons *is* open access. As Ciriacy-Wantrup and Bishop (1975: 715) state, "Common property is not 'everybody's property.'" Thus, if one distinguishes between an open-access resource and a commons, one can recast Hardin's statement as a question: If a commons has in practice become an open access resource, what historical factors have brought this about?

More intractable is the dominance of individualistic models in interpretation of commons systems. Many theorists draw on game theory to model the behavior of rational, self-interested individual users of the commons. Especially popular is the "Prisoner's dilemma." This game produces a "noncooperative" solution, namely, that the two rationally motivated individuals will act in their own self-interest but to their own ultimate disadvantage. Numerous articles, however, criticize the applicability of the prisoner's dilemma to commons issues. Kimber (1981), for example, demonstrates the muddled logic that derives from use of the prisoner's dilemma as a model for group or collective action, and argues that "it represents the perspective of one individual, but nothing can be concluded from it about everyone's choice" (1981: 187). He also suggests, in a critique of Olson's (1965) argument, that the hidden and unarticulated part of the model is *uncertainty:* the uncertainty each experiences in the face of others' action effectively constrains his behavior in respect of the collective good.

Runge (1981) presents a model based on the interdependence of decisions among users of a commons and on a need, because of uncertainty about the decisions of others, for "assurance mechanisms" among users. The outcome, he argues, is cooperative. In this view, institutions and rules are not external and imposed on the individual users, but are responses to the uncertainty of social and economic interaction. Godwin and Shepard suggest that commons dilemmas do not resemble the simple prisoner's dilemma in which doom is predetermined, but the complex and indeterminate "pluralist politics of competing elites" (1979: 277). The dynamic lies not in the inevitable confrontation between asocial individual and impersonal group but in the competition and conflict between different social groups.

The shortcomings of models premised on the behavior of "rational" individuals to explain such essentially *social* systems as the organization of a common resource are compounded by the tendency of some theorists to invest these models with a normative cast. They assume a necessary connection between communal rights and the inefficient or destructive use of resources on the one hand and individual property rights and the efficient use of such resources on the other. This hierarchical opposition thus justifies the development of private rights to property in order to avert tragedies of the commons.

These normative postulates have been contested on the ground that they are ahistorical (Carroll *et al.* 1979); they also lose validity when tested against the historical evidence itself. Thus, Beryl

Crowe's (1977) suggestion that careless use and overgrazing of the English commons led to erosion and underproduction, which led in turn to the enclosure movement of the eighteenth century, seems effectively to turn history on its head. Other studies suggest something quite different: the gradual erosion of the commons as a system of complementary and overlapping rights occurred through a long process of commercialization in which owners of private land used the commons as a "free good" for their large flocks of sheep to the detriment of those commoners without access to private land (Thompson 1976: 338). Enclosure is better explained by conflict among users and among different rights and competing uses in a situation of political and economic change.

The importance of historical and institutional analysis is emphasized by others. DeGregori chides the believers in markets as guarantors of efficient use and those who regard efficiency as the sole criterion of a "correct" set of property rights for neglecting "the historic factors of privilege that give some market power and . . . leave others powerless" (1974: 221). Robert Bates (1983a) also rejects a view that sees markets as the only preferred institution and insists that analysis *"requires* the use of a precise and detailed knowledge of cultures, structures, and institutional environments (1983a: 140, his emphasis).

The critiques are supported by empirical data contradicting the assumption that private property rights guarantee responsible and efficient management of resources (Gilles and Jamtgaard 1981). Cases from the American Midwest, Australian outback, or African plains provide contrary evidence (Gilles and Jamtgaard 1981). But the power of models is such that the process of "paradigmatic shift" is often long and painful.

Opposition to the tragedy of the commons has bred its polar opposite: romanticized notions of a precommercial, precapitalist past when communal rights preserved the land and permitted all to use it on an equal footing. This idyll serves as a foil for what are seen to be the environmentally destructive and socially corrosive qualities of later systems.

Both models are overly simple and deterministic; both reduce history to unilineal shifts; both ignore the contingent and indeterminate character of social institutions and the need to subject them to detailed historical analysis. They differ fundamentally in one critical aspect: the model positing a tragedy of the commons casts its lot with the individual actor, the social realm being at best but a context in necessary opposition to the individual's self-interest. The model of an idealized past redefines the sociocultural system and casts the individual as a nonactor, only a figure inscribing the hidden logic of the ecocultural system.

To avoid these polemic extremes we argue for the social embeddedness of a commons. It is an error to suppose that an individual calculus can explain a commons system—rather, one has to understand the socially and politically embedded commons to explain the individual calculus. Alternative models put forward by some political scientists and economists posit an interdependence of individual decision makers and, in this fashion, incorporate the institutional dimensions of individual action. An anthropological perspective gives this interdependence a more specific conceptualization, one that includes the structure of relations (of which the individual commoners are a part), the differentiation among groups, and the set of shared and/or competing meanings and values associated with a particular commons and its use.

This analytical orientation avoids the main elements of the two simplistic models of the commons—namely, the unattached, autonomous, asocial "individual" on one side, and on the other the undifferentiated, homogeneous, harmonious "community." Rather than the posited *absence* of a link between any "rational herdsman" and some group that has to be recreated or enforced to avert an impending tragedy, we expect a multiplicity of links and claims to use of the commons. These multiple claims are often competing claims, especially when changes in the use and value of common resources are taking place. The "dilemmas" of a commons emerge not from an absence of social ties between the individual user and others, but from competing rights and claims to legitimate use.

Finally, since the analyst of commons systems has to understand reality as it appears to users of a commons, the analytical framework has to incorporate *meaning*. The definitions of rights, of relative claims, of appropriate uses and users are not only embedded in specific historical sets of political and economic structures but also in cultural systems of meanings, symbols, and values.

THE CASE OF BOTSWANA: MODELS AND IDEOLOGY YESTERDAY AND TODAY

The dominant views held by the colonial authorities in the Bechuanaland Protectorate about what was wrong with the practices of range management and animal husbandry in the territory were not very different from those expressed in post-independence Botswana and embodied in the Grazing Land Policy of 1975. One is forced to suppose no mere coincidence but an intellectual line of descent.

In the nineteenth century the missionary-cum-statesman John MacKenzie, speaking from his experience among the Tswana, wished to do away with "the communistic relations of the members of a tribe" and introduce "the fresh stimulating breath of healthy individualistic competition" (quoted in Dachs 1972). The belief that certain collective or corporate forms of social organization and property relations stifled initiative and/or encouraged lackadaisical and careless use of resources was generally held by colonial officers, missionaries, and traders. It was embedded in an ideology that regarded private ownership as the superior opposite of communal forms, and whose premises were based on a long history of Western thought. It was through this lens that problems were diagnosed—overgrazing, irresponsible management of wells (including, from the 1930s, deep borewells), and low standards of husbandry, especially with respect to the breeding and culling of stock. Through that same lens, prescriptions for change were conceived and announced: the introduction of new forms of exclusive land tenure and the private ownership of wells. With hindsight, one can see that these were constructions of a reality projected by the colonialists themselves, who persistently tried to squeeze African landholding systems into a model that set private and individual in opposition to communal and group.

In addition, African social systems were increasingly dominated by a regional and world economy that was preeminently capitalist in form. The African people with whom the colonialists, missionaries, and traders were in contact were being drawn into a political, economic, and sociocultural system that contrasted in many ways with their own. As historiographic and anthropological writing of the 1970s and 1980s has demonstrated, this process involved people from different socioeconomic categories—the politically dominant and the powerless, the wealthy and the poor. They were affected in different ways, responded differently, and reacted to and used the ideological frameworks of the Europeans differently (Marks 1978; Beinart 1980; Marks and Atmore 1980; Comaroff 1985; among others). I have discussed in detail elsewhere (1984; in press) the significance that colonial ideological antipathy to communal property systems had during the 1930s for the introduction of deep borewells under private ownership to the rangelands of Bechuanaland. Equally significant was the way in which the Tswana elite—the highly ranked members of chiefdoms who were both politically dominant and wealthy in cattle—quickly learned to manipulate these ideological proclivities to their own advantage. They became the primary, though by no means the sole, beneficiaries of the new and valuable grazing boreholes (Peters 1983).

Debates in the Native, later African, Advisory Council during the 1920s and 1940s demonstrate how the weight of opinion among the Tswana elite grew to favor the new forms of ownership and control that permitted the exclusive use of resources. The object of privatization was at first the new boreholes, but over time the ultimate target became the land itself. Statements such as the following indicate the trend:

> Our [Tribal] Reserves are communal property and nobody who is willing to progress can have freedom to use his progressive ideas. (Regent of the Bakgatla in Native Advisory Council meeting, 1930)

> Where anything is used tribally no proper care is taken of that thing because any man can come along and use it, well knowing that any expenditure attaching to it he has not to bear alone. (Tswana member of the African Advisory Council, 1943)

It is important to realize that those who were explaining these opinions, raising new claims, and promoting new conceptions of landholding were also continuing to use and to benefit from the prevailing modes of communal land tenure. Even the biggest cattle owner and the most politically influential people depended in no small measure on the existing system of land use and the social relations associated with it. Nor has this wholly changed in the 1980s, when the practices of extensive, open-range cattle management are followed by all but a tiny minority of Tswana cattle owners, and these practices depend in turn on the range's *not* being divided into private ranches.

Paradoxically, the communal tenures so disfavored by the colonialists were in a very real sense created by them. The emergence of "customary" land law in colonial Africa was due to a curious mix of the colonial authorities' confusion of sovereignty with ownership, their imposition of superordinate authorities over land where none had existed before, and most significant, their conflation of several different principles inherent in many of the precolonial land systems (Colson 1971: 184). They failed to recognize the coexistence of two different principles: one gave to a "citizen" (that is, a person recognized as a member of a political group rather than as the occupant of a territory [see Schapera 1956]) a right of access to the land and the resources controlled by the group; a second "recognized an individual's right to anything he had created" (Colson 1971: 184). Colonial governments not only ignored this distinction, but in delimiting "tribal reserves," they often sought to dissolve former subjurisdictions over land. In Swaziland, for example, the government declared former "tribal" lands recognized *within* the Swazi nation to be henceforth all "national," that is, an individual Swazi could acquire rights to land anywhere and not merely in his "own" or "tribal" area. Not surprisingly, the outcome was increased conflict among political units of Swazi and resistance to the government policy (Crush 1985).

The relevant point emerging from the literature is that communal holding implies an undifferentiated, general right of all to use the specific resource held in common, whereas in fact most so-called communal systems are characterized both by multiple or overlapping rights that are not identical and by a combination of individual and group claims.

The way such overlapping rights operated in the Bechuanaland Protectorate was made clear in the 1930s by Isaac Schapera. In his description of the Tswana law, Schapera describes the chief or *kgosi* as "a trustee holding the land for his tribe" (1943: 41); he notes, though, that some chiefs might claim a wider power and that since the declaration of the Protectorate, ultimate authority rested with the Administration. In practice, chiefs distributed holdings to members of the tribe "through subordinate authorities."

They also appointed men as "overseers of the areas where cattle [were] kept and [held] them responsible for the control of local grazing and water rights."

Schapera restricted the term *communal* to *masotla*, or those fields jointly cultivated by members of the tribe on behalf of the chief (or, properly, chieftainship). He also made explicit references to "individual" rights to cultivate arable plots ("private" fields, 1943: 155) and to graze stock in certain pastures (1943: 229). Despite this careful use, *communal* came to be used far more loosely and indiscriminately by the officers of the Protectorate Administration and, in their dealings with them, by the chiefs and their representatives. The term *tribal* was used by the Administration to characterize land, property, or affairs associated with the various chiefdoms. Thus, tribal land or areas were contrasted with those belonging to the Crown or the "European-owned" areas of the Lobatsi, Tuli and Gaberones Blocks, Tati District, and Ghanzi Farms (Schapera 1943). Over time, *communal* came to be used as a synonym for *tribal*. It came to be applied to land that is neither held under individual lease nor claimed by the state. Increasingly, it connoted diffuse, amorphous, and confused rights. In the debates of the African Advisory Council from the 1920s on, this supposed *lack* of discrete rights was said to entail a lack of accountability and, hence, an irresponsible mismanagement. These misconceptions of communal landholding systems were reinforced, moreover, by the Tswana elite, who took them up in a process referred to elsewhere (Peters 1984) as strategic learning and who elaborated them in their push to privatize.

These flawed definitions persisted into the post-colonial period. Their vitality must be accounted for in part by the continuing dominance of interpretative models drawn from the West, though they are now promoted not by colonial authorities but by expatriate advisers and Western-trained nationals. The colonial era invested its paradigms with moralistic qualities: the "progressive" entrepreneur and the "backward" tribesman. In the "development" decades since the 1960s, the paradigms have recurred, but with qualities now ostensibly less moral than technical.

The conclusion of a report by the Ministry of Overseas Development in 1965 (quoted in Colclough and McCarthy 1980) that "devastation" of the range that threatened "the survival of the livestock industry and . . . the economy as a whole" could be averted only by "modifications to the present system of ownership of land in the tribal areas" not only summarizes the view of the entire colonial history in the territory but continues to be reiterated. The step from this view to the thesis of the tragedy of the commons is clearly a small one.

The preconceptions underlying the government policy and the tragedy model that influenced it continue to be invoked, but they are also under challenge both inside and outside Botswana. Spectacular failures in ranching projects have given technical experts some pause and have led critics to point out that neither private ownership of land nor fenced ranches can *per se* guarantee more efficient or less destructive use of the range (Sandford 1980; Ramatlabama Ranch Management Centre 1981).

The debate is not merely one of facts or scientific evidence. As Werbner points out, these opinions are "symbolic statements" that appeal "to a belief in proprietary incentives, in equity, in the conservation of the heritage of all" (1980: ix). The results of these policies and policy changes has produced a highly fluid situation on the ground. In Botswana the push toward new forms of private property by a privileged minority could be seen emerging in the early part of this century. In the 1980s there have been fundamental changes in property rights and in the systems governing the use and allocation of both land and water, and a clear process of privatizing pastures and water has begun. Nevertheless, the range remains unenclosed and the social relations of production and exchange as well as political organization ensure that enclosure is some way off. People's herds move across the range probably more than in the past, but at the same time claims to pastures have developed that were not possible before.

As Thompson (1976) points out, the process of gradual yet radical change in uses of and rights to English common lands took place over several generations before the period labeled *enclosure*. Enclosure was the culmination, not the commencement, of the processes that transformed the common lands. An important element in these processes is the transformation of meanings attributed to different forms of property rights.

The two principal characteristics of the precolonial Tswana system of range use were dependence on seasonal water sources and, therefore, mobility. The conceptual model governing Tswana land use was one of concentric circles: in the center was the town or village (*motse*), the place of the ruler (*kgosi*, chief or king), his court and public assembly (*kgotla*). The town was surrounded by arable lands (*masimo*), then by pastures (*mafodiso*) and cattle-posts (*meraka*) located in the range (*naga*, veld, bush, forest), which also constituted the hunting areas and merged into a "no-man's land." This outer circle might abut a similar spatial set controlled by a separate, often rival, political group. Archaeological and historical reconstruction suggests a great deal of mobility among these Tswana groups. Not only was there extensive seasonal mobility between village, fields, and cattle pastures, but also periodic movement of the whole spatial set. When water sources dried up, lands lost fertility, or climactic or political disaster struck, the entire political group moved on. Fissioning or splits of the chiefdom (*morafe*) also took place, and each splinter group left to recreate the spatial map in some other place.

The establishment of the Bechuanaland Protectorate in the late nineteenth century eliminated this political and economic option of wholesale movement. Only seasonal mobility within the areas of the erstwhile chiefdom remained possible, a restriction of former political autonomy that was captured in the new label of "Tribal Reserves." The subsequent growth of the central towns, new urban centers, railway lines, and roads and a gradual increase in human and livestock populations all further constrained a political and economic system premised on frequent and easy movement.

In the precolonial chiefdoms, the cattle pastures were named areas centering on the seasonally fluctuating water sources. These areas were allocated by the chief to political subordinates, overseers called *badisa* (sing. *modisa*, literally "herdsman"), who allocated pasture rights to their dependents, followers, and clients, and/or acted as the chief's representative in exercising authority over those already using that particular area.

In the early 1930s and especially after World War II, permanent water sources, in the form of deep boreholes, were introduced into the grazing areas. In the earlier years most boreholes were managed by groups, first by "tribal committees" on behalf of the Tribal Reserve, and later by groups of owners called "syndicates."

Under both forms, individual herders who were not members of the committee or syndicate could pay fees for the privilege of using the borehole. In the case of syndicates, though, the members were in fact private owners of the borehole, not trustees on behalf of the tribe. After the 1950s the number of individual owners of the boreholes rapidly increased. Thus there developed a system in which private owners of boreholes, either individuals or groups, operated their wells and managed their stock in areas that were still considered communal in court and by the government.

As noted earlier, the term *communal* supplanted the word *tribal*, which had been in use during the colonial era, and has come to be applied without differentiation to land that is neither held under private individual lease nor claimed by the state. This usage obscures more than it reveals about the complex interplay in the Tswana system between group control of resources and individual rights of access to them, and the political structure underlying the system of land rights. The meanings that came to be assigned to communal land included the attributes of collective ownership and a lack of individual rights, as well as their purported consequences—the absence of incentive and accountability. These have persisted into the post-independence period.

References to communal rangeland obscure the significance of the different patterns of use and of competing claims that have been developing since the 1930s. Communal is contrasted to private in official communications, yet the process of privatization has already begun on communal rangelands. It is this process in part that lies behind the new grazing land policy. The policy recognizes a process of *"de facto* control of land" and constitutes the government's attempt to regulate and direct that process in its effort to encourage further investment in range and herd management. The division of the range into commercial and communal areas is clear in principle and on paper, but in practice the small number of commercial areas that have been demarcated as such and then leased (Sandford 1980, 1983), the minute proportion of grazing land that is fenced, and the often close intermingling of grazing areas and arable blocks all create a complex situation of multiple use and competing claims over pasture land and water.

Estimates that some fifty percent of Botswana's land was grazed by livestock whereas only 0.5 percent of land was planted in crops in the reasonably satisfactory rainfall year of 1979–80 (Carl Bro International, 1982, Vol. II: 2.02–2.04) graphically capture the realities of a high-risk arable agriculture and the preference for livestock-keeping in a semiarid environment. Nevertheless, cattle ownership is highly skewed. The Rural Income Distribution Survey of 1974 found that 45 percent of rural households own no cattle, although, as has been pointed out by others, the *holding* of cattle, channeled through links of kinship and clientage, is less skewed. The poorest 10 percent of households gained only 5 percent of their income from livestock (more from goats than from cattle), whereas the richest 1 percent earned 65 percent of their income from cattle. The majority of cattle holders have fewer than twenty head and depend on "free" water sources of rivers, seasonal pools, and public dams located in the arable or mixed lands—cattle-post areas. Only a minority, the bigger cattle owners, keep their herds at cattle posts in the grazing areas (Bailey 1982), where the major sources of water are privately owned (individual or syndicate) boreholes.

The grazing syndicates range in size from four to fifty members (i.e., owners) with most having around fifteen.[2] Added to the members' cattle are those belonging to their dependents (kin or clients, sometimes friends), and to cattle owners who buy water for a fee from the syndicate. Hence, the number of cattle holders using grazing boreholes is bigger than the number of borehole owners. Moreover, the ratio of owners to users is not static but oscillates between a more incorporative and a more exclusionary mode according to general political economic shifts and specific changes in an individual's favor, fortune, or social relationships.

Can the situation on the rangelands of Botswana can be appropriately understood through use of a commons model? Should this situation be taken to exemplify a breakdown of a commons on the range? Published work (see, for example, Gulbrandsen 1980; Hitchcock 1980; Ramatlabama Ranch Management Centre 1981; Sandford 1980, 1983; Lawry 1984; Peters 1983, 1984; Odell and Odell 1980) indicates that the range in Botswana is *not* a commons. In the precolonial period the range may be seen, perhaps, as a *series* of commons; that is, each pasture area allocated to a *modisa*, a political subordinate of the ruler, might be seen as a small commons. Each unit of herders (usually a family, sometimes an individual) was formally a member of the group (a ward, sets of families related by kinship, affinity or clientage) to which the area was allocated. Each family or group of families had a cattle post around which they had prior rights to pasture and residential use, and which might be moved periodically. Other uses—hunting, gathering of grasses, wood, and wild fruits—were open to members of the larger collectivity with rights to use the allocated range areas. In order to be allocated rights to a different pasture area, the unit (individual or group) had to receive permission from those holding political authority. These areas were neither open access nor held by individuals in perpetuity: they were defined politically and with regulations about who might be admitted and for what uses (see Schapera 1943; Sansom 1974).

In seeking to understand how the situation in the 1980s on Botswana's rangelands is the product of its past, one is led to suggest that it is not a commons, a series of commons, nor an area that has been reduced to open access. In one sense, changes in the use of the the range may seem to have led to the emergence of *a* commons, in that the divisions between the former smaller commons have declined in significance. On the other hand, one might rather claim that these changes in use combined with shifts in political authority and socioeconomic organization and with the development of new property rights have led, not to a commons, but to a situation in which there are unequal claims to the supposedly common resources.

This description can resolve the paradox of the simultaneous positing of an insufficient connection between herder and land *and* an illegitimate claim to discrete areas by herders. Two processes explain this paradox. One manifests itself in the increased ability of individual herd owners to move their herds across the range which, it must be stressed, is open and virtually unfenced. A number of factors are involved in this change. Colonial rule led to the fixing of individual chiefdoms within territorial boundaries, and this in turn effectively prevented large-scale mobility. But the political changes brought about by colonial rule also facilitated greater movements of groups and individuals *within* these tribal, later district, territories. The precolonial system of political subordination and patronage between chiefly line and junior agnates or prominent commoners (nonroyal lines) was eroded by a shift to greater centralization at national and district levels. Internal boundaries became less important. As a result, the system of placing pasture areas under the control of overseers appointed by the chief gave way to one in which the tribal authority, the district commissioner and, from the early 1950s, the newly established district committees took on that power. Traditional boundaries also became less relevant after the introduction of deep boreholes, for the boreholes effectively redefined what was available for use as pastures; they led, that is, to an expansion of the available range by bringing formerly wet-season pastures into year-round use.

Changes in the relative authority of the chief and the district commissioner caused changes in the relationship between the chief and leading persons within the district. The chief's authority was diminished, and some groups were able to take up residence away from the central town in the arable and grazing areas (Silitshena 1979; Grant 1980). These same political shifts loosened many of the sanctions and reasons for tying client families to wealthy, powerful patrons. They also facilitated the movement of individuals between groups and areas. Movements across what had formerly been separate pasture areas were increased further by the new opportunity to pay fees for the right to water cattle at the increasingly numerous boreholes. Although political alliances and residential and family ties continued to be important in the patterns of access to resources, the expansion of the usable range, the decline in significance of internal boundaries, the changes in political authority, and the ability to pay for water all effectively increased the capacity of individual herd owners to move across the range more freely than formerly. Characteristics of an open-access resource are plainly revealed by this mobility.

There is, however, the countervailing trend of an increasing fixity of certain individuals in certain areas of the range. This has been associated with the drilling in grazing areas of privately owned boreholes.

Whereas a system of stock husbandry dependent on seasonal water sources in a semiarid environment entails extensive and general mobility, permanent water sources such as boreholes greatly reduce that need. Mobility remains one of the strategies employed by herd owners, both to reduce costs—boreholes are expensive to run—and to benefit from variable pastures. Nevertheless, from the late 1930s on, the secure and plentiful supplies of water available from grazing boreholes have led their owners to become less mobile, and so they have become more permanently associated with the area of range surrounding the boreholes themselves. As with the trend toward individual mobility, a number of factors interact to produce this countervailing trend. The reduction in herd mobility that is fostered by access to secure and permanent water supplies has also been promoted by the shortage of young adult men, a circumstance caused by their migration to South African mines. At the same time, the reduced need to move herds also decreased the cattle owners' demand for herding labor. As one is often told now, "the borehole is the herder" (*sediba ke modisa*), which means not only that labor is less of a constraint than in pre-borehole days, but also that the borehole is implicated in defining relations as well as pastures.

These changes in herding practices have led to a sense that the borehole owners have special claims to the areas around their boreholes. This has been encouraged by several long-held notions about land use among the Tswana. One is that anyone putting an effort (investment) into land is due the benefit. Clearest with respect to arable plots, it seems also to have been applied to grazing areas in the early years of this century, when a few wealthy individuals "opened up" territory by sinking new wells. Thus, Schapera states that when a person exhibits such "initiative" he will be "recognized as the 'owner' or 'overseer' of that [area]" (1943: 224). In the case of the Kgatleng District, the descendants of these individuals have subsequently drilled boreholes in the same areas so that their fathers' and grandfathers' rights of priority over the area as *badisa* appear to have been transferred to them even though the office itself is no longer part of the political hierarchy. This shift from a claim based on political status to one of individual occupation may be seen in other instances of the politicoeconomic transformation taking place.

The other related notion is that of "allocation," the system by which rights to particular pastures were given by the chief and his designated subordinates. This notion has since been associated with the permit to drill a borehole, though the permit is now issued by a land board. The permit is seen to include the right to use the area around the borehole, which is given further impetus by the practice, initiated under the Protectorate Administration and continuing in the 1980s, of specifying a minimal distance (conventionally five miles) between boreholes. Land-board procedures, in which map coordinates are used to define the boundaries of the areas surrounding allocated borehole sites, give a formal imprimatur to that practice.

The combined effect of the private ownership of boreholes, the persisting resonance of the conception of "allocation" of pastures around a water point, the changes in practices of herd management that reduce mobility, the increasing pressures on existing grazing land, and the growth of private property rights in lands outside the communal range is for the control of pastures around boreholes to more and more resemble private ownership.

There are still patterns of multiple use and multiple claims, and the process of privatization or *de facto* ownership is not uncontested. In the Kgatleng district, for example, when the first deep boreholes were drilled in the grazing areas during the 1930s, it was the wealthy—the owners of the largest herds and the politically dominant—who were the first beneficiaries. Wealth and political privilege as well as local control through tribal authorities of the allocation of borehole sites produced a situation in which most of the borehole owners, whether as individuals or as members of grazing syndicates, were drawn from a privileged minority. The benefits brought by the ownership of a borehole reinforced this initial advantage. Boreholes opened up pastures that were formerly used only seasonally, if at all; they reduced the amount of labor needed to lift water and, as cattle became accustomed to returning to the borehole, the amount of labor needed for herding itself; through the sale of water they provided their owners with a source of income. The government's practice of providing borehole maintenance and repair services, initially at no charge and later at heavily subsidized rates, also gave a significant, if not wholly apparent, advantage to borehole owners.

At the same time, the extensive ties of political and economic patronage, reciprocal aid and dependency also drew in poorer families. Thus, any syndicate member would have a number of "dependents" who watered their few head of cattle with his herd. Dependents could be kinsfolk, affines, and friends as well as clients, men who looked after the patron's cattle or helped him plow or whose wives helped weed and harvest the patron's fields. The persisting importance of such interdependence—the social links in the management of crop production, stock husbandry, and various services, and in the ways in which households manage the movements of members in and out of migrant labor—as well as of political alliances and factions means that many syndicates continue to allow access to more than the *de jure* members. Nevertheless, the incorporative aspects of syndicate organization as well as of individually owned boreholes do appear to be diminishing.[3]

At the end of the 1970s and during the early 1980s, Bakgatla herd owners commonly expressed the opinion that the grazing areas were "filled up" with boreholes and that there was "no more space." This perception was confirmed by the long waiting list of applicants for new borehole permits and the number of applications refused on the grounds that there was not adequate space for grazing the cattle already being held in the areas between the proposed site and existing boreholes.

Existing syndicates and individual owners were also aware of the mounting pressure, and most tried to monitor the number of members, dependents, and buyers using the water and the range. Indeed, the numbers of buyers being allowed per syndicate appeared to decline in the years immediately preceding 1980 (see Peters 1983, and in press). The increasing prices of oil and gasoline and the associated general rise in prices also caused some syndicates to feel caught in a dilemma: they wanted the extra cash income from buyers but did not wish to have the extra use. More significantly, they also feared the likelihood of buyers' claiming rights based on long usage of the borehole at a time when some district government authorities were mooting the need to compare users' existing rights, whether these were based on borehole ownership or customary and long-standing usage of areas of the range.

It is clear that understanding the patterns of use in the grazing areas of Botswana depends on investigating the multiplicity of and competition among rights to range resources and not on positing the confrontation between individual rational herders and a group demanding selfless action. Moreover, one must also attend to the level of meaning, a dimension that has not received as much attention as it deserves. Competition among rights and claims takes place through competition in meanings. These are assigned, accepted, and imposed: whose right, which meaning, whose definition are critical questions in deciphering changes in systems of land rights. The significance of certain key terms to refer to groups such as syndicates has been discussed elsewhere as central to the process of privatization (Peters 1984). Here we can consider the dispute between the owners of a syndicate borehole drilled alongside a river and other, nonsyndicate herders who brought their cattle to water at the river in the rainy season. The dispute, which remained unresolved when I left the field in 1980, turned on a conflict between two rights: the right to pasture one's cattle along a river whose water cannot be appropriated and the right of borehole owners to have usable pastures around their boreholes. Whereas the first right is well recognized and supported by custom, the second is more in the nature of a newly perceived right that *per se* is unlikely to be contested. The conflict arises because one right automatically (given the seasonal patterns) eliminates the other. Multiple uses and overlapping rights have become mutually exclusive.

When situations of changing practices occur in which rights come into competition, the outcome is frequently arrived at by arranging the rights in a hierarchy. Some rights become secondary to others. In certain circumstances, the judgments about priority are made publicly and provided with rationales: judicial decisions, for example, have these characteristics. But these judgments and decisions often emerge at a late stage in a much longer process by which hierarchies of rights and their rationales are established. A major reason for the inability to make a decision in the case of the river borehole was the fact that it was "a first"; no previous incidents, discussions, or established practices had provided the means for arriving at an acceptable solution.

In his description of the long process, over generations, of the dismemberment of the English commons, E. P. Thompson points out that rights based on impermanent, ephemeral use-rights came to be seen as secondary (1976: 339–40). That they were also referred to as nonprogressive and even as disorderly and anarchic, as Thompson notes, may be seen as only an earlier example of the deeply embedded antipathies to the commons in Western thought. These "indefinite" rights were contrasted with the "substantial" rights of others, and it was the latter that were attributed legal status and hence priority, leaving the "vaguer categories" of persons with use-rights to become, by default, illegal. The power to define, to attribute meaning, and to assign labels is clearly central here. It remains to be seen how this process will work out in the case of the river borehole.

The apparent paradox that arises from there being at once too impermanent a relation between herder and range and an excess of *de facto* control over it, and the presence of both antagonisms and incorporative practices, are challenges to any understanding of "the dilemmas of the commons." In order to achieve a finer understanding of the situation it is essential to recognize and ravel multiple uses, multiple claims, and competing rights, and to discern the interactions among three sets of processes: how existing practices affect preexisting rights, how certain constructions of rights inform practices, and how both practices and rights are fixed and transformed as they are defined and labeled.

If we are to understand the patterns of use of the open rangelands of Botswana (or the Sahel, or Kenya, or anywhere else), we are not well served by a paradigm that separates the individual user from the social, political, and economic structures in which he/she is placed. Without a keener sense of the relations in which individual users are embedded, we cannot penetrate the dynamic of a commons, which is necessarily a social system. And without an attention to the reciprocal interaction between practice and meaning, we shall also misconstrue or miss the dynamic in process. Unless we demonstrate greater caution with analytical models that are products, as they all are, of particular histories, we are in danger not only of not solving but also of producing tragedies and dilemmas in the commons and elsewhere.

NOTES

The research on which this chapter is based was supported by grants from the National Science Foundation and the Social Science Research

Council/American Council of Learned Societies, which are not responsible for views expressed here.

1. The national herd had increased from some 600,000 head in 1940 to almost 1.5 million in 1966 (Lawry 1984: 78) and to an estimate of more than two million in 1980. The human population had reached more than 700,000 by 1980.

2. More detail may be found in the author's other writings. These data were collected from one district, the Kgatleng, during a fifteen-month study in 1979–80.

3. There is no doubt of the greater exclusionary practices of individually owned boreholes—for obvious reasons. However, it would be incorrect to suppose, as Sandford appears to, that an individual owner does "not permit the watering of any cattle except his own" (1980: 36). Although this is true for some individual owners, many of them also have quite a business of selling water, that is, allowing others to water cattle for a fee, and some also allow relatives to water their cattle.

9 The Culture of the Commoners

HISTORICAL OBSERVATIONS ON OLD AND NEW WORLD FISHERIES

Bonnie J. McCay

> The proper perspective on access to, and control of, the public lands would start with our European heritage wherein only a very few could avail themselves of hunting and fishing activities. Private-property advocates overlook this institutional heritage in their quest to convince us of the current 'inefficiencies' of public land administration . . . After all, it was with a particular social welfare function in mind that our founders determined that certain natural resources would remain the common property of all—not the private property of the fortunate few. (Bromley 1982: 842)

OPEN-ACCESS COMMON PROPERTY RIGHTS in marine fisheries are backed by law in the New World, where they are also taken for granted and stoutly defended when challenged. Fishermen often cast them as inherent and natural when fishery managers, backed by economists, try to privatize them (see Townsend and Wilson this volume). It is therefore easy for Americans, including Hardin (1968), to presume that all marine fisheries, like common pastures, are inherently open access and to miss the point that common property refers to diverse institutions (Ciriacy-Wantrup and Bishop 1975) grounded in specific social and historical experience.

Even open-access common property is a social institution. Its North American manifestation derives from legal and political acceptance of the doctrine of the "freedom of the seas" in the wake of colonial expansion. The definition of the great seas of the globe as open-access common property came about in reaction to claims of exclusive dominion by Spain and Portugal. The open-access doctrine was championed by the Dutch East Indies Company in order to further its mercantile and colonial objectives in Asia (Grotius 1609; Knight 1976). The common property definition of marine resources was accepted in international law to promote the expansion of European capitalism in the rest of the world. Freedoms of navigation, trade, and fishing were essential to capitalist development (McCay 1981a: 6).

Historical evidence indicates that the American law and culture of the commons is also grounded in the experience of the enclosure of fish and wildlife commons in the Old World. In the United States the definition of some resources as common property—navigable waterways, fishes and shellfish, wild game— came about through social deliberation, enhanced by the low population density and seeming abundance of resources in colonial America. American settlers and their descendants were familiar with the European and British experience of privatization of common lands and resources, including rights to hunt and fish. Forest laws (Thompson 1975), game laws (Howkins 1979), and the privatization of great salmon streams and other fisheries (Netboy 1968) imposed hardships on the rural poor and provoked political protest and a long heritage of poaching (Taylor, this volume; McCay 1984). Knowledge of these circumstances produced numerous colonial charters and legal cases in which the new nation sought to retain the rule of the commons for hunting and fishing (Lund 1980).

The roots of North American common property law and sentiments in social class struggles seem related to a key aspect of common property in America: its claims for social equity. Its roots in the doctrines and exigencies of an expanding world system may be related to a second, sometimes competing, aspect: open access as the structure for laissez-faire competition. Both aspects are examined below in accounts of historical conflicts over fishery regulations, the rise of oyster planting, the culture of poaching, and a short-lived experiment in self-regulation in a community of New Jersey fishermen.

TRAGEDIES OF THE COMMONERS IN WESTERN EUROPEAN FISHERIES

In America the laws of the commons and sentiments behind them have roots in class struggles over access to wild game and fishes in western Europe and the British Isles and in the association of the

American Revolution with a return to basic rights. Among these is the rule of Mosaic and Justinian law that things in a state of nature—*ferae naturae*—cannot be alienated as private property but must belong to all. How revolutionary this approach was can be appreciated by a brief review of the history of wild game and in-land fishery laws in the Old World.

Best documented and most extreme were the Game Laws of England from 1671 to the nineteenth century, laws that transformed hunting into a privilege of substantial landowners and imposed severe penalties upon poachers (Howkins 1979; see Thompson 1975 for parallel developments in other uses of forest resources). The discriminatory nature of the Game Laws is evident in the fact that in 1840 only 0.24 percent of the population of England was entitled to kill game (Howkins 1979: 278). Less commonly appreci-ated is the concomitant loss of legal access to fisheries, especially inland fisheries. While the "freedom of the seas" was developing in international law and expanding throughout the globe, the free-dom to fish was being severely eroded in Europe and the British Isles.

A focused history of fishing laws and rights in the Old World has yet to be written. However, Anthony Netboy's (1968) book on the Atlantic salmon contains historical information on rights to fish in the inland, and to a lesser extent, coastal waters of Spain, France, Sweden, Norway, England and Wales, Scotland and Ireland. This information suggests that fishing, particularly for highly valued and vulnerable species such as Atlantic salmon, was also trans-formed into a privilege of the upper classes—the nobility, the clergy, and owners of land. The poor had access to fish, as to game, primarily by virtue of their social relationships to the privileged, their tenure in land, and their activities as poachers. Accordingly, claims to the freedom or right to fish came to be associated with broader claims on the part of the disadvantaged for protection against the effects of class-based privilege. During the French Revo-lution and the Spanish Civil War, for example, common property rights in fish and game were resurrected for short times in response to defiant claims by the masses (Netboy 1968: 58, 70).

Within the broader processes noted above, there were signifi-cant differences. For example, in Sweden and Norway peasants apparently fared better than elsewhere; their holdings included fishing rights that were secure enough to enable the creation of communal systems of fishery regulation and allocation (Netboy 1968: 97, 131; see also Löfgren 1979). However, the Crown owned the valuable salmon fisheries and granted them to subjects for services rendered (Netboy 1968: 97). Throughout the Old World a distinction between navigable and nonnavigable waters was relevant to fishing rights. In the case of navigable waters, kings tended to claim ultimate ownership that they used to award common rights to all subjects or special rights to nobles, the clergy, and other dependents. Fishing rights to nonnavigable waters were more often attached to feudal estates and to land ownership and tenure, although they might also be conveyable separate from land. In France, commoners could lease fishing privileges or, if vassals, could hold them as part of rights attached to a fief (Netboy 1968: 66–69).

The Magna Charta of 1215 stated a general freedom to fish in the navigable waters of England and Wales (Netboy 1968: 163–175), but this freedom was abridged and supplemented by claims of the Crown and landowners and the development of complex English common-law rights. A general freedom to fish differed from rights of "common of fishery" (Hull 1924: 12–13), which were granted to specific individuals on waters owned by others. Judging by a review of the law of fisheries of England and Wales (Hull 1924: 8–13), the allocation of fishing rights was very complex. For example, one person could be entitled to take shellfish, another only "floating" fish. Exclusive rights could be seasonal or attached to particular fishing techniques. Some rights were annexed to copyhold tenements; others, in later times, were presumed by corporations. Free rights of fishing could also be treated as a privilege. To secure military allegiance, the French monarchy granted free rights of fishing in estuaries and tidewaters to members of the Royal Navy, who remain beyond the scope of even government regulations (Netboy: 85).

In Scotland there has never been a common right of fishing, not even in the estuaries or along the coast (Netboy 1968: 227). Elsewhere, such rights narrowed or disappeared with time. A "free and general" right of fishing in certain Spanish waters became meaningless as seigneurial and riparian rights and the Crown's power to regulate fisheries enclosed most of the inland fisheries for the elites (Netboy 1968: 54). Open access to the fisheries of England and Wales was whittled away, too. Private fisheries granted before 1189 remained so; the Crown retained the right to create new ones; freedoms to fish in navigable waters became restricted to *tidal* navigable waters and the use of movable, not fixed, gear (Hull 1924: 3–5). The rights of "common of fishery" were gradually extinguished (especially in the eighteenth century, judging from Hull's footnotes, pp. 12–13). By 1923, when the government of England and Wales revised its inland fishery statutes to make them more uniform, it was observed that "it is only in very few places that the public have any right of fishing" (Hull 1924: 5).

For Old World inland fisheries, as with wild game, regulation for the purpose of sustained yield or stock restoration coincided with regulation for the purpose of class discrimination (Lund 1980: 4–10). For the sake of salmon exporters, King James IV of Scotland by the end of the fifteenth century enabled the creation of management systems for major fishing rivers run by "distinguished individuals" (Netboy 1968: 227). In the eighteenth century a similar system for the pleasure of sports anglers appeared in England and Wales. Landed gentry and their friends formed local associations. Supported by the aristocracy, they bought out the netting rights of commercial and subsistence fishermen, tried to combat pollution and obstructions to salmon migration, and pressured the government to use its powers to stamp out poaching (Netboy 1968: 200–02). After the Napoleonic Wars, English aristocrats extended the system to the rich salmon rivers of Norway, which came to be known as "lords' rivers" (Netboy 1968: 134–35). With time, national governments took over more responsibility for conservation in inland waters, pressured by sports anglers with or willing to pay for the privilege—not the right—of fishing (Netboy 1968).

Loss of rights to the *ferae naturae* of the forests, rivers, and coastal seas coincided with enclosure of the agricultural and pastoral commons and the generation of new classes of landless or dependent poor (see Hoskins and Stamp 1963). The process was one of enclosure of the commons, privatization of common rights, and breakdown of communal and feudal systems that had, to some extent, regulated the commons. Contrary to the predictions of common-property theory (which holds that private property

rights will result in resource conservation), these historical processes did little to halt and in some cases may have furthered environmental degradation (Ciriacy-Wantrup and Bishop 1975). It is
even more evident that they resulted in what Ciriacy-Wantrup and
Bishop call a "tragedy of the commoners": the generation of a class
of people robbed of their "non-monetary use-rights" (Thompson
1975: 244) in the commons. The rise of capitalism entailed the re-
ification of those rights and their conversion into objective property rights, mediated by courts of law (Thompson 1975). Those with
little property but their rights in the commons usually lost in the
process, but not without legal and violent struggle (Ciriacy-Wantrup and Bishop 1975). Evidence of their legal battles over access to
the water commons is not available; evidence of violence is:
"Pitched battles in which a bailiff or a river pirate [poacher] met his
death were not unknown" (Netboy 1968: 182).

POACHING AND OTHER CLAIMS TO THE COMMONS

Throughout and reemergent in Old World history was an "under-
ground law" (Howkins 1979: 285) that game and fish were *ferae
naturae* and thus not properly the subject of discriminatory property laws. All people had equal rights of access to *ferae naturae*. A
pragmatic version existed: "the poor themselves produced a whole
alternative morality based on the view that in a country rich with
game, it was a fool who, if he had his health and strength, went
hungry" (Howkins 1979: 285). The police often sympathized with
poor poachers, recognizing that their "crimes" were those of the
hungry. In Scotland, where salmon was both a valuable export
commodity and staple food of the rural populace, Sir Walter Scott
and other local sheriffs and justices winked at the poaching activities of those who did it "for the pot," as opposed to those who
seemed to be involved in organized profiteering in poached salmon
(Netboy 1968: 238).

Although there were sophisticated attempts to find a rationale
for the doctrine of common rights in *ferae naturae* in common and
civil law, the rationale most salient to rural poachers was based on
a combination of natural law and the Bible (Lund 1980). Howkins

(1979) shows that there could be no consensus about the discriminatory Game Laws of England, since the majority of the population held a different moral stance. The rural poor, unwilling to
allow Parliament to abrogate the laws of God and nature, "did not
regard game as property of the same type as farm animals or personal possessions" (Howkins 1979: 278). Howkins provides the
following quotation from a speech to the House of Commons in
1829:

> It had been said that the Bill would clothe game with something of
> the character of property. What was that to the poacher? Would he
> trouble his head to read the book of parliament? He read the book
> of nature. In that book he saw that the hand of nature made game
> wild, and "unclaimed of any" and he would act accordingly.
> (1979: 278)

The poor poachers were supported to some degree by the middle classes, who were also excluded from access to wild game
(Howkins 1979: 275). Sir Walter Scott expressed the popular sentiment, which he seems to have shared, that the poor of Scotland
"have as much right to the fish as the lairds have" (quoted in Netboy 1968: 238). In his time and novels, illegal salmon fishing was
an exciting rural sport for the middling country gentry, who organized poaching parties and distributed most of the illicit catch to
their dependents and the local crofters (Netboy 1968: 235). Fish
poaching was entertaining for the common folk, too, and still is, as
Taylor (1981) has shown in his study of a coastal salmon-fishing
settlement of County Donegal, Ireland. Taylor emphasizes the role
of illicit fishing as the focus of community identity in the Irish
village he studied. In nineteenth-century Scotland it was even
more, part of "the old spirit of the Border" (Netboy 1968: 237) that
kept Scottish nationalism alive.

THE COMMONS IN THE NEW WORLD

The Old World laws of inland fisheries and hunting were molded by
a class system based on the privileges of private property; lower
classes came to have least access to wild game and fishes. Accordingly, the idea of common property rights became grounded in

class struggles and the revolutionary notion of equity in access to wild resources. It was kept alive in poaching, the sentiments of the poachers and their defenders, and in debates between jurists such as Sir William Blackstone and Edward Christian on the infamous Game Laws of England. The debates led directly to the development of wildlife law in America, where they contributed to attempts by legislators and courts to create law for a New World (Lund 1980).

The American sentiment was strongly in favor of "free taking" of open-access rights in wild game and fishes, a legal theory more apt for a growing nation with abundant resources and a small elite. American courts tended to side with Blackstone in the debate "by propounding the view that wildlife belonged not to the landed but to all people in common 'by the very law of nature itself'" (Lund 1980: 24). One of the most influential of these court decisions is that of the New Jersey Surpeme Court in the case of *Arnold v. Mundy* (6 N.J.L.1, 70[Sup.Ct. 1821]) over rights in oystering lands. The court held that the American Revolution had vested inalienably and indefeasibly in the state's people the legal title and the usufruct in New Jersey's tidalwater resources. Legislative powers over those resources could be exercised only as by a sovereign, "for the common benefit of every individual citizen" (cited by Jaffee 1974: 309). Although more than a century of legislative and private derogation of common or public rights in New Jersey's marine waters and coastal beaches has taken place (Jaffee 1974), the law of the commons, based on the *Arnold v. Mundy* decision and reinforced by later U.S. Supreme Court decisions, remains as testimony of the American Revolution.

Luddism and Social Legislation

The history of American fisheries is very much a history of Luddite-like attempts by groups of fishermen to destroy or ban new and competing fishing technologies (Gersuny and Poggie 1974). Reacting to this fact, in 1953 an intergovernmental commission reviewing fisheries legislation on the eastern seaboard coined the term "social legislation":

> Except in rare instances, such social legislation seeks to protect one fishery interest at the expense of another or others, and in

some instances seeks a monopoly for the particular interest. Such acquisitive claims often cite conservation and sound management as their objectives. Rarely, however, is there sound scientific evidence to back these claims." (Atlantic States Marine Fisheries Commission 1953: 22)

The process behind "social legislation" was partly one of transfer of blame: one group experienced decline in production and tried to restrict the activities of another, as in the conflict over fish traps and "pound-nets" (large, elaborate fish traps) of the 1870s to 1890s in the southern New England and Middle Atlantic region discussed below. A more recent and successful example is the establishment of a two-hundred-mile fishing limit in 1977 and the consequent curtailment of foreign fishing.

The second half of the nineteenth century was a time of particularly vehement conflict over fishing technology on the eastern seaboard of the United States, since it witnessed major technological changes in fishing: steam and combustion engine power, purse seines, gillnets, otter-trawls, the pound-nets and fish traps to be discussed below, and more. When fish seemed scarce, there was almost inevitably a call for legislative restriction on one or another kind of fishing. That those behind most of the legislative initiatives were humbler fishermen who lacked the new technologies is what led Gersuny and Poggie (1974) to call the phenomenon "Luddite-like." But to cast it as simply the outcome of competition between groups of fishermen with different levels of technology misses the fact that the situations involved conflicts about cultural meanings and social relationships. Above all, they were social conflicts about the commons.

Pound-Nets, Fish Traps, and the Free and Equitable Right to Fish

In America, the "inalienable" right to fish has been cast in different ways, depending on the situation and on what side one is on in a particular conflict. In the nineteenth-century conflicts over the use of pound-nets and other fish traps, small-scale fishermen and their upper-class spokesmen argued that the equity notion behind common-property law was violated by open-access competition for limited resources. In other words, for users to have truly equal access to common resources, there must be some kind of check on activities in the commons. Their opponents disagreed. The situation to be described is one in which people highly dependent on common use-rights are nonetheless strongly motivated to curb what one can do with them.

Early records attribute the first pound-nets (stationary fish traps usually held within long stakes) to the New England coast in 1846 (True 1887: 22) and a similar technique, the Newfoundland cod trap, to the southern Labrador coast in 1865 (Ledoux and Lepage 1973: 10–11). Although these methods of trapping fish differ in details, both are highly labor- and capital-intensive and efficient in situations in which large schools of fish come close to shore. Their efficiency, along with a mid-nineteenth-century movement of capital from offshore to inshore fisheries, contributed to their rapid and wide diffusion. By the 1880s they were found around most coasts of Newfoundland, in Maine's Casco Bay, and from Cape Cod south to Chesapeake Bay (True 1887).

From the outset, pound-nets and other fish traps provoked controversy, and from time to time entrepreneurs trying to introduce them into new areas were driven out. Repeated attempts were made up and down the coast to restrict or outlaw the use of pound-nets and fish traps, and in southern New England the situation was so volatile that the U.S. Commission of Fisheries was created and came to investigate (Baird 1873). Commissioner Spencer Baird found that pound-nets and fish traps seemed to monopolize inshore-migrating fish and inshore fishing space: "It looks to me like a miracle how any fish get by the trap. The coast is strung all along full of twine" (Baird 1873: 27, quoting a New England fisherman interviewed in the course of the first investigation carried out by the new Fisheries Commission of the U.S.; hereafter all Baird 1873 references indicate testimonies of fishermen, lawyers, and others). They were also blamed for causing the scarcity of some species and for destroying markets by glutting them so that the price was driven down. This effect was accompanied by a seemingly paradoxical one: fresh fish had become more expensive in many coastal communities. The companies formed to own and operate pound-nets and fish traps often bypassed local distribution networks (New Jersey Commissioners of Fish and Game 1897: 23–24). They were blamed also for depleting the subsistence fisheries relied upon by the poor of coastal communities. Most to the point, the unrestricted use of the new gear was deemed by its opponents the cause of distress among fishermen who used handlines, haul-seines, gillnets, and other cheaper methods of inshore fishing (Baird 1873: 23, 28).

Debates over pound-net and fish-trap regulation were about the social meaning of common property. They were about who has rights to the commons: "if the work is given up to the pound-men, I do not know what will become of the [other] fishermen. It seems as if they cannot exist together—the rich or the poor man must have it" (Baird 1873: 52). The debates went to court.

In New England and the Middle Atlantic states, apparently, no "local" solutions were developed to manage the problem of competing technologies/competing classes of fishermen as were developed around cod-trap problems in Newfoundland.[1] Reasons for this difference are probably many, but it seems most critical that, unlike the case in Newfoundland—where capital tended to leave the activity of producing fish to the fishermen—in New Jersey, Rhode Island, Massachusetts, and other places and especially in the pound-net fisheries, capital moved more directly into fishing. Strong class differences among fishermen and patterns of absentee ownership can be found (see True 1887; this pertains mostly to places where pound-nets and traps were very large and expensive as in the Cape Cod region and along the outer shore of the New Jersey coast).[2] In any case, attempts to control the use of pound-nets and traps at the community level appear to have been limited to the use or threat of violence (Baird 1873: 52, 71; see also True 1887). It may be that the interests connected with the fishery were too powerful and farflung to allow the creation of more peaceful solutions at the local level. In southern New England and New Jersey these interests included those who controlled the offshore fishery, railroads, and food-fish and industrial-fish processing firms (True 1887). They were much too powerful to allow any political entity lower than the state or federal government to affect their activities. Accordingly, the conflicts reached high courts and legislatures, where the law of the commons was bandied about by all sides.

Two very different interpretations of the meaning of common property in fisheries are shown in the following quotations from testimonies of representatives of different fisheries interests who appeared before the Rhode Island legislature in 1871. The first points to the colonial Charter of Rhode Island, granted by the king of England, in support of the pound-net and fish-trap owners:

> Living under this charter our grandfathers and fathers continued to exercise this inherent natural right with as much freedom as they used the air to breathe and move in, choosing their implements and using them without limit or restriction. . . . The people shall continue to enjoy and freely exercise all the rights of fishery, and the privilege of the shore. (Baird 1873: 83)

In opposition, on behalf of the small-scale inshore fishermen, was testimony referring to the discriminatory effects of laissez-faire fishing:

> Are the fishermen to be driven from their fishing-grounds, are the people to be deprived of food, that a few men may be made rich out of the public treasury of the sea? And has he or they only the right to catch fish who can afford the extensive and costly apparatus of the trappers? (Baird 1873: 101)

If we go back to Hugo de Grotius, we find that the original learned argument for the freedom of the seas was based on a theory of property that justified the creation of private property only when one person's activities might endanger another's. The same point was raised in the 1871 New England debates: "nothing is clearer settled in the law than that all men have the right to catch fish in the bays, inlets, and arms of the sea, and that no man has the right to catch fish to the injury of others in their rights" (Baird 1873: 91). Overfishing violates the equity idea within common-property law. Depletion of fish stocks can be viewed as a social tragedy, depriving some fishermen of common use-rights: *"the privilege of fishing where no fish are to be found, is equivalent to no right to catch fish"* (Baird 1873: 221, emphasis in the original).

The question was not just one of abstract rights and law. Proponents for restrictions on pound-nets and fish traps pointed to the effects of unbridled fishing on community life. They advocated a system of fishery regulation that met the employment and nutritional needs of coastal communities. Restriction would, it was argued, restore more employment in inshore fishing, open up jobs in other "branches of industry" to which displaced inshore fishermen had turned, and enable more fish to remain in the coastal region as reasonably priced food (Baird 1873: 219). Moreover, if restriction helped restore fish stocks, it might also help restore something else that was seen as being lost, a sense of community on the fishing grounds: "We find out by one another where the fish are; we are all along, and we signal each other when we find good fishing. That is the way we used to fish; but now they are so scarce, we don't tell when we find a good place. It makes the people selfish as pigs. That is the tendency" (Baird 1873: 25).

Those who spoke on behalf of the pound-netters and trappers also referred to social and economic realities, such as the needs and problems of capitalism and capital investors and the demand for fish in the cities. They won. The scenario and sentiments were repeated many times, well into the twentieth century, but led to little restriction beyond licensing. Licensing was actually welcomed by some of the pound-netters: "If we could have our rights secured to us by a license, it would be better for us" (Baird 1873: 37). Much as the "non-monetary use-rights" of agrarian Europeans had been converted into objective property rights, mediated by courts of law as part of the process (Thompson 1975: 244) of alienating them from the commoners, so compromise solutions such as licensing tended to reify the laissez-faire aspect of common-property law against the more egalitarian versions of the rights of the commoners.

In later years the rich/poor dichotomy within the pound-net fishery conflict was replaced by others, especially a commercial/sports fishing dichotomy (Page 1978: McCay 1981b). In the 1980s the few pound-net fishermen left struggle to maintain their rights in the commons against the more powerful interests of the leisured classes and the businesses drawn to the coastlands that pollute the fishing waters.

The notion that common property rights are valuable in protecting the interests of those who are dependent on the commons and have little else—"commoners" in this narrative—is historically juxtaposed and in some situations sharply opposed to the laissez-faire implications of common property tenure. Open-access common property leaves open the opportunity for resource takeover by those with technological, organizational, and political advantage and provides a legal basis for ignoring or destroying localized systems of controlled or limited access (as in old and new court challenges to state laws that require state citizenship for participation in common fisheries). And yet, restricted access can result in sharp social discrimination, as in beaches reserved for the wealthy and, as briefly described below, submarine acreage taken up by the few.

Oystering and the Enclosure of the Commons

The history of eastern seaboard oystering (see McCay 1984 for New Jersey) shows (1) the process of enclosure of the commons through the creation of private or leased beds for planting oysters, and subsequent marginalization of those who depended on wild oysters and public beds; and (2) the persistence of the sentiment or culture of the commons even in the context of a strong rationale for a privatized fishery. There seems little question that, at least until depredations by the disease MSX beginning in the late 1950s, east-coast oystering would benefit from the form of management called "planting," which depends heavily on leased or privately owned grounds in combination with other measures, such as returning shell to the grounds. A major industry grew around that technique in the nineteenth century, especially in the bays of Long Island and New Jersey and in Chesapeake Bay. And yet many highly productive oystering grounds remain common property, not private property, and consequently are subject to harvest by many and cultivation by none (except, in Maryland and sporadically in other states, for occasional planting of seed oysters by the state).

Why is this so? To a very large extent because of conscious social decisions grounded in the notion that oyster planting was indeed enclosure of the classic kind; in an old New Jersey state report, the osyterman objecting to it referred to the Highlands Clearances of Scotland to make this point. In some areas the growth of the industry was constrained and regulated to prevent monopolization of oystering property in the bays through laws limiting the acreage to be held per person, forbidding leases to corporations, and restricting tools of capture to inefficient, simple ones. The intent was simple: to keep oystering a business open to large numbers of people with little capital, a philosophy still espoused in state and local policies.

The larger-scale "planters," as they were called, were also constrained by the activities of people who objected to what was happening and who from time to time engaged in near warfare to enforce their claims to disputed waters and to bring property issues to court. Reports from the late nineteenth and early twentieth centuries sometimes tersely refer to the major problem of the planting industry as the "insecurity of tenure" that arose because of these events (Hall 1894; Stainsby 1902). Moreover, the law of the commons in America as it pertains to wildlife and fisheries is heavily dependent on court cases that arose from these conflicts. As the quotation from Bromley (1982: 842) at the beginning of the chapter notes, the purported inefficiencies of shellfishing and other activities done within a common-property regime must be assessed against the fact that "it was with a particular social welfare function in mind that our founders determined that certain natural resources would remain the common property of all—not the private property of the fortunate few." Studies of the history of oystering and other activities and the conflicts over property within them indicate that the "founders' " decision had to be reinforced and reiterated many times over and is still at issue.

SELF-REGULATION AND THE COMMONS PROBLEM IN A NEW JERSEY COOPERATIVE

Most discussions of common-property fisheries assume that the only locus of intervention and regulation is an outside government. As we have seen, much of that regulation has been affected by the political interests of groups of fishermen. However, fishermen working within the legal framework of common property may also develop their own informal or *sub rosa* systems of exclusivity and self-regulation. The example to follow illustrates the dynamics of a common-property fishery and the difficulties faced by a group of people trying to manage each other and the commons. The place of this narrative is the Raritan Bay region of New Jersey. The people are the fishermen of small ports there, especially "Shoal Harbor" (a pseudonym), a bayshore port with a long history and tradition of piscatorial piracy (McCay 1981b, 1984). The major source is a document written by one of the participants around 1962 (Nelson n.d.) as part of one of many efforts, usually futile, to convince the public and state legislators that the commercial fishermen of Raritan Bay should be allowed to fish in the bay.

Background

"Social legislation" in New Jersey fisheries includes a panoply of laws that protect the interests of sports anglers against commercial fishermen. Among these is a law of 1920 (amended in 1929) that forbids the use of otter-trawl and purse-seine types of fishing gear within two miles of the outer coast of the state, a law that creates problems—and the temptation to poach—during the warm-weather months when most fishes of commercial importance migrate close to shore and into the estuaries and tidal rivers of the region.

Before 1941 the fishermen of Shoal Harbor were able to fish within two miles using other gear. The species known as "porgy" in New Jersey (*Stenotomus chrysops*; also known as "scup" in the North Atlantic) was caught with a technique called drift gillnetting. In 1941 the state, under pressure from sports-angler associations, prohibited the use of gillnets in Raritan Bay waters. The local fishermen formed an association and tried unsuccessfully to repeal the law, and they began to experiment with other ways to catch porgies. Within a few years they found that small otter-trawls, however illegal, worked even better than gillnets. Otter-trawl fishing, or "dragging," proved easier and far more profitable. More people were drawn to porgy fishing than before, and law enforcement became more difficult to carry out.

The Shoal Harbor porgy draggermen soon found that they faced a second recurrent problem: as they caught more fish, prices fell since the market demand remained fairly stable. They formed a marketing cooperative in 1953 that gave them greater organizational strength and economic power, particularly with the wholesalers at the urban fish markets of the region. However, the cooperative could not adequately handle the "glut" problem, which was intensified by greater catches due to the rise of yet another way to catch porgies: purse-seining.

In the 1950s Shoal Harbor fishermen developed a small-scale purse-seine fishery for menhaden (*Brevoortia tyrannus*), which was sold to bait-houses and, to a lesser extent, a local fish meal and oil rendering factory. Prior to that time they used pound-nets to catch menhaden. In the summer of 1953 a group of Shoal Harbor fishermen invested in an expensive purse seine. The first seine boat had a crew of eight men, working on shares. By the end of 1954 they had proved highly successful, and others were attracted to the business. By 1956 there were six seining operations, and once again, because of a limited market, profits declined.

Porgies proved more profitable to the new purse-seiners than menhaden, and thus purse-seining effort shifted to the local porgy fishery. The seiner fishermen, equipped with fish finders and depth recorders, found porgies in a small area about two miles off the coast, enabling them to extend this fishery seaward from the bay. They also extended their range to the coastal waters off the state of New York, where more liberal laws allowed them to fish "right on the beach."

Both seiner and dragger fishermen had found a legal niche for the porgy fishery. During this time the interpretation of the law was that seines and drag nets could not be used within two *statutory* miles of the shore. In 1959, however, the state attorney general ruled that the law was enforceable to two *nautical* miles. Accordingly the line between licit and illicit fishing was shifted about 1,600 critical feet farther offshore. The situation triggered escalation of an age-old "cat and mouse game" between local commercial fishermen and the marine police.

Limited Entry and Self-Regulation in the Shoal Harbor Porgy Fishery

The boundaries of the porgy-fishing commons were maintained by the illegality of the fishery. Eventually only those who had mastered the tactics of eluding the marine police and had access to local resources to do so could profitably remain in the business. Local fishermen thus tended to monopolize the porgy stock that summered in Raritan Bay and local coastal waters and overwintered somewhere out on the continental shelf. The cooperative could also limit entry by restricting membership and hence access to dock space and markets (see McCay 1980). However, within those *de facto* boundaries, the fishery remained open access. The cooperative could not easily keep its members from increasing their fishing efforts, buying bigger and more efficient boats, and entering the porgy seiner and dragger fishery from other fisheries (especially clamming, which had suffered greatly in the 1960s because of state and federal closure of the clam beds due to pollution). It could not use limits on entry to deal with the problem of overproduction for limited markets, since "every man has the right to make a living from the sea."

However, the cooperative could restrict the activities of its members in other ways. One common practice, which required little organization, was to stay in port to protest low prices. It was easy and logical, especially when prices were too low to warrant the costs of fishing. The Shoal Harbor fishermen went beyond that tactic. As the seining fleet increased in size, fishing for both menhaden and porgies, the captains developed an overall fleet quota on how much fish could be caught. The size of the quota was determined by the cooperative's manager according to what the market would bear without depressing prices. In addition, they developed a boat-quota program. It was called a "give-away" program because if a boat caught more than its quota, the excess would be given to boats that caught less. Four seiners could catch enough porgies and menhaden to supply the limited markets, but if the price remained high enough, the equivalent of their catch could support eight seining operations. In the language of one of the participants: "This was good conservation. The men caught fewer fish for more money and less work" (Nelson n.d.: 6).

The give-away program helped maintain the notion of equity inherent in the tradition, if not the written law, of common property. Equalization also took into account differences in crew size. The seiner fishing boats received larger allotments because they had crews of seven or eight men, whereas the draggers received smaller ones, having crews of only two. The notion of sharing was also extended to the costs of illegal fishing. As the catch was shared, so was the fine: "Naturally, with several boats sharing the catch, all with seven-man crews, the cost of a fine divided among them is very small" (Nelson n.d.: 10). At times the fishermen pooled funds to pay a watchman and/or shared the catch with a boat that did not fish but watched out for the marine police or harassed sports-fishing boats that complained to the police about illegal fishing.

Nonetheless, the system could not control entry into porgy

fishing, especially the most costly and productive method, seining. In 1959 there were eight seiners; in 1962, twenty-one. In 1960
draggermen changed their riggings and increased their crew sizes
for purse-seining because large and marketable porgies were unusually scarce in the bay but not farther offshore, where seiners
worked best. The closure of Raritan Bay clam beds due to pollution in 1960–61 increased participation in porgy fishing. Added to
mounting trouble was the extreme scarcity of menhaden in 1962,
to which seiner fishermen responded by concentrating almost entirely on porgies. In addition, as noted above, around this time
both law-breaking and law-enforcing had intensified, raising the
costs of fishing. Although the market had expanded somewhat,
by 1962 the porgy catch limits imposed by the cooperative were
too small to profitably support everyone involved. There were
strong pressures to disband the give-away program.

The social viability of this self-regulating system created within
the Shoal Harbor cooperative was not really tested, because the
porgy fishery ended in 1963. Porgies simply disappeared from local waters. Menhaden were scarce. A few purse-seiner fishermen
shifted their efforts to the distant waters of Long Island Sound.
Some went out of business or converted their vessels for use in
lobstering, illegal dragging in the bays, and legal dragging farther
offshore and in New York State waters for other species. The rise
of a winter whiting dragger fishery in the 1970s was accompanied
by another specialized and localized system of *de facto* limited entry and *de jure* catch limits (McCay 1980).

It is possible that Shoal Harbor fishermen were, despite their
catch limits, full-fledged participants in a tragedy of the commons.
The porgies that summered and spawned in the Raritan Bay region were apparently a discrete genetic "race" that wintered offshore but mingled little with other "races" of porgies that
summered elsewhere in the Middle Atlantic region (Morse 1978).
Shoal Harbor fishing activities might have imposed enough mortality, especially on spawning females, to reduce the stock beyond
its margin of resilience. If so—no one knows (Morse 1978)—the
contention of the fishermen that their regulatory system had conservation benefits should be viewed as propaganda in their attempt to force the legislature to change laws that discriminate
against commercial fishermen (see McCay 1981b; 1984). It is also

possible that the Shoal Harbor sea tenure system was too limited in regulatory scope. Apart from individual and group involvement in the politics of local pollution control and international fishery conflicts, Shoal Harbor fishermen could do little about pollution and foreign fishing, both of which may have played a role in the disappearance of the porgies (Morse 1978).

The Shoal Harbor cooperative was unable to halt overcapitalization, a major symptom of the tragedy of the commons. Difficulties in other fisheries—menhaden seining and clamming—forced the cooperative to allow its members to enter the porgy fishery on the principle that everyone has the fundamental right to earn a living from the sea. Its regulatory system was limited in scope and effectiveness; it was shortlived; it was perhaps unique to its time. Despite the economic distress of 1962, when porgy fishermen were forced to accept very small shares of the catch due to the escalation of the number of boats and fishermen, Shoal Harbor's spokesman still claimed in that year that the harbor was "probably the only port along the Atlantic Seaboard where the fishermen share their catch and are willing to work on a limited production program" (Nelson n.d.: 11). Nonetheless, its benefits and some of its substance were later realized in the development of similar self-regulating management systems within this and another cooperative in the area (McCay 1980). The experience showed to those involved that self-regulation could meet some economic objectives and in a way that served community notions about the fair distribution of rewards as well as use-rights.

THE CULTURE OF THE COMMONS

In most parts of North America the traditional sea tenure system is open-access common property. The basis for that tradition is found in the history of colonial and U.S. legal and political systems, informed by both the needs of entrepreneurs for free and easy access to fish and other wild resources and the idea that the New World should not carry all of the social baggage of the Old.

There are traditions within traditions. In some coastal fisheries of the United States (and elsewhere) the law of open-access property rights is modified by informal systems of regulation that in

effect narrow the boundaries of the commons, and by formal legislative and administrative restrictions on activities and uses of the
commons. Conservation of resources may be the effect and, in
some cases, the intent. It may also be tangential to the concerns of
those dependent on the resources of the sea—to protect their free
rights to fish against processes that threaten to concentrate wealth
and property rights in the hands of the few and the privileged.
Regulations and especially the creation of private property rights
(or their functional equivalents—see Townsend and Wilson this
volume) threaten to convert rights to privileges.

To uphold the notion central to the hard-won custom and law
of the commons in fishing that "every man has a right to make a
living from the sea," paradoxically it may be viewed necessary to
curtail absolute freedoms and/or to create specialized systems of
informal property rights and self-regulation based on the loosely
defined but historically strong moral position that rights of access
"belong" first and foremost to those most dependent on them. In
New Jersey's history, a line was drawn between this notion of
ownership and the creation of true private property in marine resources. The latter, shown in the history of inland fisheries and
game hunting in Europe and the oyster fisheries of North America, generates the maritime equivalent of the landless: commoners
without legal access to either common or private property. The
eastern seaboard culture and law of the sea seem to support the
sentiment that such dispossession should not take place.

NOTES

This chapter is based on research sponsored by the National Sea Grant
Program of the National Oceanic and Atmospheric Administration, U.S.
Department of Commerce, project no. R/S-3, grant no. NA81AA-D-00065,
through the New Jersey Sea Grant Program sponsored by the New Jersey
Marine Sciences Consortium. The research also was sponsored by the New
Jersey Agricultural Experiment Station, State Project 26501. This chapter is

part of the Journal Series of the New Jersey Agricultural Experiment Station, Rutgers University, New Brunswick, NJ, and is Sea Grant Publication NJSG-83-114.

1. In Newfoundland the cod traps were outlawed for a short time in the late nineteenth century, but the ban was lifted and eventually replaced by local systems of communal regulation of the inshore fishing commons (McCay 1974). Conflicts among trap fishermen and between them and other sorts of fishermen came to be managed on a community basis through the creation of a variety of ways of allocating fishing space among fishermen. These allocations helped maintain peace and a veneer of egalitarianism on the fishing grounds (Martin 1979; Andersen 1979), and many of the rules became part of official government fishery regulations.

2. In Newfoundland the local fish merchants helped fishermen obtain fish traps, either by buying the expensive gear and letting groups of fishermen use them "on the halves" (i.e., sharecropping) or by mortgaging the catch against the value of gear and supplies for the fishery. The problem of acquiring and managing the cod traps was, however, eventually met by pooled resources from agnatic kin groups. In southern New England and New Jersey, the fish traps were often owned by lawyers, politicians, wealthy investors, and fish buyers, and those hired to work on them tended to be the rural poor, former independent fishermen, and recent immigrants from the Old World.

10 The Dynamics of Communal and Hereditary Land Tenure Among the Tigray of Ethiopia

Dan Bauer

A lion, a leopard, a monkey, and a baboon had been living happily together when one day they came upon a cow, and as they had found it jointly, it was decided that it should be owned communally. (The Tale of the Good Baboon)

SOME ONE THOUSAND PEOPLE lived in the village of H'areyna in Tigray province, Ethiopia in 1970. Their primary subsistence activity was the cultivation of cereal crops, for which they used ox-drawn plows. The people of H'areyna were Tigriñña speakers and like other Tigray had practiced their own version of Christianity since the fourth century. A portion of the village's land was communal pasturage. Historically its agricultural lands had been sometimes communal and sometimes "hereditary." Of particular interest are the conditions under which the switches between systems of land tenure took place. On at least at one level the shift to a commons cannot be taken as a kind of sentimental impulse on the part of villagers, since they seemed to share Garrett Hardin's (1968) negative view of the commons, as shown in the conclusion of tale of the good baboon (see also Bauer 1973, 1977).

That evening the cow was milked and the milk prepared to become yogurt overnight. However, during the night the baboon got up, ate the yogurt, and went back to sleep. Upon finding the yogurt missing in the morning the lion was very angry, for it should have been shared. Each of the animals denied that he had eaten it. The lion declared that should it happen again he would kill the one responsible.

In spite of the lion's threat the baboon again got up during the night and ate the yogurt, but this time he saved a bit and smeared it on the mouths of the sleeping leopard and monkey. When the

217

lion awoke and found the yogurt gone and the leopard and monkey with yogurt on their mouths he was ready to kill them, but they pleaded for mercy and, on their promise that it would never happen again, he assigned them the task of caring for the cow and sent them out to the pasture.

When they returned, the leopard, who was not used to walking on the hot, thorny ground, complained that his feet were sore. The baboon said that he could help by making some shoes for the leopard. The leopard thanked him and went off. When he returned, the baboon, who had not begun, said sadly that he did not have the materials and that only monkey skin would make good shoes. The leopard promptly killed the monkey and went away.

When he returned, the baboon, who was seated by the river, had still not begun work on the shoes. The leopard was now getting angry. But the baboon explained that he not been able to work because he was very frightened. While the leopard had been away, a big animal (which looked just like the leopard) had come. This animal was still in the river growling at him. The leopard rushed over to the river and, seeing his reflection in the water, pounced on it and drowned.

The baboon now went to the lion and told him that he felt that their cow was getting very thin and that it might be a good idea for them to take the cow to the mountain where the grass was better. The baboon would go to the top to act as lookout, he suggested, in case the cow should fall, and the lion, who was strong, would remain below to catch the cow. Once at the top the baboon yelled that the cow was falling and pushed a huge rock down on the lion. The baboon was left with the cow.

The young Tigray deacon, who had been telling the story with evident pleasure, stopped here. Expecting more, I asked if this was the end of the story. "Yes," he said, "Wasn't he a good baboon? He ate all his friends!" Both a mistrust of communal ownership (the friends lived happily until they got the cow) and a positive attitude toward clever individualism are evident in the story. The lion, who once headed the group, is replaced by the clever, manipulating baboon. The old ruler is destroyed by his replacement (the story, which encapsulates the origins of social stratification, artisanry, and social mobility, is further analyzed in Bauer [1977: 85]).

The tale expresses metaphorically what Hardin (1968) says explicitly: the existence of a commons leads inexorably to disaster. The Tigray mistrust of communal institutions was manifested in many ways besides folktales (Bauer 1977, 1985), yet all Tigray villages had communal pastures, and many settlements of the region had a form of communal land tenure. Indeed, over time, village land tenure shifted back and forth between a hereditary system and a communal one. This chapter explores some of the reasons that a people who do not have a strong communalist ethic nevertheless choose to hold resources in common, sometimes. A second topic is the effect of economic constraints on the form of social stratification found in the region.

Communities of the Inderta and 'Agame regions of Tigray province fell into two types with respect to land tenure: *risti*, or hereditary, and *chigurafgoses*, or communal. Though a statistically meaningful survey of the region proved impossible, a casual sampling suggests that more villages were *risti* than *chigurafgoses* during the period of field research (around 1970), roughly at a ratio of two to one. But each of the villages visited that was then under *risti* had a history of once having been under the rule of *chigurafgoses* and vice versa. Details of Tigray land tenure are found elsewhere (Bauer 1973, 1975, 1977, 1985; Hoben 1973). What follows is a schematic depiction that suggests processes of shifting from exclusive to inclusive, and inclusive to exclusive, systems of land tenure in relation to demographic and economic change.

CHIGURAFGOSES LAND TENURE

The rules of *chigurafgoses* land tenure were relatively simple and were symbolized by its name. *Chigurafgoses* is literally translated as "bull whip land," meaning that a person could claim land by showing the wherewithal to plow it with bulls. The operation of this system shares a number of features with the German *gewanfluer* and the English common-land systems described by Gray (1915). In principle, all land was held in common by the community and allotted to individual households for their temporary use. In practice, however, the rules were not quite that simple. Households were eligible for a share of land within the village's boundaries if they had established residence in the village. In Inderta, village "residence" required a one-year period of residency in the village plus the symbolic gesture of contributing bread to serve visiting pilgrims on the village's patron saint's day. In other words, one was transformed from a visitor into a resident by acting as host to other visitors. Providing bread for the gesture was not onerous, but maintaining oneself for a year without land could be. Generally, a sponsor within the village was needed.

Once residency was established, the immigrant could apply for a share of land. Land was allocated according to the religious status of the applicant. H'areyna's land was divided into three parts: one-third for the "church," one-third for the "emperor," and one-third for the laity. The laity in fact retained the emperor's third on the grounds that they paid taxes. The "church's portion" was divided equally between deacons and priests. Depending on his ecclesiastical status, the immigrant applied to a committee of priests, deacons, or laymen for a share of land. In this distribution, being a priest had certain compensation. Ten percent of H'areyna's households were headed by priests, who shared one-sixth of the cultivable land. Deacons, due to their larger numbers, were a little less well off than laymen in terms of the size of their shares.

By 1970, when this research was being carried out, nearly all household heads were feeling the pressure of the smallness of the holdings created by the claims of new immigrants, and the political pressure to shift to the more restrictive *risti* land tenure system was becoming intense. Until about ten years before, *new* land could be carved out of the common pasturage without threatening its carrying capacity. New households, however, decreased pasturage by converting it into cultivated land, and also added new oxen to the herds supported by the pastures.

Chigurafgoses tenure systems were designed to attract people into a village. People left their home villages and regions for *chigurafgoses* villages because of land scarcity or political difficulties within their home villages or because of regional droughts. The crucial factor in a household's economic downturn was the loss of oxen. The diminished ability to plow created a dependence on others for food and use of oxen. With the loss of plowing ability came the need to rent out one's land to others. Decreased production also forced a decrease in household size: members joined other households or emigrated to other regions. People who had had several poor years might have exhausted their social resources at home but still could be attractive political clients in a new village.

In the early stages of *chigurafgoses* tenure, increased population and increasing land use had little effect on the ratio of people to cultivated land, but they increased the ratio of animals to pasturage. The overall size of the pasture was smaller, and the number of animals to feed was larger. Later, as the community reacted to the experience and perception of insufficient pasturage and took measures to limit the conversion of pasture to cultivated land, the ratio of population to cultivated land also increased.

Some changes were made in cultivation practices, including increased reliance on wheat, barley, and oats over *t'af*, a preferred cereal less suited to the area.

In addition, controls over the use of common land were sometimes instituted without changing the formal rules of land tenure. For example, Tadele Bihaylu, an energetic young villager in his thirties, told me that he had gone to a great deal of trouble to bring in new land from common pasturage. He had had special narrow plow tips made for cutting sod and through strenuous effort removed the roots and created a new field. The next year, the village committee granted a new household the field which Tadele had worked so hard to create. Such actions, needless to say, had a decidedly negative effect on those contemplating further expansion into the common pasturage. Subtler shifts in attitudes toward newcomers and outsiders could also affect the flow of people into the community.[1]

When the ratio of animals to pasture was high enough that each new household could be provided for *only by taking land away from existing households,* there was great pressure to shift from *chigurafgoses* to *risti* tenure rules. A decision of the village meeting brought back *risti* land tenure. The actual steps depended on a decision to recognize a particular claim for *risti* land as legitimate. This action required the reallocation of all village land through *risti* principles.

RISTI LAND TENURE

Risti land tenure was complex, involving both inheritance and descent principles within a highly politicized framework. The ideal way in which a person gained *risti* land was by inheritance from

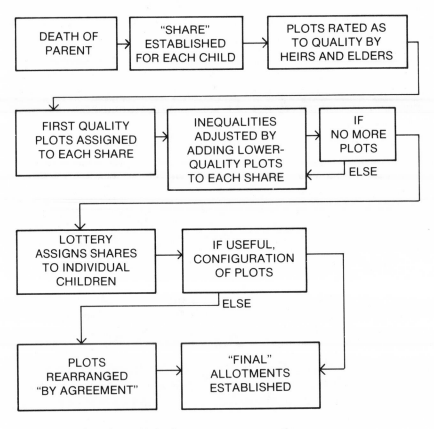

FIG. 10.1. *Flow chart of inheritance process among the Tigray of Ethiopia.*

his or her parents. All children, male or female, had rights to equal shares of land held by both parents through their *risti* claims. Each parent's holdings formed a separate estate for inheritance purposes (a fact which, given the high divorce rate, could make a big difference to those inheriting). Plots held by a parent were grouped into square shares. Once their equality was agreed upon by the inheritors they were distributed by a casting of lots (Fig. 10.1).

The second method of land distribution under *risti* was more political. Individuals could claim land by showing descent from village founders. Descent was reckoned omnilineally, that is, through any combination of males and females. The principles of *risti* land claiming were thought to be equivalent by participants, who saw descent claims as correcting ancient omissions. In fact, the two principles were not coordinate, as logically each plot from each source would have had to be divided in each generation. Individual plots were not normally divided. As a result a son or daughter could inherit his or her fair share of the total land that a parent had held without getting land in each village in which his or her father or mother had had an ancestor (see Fig. 10.2).

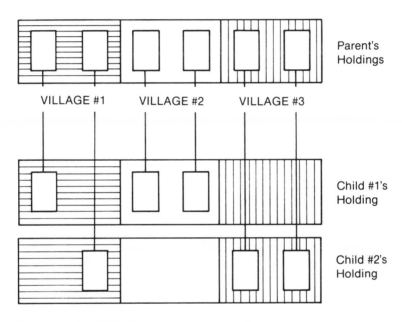

Parent's
Holdings

VILLAGE #1   VILLAGE #2   VILLAGE #3

Child #1's
Holding

Child #2's
Holding

FIG. 10.2. *Land inheritance patterns among the Tigray of Ethiopia.*

Given the logical disjuncture between these methods of distributing land, all people felt that they were owed land that they did not possess *and* each plot of land had multiple, "legitimate" claimants. Claims were settled judicially. Successful claims often led to a "chain reaction" of successes and rapid upward mobility. A person who had both gained a reputation for success in court and established the legitimacy of crucial genealogical ties could press claims in many villages without the necessity of costly litigation. Those sharing generally preferred to have such a person as an ally rather than an enemy.

DEMOGRAPHIC ADJUSTMENT AND SHIFTS IN LAND TENURE

As with the shift from *chigurafgoses* to *risti*, the reverse shift, from the hereditary to the communal system of land tenure, was done by village decision. In effect, *risti* rules were declared to be in suspension, and it was agreed that all land should be shared equally by all resident members of the community regardless of genealogical claims. Occasionally a small portion of the village would be kept as *risti* in order to retain the support of a local political figure, and there were other variants.

Switching between land tenure systems regulated population movement. The *risti* was a more exclusive and restrictive system. It limited access to village land because only those with genealogical ties (or claims to descent from founders) could make claims. Although the system allowed for a great deal of movement among villages as individuals followed their genealogies, it was nonetheless much more restrictive than the communal system. Genealogical structures, although broad, were not infinite, and the successful prosecution of land claims under *risti* depended on economic and political ability. Potential immigrants from distant areas rarely had the ties or resources needed to gain land under *risti*. It was just such people who joined a village under the *chigurafgoses* system.

Viewed from a land-use perspective, it might seem strange that a village would choose a system of land tenure that encouraged immigration, but in a region of extreme drought, political conflict, and other disasters, it is less than strange that villages desired to increase their populations at one time or another. The primary reason for underpopulation was regional drought. The folk history of H'areyna reflected this understanding:

> Once all of the land in this region was *risti*. A long time ago, perhaps a hundred and fifty years ago, there was a great drought. Everyone had to find other places to live. Three brothers who had

lived in this region went to stay in Tembien. The man they stayed with gave them protection until the drought was over. In return they promised him a fourth of the land here. When they returned he chose not to come with them, preferring to remain in Tembien. There were not enough people in this area so they declared that anyone who wished to come and plow could have the land they needed. Many people came, often marrying into one of the three families. Soon a few of the villages were quite large. Dirba [a neighboring village] changed to *risti* many years ago.

Villages apparently instituted *chigurafgoses* land tenure when they needed more people—for a variety of reasons, including political power. Communities had to be able to protect their interests in the court system and to defend themselves from outlaws and from neighboring communities that disputed the location of boundaries. Communities instituted *risti* tenure when they wanted to limit the influx of population, typically once individual landholders began to feel that giving land to new families reduced their own livelihoods. The timing of the change varied considerably from village to village and in relation to a variety of favors. For example, villages that had grown rapidly relative to the villages around them were more likely to change quickly than those that still felt a threat from neighboring communities. Villages with relatively evenly developed genealogical branches presumably had fewer problems in making the change than ones in which great disparities in sizes of holdings would have resulted from the transformation.

Both systems were flexible in terms of population movements. *Chigurafgoses* allowed for long-distance interregional movements, whereas *risti* tenure allowed a great deal of local movement. Fathers, sons, and brothers were often found in different villages, claiming *risti* land in each. The drought-famine cycle described here was also part of a general pattern of movement, much like that described by Braudel for parts of Europe (1981: 96–98). There was an overall pattern of movement to the south of Ethiopia where rainfall was more plentiful and less irregular. Movement was not always southward, however. When H'areyna was last devastated by drought, many people moved north to Tembien. It was nonetheless the overall working of the drought-famine cycle in the north of Ethiopia, modulated by village shifts in land tenure and other institutions, that led to a progressive and almost imperceptible movement of northern people into southern areas.

SOCIAL STRATIFICATION AND THE COMMONS

At the time of fieldwork, the village of H'areyna was in the process of making the shift from communal to hereditary land tenure. The process involved great internal conflict because recent immigrants, who had not yet established local kinship ties through marriage, and persons from prolific genealogical lines were to lose significantly by the change. As elsewhere, a shift in land tenure involved a shift in social structure. Although over a shorter time span, the shift described is analogous to that depicted by Ladurie (1974: 16–18) for Languedoc, an alternating of social forms (*domaines* and small egalitarian holdings) in response to population changes, with periods of coexistence. However, among the Tigray the change in social structure was not—at the point of making the land tenure change—an extreme movement from an egalitarian to a hierarchical social formation (i.e., as found among villagers of highland Burma, in the *gumsa/gumlao* shift [Leach 1954]).

Although common worship and a shared interest in the common pasture emphasized the commonality of village life, the Tigray did not accept the idea that people are essentially equal. They held instead the premise, manifested in nearly all social contexts, that no two people may be equal in terms of "honor" (*k'ibri*) (Bauer 1975). Moreover, each of the Tigray land tenure systems encouraged the development of ties of dependence between weak and strong households. As discussed above, access to oxen was a problem for weak households. A shortage of pasture prevented them from feeding a herd large enough to provide a stable supply of oxen. Since a shortage of pasture seemed to be the precipitating condition for taking up *risti*, we would expect such vertical ties to have been a regular feature of this system. In contrast, one might expect that the pressure for vertical ties would not have occurred until the final phases of *chigurafgoses* since it was initiated under conditions of low population density. But this was not the case: immigrants were dependent on strong households for sponsorship in the village. With high population density, families with little capital (i.e., no oxen) were dependent on richer households in much the same way under either system of land tenure.

SYMBOLIC AND SOCIAL ASPECTS OF THE COMMONS

The commonly held village estate is less central to Tigray than to the culture of New England. In New England, villages were often divided among competing religious sects, and the commons carried a heavier symbolic burden for the community at large. A more important symbol of community for the Tigray was the parish church. Each village was a parish and also a congregation.

In Tigray the common holding, particularly the pasture, was nonetheless of symbolic significance. A threat to the commons was a threat to members of the community. Protecting the commons was thus used symbolically as a call for social action, second only to the church. Indeed, during my stay in H'areyna and the dispute over retaining *chigurafgoses* or changing to *risti*, the church and the pasture were the major rallying points of village meetings. Those favoring the switch to the more restrictive tenure system argued that the community should protect the pasture from incursions caused by continuing immigration. Those supporting retention of the more open tenure system argued that a change would hurt the church since, under *chigurafgoses*, priests' land was not adjacent to laymen's land. Changed tenure might bring priests and laymen closer together, resulting in inevitable conflicts among neighbors over land and lessening the stature of the priests.

The commons plays a symbolic role in promoting social action (see Fernandez this volume). Groups that hold land in common are generally the ones called upon to perform common social action. In the Tigray province a village that felt itself to be at a disadvantage with respect to its neighbors was more likely to retain *chigurafgoses* after other larger villages had dropped it. Collections of descendants fighting to bring in a new ancestor under the principles of *risti* agreed among themselves to divide the land they gained in equal shares despite arguing for genealogical principles in the larger context. These "descent corporations" (Hoben 1983) probably could not act effectively as political groups if they were forced to deal with the highly divisive problems of working out their own genealogical relations while fighting a larger political entity.

All of these holders of commons were modeled on one supremely symbolic corporate entity: the sibling group. Not only was the notion of brotherhood highly charged, but the nearly sacred right of siblings to inherit equal shares of their parent's estate provided the underlying principle for the larger *risti* structure.

Highland Ethiopian villages shared few of the qualities of "closed corporate communities" described for Mesoamerica (Wolf 1957) and Europe (Netting 1981). Individuals did not allow the importance of establishing the legitimacy of their ties within the village to detract from their claims of genealogical connection with other communities. Like the Nuer (Evans-Pritchard 1940), the Tigray emphasized their ties with local founders, but unlike the Nuer, they did not downplay affiliation with lineages elsewhere. Such ties were sources of potential wealth and power. In the highland Chinantec village of Yolox, where I carried out fieldwork in 1980–81, only four males and four females were thought to have been born elsewhere and married into the village. Each Chinantec village constituted a kind of nation, with common and exclusive biology, language, custom, and property. In contrast, Tigrays expected that marriages would cross village lines.

Tigray villages were sharply different from "inward looking" Mesoamerican communities. No claims of genealogical or linguistic distinctiveness were made in different villages. Genealogical ties and shibboleths covered whole regions. It was not the community's boundary that was marked by genealogical or linguistic tags, but the position people occupied within it.

MATERIAL ASPECTS OF THE COMMONS

Apart from political reasons for having land available to attract people and the symbolic uses it may have in reducing conflict, there are material advantages to having a commons. Incentives for holding common pasturage among the Tigray were much like those for holding common lobster territories in Maine (see Acheson this volume) and common alpine pastures in Switzerland (Netting 1981:

42–69). Individual herd owners needed access to grass and water in all seasons, and yet the abundance and condition of particular areas varied greatly and unpredictably. Whereas it might have been feasible to divide pastures into separate areas in the seasons when grass was abundant, to do so when grass was scarce would have led to small plots and high incentives to transgress boundaries, as well as to difficulties in transporting animals to and from pasturage (for example, it is still legal to pasture cattle on the Boston Commons, but not to drive animals through the streets).

The political costs of keeping peace over boundaries would have been very high (see Campbell 1964 for a discussion of conflicts provoked by bounded fields among Greek pastoralists). The tragedy referred to by Hardin (1968)—that each person will add more cattle to the commons—was regulated instead by changing the definition of who has rights to the commons under varying population conditions.

Changing population density in Tigray province triggered institutional changes that encouraged in- and out-migration. It affected the internal structure of communities, since there were probably more "vertical ties" under conditions of higher density. It influenced the form of genealogical ties—those living under *chigurafgoses* kept narrower genealogical ties than those under *risti*. Though not discussed here, the composition of task groups also changed; father and sons living in separate households shared herding tasks, but could give this up when sons followed external genealogical ties to claim *risti* rights to land. The mechanisms through which these effects of changes in population density came about are discussed at length elsewhere (Bauer 1977, 1985).

The Tigray material lends general support to the thesis that high population density leads to the private holding of property (Netting 1981). However, one must be careful when comparing *risti* with "private" ownership. *Risti* land could be neither bought nor sold. It could be transferred only by inheritance or to satisfy descent claims. This fact inhibited the formation of social classes of landowners and tenants. Those losing land in one generation could regain land by activating genealogical claims in another.

Tigray villages were inhabited by people who had a deep distrust of common ownership yet practiced it. They always used some common system of land use and much of the time a pervasive communal system of landholding, which we might associate with egalitarianism. Yet they were bound by ties between rich and poor and believed that people are unequal, at least with respect to honor. Despite economic and ecological conditions that encouraged the formation of highly stratified social classes, Tigray villages had an institutional structure that opened gates to immigrants (the commons) and fences that shut them out (genealogical restrictions). Sometimes good fences make good neighbors. Sometimes a commons makes good neighbors.

ᕧᕋ

NOTES

The research on which this chapter is based was carried out between October 1968 and July 1970 with the support of the National Institute of Mental Health. I would like to thank Lawrence Taylor, Bonnie McCay, Robert Netting, and James Acheson for reading and commenting upon earlier drafts.

1. At the time of fieldwork, the local attitude toward persons from the district of 'Agame was negative. People from H'areyna preferred to be thought of as Indertans even though they lived in 'Agame district, just across the border from Inderta. 'Agames were believed to have character flaws, especially that of being more interested in hard work and material gains than honor. Most immigrants to the village were from the far end of 'Agame and could not have missed the resentment against them. Presumably only those seriously in need of new lands were willing to stay and put up with the disapprobation. The effects would be to reduce the flow of immigrants into a relatively unfriendly community. My guess is that in phases when the village needed more labor, not only was the local reception more friendly but the same characteristics later seen as negative were lauded. When the village needed people willing to cut new ground, setting hard work above honor was not so bad.

11 The Common Swamplands of Southeastern Borneo

MULTIPLE USE, MANAGEMENT, AND CONFLICT

Patricia J. Vondal

THE VILLAGE OF DESA SATU (a pseudonym) is located on freshwater swamplands between the Barito and Negara rivers in the South Kalimantan province of Indonesian Borneo. It is the focus of this essay on an indigenous common-property system, which describes multiple uses of the swamp, accepted rules of use, problems and conflicts that arise from intensified and multiple uses, and conflict resolution.

This case study exemplifies points made by Netting (1982) concerning the possibility of the coexistence of contrasting communal and individual rights to land, even within the same community, and the need to recognize economic and ecological as well as legal and political determinants of land tenure.

Desa Satu, like the district of Amuntai Selatan and the broader Hulu Sungai flood-basin region in which it is located, has high population density.[1] Its population in 1982 was 1,225, with a density of some 408 persons per square kilometer (Kecamatan Amuntai Selatan, Kantor Camat 1982). Most families are small landholders owning between 0.25 and 0.50 hectare or less. Again characteristic of the larger Hulu Sungai region is the close association between high population density and intensive agriculture focused on wet rice depicted by Geertz (1963).[2] The Hulu Sungai flood-basin region is also the locus of the highest yields per hectare of wet rice in Indonesian Borneo (Biro Pusat Statistik 1979), probably due to the relatively high fertility of soil that is inundated by swampwater and then, during the dry season when swampwaters contract, planted in rice and vegetable crops. Elsewhere in Borneo, except for some coastal areas in the provinces of West and Central Kalimantan and some sites in East Kalimantan, shifting cultivation remains the dominant mode of rice production.

In this area of high population density and intensive wet rice production, land tenure is highly privatized. Rights to swamp-waters and resources are not. The relatively high population density of Desa Satu and other villages in the Hulu Sungai region is also related to the highly diversified nature of local economies, which are in turn partly dependent on open access to the resources of seasonal and permanent swampland. The Banjarese people in this region are farmers, subsistence and commercial fishermen, traders, and handicraft producers. The swamp provides fish for the fishermen. It is also essential to the growing industry in duck and duck-egg production that has its roots in more than a century of duck farming. The swampwater is a place to herd ducks and a source of food for them. The Alabio duck (*Ana platyrhnchos borneo*) forages for fish, snails, and vegetation in the swamp, and farmers supplement this feed with additional fish and chopped sago palm. (Duck flocks are also herded on post-harvest rice fields to glean fallen rice grains.)

The case study also provides an opportunity to observe behavior in a community on the verge of a tragedy of the commons (Hardin 1968). Netting (1982) hypothesizes that population increase leads to intensified use of common property resources, in turn promoting conflict. Mediation of conflict may then lead to clearer specification of property rights and the development of exclusive tenure systems.

Although noncodified rules, to be described below, regulate the use of the swamp, Desa Satu and its swamplands are experiencing problems of the commons, including probable depletion of fish resources because of increased demand due to population increase and the rise of a duck and duck-egg industry. Commercialization of duck husbandry and intensification of duck-egg production have increased conflicts in the use of the swamplands of Desa Satu and other villages of the region. The outcome as of the mid-1980s in Desa Satu is that conflicts are resolved in favor of open access.

THE RISE OF COMMERCIAL DUCK HUSBANDRY IN RURAL NORTH HULU SUNGAI REGENCY

The western part of North Hulu Sungai Regency, where the study village is located, is the locale of the primary sources of fertile duck eggs and the largest center of Alabio duckling hatcheries in South Kalimantan. Forty percent of the entire Alabio duck population of the province is located in these districts (Dinas Peternakan Kalimantan Selatan 1981), and 60 percent of the households derive all or part of their income from duck husbandry (Kabupaten Dati II, Hulu Sungai Utara 1980).

Family-run duck farms that produce nonfertile eggs for urban markets are focal points of a horizontally integrated regional industry that includes specialists in fertile-egg production, egg hatching, duckling rearing, feed supply, and marketing. It is an industry that can be traced back to at least 1917 from Dutch accounts (Paulus 1917); it was a source of fresh and salted eggs in the region, Java, and even Singapore until the outbreak of World War II (Saleh, Interview). The industry has grown rapidly since the early 1960s. One reason is independence from Dutch colonial policies since the Indonesian Revolution in 1950. For example, Dutch officials imposed a tax on duck flocks that increased with the size of the flock (Feuilletau de Bruyn 1933). Another is rising demand, given increases in population and disposable income.

Just as important to the development of commercial duck farming are the many innovations in duck-feed composition and flock management developed by local farmers since 1970, especially the use of salt-dried fish as duck feed. This makes it possible for villagers located on seasonally dry swampland to feed ducks year-round, even when the local freshwater fish supply is depleted (Vondal 1984).

Desa Satu has taken part in the rise of the duck-egg industry in the region. According to elderly informants in the villages, in the 1950s and 1960s no more than ten to fifteen families were involved in duck farming, and the flock size ranged from 25 to 50 ducks. In 1982, 43 percent of the two hundred households surveyed were found to be involved in duck farming, and the average flock size was 100 ducks (Vondal 1984: 35–39). Like other duck farmers in the region, most have intensified duck farming even further. Ninety-five percent permanently cage their mature, egg-laying ducks, a practice that increases the rate of egg production. Only ducklings are allowed outside to forage. These examples of intensification in duck husbandry interact with rules for use of the common swampwaters.

RULES OF TENURE

All dry land in Desa Satu is privately owned. There is no local recognition of ownership claims by the village or the provincial government. Individuals, both males and females, obtain land through inheritance in accord with Islamic rules. They may also buy land in their village or other villages. Landowners are free to rent or sell their land to anyone, whether village resident or not, and to use the land and its products (such as trees) in any way they choose. Exceptions to the owners' unrestricted private property rights mostly relate to other villagers' rights of access to water—to the river and to permanent swamps—in the dry season, and to the general and contrastive principle of common property rights to swamps and their resources, as will be discussed below.

Land in this region of Hulu Sungai has been settled and farmed intensively for so long that it is almost impossible to establish how it came to be privately claimed and owned. The Banjarese are predominantly a Malay people who began settling the region from Sumatra prior to 1000 A.D. (Ras 1968). The unusually high population density in the Hulu Sungai rice-growing region was noted as early as 1824 by Dutch explorers journeying up the Negara River (Halewijn 1838). There is a general principle throughout Southeast Asia and the Pacific Islands that proprietary rights to land in frontier regions are created by clearing it and are maintained by continuous cultivation (see Moerman 1968; Crocombe 1971; Hanks 1972; Carrier, this volume). This principle plus the conditions of high population density and agricultural intensification in the Hulu Sungai region of Borneo probably promoted privatized and individualized land tenure at a very early date (see Netting 1974 for a review of the anthropological literature on relationships between private tenure and the intensification of wet rice agriculture; see also Yengoyan 1971, Drucker 1977, Netting 1982, who discuss ecological and economic factors that result in variation in land tenure and inheritance practices within this general framework).

Dutch overthrow of the Banjarese kingdom of southeastern Borneo in 1860 and subsequent labor and tax policies may also have played a role in the genesis of this highly privatized system of land tenure. Milner's (1982) study of Malay groups in Sumatra, Borneo, and the Malay Peninsula in the nineteenth century indicates that the raja of the state held absolute property rights over the soil and that individuals or households held use-rights. In the Banjarese kingdom of southeastern Borneo, use-rights required the payment of land taxes in rice and coin to the sultan and in rice to the local religious leader (Saleh 1981). Whatever limits existed on free use and transfer or sale of land claimed by individuals or households under this system are not recorded and in any case were altered by the implementation of Dutch colonial rule in 1860. Formal acknowledgment of private property claims may have developed then in the colonial period, perhaps in relation to Dutch forced labor and taxation practices (see Saleh *et al.* 1978).

Dry land becomes wet every year. Village houses in the flood-basin region are typically strung out in a line along either side of a narrow dirt road. Behind them are the marshy fields used for seasonal wet rice cultivation. After the harvest period in October and November and as the annual rainy season begins, the boundaries of privately owned and cultivated land gradually disappear with the rise of the flooded rivers and the encroachment of the swamps. The area covered by water then becomes a common property resource. This is in contrast to the dry season, when only permanently inundated swampland is considered common property. When water covers land, private property claims are submerged too, except for adjacent landowners' exclusive rights (which may be rented) to catch fish in rivers that run through or by private property.

USES OF THE COMMON SWAMPLANDS

Once privately owned rice land is flooded, residents of Desa Satu consider it an open-access resource and use their access rights for transportation, duck foraging, fishing, and gathering snails and vegetation. These uses of the swampland are critical to the diversified nature of the local economy. The custom of common use-rights or open access to Desa Satu's swamplands seems appropriate given the uses of, as well as the difficulty of marking boundaries in, flooded swamplands.

Residents and traders who use "praus" or motorized boats (*kelotok*) to transport themselves and goods between markets and other villages are allowed to cross flooded land in Desa Satu and other flooded communities. Normally these travelers would steer a course through the village via the local branch of the Alabio River because of its greater water depth, but it is permissible to journey through at any point, and at times flooding makes it more economical to stray from the river.

Access to the swamplands and flooded rice fields is essential to the success of duck farmers, who otherwise must buy or harvest duck feed. In most years, the annual flooding of the fields coincides with the harvest period of late October and November, so that farmers may be standing ankle deep in water while they harvest their rice. At the end of the harvest, duck farmers in the village are allowed gleaning rights to privately owned fields, where their ducks forage on fallen rice grains, newly spawned fish, insects, and swamp vegetation. The feed that ducks are able to glean from the newly harvested rice fields represents an important temporary reduction in supplemental feed costs for the duck farmer. Local recognition of the importance of post-harvest rice fields to duck farming is reflected in the fact that the fields become "common property" for duck gleaning and foraging even when they remain dry after the harvest, as in the drought year of 1982.

As the floodwaters deepen, the privately owned village duck flocks are allowed to swim freely throughout the village territory. Alabio ducks swim in flocks in open-water areas away from the houses. They continue to forage on fish, snails, and swamp vegetation. Their owners may or may not follow alongside in praus. Like any good herder, the owner encourages his flock to move to sites where he thinks there may be a greater concentration of food; the duck farmers lure their flocks with chopped sago palm that floats on the water. This method is also used to gather up strays when the owner wants to bring the flock back to the house to be caged for the night. In general, ducks that are caged together stay together when they are let out to forage.

A premium on flexibility in responding to variation in the concentration and abundance of food for ducks adds to the logic of maintaining the swamplands as a commons. Fishing in the swamps is also valuable to the subsistence and commercial economy of Banjarese people. Fishing is done on a daily basis by most Desa Satu men (women and girls are not allowed to fish) in addition to their duck farming, trading, or handicraft activities or their seasonal work in rice and vegetable cultivation. Fishing is for subsistence, local sale, and sale through trader-middlemen to regional markets.

Freshwater commercial fishing is a very important and traditional economic activity in South Kalimantan. It is increasingly interconnected with duck farming. Village duck farmers have long caught fish (and snails) to feed their flocks. They also buy dried fish for duck feed. As of the mid-1970s, dried fish of lower quality and smaller size have been sold as a duck-feed component, which has created another market for fishermen. Duck farmers mix fresh or salt-dried fish with rice bran or chopped sago palm and snails. Other items such as swamp vegetation or commercial poultry additives may be added.

Fishing, like duck farming, is a common-property activity. Men may fish anywhere. Moreover, there does not seem to be a rule that only local residents can fish in the swamplands within the village territory; in other words, this seems to be a truly open-access common-property system. Men from neighboring villages may come to Desa Satu waters to fish. In the rainy season, most people stay within the confines of their own villages, but during the dry season, when Desa Satu is one of the few local sites of a "swamp lake" (see below), there may be considerable movement of outsiders into local waters. The extension of fishing rights to nonvillagers is not surprising when one realizes that most residents of Desa Satu have relatives and friends in neighboring villages. Furthermore, the villages in the region were only relatively recently demarcated for purposes of local government administration as populations began to grow rapidly. As recently as 1970, Desa Satu was part of a much larger village that has since been divided into four villages.

Plants and snails are also regarded as common property. Several types of swampwater vegetation are harvested by men, women, and children for use in family meals. One plant, "ganggang" (*Hydrilla verticilata*), has become a very popular duck-feed component said to increase ducks' appetites. By using it, the farmer may reduce the amount of rice bran in the mixture, a relatively expensive component that must be purchased. Freshwater snails (*Pila ampulacea*) are also gathered from the swamp as a duck-feed component. They stay at the bottom of the swamp during the day and at night float on the water's surface where they are easily gathered. Snails in duck feed provide protein and are said to contribute to the thickness of the egg shell, an important factor in preventing egg breakage during transportation to and between markets.

There are two exceptions to the open access of the swamplands for fishing. First, fishermen avoid waters immediately adjacent to the homes of other people. All houses are built on top of six-to-seven-foot "iron wood" stilts to accommodate changes in water level. The water immediately surrounding a house is used by the family for bathing, washing clothes, washing dishes, obtaining cooking and cleaning water, and so on, and is considered an extension of the household's private domain. Second, fish found in a section of the river that runs through an individual's private property are the exclusive property of that individual. The landowner may allow others to fish there in exchange for a share of the catch. For example, one young man and his next-door neighbor set up a fish trap in the river. The catch was divided into three parts: two for the fishing partners and one for the property owner.

THE DRY SEASON AND INTENSIFIED USE OF THE COMMONS

The common-property and open-access nature of the swamplands endures through the dry season, although the swampwaters themselves are reduced to one permanent swamp lake in Desa Satu. In May rain gradually tapers off and the dry season begins. As swampwaters lower, the village road becomes visible and eventually dries up to be used for bicycle and vehicle passage. As waters recede further, the path of the local branch of the Alabio River becomes discernible. Most of the families in Desa Satu (80 percent of 200 households) begin planting rice seedlings on the edge of slopes formed by roadbanks. They will eventually transplant the seedlings to level ground as the swampwater leaves their holdings.

As the water table lowers and land becomes visible, the fields are no longer treated as open-access resources. All the available land in Desa Satu (approximately three square kilometers) is privately owned. The majority of residents own less than half a hectare of land. Landless or landpoor families commonly rent land for cultivation from more "landrich" families in the village on a sharecropping basis. Most land is planted in rice, but many families also plant cassava, cucumber, melon, squash, corn, eggplant, and chili peppers for household consumption.

Once crops begin to be planted, duck farmers confine their flocks in cages built on stilts or fence them off on ground immediately surrounding or under their homes. To protect the crops, ducks can no longer be herded in the village. No one questions this rule. In the 1982 research period there was no incident of ducks roaming by themselves as a flock or being herded by their owners in the fields during the dry season.

In the dry season an area of permanently inundated swampland in the back field of Desa Satu remains. It is said that this swampwater never dries up. Indeed, it did not during a severe drought that affected most of Indonesia in 1982. Access to this swamp lake is afforded by the river branch that cuts through the village and by public-access paths along individually owned rice and vegetable plots. Desa Satu is one of the few villages in the immediate area where permanent swampwater is found, being situated on relatively lower ground. As discussed earlier, residents consider it permissible for men from neighboring villages to fish its waters as the river branches in their own villages dry up.

The dry season is a particularly good time for freshwater fishing. The permanent swampwater becomes a rich source of fish between June and October. Fish that were spawned locally in November as well as fish that migrated from upstream rivers become stranded in such swamp lakes when floodwaters recede and small river branches dry up. The dense concentration of mature fish available in local swampwaters is easily harvested with a wide variety of nets, traps, and weirs. In contrast, in the rainy season fish are more widely dispersed and most of the mature fish have already been trapped.

Fish traps are the most common fishing implements used in the dry season. A net trap (*ringgi*) is placed in the water and hauled daily, but there are also large traps placed in the swamp lake for the season, which thus create sites of exclusive usufruct rights within the commons. In one method, rolls of tied, thin-cut bamboo strips called *temperai* are placed in a circular fence on the bottom. Every day or so the owners (typically a team) move in its sides to enclose an increasingly smaller circumference and to remove the trapped fish with the use of traps called *kapalaan*. Kapalaan are placed between the two ends of the temperai fence where they are joined to form the circle. Fish are trapped in the kapalaan as they try to leave the temperai.

Some men use *ganggang*, or hydrilla, to make much larger traps. Hydrilla is a submerged weed that carries its leaves below the swampwater and is rooted in the bottom mud (Murtisari, Interview 1983). When swampwater levels are low, it is easy to gather and pile up the weed to make the walls of a trapping fence. Because hydrilla is abundant and free, a larger area can be enclosed than with temperai, which must be purchased at a nearby market. However, the construction of hydrilla traps requires more labor, and some men combine hydrilla with temperai.

The larger traps are constructed and fished by small groups of men. For example, men from three different duck-farming families staked out an area that one of them judged to be 150 meters long by 100 meters wide, using a combination of hydrilla and temperai. He estimated that approximately two tons of fish would be caught by the end of the fishing season (when all fish are removed from the trap). The daily catch is divided per family. Smaller temperai and kapalaan arrangements are also used. One duck farmer owns five such smaller arrangements and cooperates with his neighbor, who owns another five, in their construction and the daily collection of fish from them.

Since the permanent swampland is an open-access commons, trap owners cannot hold permanent rights to sites in the swamp used by them. At the beginning of the dry season the rule is "first come, first served." Placement of traps does not preclude and interferes very little with other uses of this swamp lake. Individuals can continue to enter the swampwater to collect hydrilla for duck feed except that which forms a fish trap. Snails are taken freely as is water for cooking and drinking. However, privately owned traps do monopolize fishing space and much of the fish in the dry-season swampwater. Conflicts over this and related issues have occurred (see below).

MULTIPLE-USE CONFLICTS

Several problems arise from multiple uses of the swamp. For instance, one source of conflict in the village is the destruction of elevated potato mounds by resting ducks. After the rice and vegetable harvest is over, many families build up mounds from mud on their higher landholdings in order to get an early start at planting potatoes and cassava the following season. Because these crops take a relatively long time to mature and floodwaters do not always recede quickly as the rainy season ends, earth mounds are usually shaped from mud in order to plant early. Once the land is flooded and flocks are allowed to swim, ducks frequently rest and preen on the mounds. In the process, the mounds gradually crumble and fall into the swamp.

Another source of village conflict is unaccompanied foraging ducks. In Desa Satu, rice fields are planted at various times depending on elevation, location of the landholding, and whether or not the floodwaters have drained out of the area. Subsequently, rice harvesting too is done at scattered times throughout the village. A farmer letting his ducks loose in the fields must continually shepherd his flock not only to guide them to spots where plentiful feed can be found, but also to prevent them from eating unharvested rice from another's fields.

In each of the two cases briefly described, problems can be averted. The duck farmer continually shepherds his flock to ensure that ducks do not enter unharvested rice fields or, later in the rainy season, do not destroy others' potato mounds. This job is frequently given to a farmer's teenage son. A flock is rarely left unaccompanied for the duration of a day, though they may be for short periods.

When problems do occur, they are resolved with face-to-face

confrontations. Because the rules of use are mutually understood and accepted by everyone in the village, transgressions can often be solved in a fairly uncomplicated manner by the two people involved. In rarer instances, the village head (Pak Lurah) will be called upon to determine guilt and issue a sterner warning. The village head is the main authority in every Indonesian village. If an individual does not agree with the outcome of an arbitration, he may bring the complaint to the district level (kecamatan) in which his village is located. The district head (Camat) will then settle the issue. If serious enough, the Camat will bring the problem to the regency level (kabupaten), which is the next largest political juris-diction after the district, for the head of the regency (Bupati) to resolve. Problems such as intervillage conflicts, however, are very rarely taken outside the village. This process of conflict resolution is probably very similar to practices in many rural village societies throughout Indonesia whereby formal, third-party "dispute-set-tlers" are rarely used (see Lev 1972: 281–285).

FISH DEPLETION:
A TRAGEDY OF THE COMMONS?

In the rainy season when the boundaries of swampwater cover the entire village, there are no problems concerning issues of fishing territoriality, as fish rarely concentrate in specific areas and fish traps are generally not used. It is during the dry season when individual fish-trap territories of unregulated size are staked out that conflicts arise over fishing in the remaining swampwater.

Villagers generally agree that there are fewer fish than in the 1950s and 1960s. However, it is impossible to determine whether local and regional waters have been overfished and whether there has been a true decline in fish populations, since no measurement on local fish populations and fishing effort has ever been made. One indirect indication of depletion is that, around 1965, duck farmers began to harvest freshwater snails (Pila ampulcea) to feed their ducks. Farmers had observed that ducks dive to the bottom of the swamp to catch snails to eat and realized that snails were a potential supplement to fresh fish. I was told that the innovation in collecting snails for duck feed occurred because the ducks did not seem to be getting enough fish for optimal development, health, and egg production. However, the practice also makes sense as an adjustment to normal, seasonal fish scarcity. The use of snails as duck feed is particularly important in November, at the end of the dry season, when the local mature fishes have been almost completely harvested.

It is possible that human population increase, in the context of open access to swamplands and high demands for fish for a variety of uses, has contributed to the depletion of fish as predicted by the tragedy-of-the-commons model. The province of South Kalimantan experienced a 1.4 percent average annual growth rate in its population between 1961 and 1971, and the capital city of Banjarmasin (the major market for Hulu Sungai agricultural products) experienced a 2.79 percent average annual growth rate in the same period. Between 1971 and 1976, the average annual growth rate increased to 1.9 percent in South Kalimantan (Leiserson *et al.* 1980) and may have reached 2.4 percent by 1981 (Ardi 1982). Although data for Desa Satu and the district of Amuntai Selatan are lacking, informants' stories concerning the increase of village households since 1960 suggest a similar rate of population growth. Thus, consumer demands for fish, a major part of the diet for both rural and urban dwellers, have also grown,[3] creating an increased pressure on the fisheries products of all water resources in South Kalimantan.

Duck eggs are a major alternative to seasonally available freshwater fish in the diets of "urban" Banjarese consumers in the province. However, substitutability of duck eggs for fish does not really alleviate pressures of consumer growth on fish resources because production of duck eggs is also dependent on fish. Increased consumer demands may indeed be affecting the freshwater fish population in South Kalimantan, thus causing a decline in total fish catch. Average size of fish catch is also declining in some areas, such as Desa Satu, because of the intensive fishing practices now associated with large-scale duck farmers (see below).

How do these demands for fish on a provincial level translate to problems in the use of a common-property swampwater resource in the village of Desa Satu? This question may be largely answered by examining the growth of the commercial industry of duck and duck-egg production and marketing in southeastern Borneo and in which the village of Desa Satu participates.

Desa Satu residents, once primarily engaged in trade and commercial fishing, have rapidly become specialists in nonfertile egg production because of the profits to be made in this field. There was a 13 percent increase in the number of duck-farming families between June and December 1982. Approximately 90 percent of these families fish in the village swampwaters to obtain feed for their flocks. Commercial fishermen who have become duck farmers still fish the local waters, but they divert their catch to the flock as it is a more profitable use for the fish. In this fisheries-rich region, duck eggs yield a higher profit than do fish, particularly in the dry season when the fish population is at its highest and much of the catch is exported.

Approximately 9 percent of the 22 non-duck-farming households surveyed still earn their primary livelihood through commercial fishing. Another 9 percent of these families specialize in gathering snails from the swamp to sell to duck farmers, and 36 percent obtain their primary income from trading items between the Hulu Sungai markets and Central Kalimantan with individually owned motorized boats. Many of these traders deal in buying and selling duck eggs or duck-feed components. However, a significant number of duck farmers were formerly traders, thus adding to the total number of people who directly use the swamp for its fish resources.

Conflicts over Fish Traps

The large number of people involved in duck farming coincides with a strain in the mutually accepted regulations concerning use of the swamp in Desa Satu. One problem concerns the use of the swampwater area in the dry season for fishing. People get angry when a group of persons is perceived as staking out "too big" an area for collecting fish, thus limiting the area available for all and, more importantly, the amount of fish available for all. This anger comes out particularly at the end of the dry season as the waters become fished out. Those persons using smaller traps, and those who work individually with or without traps, have a hard time getting a sufficient catch as the dry season progresses. Since fish is a source of food for the family table, a source of feed for the flock, and a way of making some income through selling all or part of the day's catch, the seasonal depletion of fish can be a time of great anxiety.

Most of the large fish traps are built and operated by duck farmers who coordinate their activities with close relatives who are also duck farmers. Their aim is to catch as much fish as they can and salt-dry it for future use as duck feed. Although operating these traps, cleaning the daily catch, salting and sun-drying it are all labor-intensive activities, trap fishing is seen as a major way of reducing duck feed costs. This is particularly important for those owning large flocks of ducks. It also is a way to save money that can be used to increase one's flock size.[4] A portion of the catch will be used to feed the duckling flock, some will be mixed with the salt-dried fish for the mature ducks, some will be used for the family's daily meals, and the rest will be salt-dried for future duck feed. Its use is particularly important in December as the price of salt-dried freshwater fish increases, reflecting the unavailability of freshwater fish in the local areas.

A person trying to reduce his production costs this way is seen as indirectly affecting other residents in the village by having "too many ducks" and staking out "too big an area for fishing." The swampwater is not construed as private property, so the angered residents have no "right" to tell these men to get off the property, stake a smaller fishing area, or reduce its size. Rather, a great deal of grumbling is heard throughout the village. It was reported to me by one major duck farmer that some people did come to the village head to complain about the size of the large fish traps operated by small groups of men (his was one of the traps complained about). However, the existing rule *is* "first come, first served," and the village head (who is himself a duck farmer) told the men who operate these large fish traps to ignore the grumbles. The individuals who feel they are unfairly affected by big duck farmers have no direct means of addressing the situation themselves, and furthermore, they have no advocate to help them solve the problem of inequitable resource use.

This area of unresolved conflict is not addressed by traditional rules of acceptable use of the swampwater and cannot be solved by traditional means of conflict resolution. The use of the swampwater for duck-farming purposes will be increasingly problematic if participation in year-round commercial egg production continues to increase in the region, as is likely.[5] Moreover, conflicts like these may be fueled by growing stratification in income levels, due to the wealth created by families involved in big duck-farming operations, and consequent feelings of inequality within the community. For example, I was told that "only rich people have ducks" by some individuals in the village. One farmer with a flock of four hundred ducklings confined them to his own harvested rice field for scavenging because, he explained, his flock was too large to be herded in other people's fields as well. He said that the owner of a large flock is better off keeping them confined to his own fields to curtail jealous comments and strained relations among neighbors. Resentment over duck farmers' large fish traps may be another instance of this jealousy over the relative wealthiness of some duck farmers.

THE CHANGING VALUE OF SWAMPLANDS AND THE COMMONS DILEMMA

Growing pressure on the swamp and its fisheries has coincided with the rise of commercial duck farming, an increase in participation in duck farming at the village level, and increases in population. These pressures may well lead to a decline in the swamp's fish resources, as well as to inequitable patterns of resource use. New rules of swamp use and new means of conflict resolution may need to be formulated in Desa Satu.

The case is reminiscent of Hardin's (1968) theory of the tragedy of the commons in which a common resource is doomed to escalating abuse through overexploitation and population increase, particularly when individual users can profit through intensive use of that resource. In Desa Satu, an association between common property and overexploitation was not always the case. For generations swampwaters have been used for multiple purposes with no apparent problems. One gets the impression from village residents that formerly the rules regarding the use of the swamp were adequate to ensure that all individuals used the resource without adversely affecting others' rights. Although there are no formal institutions or codified regulations for the management of common-property swamplands in Desa Satu, an informal institution of historical agreement among village residents provided guidelines for mutually acceptable behavior in a complex system in which the resources fluctuate in size and quantity according to season and are used by many different actors for a variety of reasons.

The boom in the rural economy of the region caused by the rise of commercial duck and duck-egg production has had a big impact on villages such as Desa Satu. As of the mid-1980s, resources such as freshwater swamps have not come under close government scrutiny or jurisdiction. It is up to the people in the locales of swamps to create acceptable regulations among themselves, as swamps in general are still seen by outsiders as unprofitable and uninhabitable. Clearly this perception is wrong. Perhaps the capacity of land to be used for rice production led to its high value and to a system of private property, in contrast to common property in swampwater that led to the latter's devaluation. Hence a dual view of property classification may have evolved—that of private property in the dry, rice-growing season, and of unregulated, open-access common property in the rainy season when land was covered by water. The small size of landholdings in this high-population-density area means that few are able to produce enough rice in the dry season to accommodate the yearly subsistence needs of the family. Duck husbandry, which is not dependent on landownership, is one way to acquire money that can be used for the purchase of rice and other goods in the market economy of South Kalimantan. This process seems to be leading to a new view of swampwater, at least in the dry season when that remaining contains a high density of a highly valued good—fish.

The growing pressure on the swamp's resources as well as the growing anger expressed in the community leads one to expect that some new rules of swamp use will be formulated. However, because of the long tradition of solving conflicts within the village and the use of mutually derived agreement for regulating common property resources, it is unlikely that those angered residents will demand the formulation of codified regulations. Pressure may be brought to bear on the duck-owning village head to devise a compromise through the use of intermediaries such as respected village religious leaders. One plausible compromise would be to place a limit on the circumference of the large fish traps when they are initially staked out in the dry season so as to accommodate, or at least mollify, everyone who uses the swampland. Another possibility would be to limit the use of the swampwater area in the dry season to Desa Satu residents. However, this restriction would undoubtedly create feelings of animosity between Desa Satu residents and residents of surrounding villages who have historically fished these waters as well.

The interests of village duck farmers are not favored by increasing regulation of swampwater use. Rather, through open access and the "first come, first served" arrangements, those farmers who have been able to marshal the labor to build and work large fish traps are able to maintain large duck flocks and to progressively increase their flock sizes. This has clearly led to a less equitable distribution of access to the commons, and the intensity of these fishing practices undoubtedly contributes to depletion of fish in this area. Yet the growing wealth of these duck farmers may also be leading to greater influence in local politics; wealth earned from one's labor is highly respected in the Banjarese rural culture in South Kalimantan. If the open-access arrangement is maintained, a tragedy of the commons *and* of the commoners may indeed occur. The manner in which residents of Desa Satu eventually choose to deal with these new problems of swampwater use will be instructive for future studies of natural resource management in conditions of complex environmental and economic circumstances.

NOTES

This chapter is based on fieldwork carried out in South Kalimantan province of Indonesia in 1981–82. The research was supported by the National Science Foundation under Grant No. BNS-8107626 and by Cathay Pacific Airlines. In Indonesia the research was sponsored by Lembaga Ilmu Pengetahuan Indonesia, Jakarta, and Universitas Lambung Mangkurat in Banjarmasin. I wish to thank Bunnie McCay and Victor Caldarola for their thoughtful comments and editorial suggestions on earlier drafts.

1. The population density of the Hulu Sungai flood-basin region is about 202/km², making it the highest in any region in Borneo. Compare this figure with that for South Kalimantan province as a whole, 53/km²; for West Kalimantan province, 16.2/km²; Central Kalimantan, 5.8/km²; and East Kalimantan, 5.0/km² (Biro Pusat Statistik 1980).

2. The proportion of land dedicated to wetland rice is greater in South Kalimantan, particularly in the Hulu Sungai flood basin, than anywhere else in Indonesian Borneo (Biro Pusat Statistik 1980).

3. The World Bank (Leiserson *et al.* 1980) estimated a per capita consumption growth of 5 percent per year in urban areas and 2 percent in rural areas between 1971 and 1976 for all areas in Indonesia "outside Java." Ardi (1982) cited an annual increase in disposable income of 3 percent for South Kalimantan.

4. These duck farmers were raising a large flock of ducklings to replace their current flocks of mature egg-laying ducks once they passed their prime production phase (ca. 12 months of age). A higher level of profit is gained by raising one's own replacement flock (Vondal 1984). Although it is believed that ducklings should only have fresh fish, salt-dried fish can be used for mature ducks.

5. As long as the market for duck eggs is favorable, it is likely that commercial duck farming will continue to spread. Although the average monthly price farmers receive for their eggs fluctuates throughout the year, they are able to make money beyond what they need to maintain their flocks and often beyond what they need to support their families. Many families have used their profits to expand their flocks, improve and enlarge their homes, educate their children beyond grammar school, and help finance pilgrimages to Mecca in Saudi Arabia. Everyone is Moslem in this region, and making the holy pilgrimage in one's lifetime is one of the highest goals.

12 Institutional Arrangements for Resolving the Commons Dilemma

SOME CONTENDING APPROACHES

Elinor Ostrom

MANY OF THE WORLD'S RESOURCES share characteristics that enable us to classify them as common-pool resources (see Blomquist and Ostrom 1986). All common-pool resources produce a fixed flow of "use-units" per unit of time. When the resource is a groundwater basin, the use-unit is the quantity of water pumped per year. For a grazing commons, the use-unit is the number of animals fed per season. For an air shed, it may be the quantity of different pollutants emitted into the air per year.

When the number of use-units consumed by those sharing access to a common resource is considerably less than the "sustained yield" of the system, few problems exist. As the number of use-units consumed or withdrawn from a commons approaches or exceeds sustainable yield, serious problems may emerge. However, unless some form of regulation is achieved, all participants have incentives to increase their use of the resource.

The tragedy of the commons (Hardin 1968) is created when these incentives remain unchanged and those involved continue to follow strategies that destroy the very resource that is potentially capable of yielding valuable use-units for generations to come. Most policy proposals to avert this tragedy recommend changes in institutional arrangements. Institutional arrangements are the rules in use by a community to determine who has access to common-pool resources, what use-units authorized participants can consume and at what times, and who will monitor and enforce these rules (Ostrom 1986).

Two fundamentally different institutional arrangements are typically posited as necessary for resolving the commons dilemma. The first is the allocation of full private property rights to a set of participants. W. P. Welch, for example, advocates this institutional solution when he asserts that "the establishment of full property rights is necessary to avoid the inefficiency of overgrazing" (1983: 171). He believes that privatization of the commons is the optimal solution for all common-pool problems, and his major concern is how to impose private ownership when it is opposed by those using a commons.

A strikingly dissimilar institutional arrangement—allocating full authority to regulate the commons to an external authority—is assumed to be necessary by others. Carruthers and Stoner, for example, made the following analysis for the World Bank:

> Open access to exploitable communal resources without public control means eventually losses for all involved, whether it is in the form of less or more costly irrigation and drinking water . . . overgrazing and soil erosion of communal pastures, or less fish at higher average cost from surface water sources. Common property resources require public control if economic efficiency is to result from their development. (1981: 29)

Advocates of both positions share the assumption that a particular form of institutional arrangement is necessary.

In contrast is the view that, left to themselves, individuals who are dependent upon common-pool resources for essential inputs to their economic activities will work out a system that achieves regulation over the commons. Institutional arrangements developed will be determined by their uses of the resources. Robert Netting (1976: 137) expresses this view:

> My contention will be that, in the absence of decisive legal or military controls from the larger society, the system of property rights in the peasant community will be directly related to the manner in which resources are exploited, the competition for their use, and the nature of the product products—more specifically, *land use by and large determines land tenure.* [Italics added]

This approach differs in two important ways from the others. First, it assumes that when relatively isolated sets of individuals live in a slowly changing environment, they will be able to devise institutional arrangements well matched to their situations and problems. Second, it acknowledges that communal ownership, rather than private ownership or central control, can be an optimal institutional arrangement for some types of common-resource problems.

TESTS OF THEORETICAL STATEMENTS ABOUT THE COMMONS

Statements of Impossibility and Necessity

Theoretical statements that X is related to Y are difficult to challenge effectively with empirical evidence. On the other hand, two types of theoretical statements can always be clearly confronted with empirical evidence. They are:

1. It is *impossible* for Y to occur if X occurs.
2. For Y to occur, X must *necessarily* occur.

In regard to Statement 1, finding a single case in which Y occurs when X is present is a powerful challenge to the empirical validity of the statement. In regard to Statement 2, finding a single case in which Y occurs and X is not present is similarly effective.

Welch's statement quoted above about the necessity of full property rights is a clear version of Statement 2, and we can reformulate it as a hypothesis:

H1   To avoid the inefficiency of overgrazing, it is necessary to establish a system of full property rights.

To examine the empirical validity of this statement, we need to define *full property rights* and how this institutional arrangement differs from others. Welch distinguishes three types of property rights: "*Common property* can be used by anyone. . . . *Usufruct property* confers a nontransferable right to exclude others from use. . . . *Full ownership* confers both excludability and transferability" (1983: 166).

The statement made by Carruthers and Stoner quoted above can also be converted into a hypothesis, using the form of Statement 2:

H2   To avoid inefficient development of common property resources, it is necessary to establish public control over their use.

By "public control" is clearly meant that all major allocative decisions concerning who could use how much of a common property resource would be made by central, bureaucratic agencies (Carruthers and Stoner 1981: 31, 38, 41).

It is more difficult to isolate a similar hypothesis from Netting's position that environmental characteristics and economic activities determine institutional arrangements. In his study of a Swiss alpine village (to be described below), he reacts to the assumption that private ownership is the optimal form of land tenure and that communal patterns of ownership are anachronistic holdovers of ancient tribal communism. He argues that communal patterns may allow more efficient use of some types of resources than private ownership would. He slips, however, from this argument into the assertion quoted above that "by and large, land use determines land tenure." He is clear about what he means by "land use," (see Table 12.1 below), but less clear about what he means by "land tenure." Netting distinguishes between "communal" and "individual" tenure without further definition and is ambiguous also about what he means by "determines."

At least three hypotheses can be formulated in an effort to clarify what Netting and others making similar arguments mean. The most determinate one would be:

H3a In small, isolated communities with authority to make their own rules, land-use patterns characterized by attributes A_1, A_2, . . . , A_n will always be found with institutional arrangements characterized by rules R_1, R_2, . . . , R_n that facilitate an efficient solution to the problems involved in this land-use pattern.

Hypothesis H3a is a statement of necessary relationship and asserts that all rules affecting the regulation of land use will be similar in similar land-use settings. This formulation assumes that "land tenure" includes all such rules.

A somewhat weaker version of the hypothesis is:

H3b In small, isolated communities with authority to make their own rules, land-use patterns characterized by attributes A_1, A_2, . . . , A_n will always be found with institutional arrangements containing one particular rule, rule i.

This version picks out a particular rule or subset of rules as necessarily related to a particular set of attributes of land-use patterns.

Still further weakened and more probabilistic is the third version:

> H3c In small, isolated communities with authority to make their own rules, land-use patterns characterized by attributes $A_1, A_2, \ldots, A_n$ will frequently be found with institutional arrangements containing at least one particular rule, rule i.

This states a predicted association rather than a necessary relationship.

Communal Tenure in a Swiss Village

Netting's study is of Törbel, a Swiss village of about six hundred people located in the Vispertal of the Upper Valais region. Netting (1972: 133) identifies the most significant features of the environment as "(1) the steepness of its slope and the wide range of microclimates demarcated by altitude, (2) the prevailing paucity of precipitation, and (3) the exposure to sunlight." For centuries, Swiss peasants have planted their privately owned plots with bread grains, garden vegetables, fruit trees, and hay for winter fodder. Cheeses produced by a small group of herdsmen, who tended village cattle pastured on the communally owned, alpine meadows during the summer, have been an important part of the local economy.

Written legal documents dating back to 1224 provide information about the types of land tenure and transfers that have occurred in the village and the rules used to regulate the five types of communally owned property: the alpine grazing meadows, the forests, the wastelands, the irrigation systems, and the paths and roads connecting private and communally owned properties. On February 1, 1483, Törbel residents signed a law formally establishing an association to achieve a better level of regulation over the use of the alp, the forests, and the wastelands.

> The law specifically forbade a foreigner (*Fremde*) who bought or otherwise occupied land in Törbel from acquiring any right in the communal alp, common lands, or grazing places, or permission to

fell timber. Ownership of a piece of land did *not* automatically confer any communal right (*genossenschaftliches Recht*). The inhabitants currently possessing land and water rights reserved the power to decide whether an outsider should be admitted to community membership. (Netting 1976: 139)

The boundaries of the commonly owned lands were well established long ago, as indicated in a 1507 inventory document.

Not only was access to well-defined common property strictly limited to citizens, who were specifically extended communal rights, but written regulations specified in 1517 that "no citizen could send more cows to the alp than he could feed during the winter" (Netting 1976: 139). Matters such as these were handled by an alp association that included all local citizens owning cattle. This legally constituted group, in the past coterminous with the closed corporate community, had annual meetings, hired the alp staff, imposed fines for misuse of the common property, organized annual maintenance work, and democratically elected officials.

Regulations also stated the responsibilities of those with access to the commons to provide labor inputs for cleaning springs, maintaining the dam and major ditches of an extensive irrigation system (irrigation rights themselves were privately owned), building and keeping up roads and paths, rebuilding avalanche-damaged corrals, and redistributing manure on pasture lands. A codification of these regulations signed in 1531 included twenty-five separate statutes regulating even more diverse activities, including hunting, the spread of cattle disease, dispute settlement, damage done by stock to private plots, communal house building, and alp pasturage rights (Netting 1976: 139–40).

Private rights to land are well developed in Törbel and other Swiss villages. Not only are most of the meadows, gardens, grainfields, and vineyards owned by separate individuals but complex condominium-like agreements have been worked out for the fractional shares that siblings and relatives may own in barns, granaries, or multistoried housing units. The inheritance system in Törbel ensures that all legitimate offspring share equally in the division of the private holdings of their parents and consequently in access to the commons, but family property is not divided until surviving siblings are relatively mature (Netting 1972). Prior to the nineteenth-century period of population growth and hence severe population pressure on the limited land, the level of resource use was held in check by a combination of late marriage, high celibacy, long birth spacing, and considerable emigration (Netting 1981).

Netting (1976: 140) dismisses the notion that communal ownership is simply an anachronistic holdover from the past by showing that for at least five centuries these Swiss villagers have been intimately familiar with the advantages and disadvantages of both private and communal tenure systems and have carefully matched particular types of land tenure to particular types of land use. Then, to support his argument that "land use determines land tenure," he associates five attributes of land-use patterns with the differences between communal and individual land tenure (Table 12.1). He argues that communal forms of tenure are optimal (a) when the value of production per unit of land, the frequency and dependability of use or yield, and the possibility of improvement or intensification are low; (b) when large areas are required for effective use; and (c) when relatively large groups are required for capital investment activities (see Runge 1983 and Gilles and Jamtgaard 1981 for similar arguments).

TABLE 12.1

Attributes of Land Use by Type of Land Tenure System

ATTRIBUTES OF LAND USE		TYPE OF LAND TENURE	
		COMMUNAL	INDIVIDUAL
A1	Value of production per unit area	Low	High
A2	Frequency and dependability of use or yield	Low	High
A3	Possibility of improvement or intensification	Low	High
A4	Area required for effective use	Large	Small
A5	Labor- and capital-investing groups	Large (voluntary association or community)	Small (individual or family)

SOURCE: Netting (1976)

Communal tenure "promotes both general access to and optimum production from certain types of resources while enjoining on the entire community the conservation measures necessary to protect these resources from destruction" (Netting 1976: 145). Although yields are relatively low, the land has maintained its productivity for many centuries, and land values have been among the highest in Switzerland. Overgrazing has been kept within tight controls. Not only has the commons been protected but the community has been enhanced by the construction and maintenance of commonly owned facilities. This study is a strong challenge to the empirical validity of either Hypnothesis H1 or H2. It does not appear necessary either to divide the commons into privately owned land or to place such land under a central, public authority to achieve development patterns that avoid overuse or underdevelopment of common resources.

Communal Tenure in Japanese Villages

In Japan, extensive common lands have existed and have been regulated by local village institutions for centuries. In an important study of traditional common lands in Japan, Margaret A. McKean (1984) estimates that about 12 million hectares of forests and uncultivated mountain plains were held and managed in common by thousands of rural villages during the Tokugawa period (1600–1867) and that about 3 million hectares are so managed in the 1980s. Although many villages have sold or divided their common lands, McKean (1984: 2) indicates that she has "not yet turned up an example of a commons that suffered ecological destruction while it was still a commons."

McKean provides both a general overview of the development of property law in Japan as well as a specific view of the rules developed in three Japanese villages—Hirano, Nagaike, and Yamanoka—for regulating the commons. The environmental conditions of the villages studied by McKean have a remarkable similarity to those of Törbel. The villages are also established on steep mountains where many microclimates can be distinguished. Peasant farmers cultivate their own private lands, raising rice, garden vegetables, and horses. The common lands in Japan produce a wide variety of valuable forest products, including timber, thatch for roofing and weaving, animal fodder of various kinds, decayed plants for fertilizer, firewood, and charcoal.

Each village in traditional times was governed by an assembly, usually composed of the heads of each of the households assigned political rights in the village. The basis for political rights differed from village to village. Rights were variously based on cultivation rights in land, on taxpaying obligations, and on ownership rights in land. In some villages almost all households had political rights and rights to the use of the commons. In others, these rights were more narrowly held (McKean 1984: 26).

Each village assembly established a relatively complex set of rules regulating both the use and enhancement of the village commons. Boundary rules clearly indicated which lands were held in common and which in private ownership. Entry rules unambiguously specified who was authorized to use the commonly owned land. Ownership of the uncultivated lands near a village devolved from the imperial court to the villages through several intermediate stages involving land stewards and locally based warriors. In the earlier systems the owners of local estates employed agents in each village and authorized these agents to regulate access to the uncultivated lands. As villages asserted their own rights to these lands in the late sixteenth century, they shared a clear image of which lands were private and which were held in common and the view that those lands held in common needed management in order to serve long-term interests of the peasant agriculturalists dependent upon them.

In traditional Japanese villages, the household was the smallest unit of account. Rights of access to the commonly held lands were accorded only to a household unit. Consequently, households with many family members had no advantages, and had considerable disadvantages, in terms of access to the commons. Population growth was extremely low and ownership patterns within villages were stable (McKean 1984: 29).

In addition to delimiting the ownership status of all lands, village assemblies also created detailed partitioning rules (Oakerson 1978) that specified in various ways how much of each valued product a household could harvest from the commons and under what conditions. For example, to enter a commons to collect plants, one might have to obtain an entry permit from the village authorities and abide by rules concerning the tools and methods used (see McKean 1984: 33 for more detail).

Rules were tailored to the specific needs of each village and the ecological condition of a particular commons. Villagers were also required to work to enhance and maintain the yield of the commons in collective work such as annual burning or specific cutting of timber or thatch. Each household had an obligation to contribute a share to such efforts (McKean 1984: 39). The establishment of rules, monitoring of behavior and of conditions in the commons, and the assignment of punishment were all conducted primarily in the villages. McKean concludes that the long-term success of these locally designed rules systems indicates "that it is not necessary for regulation of the commons to be imposed coercively from the outside" (1984: 56).

Comparison of the Two Cases

The McKean study complements and supports the Netting study, providing further evidence to reject Hypotheses 1 and 2 stated above. Small, isolated villages have been highly successful in two different regions of the world in creating communal systems for regulating common-pool resources.

The remarkable similarity in the environmental and economic patterns of the Swiss and Japanese villages tends to support Netting's argument about relationships between these patterns and land-tenure arrangements. Where the value of production per unit area, the frequency and dependability of use or yield, and the possibility of improvement and intensification are low; the area required for effective use is large; and a large group is needed for labor or capital investment, a form of communal land tenure is used in both the Swiss and the Japanese villages. Private ownership exists where intense cultivation of small areas of highly productive and dependable land can be organized by small family units.

There are, however, differences in institutional arrangements concerning land use. In both villages access to the commons depends on the inheritance (or purchase) or private land with associated rights to communal property. But the inheritance rules are different: equal division among all heirs is the Swiss rule, and nonpartible inheritance is the Japanese rule. There are also differences in opportunities to increase private or communal holdings. In the Swiss system, those with citizenship in the village can buy private land from siblings or other villagers who emigrate, enabling those who have been able to earn money from external jobs to greatly enhance their private holdings, which in turn affect their communal holdings (although the purchase of land beyond what was needed for household subsistence was a relatively poor investment [McGuire and Netting 1982]). In the Japanese system, although private holdings change as families split, each sibling receives a constant and unchanging allocation of private holdings as well as communal holdings.

The ability of individuals to emigrate also differed substantially. Although migration from Swiss villages has been more tightly restricted in some areas than in others, moving out of the village has been a realistic option for centuries. Movement from one village to another was far more tightly controlled in the Japanese villages of the Tokugawa period. Even traveling overnight to another village required prior approval from the village head and domain authorities (McKean 1984: 25). There may also have been differences in control by parents over entry to the land and the commons. In both settings, population growth was low but the reasons for it varied. Törbel's low rate depended heavily on emigration as well as late marriage, high rates of celibacy, and long birth intervals. In the Japanese villages the low rate was maintained by severe birth-control measures, including abortion and infanticide.

Given the differences in rules relating to inheritance, emigration, and the control by parents over entry to the commons, one cannot conclude that the full sets of rules related to land tenure in these similar economic and ecological environments were similar. Hypothesis H3a, the strongest version of the third hypothesis, is thus rejected. The evidence is instead consistent with Hypotheses H3b and H3c. (More extensive research would be needed to distinguish between these two.) "Communal" ownership was used in both settings to specify some of the rights and duties of participants related to similar types of economic activities and similar environmental conditions. The rather vague reference to communal ownership can be translated in both cases to mean the existence of the following two specific rules:

R1   Any co-owner of communally owned land can exclude any nonowner from consumptive use of this land. (This rule

converts the commons from a free and open-access resource to a system of true communal property [Ciriacy-
Wantrup and Bishop 1975; Runge 1983].)

R2 No co-owner of communally owned land can exclude any
other co-owner from use of this land as long as the use is
consistent with R_1 . . . R_n regarding timing and amount of
use.

The specific operational rules used to define timing and amount of
use differed. For example, in the Swiss village, rights in common
pasturage were distributed according to the number of cows that
could be overwintered using hay supplies produced on the owners'
meadows, a practice known elsewhere as "stinting." In the Japanese village, rights to pasture animals on the communal pasture
were simply distributed in equal shares to village households.
Moreover, each of the Japanese villages had developed a different
intricate array of specific regulations for the use of commonly
owned land.

It may be possible to produce coherent explanations for variation among some of the particular rules discussed (see, for example, McKean 1984: 33). One plausible explanation is that the
strictness of the rules governing access and use is closely related to
the relative scarcity of a particular use-unit in the commons. This
hypothesis, however, is not sufficiently robust to explain all the
differences among rules of access and use.

Rules governing property and inheritance often go far into the
cultural past, and although they may be adapted to ecological conditions, they did not necessarily originate from them (see, for example, Cole and Wolf 1974 for alpine villages in the same environment
with partible and impartible inheritance rules). An alternative hypothesis is that the rule currently in use is the first one adopted in
the village for which conformance is sufficiently high and the results sufficiently beneficial that villagers were satisfied with its consequences. Such a hypothesis is fully consistent with the view that
institutional rules start from a process of trial and error and are
changed by efforts to improve on the results through analysis and
design. Trial-and-error efforts combined with learning may produce quite different solutions to the same problems.

In both the Swiss and Japanese villages, people had to solve
the problem of limiting the total amount of use of the commons to

less than or equal to its sustainable yield. Both systems did this by limiting the use of the commons to those in the village, but within this general restriction they allocated the flow of benefits differently. Both systems had to solve the problem of granting rights to the next generation, but one opted for partible and the other for impartible inheritance. Both had to deal with problems brought about by population growth and limited resources, but as we have seen, the methods used to control population growth varied. Finally, both systems had to devise specific rules concerning access to and use of each type of consumption unit from the commons. The variety of rules used to accomplish this general task is very broad.

The ethnographic and historical studies reviewed are important to our understanding of the role of institutional arrangements in solving common-pool resource problems. Given the longevity of the locally designed rule systems described, we suspect that it is possible for those involved in a commons dilemma to arrive at a set of rules that enables them to keep total use within the limits of sustainable yield. We saw in both examples that neither developing fully individual property rights nor allocating control of the commons to a central, outside authority is necessary to solve the problem of resource overuse. These studies provide strong evidence against the assumption that there is only one institutional way to solve all problems related to common-pool resource systems.

The discussion of Netting's hypothesis that environmental and economic conditions "determine" the types of land tenure points to the dangers of simple acceptance of a deterministic view. Although Netting himself may not have intended the level of determinism stated in the "strong" version of this hypothesis, it is found in other studies. A simplistic acceptance of economic determinism can lead scholars to assume that all institutional change increases general social welfare and that the direction of change in all societies is toward an ever-improving economy.[1] The institutional rules used when changing other institutional rules may play as large a role in affecting the direction of future changes as the economic activities involved.

Several additional lessons can be learned from the Swiss and Japanese case studies. One relates to the importance of rules to complement cultural value patterns. All too frequently, analysts of common-pool problems assume that only a change in human value patterns or concepts of morality will lead to the type of behavioral change needed to avoid the tragedy of the commons. Alternatively, it is sometimes asserted that the tragedy of the commons only occurs in modern, westernized cultures. Members of these cultures are exhorted to emulate the "selfless" value systems of other cultures. Without denying the importance of cultural values, it is apparent that Japanese villagers have not been willing to rely entirely on socialization as a means of ensuring behavior that avoids the tragedy of the commons. McKean's own conclusion in this regard stresses the point.

> The Japanese experience also demonstrates that no rules are self-enforcing. Even though Japanese villagers had a strong community identity and were very concerned about social reputation and bonds with the group, and although they were capable of internalizing as a vital goal the preservation of the commons, even this most cooperative, compliant group of people were vulnerable to temptations to bend, evade, and violate the rules governing the commons. Thus there had to be a scheme of penalties and these had to be enforced. (McKean 1984: 54)

A second lesson relates to time. These systems were not created by a single sweeping administrative reform that set up local councils in all communities. The power of local villages to regulate their own common properties was wrested from feudal lords during an epoch of struggle. Trial-and-error methods could be used as villagers became aware of the consequences of the current rules. One can only speculate on the type of conclusions that an evaluation team might have expounded in 1603 upon examining the first two years of a Japanese village's efforts to regulate its newly acquired commons. No doubt considerable confusion still existed about who had access rights and for what purpose. Such a team might even have strongly urged that national authorities be asked to take over responsibility before the irresponsible villagers destroyed their valuable common property.

A third lesson relates the ease and capacity of monitoring behavior and performance. The villages were small, the commons they managed were nearby, and the local managers of the commons could directly observe how the rules they were using affected the yield of the commons. The rules in use were understood by the participants.

> Moreover, the villagers—certainly village elders and *kumi* chiefs, and probably heads of all households—thoroughly understood the direct relationship between the rules and the preservation of the commons. These people lived with the seasons and natural cycles and knew their commons very well. Every time I asked about the reason for a particular rule, my informants explained the rule in terms of environmental protection and fair treatment of all the villagers. There was always a sophisticated and sensible explanation, and never "well, we've always done it that way." Even if the village elders were the prime repositories of accumulated scientific knowledge of this sort, this information circulated regularly through the village. Obedience to the rules was almost certainly based on an appreciation of the value of the rules, and not merely on compliance to avoid penalties. (McKean 1984: 45)

The combination of sufficient time to learn how to create successful rule systems and the capacity to monitor the results at relatively low costs are probably major factors in the long-run success of these systems.

NOTES

This chapter is drawn from a paper presented at the 46th Annual Meeting of the American Society for Public Administration, Indianapolis, Indiana, March 23–27, 1985. I appreciate the useful comments made on the first draft by Ed Connerley, David Feeny, Margaret McKean, Robert Netting, Vincent Ostrom, Mark Sproule-Jones, and Norman Uphoff. I also appreciate the support received from the National Science Foundation through grant number NSF SES 83-09829.

1. An important intellectual tradition in economics has attempted to view institutional arrangements as inherent in an economic model rather than simply seeing institutional arrangements as external factors that help explain the processes and results of economic activities (see Davis and North 1971; Binswanger and Ruttan 1978; Hayami and Kikuchi 1982). The theoretical work has led to some careful empirical studies (see, for example, Feeny 1982 and Hayami and Kikuchi 1982)

whose evidence is consistent with Hypothesis H3c. In their empirical work and detailed theoretical discussion, these scholars are careful to stress not only factors leading to a demand for institutional change but factors affecting the supply of institutional innovations. Thus, the more recent work in this tradition has attempted to address the question of how suboptimal institutional arrangements evolve as well as improvements in institutional arrangements.

13 The Call to the Commons

DECLINE AND RECOMMITMENT IN ASTURIAS, SPAIN

J. W. Fernandez

Lo de común ye de ningun.
["That which is everybody's is nobody's."]
Asturian saying

THE GRAIN OF ASTURIAN FOLK WISDOM in this epigraph pithily anticipates Garret Hardin's (1968) exploration of the logically negative and systematically pejorative consequences of acquisitive individualism for community interests. Hardin's "tragedy of the commons" is one of the revelatory concepts in the literature of the human condition of the second half of the twentieth century. It may be more accurate to say that it has been revelatory in those parts of the West whose liberal instincts—in the economic sense of "liberal"—and whose confidence in technical solutions and the human capacity to create and administer rational systems of governance and distribution has not been effectively challenged, at least since Adam Smith's "invisible hand." Hardin's "invisible hand," the sum total of self-interested calculations (working on population and common resource use rather than industrial production), has quite a different consequence than Smith's.

The debate over the commons is much older than either Adam Smith or Garrett Hardin's thinking about the relationships between individualism and collective or systematic interests. The vicissitudes of the commons, the struggle for and against "agrarian individualism" (Bloch 1930), is a major theme of studies of the rural areas of Western Europe at least since the agronomist movement in mid-eighteenth-century England and France and its resonance in Spain from the 1830s on. In this chapter I examine aspects of the problem of the commons as it has arisen in the northern Spanish province of Asturias over the last several hun-

266

dred years and as it is present in Asturian villages in the 1970s and 1980s.

Despite the drastic decline of the commons in Asturias as elsewhere in Western Europe, it still exerts its call, its attraction. In Asturian villages a complex web of usufruct rights and communal obligations Thompson 1971, 1976) made manifest to the country people, more clearly than anything esle perhaps, the meaning of community (see Behar 1983 for a comparable analysis in neighboring León). I concentrate here on only some of these: for cooperative activities, *sextaferia*, *andecha*, and *esfoyaza*, and for use-rights, *derrota* and *vecera*. My interest in these practices is essentially Durkheimian. I want to see in what systematic way they convert individual interest into system interest, making the obligatory the desirable. The historical question, of course, is just the opposite: one wants to know the ways in which allegiance to the commons degenerated.

AGRARIAN INDIVIDUALISM AND THE CALL TO THE COMMONS

Insofar as anthropology is the discipline that seeks to derive general principles of human behavior and human nature, we are led to ask an anthropological question: What is it that inspires people to take an interest in a superordinate system that surely surpasses their immediate everyday and inevitably self-oriented sense of reality? What is it about the commons that is worth preserving or restoring? Despite the triumph of agrarian individualism in Western Europe, that question has not receded. Societies vary in the feelings of mutual obligation and willingness to sacrifice for the common good that they instill in their members. In Western Europe, the struggle over agrarian individualism was in a profound sense a struggle over society's obligations to instill just these feelings and enforce that willingness. In England, for example, the struggle for and against enclosure of common lands since the Middle Ages was fought out over the right of the Crown or Parliament to inspire or impose respect for the commons—by means of statutes, acts, commissions, tillage laws, and so on—against increasingly laissez-faire attitudes appropriate to an Adam Smithian view of the world.

The enclosure debates were couched mainly in terms of

entrepreneurial freedom and production efficiency on the one hand, and depopulation, unemployment, and rural misery on the other. Behind these issues were questions of society's role in the enforcement of obligation so as to assure respect for the commons. And behind these questions, in turn, was the issue of what it is about the commons that seemed to be worth preserving or restoring. More than economics was at stake. From the mid-nineteenth century on, the appearance of various kinds of Commons Preservation Societies—in the interest mainly of that modern use-right, public recreation—testifies to how dignifying, humanizing, revitalizing, regenerating the commons is still felt to be.

ASSAULTS ON THE COMMONS IN ANDALUSIA AND ASTURIAS

The tragedy of the commons is not only a tragedy for resources. It is also a tragedy having to do with the loss of the commons, its appropriation for private use, and the consequent destructive impact upon human relations. A well-known example of this second and perhaps more authentic tragedy of the commons occurred in Andalusia, southern Spain (Gilmore 1980). There the medieval and early modern rights of the poor and subtenant classes to rent and cultivate common arable lands, to pasture on common pasturage, and to gather on and otherwise exploit the wastes were gradually withdrawn from them by connivance between the nobility and prosperous farmers. The use of these lands, along with the right to pasture animals on the stubble of private croplands ("free forage," or *derrota*) were rights basic to the well-being of the lower strata. Their loss because of various kinds of enclosure was a primary factor leading to the rural poverty of Andalusia in the nineteenth century and the conflict-ridden agrarian crisis that has continued to plague this area of Spain.

Asturias has also seen recurrent assaults on the commons. However, the conditions and outcomes are different from those of Andalusia. For a variety of reasons having to do with (1) rough mountainous terrain containing extensive wastes, (2) relative absence of large manorial or seigneurial possession, (3) a large class of privileged freemen (*hidalgos*), (4) a mixed agricultural-pastoral lifeway coupled with late-nineteenth- and early-twentieth-century industrialization (mining), the Asturian assault upon the commons did not result in a dispossessed class of rural proletariat or the disappearance of common land. When the commons was individualized it was done without pauperization of the kind experienced in Andalusia, and much common land remains.

From very early medieval times village-level tension existed between private and public lands, with a tendency for the latter to be converted into the former. The Fuero of Llanes granted to a town by that name in eastern Asturias in 1168 by Alfonso IX recognizes two classes of property, individual and collective, and strives to maintain a distinction between the two lest the latter collapse into the former. It also recognizes the right, under the pressure of population increase, for the individual to extend into the collective through *presura* and *escalio*, the ancient or at least early medieval right to make use of unused or common-use land by clearing, occupancy, and cultivation. In Asturias the right was generally limited to four years, after which the land was to return to common use, but as long as land was relatively abundant, as it has been in most parts of Asturias, this occupancy tended to become lifelong or permanent. Private lands thereby expanded into the commons.

Another assault on the commons resulted from expanding seigneurial claims. Over the centuries, monasteries, abbeys, military orders, and the nobility were given large land grants throughout Asturias. Perhaps as much as fifty percent of the providence fell under their jurisdiction (Anes 1977). At times seigneurial entities were also given rights to expand agricultural production into uncultivated areas. This trend was particularly evident in the thirteenth century (Ruiz de la Pena 1981) and later in the seventeenth century, when the novelty of maize cultivation led to a departure from extensive cultivation, the abandonment of fallowing, and further population increase in both man and animals. The result was local pressure on land and intense struggle between the seigneurial elite and local groups with parochial or *concejo* perspectives over land use and rights.

The late seventeenth and early eighteenth centuries were times of particular struggle over the commons. At one point the Royal Junta of Castilla sent a judge to Asturias to investigate the complaints; he stayed more than two years. In most cases he found against the "powerful" and in favor of the "poor villagers and parishioners" (Anes 1977). Though his judgments were subsequently challenged successfully by the elite, his efforts in favor of the commons were not forgotten.

In the nineteenth century two laws of disentailment[1] also worked against common land and the commoners. One acted to sell off seigneurial land, mostly of the church, into private hands, mostly of the wealthy. The second helped villagers acquire land but also sought to sell off common lands belonging to municipalities. This infringement of long-established municipal commons prompted strong village reactions. Tension over the control of parish commons among villagers, municipal governments, and organs of the state continues. By the 1970s the state conservation agency, ICONA (Instituto Nacional por La Conservación de la Naturaleza), with its interest in the rational use of the forest and mountain commons of Spain, had become the chief object of village antagonism.

Although the predominant trend has been agrarian individualism and privatization of land, communal land in the form of uplands and mountains for public use (*monte de utilidad pública*) remains. Approximately 27 percent of the province is so designated. The really mountainous communities have as much as 50 to 60 percent, mostly precipitous, rocky, or high windswept barrens incapable of supporting more than a brief summer's pasturage. In every community there is, however, potentially arable common land. Because of rural population exodus there is virtually no pressure to clear, enclose, and cultivate it by *presura* and *escalio*.

Considerable common land remains. Moreover, there have been recurrent attempts to defend and reclaim the commons. The vicissitudes of the commons in Asturias is instructive in its own way with respect to the regeneration and degeneration of human relationships—which is what the call to the commons is mainly about.

The Call to the Commons: Three Cases

The communal and cooperative institutions that will be described are moribund or have entirely disappeared in the Asturian countryside. But even when they are vestigial they have a psychological reality, as a testimony of something meaningful, and they can provide us with useful data, as shown in these three cases:

1.   In the post-Franco era, neighborhood associations (*Asociación de Vecinos*) have sprung up in the cities, towns, and countryside of Asturias. Between 1978 and 1980 the Municipality of Aller saw the passage of fifteen of these associations through municipal approval and into provincial charter. The thrust of the associations has come mainly from the political left although the most successful have tried to remain apolitical. This is a necessity in rural areas with large conservative factions.

In Aller the membership of the Asociación de Vecinos de El Carmín de Felechosa has, since 1977, come to include more than 75 percent of the families in the village and more than 55 percent of the adult population. The presence of a dynamic outsider, a socialist schoolteacher, was important in the organization, but villagers responded strongly, particularly those families with coal miners as members. Projects were undertaken quickly: refurbishing and painting a decaying schoolbuilding; establishing an adult social center; building new quarters for the visiting doctor; repairing plaza foundations; building sidewalks; paving streets. All of this and more occurred in a town which in its very recent past had been devoted mostly to animal husbandry, a lifeway that had become family-oriented and not very civic-minded, certainly not with regard to the development of public space. No doubt the miners' presence was important. The solidarity and potential for coordinated interaction of the miners' ethos was central to the association's success.

The old institution of communal prestation called *sextaferia* was revived by the Asociación for projects beyond the scope of small groups of unemployed men paid with association funds. *Sextaferia* applies mainly to work, by communal prestation, on hamlet roads and wagon paths and for general village improvement. For example, water shortage in Aller in the summers of 1979 and 1980 triggered long and turbulent debates about who or what was to blame and who had responsibility for solving it. A young, unemployed miner defused the debate by calling for *sextaferia*—"as our grandfathers did"—in repairing leaks in the water supply system. Ten men volunteered. In two days they had repaired the leaks, and the water supply increased by 20 percent.

2. In the same municipality around the same post-Franco period another social group was formed. Some twenty young and middle-aged professionals with village origins but living in more urban areas of Asturias formed the association *Amigos de la Escanda*. Their purpose was to meet to plant, cultivate, and harvest the spelt wheat (*escanda*) that was formerly the typical cereal of the Asturian Catabrian slopes but had been almost entirely abandoned. Their motive was nostalgic celebration of traditional practices. The planting, cultivating, and harvesting was to be done in *andecha*, which meant cooperative and convivial work in the difficult tasks associated with cultivating spelt wheat. After the *andecha* harvest, the group capped a yearly round of meetings with a large banquet of traditional dishes, particularly *pan de escanda*, spelt wheat bread, formerly the blessed bread of church portal distribution, religious processions, and church portal auctions.

After several years the task of coordinating the schedules of so many professional people proved too difficult and the plan of cooperative harvesting and bread preparation was abandoned. Only a handful showed up for the *andecha*. Eventually the group changed its name to *Amigos de Aller* and settled on one banquet a year, accompanied by lectures and papers on traditional topics, that celebrated their accession to the professional elite.

3. The third instance of reassertion of claims of the common or of activity in common is expressed in forceful though surreptitious actions: the burning of public forests in the *monte*. The common lands of the mountains were largely under local parish or municipal control until the mid-nineteenth century, when this control was alienated and given to more central authority. Since then there have been periodic village attempts to reassert local control, attempts principally to block entrance into common mountain pastures of cattle from other villages that traditionally had not had grazing rights there. Often the Civil Guard had to be sent in.

In the twentieth century the government planted pine forests in selected uplands in an attempt to maximize income from wastelands. These forests became the object of local antagonism. Periodic attempts were made to burn them and return the *monte* to potential summer grazing for the community. In the 1960s and 1970s the government agency ICONA became the target. The new conservation ethic of the period made ICONA particularly vigilant about local mountain use, particularly fires. Periodically during my fieldwork, fires were set by unknown villagers or allowed to escape control by known villagers, destroying some mountain pine forest or scrub growth. In so humid a climate, naturally caused raging fires are unlikely. Nonetheless, significant amounts of upland were, in effect, thus returned to grazing commons.

The Regeneration of Cooperation

These three instances of the resurrection of moribund cooperative practices in the Asturian countryside show important differences and yet a common practical and symbolic theme. The first was a practical attempt to use the force of tradition to stimulate communal effort. But there was also a symbolic appeal being made in the call for allegiance to an ancestral lifeway and the cooperative activity characteristic of it. The second was a nostalgic attempt to recapture and celebrate the virtues of rural life by a group of people who, because of their professional responsibilities and urban lives, felt increasingly alienated from their rural roots. Their effort, with its focus upon spelt wheat and spelt wheat bread, was more concerned with symbolic issues than with practical matters and indeed foundered on practical problems. The final case was a gesture both symbolic and practical: a protest against government control of public forestland, against its alienation from local use and control, and an attempt to return that land to the possibility of summer pasturage.

The use of, search for, and celebration of a communal heritage and the cooperative traditions of the past is one of the major themes of our times. It may be a theme of any historically situated people propelled by acquisitive individualism and/or rationalized bureaucratization—that is, by "modernization"—away from small communities and the cooperative endeavors and well-understood reciprocal obligations supposed to be characteristic of them.

The "Lost Commons" in Spanish Social and Intellectual History

Nostalgia for the imagined conviviality and diffuse solidarity of the past—the commons embedded in human relationships—and the desire to put them into practice again is by no means confined to the Asturian countryside. Nor is it confined to the twentieth century. It is a recurrent theme in Spanish social and intellectual history. The late-nineteenth-century work of Joaquin Costa (1902, 1915) on the history of collectivist thought in Spain and on collectivist agricultural practices and collectivism in customary law was based on the work of other Spanish writers dating back to the fifteenth century. Three of these early writers were not only statesmen and national political figures of their time but also Asturians, who maintained close association with Asturian rural life and derived support for their arguments from close observations made upon it.[2] Their centrality in Costa's work argues for the enduring preoccupation with the question of the commons in Asturias.

In the twentieth century the theme of the lost rural community is taken up again by the Asturian legal historian Ramón Prieto Bances. In a series of collected studies (1976) Prieto Bances uses parochial legal codes, or *ordenanzas*, and other materials to delineate the nature of the Asturian rural community in the past. He sees it as comprised of extended families bonded by a strong sense of neighborliness (*vecindad*) that materialized in institutions such as the *andecha*, in which neighbors gave freely of their help in the harvest or in the care of the sick, the old, and the needy.

The "large family" of the rural community was embedded in a larger, Christian one, localized in the reality of the parish and in a rural class structure defined mostly in terms of generous patrimony and patronage. This rural conviviality was shattered by the doctrinaire policies of the nineteenth century working through disentailment of seigneurial rights over land and through bureaucratic centralization. Prieto Bances interpreted the *ordenanzas* as local attempts to preserve community autonomy and reassert the reciprocal responsibilities of community life in the face of threats to them, such as the Law of Municipal Centralization in 1845. They were an attempt to reassert an image of community life that Prieto Bances, a hundred years later, could easily read out of them.

Other images, including that of cultural geographer García Fernández (1976), showed instead a system of domination and subordination in which the propertied classes greatly benefited, rather than a patrimony structured along family lines down which resources flowed with distributive justice. It was the propertied classes after all who had the power and influence to organize rural life by effecting *ordenanzas* at parochial and provincial levels. This organization was to their benefit in appropriating the surplus values generated by the rural community.

From the 1870s on, images of exploitation and of systematic failures in communal cooperation and equitable reciprocity arose in conjunction with the industrialization of Asturias. It is not our purpose here to pursue the idea and image of the commons in the industrial milieu or the rise there of militant class consciousness and other pejorative visions of traditional distributive and administrative justice. What is important is that the commons remained a central and motivating image as seen in the short-lived but nationally reverberant October Revolution of 1934 in Asturias, the first socialist revolution in the history of Spain. It is sufficient to say that this revolution aimed at establishing, or regenerating, nothing less than the *comuna Asturiana* (Diaz-Nosty, 1975). Let us turn to some of the traditional communal (and cooperative) institutions that lie behind these recent attempts at restoring community.

TRADITIONAL COOPERATIVE INSTITUTIONS

Sextaferia

Sextaferia, long recognized in local laws, is the most active of the various cooperative institutions to be considered here. The provincial press in the 1970s has reported on hamlets that built roads from their isolated locations or performed some other communal effort by means of *sextaferia*. The term applies mainly to work, by communal prestation, on hamlet roads and wagon paths, but it is also used for work toward general village improvement. It is understood as a system whose purpose is creating or maintaining routes of communication between neighbors (*vecinos*), between *vecinos* and their fields and upper pastures, and between the collectivity of neighbors and other collectivities. Its communicative importance derives from the problems of a land of *minifundia*—many scattered plots of family property—and scattered small hamlets in a steep mountain landscape with many watercourses.

The church may have played a role in the origin or the systematization of *sextaferia* in Asturias. The term is the Christian ordinal day name for Friday, the sixth day of the week, perhaps reflecting efforts to make communal prestation part of an orderly religious week: setting aside Friday for communal work as Sunday was set aside for worship. The church was less than successful in defining the day or clarifying whether the locus of responsibility was the household or all able-bodied men between eighteen and sixty-five.

In 1835 the central government tried to impose clearer definitions of *sextaferia*, particularly of the structures of authority for overseeing the work. However, in so doing it vitiated the autonomy of the institution[3] and brought to the fore a problem of the centralized state. It created an attitude of "let the municipality or the state do it" (*"¡Que lo facen ellos!"*). The *alcalde* of a barrio in Aller who otherwise took pride in *sextaferia* resisted calling it when it seemed possible that the government might contract out the job. Calling *sextaferia* usually provoked disgruntlement among his neighbors. In 1835 and thereafter it proved much easier to proclaim local initiative than to recapture it by the systematization of rules from above.

Sextaferia has always been subject to abuses and unsystematic procedures. In his recommendation of the custom, which was almost uniquely Asturian, to Carlos IV, Jovellanos (1753) nevertheless pointed to some of these abuses. One was that some members of the community (for example, the ecclesiastics) claimed privilege or used an absence to avoid their obligations. Another concerned unequal contributions to the task: a man with a wagon contributed more than an ordinary workman. These abuses reflected problems of rural class structure.

Another abuse was that of using *sextaferia* to force people to do road work on private, ecclesiastical, or seigneurial roads or on roads that manifestly were the state's to maintain. A problem that has plagued *sextaferia* since nineteenth-century centralization is how the commons on which the work was to be performed was to be defined, falling as it does between private property and state property. As the commons itself shriveled in size, the question became ever more difficult to answer. People often resisted the call to *sextaferia* on the basis that it was work that belonged either to proprietors or to the state. During the Franco regime, the state's attempt to exert control for conservation and communal purposes over the upland commons of Asturias acted to further reduce the villagers' sense of the common in whose service they might be called upon to work *sextaferia.*

The *ordenanzas* frequently mention fines for nonparticipation, but these apparently were rarely applied. The commitment to this call to the commons was otherwise motivated. Some communities were constantly attentive to men in *sextaferia,* stopping to observe their work, joking with them, sending food out to them, and making their work reverberant in the community. Some villages had particularly rich folklore—jokes, work songs, rhymed verses (*coplas*)—useful for making the communal effort more pleasant. Some had priests, *alcades,* and other men and women of perceptive and persuasive powers who could evoke and envision the common weal. Such cultural factors were crucial to a successful *sextaferia* and the conviviality it achieved. The repeated codification of rules did not address these factors.

A recent example of *sextaferia* suggests that the custom has very much to do with reproduction, in the social sense surely, and perhaps the biological sense as well. The custom was used by isolated hamlets in Gamonedo in the Peaks of Europe, eastern Asturias, to build a road over very steep ground in a little over two years of intermittent effort. Then in the summer of 1981 the young men of the lower hamlets of this municipality gathered in *sextaferia* over several days to cement in a plaza to provide an all-weather dance floor. They were motivated by demographic accident: there was a ratio of only two young women to twenty marriageable young men in the community. *Sextaferia* made the town attractive on festival days to marriageable young women. Although that seems to be a special goal, the much greater investment of time in prestation for the all-weather road was intended to make the parish attractive as a year-round residence, particularly for young couples whose tendency it is to escape the isolation and migrate to the seacoast towns and cities.

Andecha and *Esfoyaza*

The increasing assertion of the powers of the state over collective matters and the commons tended, we see, to vitiate local initiative. State interest in *sextaferia* helped to preserve it, whereas

other cooperative institutions in which the state had little interest
have almost entirely disappeared. *Andecha* and *esfoyaza* and similar
institutions are systems of cooperation less evidently tied to larger
systems. They were systems of mutual aid in the countryside, and
their record is mainly found in the folk literature of proverb,
maxim, song, and poem rather than the literature of rural *ordenanzas* and *reglamentos*. These institutions are evocative and are
nostalgically recalled even though no longer practiced. Their evoca-
tiveness and nostalgia arise from the commensality almost always
involved and from the relationships between the sexes that these
institutions facilitated.

Andecha   *Andecha* is a practice accompanying the difficult harvesting of the spelt wheat of Asturias, the only wheat that grows
well in the upland areas and the mountains. It is spiny, double-
shelled wheat difficult to remove from the stalk and to thresh free.
It is harvested with two sticks tied together at one end that are
clamped around the spikes of wheat. The spikes are then yanked
off into large baskets. *Andecha* is also associated with the threshing
of the wheat by cooperating groups of men. In the zones with
which we are familiar both men and women participated in a day-
long activity. There was a certain complementarity, men preceding
in the harvesting row and women following after gleaning. The
day's work was followed by a large meal and a dance (see Castanon 1970). In a more general sense, *andecha* refers not only to
help with the harvest but to help with other arduous tasks of rural
production (Prieto Bances 1976, 2:1177–1204). Often it was help
offered by the able-bodied to those afflicted by sickness, old age,
or other loss associated with moral obligation.

A spirit of challenge and competition was part of the evoca-
tiveness of *andecha*: who would discover a certain insect or bird's
nest, a double or triple spike? *Andecha* in the field relieved the
work of the day. Curdled milk was given as prizes for work done.
The work was accompanied by song and poems often invented
especially for this work and expressive of its convivial and competitive atmosphere. One senses that a good deal of cultural creation and celebration of village culture went on. Comments—folk,
literate, and academic—suggest that the games and festivity of
andecha often took precedence over the quality and quantity of the
work performed.[4]

The folklore emphasizes the sexual relationships facilitated, as in this *cantar* recalled by old people. It is understood that a young man is speaking to a woman. The word "to gather" is understood metaphorically, as are the forked harvest sticks:

> I'm not going to *andecha*
> Because I don't have the harvest sticks.
> Lend me yours
> And we will go gather alone.
> *[Translation by the author]*

The folklore also emphasizes the festive, suggesting the importance of the reciprocal, social element of the activity as an expression of the autochthony and conviviality of the rural community (Prieto Bances 1976). But as we have seen, this and other collective institutions have also been interpreted (García Fernández 1976) as either promoted by propertied classes to increase production or used by countrymen to gain some margin over the double demand of meeting rental obligations and minimal family needs. The poverty of the daily rural diet made the abundant food offered after *andecha* another attraction to the participants. Reciprocity was not involved, García Fernández argues, as most villagers did not have either the property or the food surpluses to justify calling *andecha*.

The other sense of the term *andecha*—help given to the needy, sick, and aged on any occasion—is closer to contemporary reflections of countrymen. Although it may often have been the case that only a few village families had large enough landholdings in property or tenancy to need and be able to call *andecha*, any villager could benefit from *andecha* in this second sense. Here also the literature tends to argue the gratuitous and nonreciprocal nature of this aid. But informants emphasize at least the mutuality, if not the reciprocality, of aid. They take a very long view of the life cycle. The aid one lends now to a needy neighbor will be reciprocated later at a time of one's own need.

Esfoyaza One understanding of the origin of *andecha* (Jovellanos 1753) derives the word from the Latin *indicta*, "to point out." Participation in *andecha* of both kinds seems to have been brought about first by being "fingered" and thus made aware of an obligation or responsibility to work, which was resisted, although not as much as *sextaferia*. The folklore of *esfoyaza*, cooperative cornhusking bees, gives no instance of resistance or any indication that these affairs were the privileges of certain village families. *Esfoyaza* was a cooperative institution of more spontaneous convivial quality, and in modern times it is a metaphor for any happy productive gathering of people and things.

Commensality and courtship were part of *esfoyaza*, also. Roasted chestnuts, hazelnuts, and cider were provided. Games typically involved the discovery of colored or black grains of corn followed by the embracing of a chosen member of the opposite sex. Humor focused on ears of corn, which young men poked at or tossed at young women. The conviviality of the occasion and the solidarity that it achieved rested in good part on the contact between the sexes that it facilitated or recalled.

The Limits of Reciprocity   One elemental commitment and primordial source of solidarity is the mutually shared need to recreate society and to find occasions to do so. Cooperative harvesting becomes an excellent occasion for doing so, for celebrating and facilitating the reciprocal relations of the sexes upon which, in the end, interfamily solidarity is based.[5] The call to the common threshing ground out of which the seed of the next generation is produced is powerful indeed. With regeneration in mind, the individual recognizes his isolation and readily enlists himself in cooperative activities that, whatever other purposes they might serve, offer the opportunity to find common ground with those in whom he can invest himself in such a way as to reproduce himself.

At the same time the question of the nature of these cooperative systems and their self-sufficiency and subservience to larger systems should be raised. García Fernández (1976) points us toward questions of property rights and the relation of private property to the commons. Property relations in the villages were part and definitive of a larger system that retained its legitimacy on the basis of objectively unjust and largely symbolic systems of reciprocity—for example, seigneurial protection in exchange for surplus agricultural production.

In contrast, the reciprocity found in the cooperative institutions reviewed was very elementary. There was a general sense that able-bodied adults, especially younger ones, should take turns in going to *sextaferia*. There was a sense that those house-

holds that were able should reciprocate and take turns in the holding of *andecha*. And there was the sense that *esfoyaza* should
circulate around the village. Two other cooperative institutions of
Asturias, *la derrota* and *la vecera*, involved a more complex, codified set of reciprocal relationships that are better interpreted
within the context of privatization of the commons and the rise of
agrarian individualism.

Derrota and *Vecera*

La derrota and *la vecera* are cooperative pasturing institutions
that represent continuing claims upon the commons in the face of
privatization of land and the individualization or familization of
production. Each has declined or disappeared in Asturias, but the
underlying principle of reciprocal responsibility for the supervision of grazing remains. They are systems of administering the
commons that take individual or state property claims into account but seek to interpose the rights of the community against
them.

Vecera   The *vecera* is the custom of communally supervised
grazing by the taking of turns or by the communal payment of a
herder or drover. It is still widely practiced in the neighboring
province of León in the 1980s but is rarely practiced in Asturias. It
appears in the *ordenanzas* of Aller and is remembered by villagers.
The principle of reciprocating responsibility in the supervision of
grazing is the center of more elaborate institutions of *mancommunidad* that have appeared here and there in the Asturian summer
grazing zones. Agreements of *mancommunidad* enabled parishes
and towns to defend upland commons lying between parishes or
municipalities. They also dealt with alternating pasturing rights
and reciprocating obligations to supervise summer herds.

Derrota   In the *derrota*, still found in some parts of Asturias,
what is private land becomes, after harvest, common until the
next planting. While common, it is open to grazing by animals
owned by others in the community. The *ordenanzas* of Aller fix
precisely, by saints' days, the entrance and exit of the animals. The
term *derrota* refers especially to the throwing down of the gates

after the first picking of the corn or scything of the hay. The term thus implies the breaking into privately owned lands *en cultivo*, or in pasturage, opening them up to common grazing.

The near disappearance of *la derrota* in Asturias corresponds to a shift away from grain cultivation to forage crops in the late nineteenth and early twentieth centuries in response to commercialization of meat and milk production. Increased emphasis on meat and milk productivity brought the decline of stubble grazing, which was replaced by more intensive feeding methods.

The *derrota* may have represented a continued claim upon common lands that had been privatized through *presura* and *escalio* or by other means. The custom was, as Joaquin Costa (1915) argues, part of a transition between agrarian communitarianism and modern agrarian individualism. To San Miguel (1956), on the other hand, it was a reasoned attempt by landowners and renters to preserve some of the labor-efficiency advantage of pasturage in common as the commons themselves receded. The *derrota* saved individual families the burden of constant supervision of their animals or of hiring this supervision out to be done. With the disappearance of the *derrota* from most rural zones in Asturias, the care of cattle—the day-in and day-out, year-round responsibility of shifting them among widely scattered meadows—has put a burden on families captured in the phrase *la esclavitude de las vacas:* "enslavement by the cattle."

LESSONS FROM THE COMMONS EXPERIENCE

From the communitarian point of view the evolution of the commons in Asturias qualifies as a tragedy. Everywhere, with such exceptions and survivals as we have noted, family-centered rural production seems to be the norm. For most Asturians the saying in the chapter's epigraph is taken in this sense: "As the commons belongs to no one, anyone is entitled to use it as he can for his own best purposes." Whereas the *ordenanzas* mandated the periodic cleaning of public ways, riversides, and riverbeds through *sextaferia*, these commons, when they lie beyond limited municipal supervision, have become trash heaps for the furtive dumping of garbage. Whereas *andecha* brought families together in cooperative labor in an atmosphere of conviviality and courtship, television now separates them, dance halls and discos and pubs privatize courtship, and patronal festivals tend toward desultory entertainment overwhelmed by blaring loudspeakers. Whereas the *derrota* asserted common and community interest against private property, cattle raising has become very much a private enterprise.

Nevertheless, the commons still exerts its call. The awareness periodically asserts itself that it belongs to everyone. The hope periodically arises for a new or revitalized social contract that will bring country folk together on a common ground that is not simply a marketplace. Tuero Beltrand, an Asturian student of these collective institutions, ends his review of them by pointing out how much they once contributed to the distinctive personality of the Asturian landscape (Tuero Beltrand 1976: 165). He also suggests in a general way that their characteristics are worth considering and their study is justified in itself. Can we be more specific? Can our knowledge of these institutions of the past inform the future? The lessons are not easily derived and require some rethinking.

1. THE INDIVIDUAL AND THE SYSTEM: Almost all modern, Western social science lies in the context of Mandeville and Adam Smith, who showed how utilitarian individualism—individuals pursuing their own best interests—produced, by means of markets, an impressive and intricately constructed social system. The first question we asked of these materials was, What is the relation between individual and system interests? The received answer, of course, was that there need be no system interest; the system produces itself by the invisible hand. It is the job of social science to discover these self-produced systems, especially when they seem to lead not to the wealth but to the pollution of nations.

There are difficulties in bringing our discussion to bear upon the question of individual and system. First, in the Asturian historical materials we are really not dealing with individuals but rather with households that have corporate character (see Freeman 1972). It is the household (*hogar*) and its representation (*vecino*) that hold responsibility for cooperative, communal action. So we are already dealing with the individual embedded in a cooperative system in which he has natural interest, and upon which he can fall back when the attraction toward larger systems fails.

Nevertheless, the motivation of the household to join the cooperative activities discussed above poses problems similar to those of
the individual's engagement with the system. The household must
take a more complex social dynamic into account, that of its members; it has greater self-sufficiency, but it is not entirely self-suffi-
cient. It must engage itself with the system to reproduce itself.

A second difficulty is that of identifying self-interest in any economic sense in these institutions. One of the chief attractions for
participation was their conviviality, especially in commensality and
courtship. These varieties of "social euphoria" are usually seen as
the consequence and not the cause of interaction. But Asturians
were often motivated to engage in *sextaferia* and *andecha* because of
the promised conviviality and commensality. They were in that
sense revitalizing experiences. These psychophysiological states
are important payoffs for the work invested, and may be the fundamental ones.

2.   METAPHORS OF RECIPROCITY: Reciprocity of one kind or another defines a successfully functioning system of cooperation.
Without its presence or promise, participants quickly defect (see
Axelrod and Hamilton 1981). At the level of the *ordenanzas* we can
identify some of the systematics of these institutions although we
must be cautious about their actual operations. It has been difficult, however, for either anthropologist or informant to identify
reciprocity in them.

Our materials push us to a different and longer-term notion of
reciprocity, following Annette Weiner (1980). She argues that our
customary analysis of "norms of reciprocity as a core principle of
social systems" is too concerned with discrete acts of giving and
receiving. Her premise is that norms of reciprocity must be seen as
part of a larger system in which the reproduction or regeneration
of persons, objects, and relationships is primary. The observations
of A. I. Hallowell (1955), including his view that the modern conception of the world as mechanism has been too influential in anthropology, influence her thinking. Counterposed are views of the
world as alive and flourishing yet susceptible to death and decay
and as a consequence, we might add, constantly in need of revitalizing. We need to think about an animate world view, she tells
us, in which the life cycle of persons and things is primary and
regeneration is preoccupying.

This animate world view was, and to some degree still is, central to Asturian villages. Indeed such a world view and its emphasis on the stages of the life cycle and ultimate death, plus conditional resurrection, was assiduously cultivated by the church, which was central in motivating some of the institutions we have depicted. To say of these institutions that they were convivial and revitalizing is to use terms resonant with this animate world view. But what does the commons have to do with this animate world view?

In the most elementary sense, certain of these institutions provided unique opportunities for courtship and thus for regeneration. Activity in, upon, and for the commons is an investment that is reproductive and regenerating because it maintains the pathways by which regeneration and reproduction can take place. It provides an arena for the celebration and reproduction of cultural commonalities and it promises enduring interactive commitment.

Humans—like most organisms, it seems—will engage in cooperative activities, even when the payoff is not very clear and certainly not immediate for some of the parties participating, as long as there is an expectation that the interaction has long-term and enduring potential (Axelrod and Hamilton 1981: 1395). The commons gives that guarantee as no other arena or engagement can—certainly not contracts between private persons and properties, even those contracts lasting "three lives plus twenty-seven years" typical of seigneurial land leasings in an older Spain. However long these contracts, they were still tied to the life cycle.

3. DEFECTION: The nineteenth and twentieth centuries have seen defection *en masse* from the institutions we have discussed. This is epitomized in the shift from a commons that was everyone's to a commons that is no one's. Why? We know that there were many abuses in the systems that were resented by participants and that raised questions about equality of participation and how the commons was defined in relation to private and state property. When there is uncertainty about who will participate and whose commons is involved, and where others seem to be cooperating, defection is likely.

The expansion of the scale of human relations in the last century has brought the countrymen fully into a market and money economy and has promoted defection. It opened up villagers to other ways of doing things, and it reduced the church's epistemological powers of explanation. This happened slowly and unevenly in the Asturian countryside, but it gradually intruded on the moralizing ability of the local priest to motivate cooperative acts or acts of benevolence and mutual aid. At the same time, the short-term contractual relationships of the market economy tended to shift mentalities away from an animate orientation embedded in the life cycle to a more mechanical one focused on a present marked by marketing operations and not by human passages. Finally, as has been often enough said, when country folk engage in market economies they are politically marginalized and ontologically decentered. Decisions that exploit them are made elsewhere, not to mention the products they increasingly covet, and their participation gradually convinces them that the preponderant reality is elsewhere. The belief that the center of gravity is outside the community can be an important cause for defection. The suspicion that one's cooperating partners are dependent on or in the service of third parties whose interests do not really enter into the cooperation affects its quality and makes defection more likely. This is one of the destructive effects of any kind of patronage system. Alienating influences have long been experienced by Asturians, and have been enhanced in their effects by a long history of emigration that has, in turn, increased the decentering of reality.

Finally, we have mentioned the effects of the disentailment laws of the nineteenth century, which helped privatize land and led the assault upon the commons. Disentailment represents a significant assault on cooperativism by moving against the arena in which cooperation best takes place and creating on ethics and atmosphere that promotes contractual obligation rather than cooperative opportunity.

PRINCIPLES FOR A NEW SOCIAL CONTRACT

Some of the cooperative and commons institutions of Asturias are still practiced sporadically in the 1980s. Most are remembered with nostalgia. We have tried to relate our materials to one of the most pertinent of contemporary ideas: the tragedy of the commons. True, we have been concerned more with the tragedy of the abandonment of the commons than with the tragedy of its degradation, though these are related processes. We have also been concerned with propensities to reciprocate or defect from cooperation and with convictions about the necessary presence of the commons.

Our discussion also relates to the *regenerationalismo* of such recurrent interest in Spain. Articles regularly appear in the Asturian press in defense of the commons. If we were "present at the creation" of a new social contract—and "regenerationalists are always present at that possibility"—we would have some ideas to offer and some anthropological principles to take into account:

1.   Contracts based on individual or corporate-group interest and not on system interest lead to degradation of the commons.

2.   Although a social system without a commons is conceivable, the commons is the only satisfactory arena for truly long-term, confident cooperative acts. It is the only truly convivial arena. A convivial society will mandate the preservation of its commons and contract periodic cooperative activities upon it.

3.   The value of conviviality is based on the requirement for regeneration imposed by the life cycle, and on the need for the reproduction of cultural goods imposed by the evanescence of memory.

4.   Humans will most reliably participate in cooperative institutions when they see some possibility of regenerating themselves or reproducing the culture with which they are most intimately associated.

5.   Reproduction and regeneration carried out on common ground are essentially convivial acts of mutual investment and aid.

6.   Social contracts based on the metaphor of the life cycle and on an animate world view are less susceptible to defection than contracts based on the metaphor of short-term contractual objection and a mechanistic world view.

7.   Contracts are not written in a vacuum but at historic phases in the dynamic interaction of dependency and autonomy. Awareness of these swings of commitment is essential in the writing of an enduring contract. The writing of a contract is always the

negotiation of contraries in a situation in which parties are centered or decentered. Contracts written too much in the spirit of the times are most susceptible to subsequent defection.

NOTES

This chapter is a much-abbreviated version (thanks to the editing of Bonnie McCay) of a paper presented at the Social Science Research Council Conference on Institutionalized Forms of Reciprocity and Cooperation in Rural Europe held at St. Anthony's College, Oxford University, September 9–11, 1981. Sandra Ott and John Campbell were the organizers. I thank, as always, Renate Lellep Fernandez, Ruth Behar, and Richard Detwiler for their contribution to this work. The field research on which it is based is part of a longitudinal study begun in 1965 that is continuing through the present.

1. By disentailment is meant the process in nineteenth-century Spain that freed for sale, by the state, the real property previously held in perpetuity (since the Middle Ages) by ecclesiastical, civil, and seigneurial corporations. It was a process widely promoted in Europe by liberal regimes anxious to rationalize agriculture. In Spain this process was called "desamortización," and aimed to open up lands held in unproductive "dead hands" ("manos muertos," hence "desamortización"). It occurred in two phases. The first, that of Mendizabel (from 1836), primarily affected church lands. The second, that of Madoz (from 1855), affected municipal holdings and thus was more important in the loss of the commons.

2. I am referring here to Alvar Flores Estrada (1766–1853), Pedro Rodriquez Conde de Campomanes (1723–1802), and G. M. Jovellanos (1744–1811). The first two promoted collectivist and communal institutions; Jovellanos did not.

3. The early nineteenth-century shift to a municipal and centralized bureaucratic state was accompanied by reiterated emphasis on the custom of *sextaferia*, recognition perhaps that the newly centralized governments were unable to maintain a road system without it. A note di-

rected to the reanimation of the laws of *sextaferia* appears in a very early issue of the *Boletín Oficial del Principado de Asturias,* the organ of the centralized states (no. 9, 21 de enero de 1835, p. 21). The civil governor promised complete codification of the rules and responsibilities of *sextaferia* as well as some modern revisions of its requirements, and these appeared in 1839.

The institution has been as much an instrument of centralized administration as of communal well-being. This may have reinforced ambivalences about it, expressed among other ways in the use, instead, of the term *peonada,* the deprecatory term for a gang of day laborers at the beck and call of a more powerful and usually more exploitative authority. There was also the problem of the interference of municipal and provincial authorities in processes of local selection of *sextaferia* organizers and leaders; local authorities were imposed rather than locally selected and thus lacked authority for an essentially voluntary commitment.

4. As in the following *cantar* (Castanon 1970, 1: 326):

   Damned by the curdled milk
   That the harvesters are eating
   They neither sing nor dance
   Or fill the baskets with grain.

5. From the church's point of view, the possibly licentious character of these reunions was cause for periodic attempts to supress them. See Matías Sangrandor y Vitores, cited in Costa *et al.* (1902, 2: 128–29).

14 "The River Would Run Red with Blood"

COMMUNITY AND COMMON PROPERTY IN AN IRISH FISHING SETTLEMENT

Lawrence Taylor

ON A SUMMER'S EVENING IN 1973, Father John McDyer, parish priest of Glencolumbkille in southwest Donegal, Ireland, called a meeting of the fishermen of Teelin, an estuarine settlement of one hundred households in one corner of his large and mountainous parish. Father McDyer had earned a reputation throughout Ireland, and even abroad, for his apparent success in organizing cooperatives in this poor, west-coast region. These included knit-wear, agricultural produce, and fish-processing ventures run by committees for the common profit of their members.[1] On this particular evening the priest proposed to extend such cooperation into a new field: the estuarine salmon fishery of the Glen River and its small estuary, Teelin Bay.

Several dozen men, ranging from teenagers to septagenarians, filed into the parish hall and arrayed themselves in crews about the room. McDyer proposed that the fishermen form a cooperative in order to buy the fishing rights to the river and estuary from Gael-Linn, a nonprofit, Dublin-based corporation that had owned them since 1959. If they owned the rights to the fishery themselves, in common, the cleric reasoned, they would refrain from poaching and generally act to better husband the resource. Several fishermen took turns speaking, as did a few others not currently involved in the pursuit but quick to claim "I'll kill a fish fast as any man here," but none directly addressed the priest's proposal. Later it became apparent that although none of the men much favored McDyer's plan, they were unwilling to voice their opposition to a priest so bluntly. With me they were more straightforward. On the road back down to Teelin I asked one of the "retired" fishermen what he thought of Father McDyer's suggestion. "The river," he answered, "would run red with blood."

This chapter will explore some of the reasons that the priest's "call to the commons" was not, in this case, answered. Although the problem, thus stated, is ethnographic and some of the reasons for the priest's failure may lie in the realm of local particularity of person and event, the case study may shed some light on more general matters. Informants' discussion of the priest's proposal, when examined in the context of the local history of common property and a current system of apparent common property management in the very same salmon fishery (to be described below), illuminates the overall character of communality in this Irish settlement. The case study further suggests that the social and cultural structure of any community may be important variables in any such cooperative venture.

Such an observation will probably strike few anthropologists as novel, but the specification of which sorts of communal characteristics are most relevant to common-property systems may be the most significant contribution anthropology can make to the general debate on tragedies, or successes, of the commons. Following Hardin (1968), the theoretical literature on common-property systems has so far been dominated by the classical economic model of self-seeking and essentially unconnected individuals. Communities, from that perspective, have only a hypothetical and largely irrelevant existence. Indeed, they may be shown to be impossible *per se*. Many anthropologists find such a model inadequate, given the fact that they often find themselves in actual communities possessed of some common resource more or less successfully managed. In the real world, property is never absolutely individual or unrestricted. The commons is typically some delimited piece of the world claimed (not always in accordance with others' perceptions of the matter) by some equally delimited group of people, a corporate group—corporate, at least, with respect to the property in question. Moreover, such groups do not often allow unrestricted use by individuals, but manage the resource through a variety of formal and informal means.

How is this possible? A romantic response to the classical economic model might hold that "community" is the natural condition of man and that economic man is the late result of cultural perversion, capitalist or otherwise. Such a position is no more helpful in accounting for actual cases, however, than the tragedy-of-the-commons thesis. A more productive stance would be one that notes that, whatever the "natural" inclination of human beings, actual communities act differently, not only from one another, but with respect to various resources, and that where such resources are held in common the group manages access and use through cultural means. Those cultural means include not only formal rules and informal customs, but also primary values and assumptions about human nature that underly and buttress more visible institutions. Indeed, culture works best when it appears "natural."

The anthropologist, therefore, needs to discover both why and how specific communities hold particular resources in common, and by what means they are able to manage their use. Case studies of failed attempts to establish common property, like the one under discussion here, can shed a special light on these matters because they provide occasions for the voicing of objections that reveal the basic cultural values and assumptions mentioned above.

COMMON PROPERTY IN LAND

Although Father McDyer made no detailed references to Teelin's past in his appeal to the fishermen, he could have found relevant precedents. As with many western Irish settlements, Teelin had historically been the scene of a common-property landholding system of the standard Atlantic fringe infield/outfield sort (see Evans 1939, 1964, and McCourt 1954, 1971). The typical form of settlement up through the early nineteenth century in some areas, including western Donegal, was the small hamlet or *clachan*. This cluster of homes was surrounded by a limited area of arable land, divided into strips or small parcels. Until the adoption of potatoes as the principal food crop in the late eighteenth century, such land was mainly devoted to oats, intensively cultivated with the aid of seaweed (where available) and cattle manure. Individual households claimed usufructory rights over these parcels for varying lengths of time, but the ultimate tenure was vested in the hamlet community, and use-rights were apparently rotated on a regular (again variable) basis (sometimes called "rundale"). Hamlets also claimed corporate rights to extensive grazing-quality land and bogland for fuel. This system survived intact in regions such as western Donegal until the eighteenth century, when British landlords began the process of replacing such communal tenure with individual tenancies. Even then, however, complex systems of landholding and inheritance survived in remote areas such as Tory Island (Fox 1979) well into the nineteenth century.

As for the older, "traditional," corporate-tenure system of the *clachan*, it is not clear what the local social basis of the system was in pre-British times, although some Irish historians assume a lineal (*fine*, patrilineage) basis to these local communities (Byrne 1967). Kinship and descent ideology may well have been important in at least justifying local cooperation (as in the twentieth century), but it may also have been the basis of authority for those persons making allocation decisions. Although the actual, local decision-making process is not known, medieval and later literature speaks of a *ceannfine* (literally, "lineage head") invested with such authority and, most important, answerable to clan subchiefs and chiefs above him. Descent, in other words, was the basis of vertical as well as horizontal ties, and the local community was incorporated into larger hierarchical political units whose authority may have been the ultimate basis of local corporateness (see Taylor 1980). Later, as Evans (1939: 51) instructs us, an "appointed leader" in a townland or group of townlands oversaw the casting of lots used to reallocate strips of land. On islands as far apart as Tory, off Donegal, and The Great Blasket, off Kerry, such an individual was called *An Ri*—the king (see Fox 1979: 16 for a discussion of the possible historic character of the *An Ri*). A similar role seems to have been taken by priests elsewhere in the west when permanent land division took place in the late nineteenth and early twentieth centuries. The source of authority of such "officials," except in the case of priests, remains unclear.

The *clachan* as a social, as well as territorial, unit survives in the 1980s in the townland (*Baile Fearainn*), which constitutes a rural neighborhood. Even in the predominantly dispersed settlement pattern of western Ireland, clusters of households sometimes called "towns" survive (Evans 1942: 48–51). Although their farms are fully private property, residents in such nucleated settlements seem especially closely bound by the cooperative customs of exchange due to "friends" (meaning in this usage relatives: see Arensberg 1968: 122f, and L. Taylor 1981). British landlords eventually succeeded in fully enclosing and individualizing tenancies in arable land, but these townlands continue to hold common rights in mountain pasture and peat bogs, perhaps because these two resources are under little pressure from population. Both human and livestock populations have been greatly reduced over the last century (from 1,017 people in 1876 to fewer than 300 in 1976 for Teelin as a whole, a reduction mostly due to emigration). The lack of pressure on these resources, however, means that they do not really need management as common property.

Teelin is a loosely nucleated settlement comprising seven of these townlands, nestled in the narrow space of semifertile land between the mountain Slieve League and the Glen River and its estuary, Teelin Bay. Within Teelin, the names of townlands are frequently used to designate a home territory. Outsiders more frequently speak of Teelin as a whole. Geographically and socially, Teelin, over and above its constituent townlands, is a community for insiders and outsiders alike, but never more so than in salmon season.

THE SALMON FISHERY

Beginning in the early spring of each year, schools of salmon make their way south along the Donegal coast, heading in each case for the stream of origin, where they will spawn and die. As long as Ireland has been inhabited, beginning with mesolithic hunter-gatherers, salmon have been taken, typically in the course of their upstream swim in any of the many salmon rivers. Methods have included everything from using hooks, spears, and hand-held nets, to what are called "fixed engines" (stationary weirs and nets).

Evidence from various regions suggests that riverine salmon have long been a privately or institutionally owned and managed resource. In particular, important salmon fisheries were, from medieval times, controlled by monastic settlements in many areas. Later, landlords claimed such fisheries as adjoined their estates, frequently treating them as separate and alienable assets. Such fisheries were noʈ open to the peasantry. Locals might be employed to tend the landlord's weir or crew his net-boats, but unauthorized fishing was theft (Netboy 1974: 91–110).

Although Teelin's sea fisheries have always been in the public waters of Donegal Bay, the estuarine salmon fishery has followed the typical path of ownership, and was bought and sold among several of the region's large landlords in the course of the nineteenth century. In the 1980s, more than sixty years after independence from Great Britain, most Irish salmon streams remain private property. Teelin's Glen River is unusual, however, in having been purchased in 1959, along with other remnants of the Musgrave estate, by Gael-Linn, a nonprofit, Dublin-based organization dedicated to the resuscitation and preservation of life in the *Gaeltacht* (the Gaelic-speaking western fringe of Ireland).

It was Gael-Linn's intention to make a working farm or tourist attraction of the remains of the estate site and to maintain a public, well-regulated salmon fishery in the river and its estuary. Toward the latter end they require licenses for fishing there. The estuary also comes under the jurisdiction of the national Inland Fisheries authority, which requires licenses and further restricts the fishery. It determines mesh size and prohibits weekend, after-dark, and "fixed engine" fisheries. The general intent of these limitations, most of which originated in the 1863 Salmon Fisheries Act (under British rule), is to conserve the resource. Neither Gael-Linn nor the Irish government intends to deprive the local populace of access to this resource, but rather to create, in effect, an externally regulated commons.

Lack of funds and manpower, however, has made enforcement of fishing regulations by both Gael-linn's bailiff and government agents far from effective. In the summer of 1973, when Father McDyer called his meeting, most of the river and estuarine fishery was in fact illegal. Nonetheless, there were far more seine crews fishing in the off-limits channel, where the narrow river makes it difficult for salmon to escape the net, than down in the more open, and legal, bay. Illegal "fixed engines" in the form of bag-nets studded the coast outside the estuary. There were even a few individuals who would venture out at night and stretch a net across the entire width of the narrowest part of the river, catching all the fish that made it that far. Should any salmon survive to travel further upstream, they would be (illegally) dynamited out of the water for their trouble.

Although all these fishing methods were illegal, in local eyes they were not equally illegitimate. All, including those governed by the rotation system described below, could be called "poaching," depending on the context of discussion. Dynamiting was generally considered a heinous crime and suspected only of outsiders and other moral degenerates. All nocturnal fishing was beyond the pale of local standards, though perpetrators might be admired as well as blamed. No one concerned himself with the fixed bag-nets as long as they were set up on the sea coast, outside the estuary. The haul-seine fisheries, conducted from small boats in either the legal bay or the illegal channel, were both socially legitimate and regulated by locals without interference from external authorities. This informal regulation, which amounts to the management of access to a common resource, seems striking evidence of communality and hence relevant to the case at hand. I will describe the fishery as I witnessed its operation on my first day in the community in 1973 (see also L. Taylor 1981).

Seven eighteen-foot open boats sat motionless around the perimeter of Teelin Bay, half a mile across at its widest. Each boat was manned by four or five men sitting quite still and staring in various directions over the water. A seine net lay in the stern of each boat, from which a single line led to another crew member standing on shore. After a while a salmon leaped just downriver from one of the boats, the crew of which immediately began to row furiously upriver and around the leaping fish, paying out the net as they went. The shore man held the line taut, holding one end of the net stationary as the crew rowed and brought the other end of the net around to complete the circle. All boat hands then pulled the bag thus formed, and its contents, aboard. Having stowed their salmon in one end of the boat and neatly piled their net for the next *dol* (as each casting of the net is called in Gaelic), the crew looked up and around toward the other boats scattered about the estuary. One of these boats was in fact rowing toward the crew that had just taken a *dol* and yet another vessel was heading for the position vacated by the second boat. Within a few minutes, about half of the boats had thus exchanged positions, and all with no words other than a polite greeting. The same system operated upriver in the illegal channel, where each boat, after taking a *dol*, would simply row upstream to the end of a virtual queue.

The management of this scarce and important local resource, at least to the extent of ensuring equal access to all members of the community, would seem impressive evidence of local cooperativeness and general communality. Why, if they were accustomed to such a system, were the fishermen so averse to the priest's suggestion that they more completely regulate their own fishery by first corporately buying it? A closer look at how the fishermen themselves regard their rotation system may shed some light on the matter.

Considering the Irish propensity to use history as ideology, an inquiry into the origins of the rotation system should yield interesting results. The views of the fishermen were nearly uniform: fishing for salmon by small boat in the river and estuary is not reported by locals to be an ancient pastime. Older fishermen told me that a generation previous, weirs were used; they were then supplemented or replaced by ring-seine crews under the hire of the landlord. Few Teelin men, locals claimed, fished on such crews, but were rather to be found netting salmon by the same method out in the open waters of Donegal Bay. In the winter, herring were taken by the same method, using two boats, one moving and one stationary in lieu of a shoreman. But the rotation system, they claimed, applied in the outer waters as well, where the same rules were followed as in the estuary and river.

When asked about the origin of rotation *per se*, fishermen answered with great consistency: "Not in my time, or my father's time," "I wouldn't know . . . very far back," "*fado, fad o shoin*" (long, long ago), "they always did that." How did it begin? The answers to that question were of two related kinds: (1) "the fishermen made it up themselves," "it's a kind of 'by-law' the fishermen have," or (2) "it's a natural way," "it's only natural." Even when the first sort of answer was offered, there was no implication of any formal decision-making process. Rather, it was perceived as a natural response to the exigencies of the situation. One particularly eloquent fisherman explained it thus: "It's two completely different things on land and on the water. On land"—and here his hands fell on the table one alongside the other illustrating adjoining farms—"if there's trouble between these men, say cows wandering across, it's only between them, but on the water, if one man would refuse to move after taking a *dol*, well . . . it's unthinkable, *ta se* [it is] unthinkable!"

The origins of the rotation system, however, become even more problematic if we read surviving committee reports and travelers' accounts of the Donegal inshore fisheries from the late eighteenth and nineteenth centuries. For this portion of the coast, the constant report is of piscatorial strife, of herring fishermen shooting their nets across one another's, with resulting fights and even lawsuits.

Why the complete contrast between the fishermen's collective memory of cooperation and the historical record? When I told older fishermen what the reports described, they were either puzzled or uninterested; it did not register as any part of the past as they remembered it. Several possibilities suggest themselves: (1) the strife reported by commissions was true, but it was between and not within communities in the many coastal zones between the small fishing ports dotting the coast; (2) the strife was general and the rotation system was consciously invented by either external authorities or a number of fishermen in the face of maritime mayhem; or (3) the commissioners were less accurate or more selective in their reporting than historians might allow.

Whatever the actual roots of the practice, it is noteworthy that the rotation system is not now explained or justified as the result of any historic—democratic or autocratic—decision. This is especially interesting in that a local antiquarian, not a fisherman, remembered having been told that the rule *did* originate in a "meeting" within recent historic time. The fishermen's insistence on the traditional/natural origin of the system is in fact consistent with the general historicity of Teeliners. Specific practices are represented as originating through decision making only if the decision was made by such external authorities as priests or landlords.

A case in point is the division of the rundale fields and a portion of the commons into consolidated "stripe" farms, which historical records indicate was performed by a surveyor under the direction of landlord Thomas Connolly sometime between 1835 and 1860 (according to surviving maps). Older locals "remember" this as a specific event, that is, they recall the name of the surveyor and that he said, "These lines will stand forever," and they are in fair agreement on the relevant landlord. They are less sure of the date. Thus Teeliners view their community's past as one of periods of unvarying practice interrupted by transforming events in the guise of visitations from outside powers. Practices seen as arising from the community are considered more or less "natural," and that is their legitimization. Specific social origins are accorded only to external powers impinging on the local, natural world.

The "naturalness" of the rotation system arises again if we ask, What permits the system to function so smoothly? As always, the character of law is clearest in the response to violation. I was aware of only one, when a crew threw a *dol* in the declining light one evening and claimed on the following morning that they had not, and so refused to relinquish their position. I witnessed no direct confrontation, but rather an enormous amount of pointed whispering gossip in pub and household. The trangression was not repeated. In this case, the offender's behavior was not so much unfair as unnatural. Salmon, they reason, "brings out the greed in a man," but that is a natural selfishness balanced by an equally natural cooperativeness. The offender was thus "unbalanced." No one, however, is perceived as having the authority to directly reprimand or punish the offender in such cases, and such incidents seem to be either forgotten or remembered only reluctantly. Instead, the rule is remembered as applying without constraint and without infraction. Cooperation, in this instance, is perceived as merely the "natural" expression of local behavior.

Such cooperation, however, is restricted to the community. During the salmon season, at any rate, a kind of "amoral communalism" applies. Although there are fishermen on the far side of the estuary, the ring-seine fishery described above is almost entirely restricted to Teeliners. "Far-siders" (*daoine taobh thart*), as they are unaffectionately called during salmon season, generally use fixed bag-nets set out on the coast. When they try to set such "fixed engines," which are illegal, inside the estuary, Teeliners have resorted to slashing nets or even calling in the outside authorities. Thus the Teelin fishermen cooperate to defend a territory (unsanctioned by law), as fishermen do in many parts of the world (for example, Maine, as described by Acheson, this volume and 1975). Indeed, Teelin may be said to achieve its most real existence as a competing and cooperating community in the context of the salmon fishery. Why then the reluctance to adopt Father McDyer's plan, to answer his call to the watery commons? Why would the river, in the words of that eloquent fisherman, "run red with blood?"

THE PRIEST'S COOPERATIVE

The point of Father McDyer's proposal was to create a situation that would eliminate poaching, that is, all illegal fishing perceived as harming the continuing stock of available salmon. Were the fishermen convinced, however, that there had been a decline in the fishery, and that poaching was indeed responsible for it? If so, were they willing to give it up?

Although statistics are not available for such local units as one river, official reports on the general decline in runs of spring salmon coincide with local memory and opinion (see Inland Fisheries Commission 1975). The fishermen were well aware of the vast migration route followed by the salmon and frequently argued that the entire fishery was being destroyed by foreign fleets catching thousands of fish in their feeding grounds off the coast of Greenland. Yet most people also expressed a belief that poaching was taking a significant toll on the local resource, especially considering the "homing" habits of the fish.

Poaching, however, was also a valued tradition. Just as the landlord's role was to police his holdings, the tenant's role was to poach. Old men spoke with undisguised relish about the good old days, when close watch over the waters made poaching a true challenge. Otherwise law-abiding men would wink and smile at their own reminiscences of successful expeditions and even of capture and confinement. Today, small fines and the lack of effective enforcement seem to have made poaching a somewhat less challenging sport, but sport it remains. Evidently the fact that the landlords are gone and the Irish government or Gael-Linn's bailiffs are now the regulators makes little difference in the local perception of the "sides"; it is still locals versus outside authorities. Yet fishermen still claim it would be better if everyone would stop poaching. The problem, as they see it, is that poaching, as long as it does not violate local rights of access as defined in the rotation system, is a "natural" local characteristic. No one could imagine giving it up.

Father McDyer may well have appreciated the local cultural significance of poaching as an expression of hostility and opposition to outside authority. He apparently reasoned that if that outside authority was, in a sense, eliminated through group purchase, then the motivation for poaching would be likewise removed. People would not want to poach against themselves and each other, and if anyone did, his neighbors would presumably be vigilant in their own interests, as the rotation system seemed to show.

The fishermen, however, did not see it that way. Whenever I asked them why they opposed the priest's plan when they cooperated so easily in the rotation system, they seemed genuinely puzzled by my juxtaposition of the two matters. They apparently saw them as distinct phenomena operating on very different principles. As discussed above, they were inclined to see the rotation system as an expression of the more or less natural reciprocity of kin and community neighbors. The rotation system was simply "taking turns."

From this perspective, the priest's proposed cooperative was indeed problematic. First, the fact that it was proposed by the politically powerful priest made it seem the latest imposition of external authorities rather than "their cooperative," as the priest put it. It was Father McDyer's cooperative, as the fishermen saw it, yet they were supposed to pay for it and police it. To the older fishermen this combination seemed particularly confusing. Indeed the priest's vision was a bit of a mixed metaphor. He spoke of a rational corporation, of the purchase of private property to be used by others. However, his notion of management seemed rooted in a romantic view of the "traditional" ties of the local community. Being so interrelated, he apparently reasoned, Teeliners would find it easy to cooperate in managing the resource. But this meant that McDyer was asking them to act like businessmen and even landlords on the one hand, and kin and neighbors on the other.

Ownership was a critical issue. Common ownership does not imply cooperation. From the local point of view, successful common ownership did not extend past the household. "Any nice house you see empty with its roof caving in," one local advised, "you can bet the owner died without a will and his children can't agree on what to do with it." Despite the "fish-ins" then occurring in other, perhaps less isolated, regions of Ireland, here locals, and particularly the older men, saw nothing wrong with the institution of private property. They even seemed to take it for granted that rivers were typically so held. Although a man might speak in a general way about British and landlord tyranny and the fact that they had no collective right to be in Ireland, he might also imply that since the particular landlord had in fact purchased the estate, he did after all own it legitimately. It was his river and his right to enforce his restrictions with bailiffs. Since Gael-Linn and the Irish Government in Dublin now owned the river, they should act like better landlords and watch it more closely. As for the rotation system for salmon, like that for herring it amounted to standing in line for fish that nobody pretended to own as they passed through the local environment on their way around the North Atlantic. To purchase the river as the priest recommended was to confuse, first, group with individual activity, and second, common ownership with cooperation. Not only did the second two concepts not necessarily go together, but in the local view they seemed mutually inimical.

The rotation system seems analogous to the old rundale distribution of arable land, in which a longer-term rotation was involved. The crucial difference, of course, is in the matter of ownership. Neither the waters nor the fish swimming through them are "owned" by the fishermen in the sense that their forebears owned the land redistributed in rundale. In the case of rundale, however, that corporate ownership was vested in the group by virtue of their membership in a larger polity. Although descent and kinship may have been evoked in that system to justify the horizontal reciprocity of access involved in redistribution, the vertical ties of clanship may have been equally necessary to underwrite the authority of the *ceannfine*.

The cooperation of the salmon rotation system rests, on the other hand, only on the egalitarian ethos of communal reciprocity, which is, in turn, understood as natural. Evidently the value is truly constraining, because few would or did try to violate the rotation rules. When a violation does take place, as in the incident described earlier, communal punishment does not have to be organized. Perpetrators are perceived as deviants rather than criminals, and hence the opprobrium of informal social control follows, as it were, naturally.

The priest's cooperative, however, would depend on uncommon restraint, and fishermen expected infractions requiring some sort of official enforcement, for such had always been the response to poaching. Here for them lay the real crux of the problem. "What could I do," one fisherman put it, "if I saw that man down pooching [sic] and he's my cousin, or my wife's relation. I couldn't tell him to stop. We're all too close here. We want a bailiff to stop the pooching . . . and he should live on the other side [of the river], and we shouldn't know him or his family!" Anthropologically inclined as he evidently was, the fisherman was speaking of severe role conflict and the problem of authority in an egalitarian social system. Rather than eliminating the need for enforcement, buying the river would turn everyone into a bailiff. The fisherman was also aware of the value of the "stranger" as scapegoat and enforcer in such communities. It was this anticipated crisis of authority that would cause the "river to run red with blood."

COMMUNITY AND COMMON PROPERTY

In pre-British times, Teelin's common property may have been vested in small, local, corporate descent groups (*clachan*), but such social groups were parts of larger, hierarchical clan and chiefdom polities. The local decision-making process involved in managing common fields remains unknown, but whatever it was, the community was defined in relation to external sources of authority as well as local resources. That is not to say that local decision making required intervention from actual outsiders, but that "kinship," for example, as a source of local authority was more than local in origin (as in the case of segmentary lineage systems even in the absence of political authorities).

The Gaelic chiefdoms were replaced by a new external authority, British landlords. Estate-agent papers for the 1870s suggest that such representatives of the new ruling class played at least some role in regulating the use of common resources, such as mountain grazing and peat bogs. In that period, common grazing was allocated according to arable holdings and a section of the bog went with each household.[2] Whatever local, informal regulation was going on, once again external authorities were often turned to in the case of property disputes. Indeed, priests and agents competed for just such a position (Taylor 1985). That is not to say that Teeliners did not cooperate during the landlord regime. Where common property was concerned, however, such cooperation always rested on specific, restricted use-rights—no free-for-all—buttressed by an ultimately external source of authority. The community also expressed itself as such through attacks on that very same source of authority in the form of poaching.

In the 1970s and 1980s Teeliners expressed the same ambivalence toward external sources of authority as they did under the landlords.[3] On the one hand, they poach, and on the other, they wish outsiders did a better job of stopping them. Further light is shed on the matter by the salmon rotation system, which exists without reliance on anyone outside the community. The rotation system is thought of as "taking turns," a reciprocity between equals. As in the case of "cooring" (from the Gaelic *comhair*, "to help") described by Arensberg (1968: 72–73), wherein farmers exchange labor in times of need, the exchange of fishing position is obligatory only in the sense that any good kinsman or neighbor would "automatically" do it.

It may be that it is precisely because they do *not* own the resource in common that the fishermen are able to cooperate in this way. By unofficially claiming a fishing territory, as well as by poaching, Teeliners define their community in opposition to outsiders (either the neighboring "far-side" community or officialdom). This fact, and the public nature of the fishery, make it the preeminent communal pursuit. Thus, insofar as the internal relations of the community (as opposed to household) are perceived as egalitarian, that equality is acted out in the rotation system. Breaches of that custom, it also follows, must be seen as signs of moral deviance inimical to the very definition of community.

In his proposal to create a cooperative for purchasing and managing the river, Father McDyer called for an "artificial" corporation to purchase the rights, which would then, in his view, be managed by the "natural" community. Garrett Hardin might argue that the poaching was in fact causing a tragedy of the commons and that the priest's solution really involved privatization through the creation of a corporation. The priest would no doubt counter with the observation that the local fishermen did not view either government or Gael-Linn property as *theirs* (the fishermen's). The formation of the cooperative would make it common with respect to the real community.

The natural community, however, existed most strongly, most cooperatively, precisely in its opposition to the authorities the priest planned to eliminate. Moreover, if McDyer was right in his assumption that locals did not see "public" or nonprofit, for-the-public waters as commons, he was wrong in thinking that his own cooperative would be perceived as such. The fishermen saw the purchase, even by a group, as the creation of private property. Community was not, in the local view, based on the ownership of common property. With property, as they saw it, came the competing interests of individual households rather than corporate interest versus outsiders: amoral communalism giving way to less-than-moral familism. Property needed regulation, and regulation rested on authority. Hence, the fishermen properly understood that the priest's notion of community was not their own, and that the adoption of his plan would require management based on a different set of social relations. The social costs of that change—if not literal blood, then blood as symbol of the reciprocity and egalitarianism of kin and community—would far exceed the benefits accrued by the increased flow of salmon.

This case suggests some interesting possibilities concerning the conditions under which communities may adopt, or at least adapt to, common property and its management. The key issues may lie in the definitions of "community" and "property."

One species of egalitarian community, which we can call "traditional," has difficulty with authority, at least when that authority is not rooted and hidden in local conceptions of what is traditional or natural. Moral arguments justifying local authority or cooperation must be based on these categories. The location of ultimate authority outside such communities safeguards their egalitarian ethos and strengthens the conditions for cooperation among equals. In such communities, resources such as mountain, bog, and fishing territory may be viewed as "common property": that is, held by the community in opposition to other communities. In that case "ownership" is understood as a traditional, collective right to use something, rather than as a right based on contract. That is not to say that contractual rights have no place in such communities, but rather that they are understood to apply in other spheres and do not define community relations. The point, for those wishing to introduce a new version of common property and management, is not to confuse such spheres.

There are other sorts of equally "close-knit" communities, of course, based on very different notions of both community and property. Indeed, common property is perhaps more typically associated with "associational" or "intentional" communities whose vision of the relations of both community and property may be called "contractual" (see Taylor 1983: 9–16). In these communities, common property may well be understood as specific and contractual in the same sense as individual property. Contractual communities, however, are characterized by institutions (churches, committees, etc.) that offer a means for managing resources and each other's behavior that is different from the means used by communities such as Teelin.

Father McDyer's proposal might have found a better reception in a contractual community. Managing a resource in the context of the priest's cooperative would probably involve much argument and conflict in an egalitarian contractual community, but such conflict would not be viewed as a threat to the community or a sign of the demise of sociability as it would in Teelin. Rather, such conflict could be seen as part of the very substance of community as locally defined.

Ideologies can, of course, be manipulated by the creative re-use of tradition. Perhaps Father McDyer would have done better had he been able to convince the fishermen of Teelin—as Nyerere told Tanzanians—that they were socialists all along, or that he was merely reinstating a historic and natural system obliterated by the perfidious Saxons, rather than urging them to adopt a rational system based on an essentially contractual idiom. The social, after all, may be eventually perceived as natural. There is the intriguing possibility that the rotation system itself originated with just such a conscious decision in rather recent historic time, made by the landlord, the fishermen, or some combination of the two. In order to justify and legitimate the decision, however, it must now be remembered as eternal and natural.

NOTES

This chapter is based on fieldwork conducted in the summer of 1973, for nine months in 1976, and during a short visit in the summer of 1983. It has greatly benefited from the editorial comments and suggestions of Bonnie McCay, James Acheson, Dan Bauer, and John Gatewood.

1. The other cooperatives organized by Father McDyer have had a controversial history. An unpublished study by a team of cultural geographers from St. Patrick's College in Maynooth, Ireland, blamed their eventual financial failure on the priest's unwillingness to cede control of the cooperatives to others. None of the other cooperatives relied on a local community for management to the extent of the proposed fishing cooperative discussed here.

2. Informants described these contractually defined rights to Heinrich Wagner (1943). They are no doubt traditional in origin, but were probably specifically and contractually limited under landlords who were seeking to precisely define tenants' rights.

3. Larger communities may also be defined in opposition to outside authorities. In the summer of 1983 an Irish navy vessel attempted to board a fishing boat suspected of carrying illegal gear in Donegal Bay. The fishing boat refused to stop, and the navy vessel fired at the escaping culprit, who made it safely into port. The next day an ad hoc armada of Donegal half-deckers crewed by angry armed men steamed out into the bay. The naval vessels were ordered out of the area, but for the next week or so there was more friendly interaction between fishing fleets up and down the entire west coast of Ireland than in recent memory.

Part III

THE STATE
AND THE COMMONS

15 An Economic View of the Tragedy of the Commons

Ralph Townsend and James A. Wilson

HARDIN'S (1968) THESIS OF THE TRAGEDY OF THE COMMONS challenged the appropriateness of the social institutions that governed the use of many renewable resources. In theory, these resources could provide an endless stream of benefits, but in practice, they were often destroyed by shortsighted behavior. The institution that encouraged such destructive behavior was open access.[1] When no one owned the resource, each user's self-interest dictated overuse.

This simple idea was not new. Indeed, economists since Adam Smith have extolled the virtues of the institution of private property over alternative property institutions. But prior to Hardin, most economists viewed open access as a theoretically interesting, but otherwise minor, institution in Western economies. The seminal contributions by economists typically chose insignificant examples to illustrate the problems of incomplete property rights. Meade (1952), for example, used the external benefits of apple blossoms to honey production, and Coase (1960) cited the archaic example of fires created by sparks from railroad engines. Hardin emphasized that the absence of private property rights characterized the most crucial resources: air, water, and other essentials of life. Moreover, the establishment of private property rights was clearly difficult if not impossible for these resources.

The practical issue of how best to solve the tragedy of the commons was first explored in the case of fisheries. The evident overfishing of stocks by technologically sophisticated fishermen in the 1950s created unmistakable symptoms of the tragedy of the commons. The roots of this overfishing were widely believed to be biological. The science of fisheries management was the exclusive province of biologists, who proposed conservation measures such as quotas, closed seasons, minimum mesh sizes, and prohibitions on the use of efficient gear. Gordon (1954) extended the multi-disciplinary field of fishery science to include social science when he argued that the roots of the problem lie in the institutions and economic organization of the fishery. As long as access is open, no user has incentives to conserve the resource. The problems of management of an open-access resource are caused by the absence of the right to control the resource. The fundamental issue in the management of these resources is the nature of economic institutions.

As Scott (1955) suggests, this fundamental issue can best be understood by comparing the actions of a sole owner with the actions of the user of an open-access resource. Private property bestows upon the owner a well-defined set of rights and responsibilities. The benefits produced by the property, as well as the costs of maintaining and improving the property, fall to the owner. When an owner faces a decision about alternative uses of a particular resource, he or she has economic incentives to put the resource to its most productive use. When the effects of the decision involve many years, the decision faced by the owner is more complicated but the principle is unaltered. For example, a landowner who must decide whether to farm the topsoil or dig up the minerals below can compare the streams of income and expenses from the two alternative uses. Moreover, the institution of private property is supplemented by the market for property. In theory, a piece of property will be most valuable to the most efficient and farsighted owner. Thus, sale of property to the highest bidder should place property in the hands of the most efficient and farsighted user.

When anyone may use a resource, the resource is in effect unowned. Anyone may try to reap the benefits of the resource but no one may claim exclusive rights. The incentives created are extremely destructive. Because no one may lay claim to any benefits from husbanding the resource, conservation is not in any individual's self-interest. Even when the investment involves merely waiting for the resource to mature, incentives exist to deplete the resource immediately. Consider, for example, a piece of farmland with unrestricted access. Clearly, no one has incentives to plant crops, to control disease, or to cultivate. As soon as the crop reaches minimum usable size, however, everyone has an incentive to harvest the crop. To leave the crop to grow is foolhardy: someone else will immediately harvest it.

Most of the important fisheries of the world have been exploited under conditions of open access. Fishermen have strong incentives to rush to catch the fish before others do. This incentive has many inefficient results. Boats may be so dense on rich grounds that collisions and gear entanglement occurs. In their race to be first, fishermen build large, fast vessels that catch an entire season's catch in a few days or even hours. An increasing portion of the catch comes from small fish that neither reproduce nor grow to an efficient size, so catches diminish over time. In extreme cases, commercial or even biological extinction may occur.

Economists built an empirical literature to substantiate the inadequacy of biological controls. Crutchfield and Zellner (1962) pointed to the need for ever-shorter seasons in the overcapitalized Pacific halibut fisheries. Crutchfield and Pontecorvo (1969) found similar overcapitalization and low economic returns in the Pacific salmon fisheries. Pontecorvo (1962) pointed to the overexploited lobster fishery in New England. In nearly every fishery examined, economists found excessive investment in harvesting capacity, low economic returns to fishermen, and increasing signs of stock decline which they attributed to the institution of open access.

THE SCHAEFER-GORDON ANALYSIS

A simple mathematical model based upon the work of Gordon (1954) and Schaefer (1957) illustrates the essential elements of the losses caused by open access. The Schaefer-Gordon model captures the interaction of biological and economic forces. The fishery resource, or stock, is assumed to have an intrinsic ability to grow that depends only upon the size of the population. Because fishing reduces its size, fishing activity indirectly affects its growth. When this simultaneity is ignored by man, the resource will be reduced or even destroyed.

In the Schaefer-Gordon model, as stock size increases, the growth of the stock increases at a decreasing rate. The effects of more births (because there are more sexually mature adults) are gradually offset by competition for food and habitat. Such a stock-growth/stock-size (or stock-recruitment) relationship is illustrated in Figure 15.1. Growth rises until the stock reaches S_{MSY} and then falls until growth reaches zero at the maximum on the sustainable yield line.

The economic side of the Schaefer-Gordon model is determined by the amount of fishing activity, or "fishing effort." Each unit of fishing effort is assumed to catch some fixed percentage of the stock. Given a level of fishing effort, catch is proportional to stock size. In Figure 15.1 the relation between catch and stock size is drawn for two levels of fishing effort, E_1 and E_2. The higher level

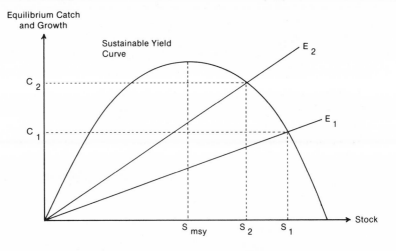

FIG. 15.1. *Relationship between fish stock size and recruitment.*

of fishing effort is E_2, because more fish are caught at any level of initial stock size.

The economic and biological factors are linked, because each depends upon stock size. Stock size determines both catch and growth of the stock. Moreover, catch and growth together determine if the stock is increasing, decreasing, or remaining constant. If catch exceeds growth, the stock must be falling. If growth exceeds catch, the stock must be increasing. The system can reach a steady state only when growth exactly equals catch. In Figure 15.1, for any level of effort, the equilibrium occurs when the growth line and the catch line intersect. For effort level E_1, the equilibrium stock size is S_1 and equilibrium catch is C_1. For effort level E_2, equilibrium stock size is S_2 and equilibrium catch is C_2. Note that as the effort increases (i.e., as the effort line becomes steeper), the intersection of the two lines occurs at lower and lower stock sizes. Consequently, an inverse relationship exists between fishing effort and stock size. As we would expect, more fishing causes stocks to decline.

The relationship between fishing effort and catch is more complicated. Two forces are interacting. As fishing effort increases, a larger percentage of the available stock is caught each year. But higher fishing effort reduces the stock. So catch at first increases, but eventually decreases as fishing effort increases. Such a relationship between fishing effort and catch is illustrated in Figure 15.2. This is usually called a yield-effort curve, or simply a "Schaefer curve." The highest possible equilibrium catch is called maximum sustainable yield (MSY).

Although the curve in Figure 15.2 appears to be analogous to

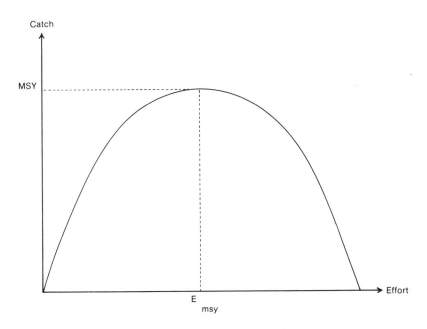

FIG. 15.2. *Relationship between fishing effort and yield.*

the sustainable yield curve in Figure 15.1, they are in fact mirror images. When effort equals zero, the stock is unexploited and stock size is at its maximum. As effort increases, stock size falls. When effort reaches its maximum, stock size is zero.

To complete the Schaefer-Gordon model, the effect of economic incentives upon the level of effort must be incorporated. Better economic returns to fishing will attract more effort; poorer economic returns will cause effort to leave the fishery. The economic system reaches an equilibrium when there are no incentives to enter or leave the fishery. This occurs when no excess profits and no losses occur.

Economic returns are determined by the catch rate, the price of fish, and the costs of fishing. The total revenue received from the sale of catch equals price times quantity caught. Therefore, the relationship between fishing effort and total revenue is just the yield-effort curve of Figure 15.2 scaled up by the price of fish (see Fig. 15.3). The effort-revenue relationship at first increases and then decreases as effort increases. Total cost equals the quantity of fishing effort times the cost per unit of effort. Note that the cost of effort includes the opportunity cost of the fisherman's time and of any equipment. Because total cost is equal to the level of effort scaled up by the cost of a unit of effort, the total cost-effort relation is a straight line.

The economic incentives cause the system to reach equilibrium when total revenue equals total cost. This occurs when the total revenue and total cost lines intersect in Figure 15.3. At this point, there are neither profits to attract new fishermen nor losses to encourage exit.

The analysis of economic incentives in Figure 15.3 can be used to illustrate the effects of three different management options: no management, maximum-sustainable-yield management, and maximum-economic-yield management.

When the fishery is unregulated (i.e., access is open), effort will enter the fishery as long as economic returns, or profits, exceed those that could be earned by fishermen in other occupations. But more effort in the fishery tends to reduce profits for everyone. Eventually, with enough new effort, profits are reduced to the point at which no further effort is attracted to the fishery. This equilibrium level of effort in the fishery will occur when total

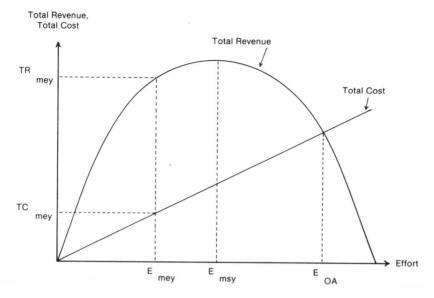

FIG. 15.3. *Relationships among fishing effort, cost, and revenue.*

cost equals total revenue. This level corresponds to E_{OA} in Figure 15.3. Under open access, the total value of production exactly equals the cost of production in equilibrium.

The biological proposal to regulate catch at maximum sustainable yield (compare MSY in Fig. 15.2) amounts to maximizing total revenue in Figure 15.3. This would occur in Figure 15.3 at an effort level of E_{MSY}. However, economists have proposed that the value of production in excess of costs be maximized. Such a maximum economic yield (MEY) would be analogous to a farmer's maximizing his net income. The economically efficient level of effort occurs at E_{MEY} in Figure 15.3. The difference between total revenue and total cost, called "economic rent," is the distance $(TR_{MEY} - TC_{MEY})$ in Figure 15.3. Management under the criteria of maximum economic yield implies less fishing effort and larger stock sizes than either open access or maximum-sustainable-yield management.[2] (Recall that lower levels of fishing effort cause larger stock levels.) It may seem paradoxical that economic management implies more conservative management than the biologist's maximum sustainable yield. Economically efficient management requires larger stock sizes because fish are cheaper to catch when they are more abundant.

ECONOMIC MANAGEMENT OF FISHERIES

For economists, the model just presented provides the standards by which to judge the effectiveness of management institutions. Appropriate institutions must reduce fishing effort to the efficient level, E_{MEY}.[3] If the institution of open access lies at the heart of the tragedy of the commons, the obvious solution is to institute private property rights. That apparently simple solution presents significant issues in most fisheries. Property rights cannot be simply copied from our experience on land: stocks of fish usually cannot be carved up by lines drawn on a map. Management must choose among various types of imperfect approximations of private property rights.

For a few fisheries the analogy to land-based property rights is not difficult. For example, sedentary shellfish stocks can be assigned to specific owners. The right to harvest anadromous species when they return to spawn can likewise be assigned. Not surprisingly, marine aquaculture has developed in shellfish and anadromous species. The economic effectiveness of these rights has been documented for American oysters (Agnello and Donnelley 1975; see McCay, this volume).

It is far more difficult to create private-property rights for more mobile species. For mobile fish and shellfish, economists have generally urged administrative reductions in the number of fishermen. Usually this reduction is accomplished by issuing a limited number of permanent, transferable licenses. Such programs have come to be identified as "license limitation" or often just "limited entry." The roots of this management idea may be found in the presentations of Scott, Sinclair, Crutchfield, and Pontecorvo at a 1961 conference of the Food and Agriculture Organization of the United Nations (Hamlisch 1962).

Many practical problems are created by management systems that simulate the outcome rather than the institutions of a property-rights system. Under license or effort-limitation programs, fishermen face a set of "disharmonious incentives." Each fisherman has a competitive incentive to defeat the effort-limiting rule by building bigger boats, misreporting landings, and so on. Fishing effort is composed of a variety of inputs—size of boat, horsepower, type of gear, skill of the fisherman, and others. Rules that limit one component of fishing effort encourage the substitution of other components, thereby increasing fishing effort. For example, a rule limiting the length of boats is very likely to result in wider boats, boats with more horsepower, more electronics, bigger nets, and other compensations. The practical extent of this problem depends upon two characteristics of the fishery: the nature of the harvest technology and the level of effort relative to the level appropriate for a sustainable fishery. If the harvest technology is limited to a single technology, substitution of unrestricted inputs for restricted inputs will make little difference to overall effort. Similarly, if the initial management program limited effort to a level well below the maximum necessary to sustain the fishery, the practical effect of rule-defeating substitutions will be minimal.

These disharmonious incentives stand in contrast to those of a true private-property system, such as found in Western agriculture. The individual farm owner's self-interest is served ostensibly by wise cultivation of the land and conservation of the soil, at least more so than that of the non-owner. This self-interest corresponds with society's collective interest in the resource. There is less need for the state to stipulate the size of tractor, the kinds of crops, or methods of cultivation. Moreover, the system provides a set of harmonious incentives that reinforce its operation. If someone chooses to break the rules of the property-rights system—by stealing, for example—each property owner has strong and very apparent incentives to defend not only his own property but also the property of others.

When fisheries are managed to imitate the outcome of a property-rights system, no comparable set of individuals has an incentive to defend the rules of the system. When a fisherman builds a bigger boat or misreports his catch, the immediate harm to any single individual is negligible and the long-term collective harm is very difficult to perceive. In short, imitating private-property rights without in fact creating exclusive property rights creates neither the incentives for socially appropriate behavior nor a spontaneous enforcement mechanism.

The tendency poses a distinct dilemma for management. In order to reduce fishing effort to the level appropriate for a sustainable fishery, managers must create rules that encourage the use of inefficient technology. Because of the imperfections of the system, management must continue traditional biological rules—quotas, mesh size, and other restrictions that protect the resource. The extensive rule structure that results leads to high enforcement costs and/or fishing effort that exceeds the level desired. In short, management systems that alter the manifestations of the tragedy of the commons by simulating a property-rights regime through license limitations have built-in incentives that tend to defeat both conservation and efficiency objectives (see Pinkerton, this volume). The result is higher social costs and lower social benefits from management.

The practical response to these problems has been twofold: first, under "buy-back" programs the state purchases and retires a fisherman's license. These programs reduce fishing effort through a reduction in the number of fishing units rather than through a reduction in the efficiency of a larger number of units. These programs have very high costs relative to the social benefits that are achieved. In a fishery the expected value of the license will vary greatly among fishermen according to skill. The market value of that property right will reflect the expectations of the most optimistic potential entrants to the fishery. This market value will be well above the value of the license to the most ineffective fishermen in the fleet. An offer by the state to purchase licenses "at fair market value" will be most attractive to the least effective fishermen. The state pays very high prices to get rid of the most marginal fishermen. As a practical matter, however, the state will rarely be able to spend enough to make a difference to the efficiency and conservation status of the fishery.

A second response to the problems of limited licensing programs is the "enterprise quota system." Overall fleet quotas are divided up and assigned to individual enterprises. This approach contrasts greatly with the traditional one in which quotas of fish that can be caught apply to a fleet of boats as a whole. The outcome of a fleet-wide quota is a race to catch as much as possible of the quota before others. The race leads to investment in bigger, faster, better-equipped, and sometimes more boats to allow the fisherman to maintain or increase his share of the overall quota. The result is growth in total fishing effort. In contrast, the allocation of shares in a quota to individual enterprises decreases the incentive to increase the effort of the individual boat or enterprise and, assuming that the quotas are tied to specific vessels, eliminates the possibility of adding new boats or enterprises to the fleet. Each enterprise is free to catch its quota whenever it chooses and is likely to search for ways to minimize its costs of doing so.

Like all these regulatory systems, the enterprise quota creates its own problems. Fishermen are likely to engage in "high grading," landing only the fish of the highest market value or grade and throwing the rest overboard, dead or dying, so that it does not count against the enterprise's quota. Similarly, there are strong incentives to evade the proper reporting of catch. Finally, the quota race is not entirely ended. The costs of catching fish and the quality of fish are usually functions of the location of the fish and the season of the year. As stocks decline, the costs of fishing increase. Consequently, enterprises with their own quotas may compete in the race to get to the highest quality fish in the most accessible fishing grounds.

AN ALTERNATIVE VIEW OF MANAGEMENT

A different model of the dynamics of fish population leads to a basic criticism of the standard economic approach to fisheries management. The standard approach relies almost universally on the idea that there is a strong relationship between the size of a fish stock today and the number of recruits, or young marketable fish, in the next generation of fish. Simpler models view this relationship as strictly deterministic; others introduce stochastic variability into the stock-recruitment relationship. The idea is the basis for long-term control of the fishery: if current catch can be controlled by controlling the level of effort in the fishery, the size of the catch in the future can be controlled also. Controls on the current level of effort, although costly in economic and social terms, are worthwhile because they yield a more valuable resource and sustain it into the future.

A new line of criticism asks, if the population dynamic of the fishery does not exhibit a strong relationship between current and future stock sizes, is the traditional approach likely to work? Hennemuth (1979), for example, suggests a population dynamic that is very different from the Schaefer growth curve of Figure 15.1. He emphasizes the multiple-species or system-wide determinants of fish-population dynamics. The foundations of his approach can be summarized as follows: for any individual species in a system, there appears to be almost no relationship between current and future stock sizes when populations are above some "critical minimum" size (Hennemuth 1979: 512). Above the minimum, recruitment is highly variable with an annual average that is largely independent of stock size. Below the critical minimum, average annual recruitment falls dramatically, although the variation among classes of recruits may be as large as that observed at larger spawning stock sizes. The likelihood of a high level of recruitment is much lower below than above the critical minimum.

Unlike its components, the system as a whole appears relatively stable (Hennemuth 1979: 522–23). There is a relatively stable amount of total energy going into the system each year, primarily from sunlight. The total biomass produced from this energy is also relatively stable, but it may accumulate in different species. Which species accumulate the energy in a given year depends in large measure on the survival rates of eggs spawned in that year and earlier years.

The determinants of survival of the young of the year are extremely complex and outside the effective control of fisheries managers. Most marine fauna are very fecund. A female codfish, for example, lays millions of eggs each year. The survival of any one of these eggs is dependent upon a large number of factors. Water currents, temperature, salinity, wave height, turbulence, the availability of food of the right size at the right time, predation, and a variety of other factors create the great variability of recruitment from year to year. If only a small number of eggs laid by a very small spawning stock encounter the right conditions, very good recruitment—or rate of replacement—could still occur. For the system as a whole, however, it appears that additions to total biomass, primarily from the growth of young, are relatively stable and approximately equal to reductions from the biomass due to mortality (including fishing mortality).

If this is the population dynamic of fish communities in marine ecosystems, management that is ecologically, economically, and socially reasonable is likely to be very different from that traditionally advocated and used. This kind of population dynamic provides little justification for control of the population sizes of individual species, except to the extent that management can avoid their reduction below critical minimum levels. As long as populations remain above the critical minimum level, traditional management measures such as quotas, enterprise quotas, limits on fishing effort, and so on are likely to be irrelevant to the future size of the stock.

Consequently, traditional measures are only likely to be useful when they prevent a population from falling below its critical minimum level. However, this benefit of the traditional approach can be achieved only at the expense of significant short- and long-run social costs. The social and economic costs of limited entry appear reasonable if the results are sustainability of the fishery at maximum economic yield, but if the only goal is to maintain the fish population above the critical minimum level, it may be achieved in less costly and perhaps even more effective ways.

On the basis of this alternative population dynamic, Wilson (1982) has suggested a new approach to the management of fisheries. The problem is not seen as one of direct "cultivation" of the resource, that is, one in which private-property rights or their simulation are appropriate. Instead, the management problem is one of finding the institutions that promote efficient adaptation to a highly variable and largely uncontrollable multiple-species resource.

In this approach the management objective is to avoid reducing fish population sizes below the critical minimum level. The solution is to switch fishing effort away from stocks with declining populations and toward stocks with increasing populations. At first glance this appears to impose a control problem that may be even greater than that required by traditional management approaches. However, many economic and social aspects of unregulated multiple-species fisheries tend to produce spontaneous (i.e., self-interest-induced) switching (Wilson and Acheson 1981; Acheson 1981b). The switching may not ensure the maintenance of stocks above critical minimum levels, but it does provide a tendency toward that goal that can be reinforced by management.

For example, information systems among fishermen are highly sensitive to the state of the resource. When a stock is abundant, information about its location and catchability is widely shared among fishermen. Because information is so important to the efficiency of harvesting, the fleet as a whole is relatively efficient. As a stock begins to decline, however, fishermen become less inclined to share information about the location and movements of fish. Collective, fleet-wide information about the stock declines as does the efficiency of the fleet, increasing the incentive to switch. Given the objective of avoiding critical minimum population levels, these responses to declining abundance work in the direction desired for management.

Market prices and other factors have the effect of attenuating self-regulated switching behavior. A decline in landings can lead to an increase in the price of fish. If price rises are high enough, switching may not occur, and the possibility of depleting the fish population below critical minimum levels is increased. Traditional management techniques such as licensing rules that are species- or area-specific or the use of rigid harvesting technologies are also likely to reduce the tendency of fishermen to switch away from declining stocks.

The management approach suggested (Wilson 1982) would reinforce the species-switching behavior of fishermen and cause them to switch earlier in the decline of a stock. Management measures would assure that fishing effort is continually reallocated from scarce to abundant species in response to normal variations in population sizes over time. These management measures would indirectly influence the fishing decisions of individual fishermen. On the biological side, the most appropriate rules ensure that the spawning biomass of a species is not threatened. They prevent (or strongly constrain) fishermen from fishing on immature fish and/or spawning aggregations. Traditional measures such as large mesh sizes and time or area closure can raise the relative returns to fishing on larger fish or on other species and lower returns to fishing on small or spawning fish and sharply declining species.

The removal of species-specific licensing programs—which encourage fishermen to continue in a fishery for fear of losing the right to participate—and the encouragement of more flexible harvesting technologies, which reduce the cost of switching, can lead to earlier switching. Moreover, prices can behave in ways that cause fishing effort to switch from a population either early or late in its decline. Prices contribute to the management problems when the increasing scarcity of a stock is accompanied by large increases in its price. Such price increases provide incentives for fishermen to continue fishing on a declining or depleted stock. The role of prices in switching behavior leads to consideration of intervention in markets as a means of fisheries management. The relatively low price elasticities for species such as haddock and salmon exist not because of consumer tastes, but because of the fairly narrow trading possibilities in most fisheries markets. The structure of trading can be modified, however, through the introduction of more public trading arenas, making the structure of contracts more flexibile and responsive to changes in abundance. Additionally, the introduction of new fisheries commodities—such as cultured fish and surimi—can be expected to create substitutes and thereby affect the price elasticity for wild and fresh fish.

In summary, this alternative to the standard approaches in fisheries management and economics argues that when there is little ability to control the long-term size of the populations of different species of fish, management must address those aspects of the system that achieve the objectives of ensuring successful spawning and avoiding critically low population levels. Measures that reinforce the normal tendency of fishermen to switch away from declining stocks conform best to these objectives. Traditional management measures such as quotas and effort limitation, including limited entry, are based on an unrealistic assumption about the extent to which human intervention can control fish populations. These programs are, at best, only incidentally conservationist and, at worst, impose expensive and irrelevant regulations on a fishery.

NOTES

The authors wish to acknowledge financial support provided by the National Sea Grant College Program, National Oceanic and Atmospheric

Administration, Department of Commerce, under grant #NA81AA-D-0035 through the Maine-New Hampshire Sea Grant program.

1. Early writers called any institution lacking property rights "common property." Ciriacy-Wantrup and Bishop (1975) make the crucial distinction between "common property," when a well-defined community collectively uses a resource, and "open access," when anyone may use the resource, one that we follow.

2. It is clear that E_{MEY} must be to the left of E_{OA} and E_{MSY}. Using geometry, we see that the maximum distance between total revenue and total cost must occur where the tangent to the total revenue line is parallel to the total cost line. This must obviously occur somewhere between the origin and E_{MSY}.

   Although Figure 15.3 represents the typical case for an exploited fishery, it is possible for E_{OA} to occur to the left of E_{MSY}. This is a so-called "underutilized species," for which price is so low or costs so high that even under open access the catch is less than maximum sustainable yield. Thus E_{MEY} will still occur to the left of E_{OA}.

3. The reader should not assume that the simple Schaefer-Gordon model encompasses all of the theoretical economic issues. Mathematical models of a variety of complicating issues have been produced. For example, Turvey (1964) discusses the economic significance of mesh-size rules. Clark (1976) moves the entirely static Schaefer-Gordon analysis into a dynamic model and obtains rather surprising results. The reader interested in more sophisticated analyses is directed to Scott's (1979) review article and to texts by Anderson (1977) and Hannesson (1978).

16 *A Malaysian Tragedy of the Commons*

E. N. Anderson, Jr.

IN ITS CLASSIC AND SIMPLEST FORM, a tragedy of the commons (Hardin 1968) occurs when unrestricted access to a resource leads to depletion, as each individual is forced to maximize short-term gains or be displaced. One might expect that when such a situation develops people will get together to exercise control before their livelihood is destroyed. One might expect people to "specify the commons," that is, to establish some kind of responsibility over resources such that use-rights are restricted by law or custom: through use of quotas, limited access, property rights, enforced restoration of stocks, or the like. Indeed, such specification is often invoked, maintained by anything from force to religious taboo. Yet tragedies of the commons occur everywhere, and measures to specify resources are frequently too little and too late. Why do people not act in their own long-term self-interest? Why is there such a failure of control?

In many cases, failure occurs when government asserts control at too high a level and finds itself caught by conflicting demands that are exceedingly hard to clarify or resolve. In such cases local polities may attempt to assert control despite the wider authority (see Pinkerton, this volume). In any case, failure seems to be associated with the level and locus of control and the context of decision making at that level. The case of the west Malaysian fishery in the early 1970s represents a classic tragedy of the commons and a case in point.

THE MALAYSIAN FISHERY

A Tragedy of the Commons

The west Malaysian fishery occupies the Indian Ocean coast of peninsular Malaysia, a complex shore lined with extensive mangrove swamps protected by the off-lying Indonesian island of Sumatra. Due to the swamps and to nutrient inflow from many rivers, the area supported an exceedingly rich fishery, unusual in tropical waters. The entire coast was heavily fished. In particular, the coasts of the provinces of Penang and Perak once supported huge fishing communities that regularly caught more than one hundred species of marine life of commercial importance.

Intensive fishing of the area—that is, fishing by fairly large motorized boats—began in about 1960. By the late 1960s hundreds of medium-sized boats and thousands of small boats were active in the area. Yields of high-value fish and shrimp began to decline rapidly. In the 1970s yields continued to decline. Fishing is far from extinct in the area in the 1980s, but stocks—especially of the more valuable fish—have declined catastrophically, and whole communities of fishermen have been ruined or nearly so. Pollution and landfill had much to do with this (Consumers' Association of Penang 1976), but overfishing is clearly the major problem (Anderson and Anderson 1978).

Marja Anderson and I studied one of the central communities in 1970–71 and visited all the fishing communities of any size on the affected part of the coast. The community on which we focused, Kampong Mee (a pseudonym), was particularly unfortunate. Located near the urban areas of Penang and near several other large fishing ports, it was affected by pollution and overfishing more than were the more isolated towns. Also, for reasons that will appear, it was home port to a large number of boats. About 150 small and medium-sized vessels operated all or part of the time from Kampong Mee, with half to two-thirds of them present at any one time. Most of them were motorized trawlers about twenty to thirty feet long—imitations of British vessels of perhaps fifty years before that nonetheless represented a great concentration of catching power. No other port on Penang Island had so many boats. Several of the large mainland ports had many more; however, those boats were almost entirely purse-seiners of very small craft. Motorized trawlers had been driven out of most of the nearby mainland ports and had usually taken refuge at Kampong Mee due to conflict with other fishermen, an instance of local-level specification of the commons.

The extent of overfishing was indicated by the reports of the fishermen and other witnesses and observations of catches (no accurate figures were available). The accounts of the fishermen were consistent. They reported making one to two trawl-hauls (about three to four hours each) on a typical day during the 1960s. By late 1960s, the necessary number of hauls had increased. In 1970–71 the number I observed was invariably four (on a full working day). This represented the maximum possible in a day, since boats had to return to port each night for maintenance, to sell the fish, and for safety. It was a grueling schedule. The reason for the increase was that the fish and shrimp had greatly declined in number—particularly the valuable species and sizes. Some species formerly important to the fishery had disappeared completely, notably the highly prized *chi kaq hu* and *kuan im hu*, the first of which had once been abundant.[1]

By 1970–71 all valuable species had declined precipitously, especially those of the larger size ranges. The trawl-hauls were made up almost entirely of small organisms—especially the young growth forms of fish and shrimp and crabs that would have been valuable if mature. As tiny young, they were usable only for fish-meal fertilizer. There was a fish-meal plant in the village and another in the city. They paid a few cents a pound for fish that, if they had grown up, would have brought up to two or three dollars (U.S.) per pound. The fishermen were as aware as modern marine biologists that trawl-hauls consisting almost entirely of small organisms are prime evidence of extreme overfishing. Adult sizes were fished out. The young were not given a chance to grow up.

Specifications of the Commons: The Fishing War

Trawling began on this part of the coast in 1962. Fishermen using older methods already knew that motorized trawling would endanger their livelihood. They had heard about what had happened in Thailand (not many miles north). They reacted with admirable directness, if not restraint: they turned out in force, seized the first trawler and burned it, threatening the life of the enterprising fishermen who had introduced the threat of disequilibrium.

Thus began the great fishing war of the Penang and Perak coast. Many of the fishermen, especially on the Perak coast, had been or were smugglers and sometimes pirates. They were quite used to handling their own problems by force. However, trawlers were so profitable that they continued to proliferate throughout the area. But since the number of purse-seiners and other small craft was always several times the number of trawlers, the so-called "inshore fishermen" were able to drive the trawlers out of all the mainland ports of any significance. ("Inshore fishermen" was a Malaysian government term for the purse-seiners and small net operators. It is a misnomer; they stayed a little more inshore, on the average, than the trawlermen, but both groups fished primarily close to shore). In only one mainland port were the trawler fishermen so united and tough that they could hold their own militarily against the more numerous inshoremen.

Thus the commons was specified. The coastal inshore men controlled much of the best fishing ground and breeding areas for the fish and shrimp in question and could give some protection to them. However, they were themselves so numerous that they were quite capable of overfishing without the trawlers' help. In addition, the trawlers poached regularly on their patrolled waters, leading to recurrent and often violent confrontations. During our stay in Kampong Mee, a trawler was captured and burned. In this episode one fisherman was killed and another badly slashed. In another area some fifty boats met in what amounted to naval battle on the open sea. The total amount of killing, burning, and damage is unclear, for both the government and the fishermen were understandably anxious to keep the matter quiet, but there were many deaths and boat-burnings.

Attempts to specify the commons by excluding certain groups (who took refuge nearby) were not successful at restricting access to the commons. Further conflict, in the absence of any external control, might have led to a final accommodation that would have protected the resource. At least as likely is the possibility that it would have led to final victory by one strong-man who would have deployed a controlled fleet that could have wiped out the resource rapidly. In any case, conflict was eventually reduced to a low level by military and police intervention. Meanwhile the government tried to control the tragedy of the commons in its own way.

Government "Management" of the Commons

The Malaysian national government intervened in two ways: by passing restrictive laws enforced by the marine police, and by creating fishermen's cooperatives modeled on cooperatives introduced elsewhere in the British Empire and former British Empire states (Anderson 1973; Anderson and Anderson 1978). Cooperativization was to benefit the fishermen by providing them various services, of which the most important was a means of conveying their views and concerns to the political arena. It also provided a way to restrict entry to the fishery: only members of the cooperatives could operate boats in the trawler fleet. The major government attempt to cut down on overfishing was by legislation that prevented the trawlers from operating within nearshore waters. A law against trawling at night was also passed, since there was no other way to prevent poaching on the inshore waters at night.

Neither law was adequately enforced. It would have taken a whole navy of utterly uncorruptible and zealous police to oversee the Penang-Perak shore. Fishermen poached regularly, operated at night, bunched together so that a police boat could chase only one at a time while the others saw and escaped, and souped up their engines so that they could (with a fair start) outrun the police boats. A pursued boat had to cut loose its net to flee if the net was out, and this represented a substantial financial loss. The threat of this loss was the only serious deterrent to poaching.

THE GOVERNMENT'S DECISIONS

Options Foregone and Unforeseen Consequences

I had gone to Malaysia to study decision making, but the fishermen were hardly in a position to make many decisions. The

trawlermen could not deal with the inshore fishermen; the trawlermen were outnumbered and outgunned. They could not stop
fishing; there was no other way to earn a living. They could not
make decisions about the organization, management, direction, or
development of the fishery. The government had preempted that
role. The cooperatives were tightly run by a group of local Malay[2]
political figures and Chinese businessmen and in accord with government directives; the fishermen had no direct voice in either
management or policy-setting. The cooperative boards were not
by any means unresponsive or intransigent, but the fishermen felt
excluded and powerless. Poaching was necessary to make a living.
The alternatives were starvation or leaving Kampong Mee to seek
work elsewhere.

Colin Leys describes developmental decision making as follows:

> The process of "choice" rarely consists of an explicit "moment" at
> which some appropriate person or committee reviews the alter-
> natives, weighs the pros and cons and consciously selects one of
> them. It is, generally, a continual process of options foregone,
> through the passage of time, and through the taking of other deci-
> sions which have the often unforeseen consequence of closing off
> possibilities in spheres not considered at all in the context of the
> decision. (Quoted in Johnston and Kilby 1975: 156)

The fate of the Malaysian fishery follows Leys's law. At the time of
our research Malaysia was exceptionally well run. The government had just survived the riots of 1967–69 and was strikingly
independent of foreign influence. The government tried to respond to the fishermen's needs.

The government just imposed the two regulations described
above. The cooperatives were then tried. All trawlers had to be in
cooperatives to be licensed; other boats did not. The cooperatives
gated entry to the fishery. However, by this time, few were entering the fishery. Far too much catching power was already mobi-
lized. Regulation of entry into the inshore fishery was impossible.
Many of the inshore-fishing towns were isolated and independent
hotbeds of smuggling and occasional small-time piracy. Regulation
of behavior in these communities was no easy matter for any
authority.

The cooperatives had another handicap as regulatory institutions. Their main function was to help the fishermen, and thus (among other things) to represent fishermen's interests. The persons actually in charge of them were not fishermen but Malay bureaucrats and Chinese businessmen. Aware that they did not have the full trust of the fishermen, who viewed them as outsiders, they attempted to establish their credibility by carrying to the state and national level the fishermen's many complaints about the police, the regulations, and all controls on fishing. Moreover, their income depended on the fishery, which meant that it depended on the continuation of inshore and nocturnal trawling and of a large fishing effort. The men in charge of the cooperatives were less than enthusiastic about enforcing the new regulations.

After the trawler-inshore conflict escalated to nearly a small-scale civil war, the government sent in troops and ships, forced arbitration, and ended the more extreme forms of hostility. After that the fishermen were more or less left alone, and overfishing led to decline of the industry. Pollution and filling in of fish breeding grounds took a terrible toll of the fishery in many areas as well. The government did not react to this problem; apparently the benefits to industry were considered greater than the costs to fishermen and consumers (see Consumers' Association of Penang 1976).

It should be noted that at this time, the government was also active politically in the villages. Malaysia's reigning political parties represented an urban—in particular an educated urban—population and had little contact with fishermen. The fishermen were fairly liberal to radical when politically active at all and had often supported the Labour Party (*Partai Buroh*). This left-wing party was suppressed by the government in the 1960s. None of the still-tolerated parties was very attractive to the politically involved fishermen, and many fishermen were apolitical. A mood of apathy and despair settled over the political life of the villages. Most fishermen stated that they felt the government was out to suppress them rather than to help them. This left the cooperatives as the one viable channel for the fishermen to deal with the government. The cooperatives were considered an imposition because a small fee was charged for their services. Fishermen felt that the benefits of cooperativization were not worth this fee and found ingenious ways to cheat (Anderson and Anderson 1978).

Preemption of Control over the Commons

In summary the only effective measure the government took was to reduce overt conflict. Although reduction of conflict was a worthy goal and necessary to maintain public stability, it also prevented the fishermen from coming to their own solutions to the overfishing problem. What the fishermen were trying to do was "capture the commons" in the most literal possible sense: by use of force. Had they been allowed to continue, the fight would have been long and bloody and very possibly unsuccessful. But the government had even less to offer.

Governments have preempted much control in many sectors of life, even in the so-called free-market countries. Malaysia is a capitalist country with a great deal of free enterprise, but the power of government in ultimately directing that free enterprise is seen not only in the present case, but in all sectors of the economy. By following specific policies of regulation, arbitration, selective outlawing of pressure and political groups, infrastructure development, and so on, the government can act on the economy not so much by advocating or initiating specific courses of action as by preventing many courses of action. A government often acts by default, making its decisions by gradually ruling out courses of action until only one remains. The one ultimately followed is not always (or often) the optimal one that would have been chosen if anyone had ever looked at the problem as a whole and tried to come up with an ideal judgment.

In the present case, the government choked off all efforts by the fishermen to help themselves or adapt to their situation. It replaced grassroots democracy in the cooperatives and elsewhere with appointed party men; it abolished the one political party that spoke to and for the fishermen; it stopped the conflict over capturing the commons; it tried to regulate fishing effort. Some of these moves were reasonable, some not. None of them effectively addressed the problem, but all ruled out possible avenues for the fishermen.

Another government act eventually seen as a mistake was the

replacement of private-fish-marketing by government marketing. The private wholesalers were in fierce competition with each other, knew the field thoroughly, and existed on razor-thin profit margins. The government quickly found that even operating at a loss it could not offer the benefits and services that the private marketers did, unless it wished to operate at a level of loss in which it was prepared to write off all salaries, which it was not anxious to do (see Anderson and Anderson 1978).

What the Government Should Have Done and Why It Did Not

It is rather easy to see what the government should have done. A long series of reports, increasingly desperate in tone, had been presented to the government and to its British imperial predecessors (see review in Anderson and Anderson 1978). Active intervention to improve equipment and train fishermen was an obvious first step, along with exploration of marine resources. This may sound paradoxial—why increase fishing effort?—but is reasonable, for with improved gear and knowledge the fishermen could have ranged much more widely instead of concentrating their effort on a narrow band, the inshore zone. The government also could have stimulated development so that fishing would not be so narrowly targeted toward a few choice species.

Another need was regulation of water pollution and landfills (Consumers' Association of Penang 1976). Finally, huge areas of mangrove swamp, salt marsh, and inshore waters should have been absolutely ruled out of bounds for all fishermen, for these were the breeding areas of the main species caught. If the protected areas were made large and *all* fishermen—not just trawlers—were banned, enforcement would have been feasible. But Malaysian governmental involvement in agriculture and food production was limited to what was perceived as key: rice and export crops. Rice provided the real *food*. In the Malay and Chinese languages, "food" and "rice" are synonymous, and the government officials simply could not see the need to devote effort to other foods. Fish is not food, but *lauk*—a Malay word meaning, essentially, flavoring for the rice. Export crops were different; they brought foreign exchange.

Fish was exported, too, but was not considered by the government as a candidate for export-oriented development.

For at least partial explanation we must also turn to matters of ethnicity. The government of Malaysia is dominated by ethnic Malays. Malays in general regard fish as low-prestige food—the rich tend to eat red meat and poultry instead—and that was part of the problem. Most of it, however, was caused by the domination of the fishery by Chinese. Malay-Chinese rivalry was intense at the time. (In the 1980s it has died down as a public, visible problem, largely because the Malays have consolidated their dominance over political life.) With development of Chinese sectors of the economy at a low level of priority, the government naturally concentrated its efforts elsewhere.

However, this begs the question of the development of the Malay fishery. There were many Malay fishing villages in the area with their own distinctive lifestyles and methods. Why were these not developed? The answer here is the final one in our equation: these fisheries were small, impoverished, and peripheral, and the Malaysian government was concentrating its development effort on large-scale projects. It did, for instance, assist in the development of large trawlers—an abortive development, for the big boats turned out to be unable to pay for themselves. A close investigation would have shown that struggling small-scale fisheries needed little help to become viable, whereas highly capitalized new enterprises produced dangerously low returns because of poor knowledge of offshore grounds.

The government operated on the basis of certain rules of thumb. Large, mechanized enterprises were preferred to small ones. Chinese-dominated industries were in low esteem. Regulation was preferred to development, perhaps because it was considered cheaper. Rich, established sectors of the economy were preferred to minor ones. Beliefs and attitudes about food were also important. The government acted on assumptions that were not examined and were sometimes quite counterproductive. At no time was a clear decision made about the fishery as a whole.

The difficulty of making decisions about complex policy issues is demonstrated in the real-world behavior of firms (Winter 1975) and of people in general (Rappoport and Summers 1973; Nisbett and Ross 1980; Hammond, Rohrbaugh, Mumpower, and Adelman

1977). In making judgments, particularly about complex matters, people simply cannot weigh all the cues or variables properly. Moreover, when decisions are made (or not made) according to Leys's Law there is maximum chance of distortions entering the picture.

Even—or perhaps especially—multinational corporations and superpower governments make mistakes. Maximization of power or wealth is not their only motive. Also involved in decision making are desires to suppress those who are disliked, to save time and effort, and to deal with cultural preferences. These factors may not be very important, in some cases, as operatives. However, what they may do is *confound the decision-making process* by introducing so many confusing variables that making a clear decision becomes impossible without special techniques. Under some circumstances, it is questionable whether enlightened self-interest or even un-enlightened self-interest would be worse in managing the commons. Only an *extra*-economic authority or control mechanism can discourage overusers in a commons. There is also a need for special techniques for making informal decisions, such as social judgment theory (Hammond *et al.* 1977) or the Carkhuff model for clarifying problems, goals, and tactics (Carkhuff and Berenson 1977). The only way to solve problems as complex as those of the Malaysian fishery is to use more sophisticated methods of decision making.

CONTROL AND SPECIFICATION OF THE COMMONS

A tragedy of the commons is a loss of control. The alternative to reasserting control is either inaction or scapegoating. Often such maladaptive behavior is an expression not of greed or of too much power, but of too little power. People have too little; they fear to use what they have; or—perhaps most commonly, and the under-lying theme in these events—they do not know how to draw on the power they have. Social judgment theory (Hammond *et al.* 1977) and other decision-making formalizations and psychological aids to focusing and studying can thus have a much wider impor-tance in the world than one might think. The development of skills in coping with problems has been stressed by modern counseling and therapy techniques (Carkhuff and Berenson 1977); this philosophy of growth and personal empowerment is adaptable to the public sphere and conformable with social judgment theory.

A key question is the *locus* of control. Where in the decision process are the real goals? What are the real goals about which decisions are made? (see Randall 1977). Where is the locus of control? Who is making the decisions that actually affect the fate of the resource? What is the place to focus our research—local community, government, or international economic order? In the Malaysian case, the national government was all-important. In other cases, the locus of real control is elsewhere, or two or more levels of polity may have some control.

Systems theory is also useful. The locus of control and optimizing the mix of delegation or concentration of authority is a matter of central concern to systems theory. Preemption of control by high-level authority when control is more efficiently located at the lower levels is known as "meddling" in systems analysis (Flannery 1972). One major cost of meddling has already been noted in the present case. The higher polity is concerned with wide issues, apt to forget or ignore the relatively "minor" problems of local communities, and behaves in a way that diminishes lower-level control.

The importance of emotional involvement with a resource base has rarely been stressed, except perhaps for the involvement of hunters with their game (see, for example, Ridington 1982), but obviously those who derive their livelihood from a fishery are necessarily involved emotionally in preserving it. The extreme importance of emotional involvement in detection and cognitive processing of information is now established (Zajonc 1980; Clarke and Fiske 1982). It is folly to think that fishermen are always going to control the resource base in their best interest, but it is probably a greater folly to think that a high-level polity can do it better by taking over entirely. Classic political theory would tell us that the government should simply impose regulations, serve as a facility for arbitration in disputes, and leave other matters to the local level. This, I feel, would have been the optimal strategy in Kampong Mee: the government could have closed the fishery entirely until the fishermen of the various coastal towns worked out a mutually acceptable policy for specifying the commons, limiting the catch, and preserving breeding stocks.

There is, however, a more interesting effect of the policy of national-level intervention followed by relative inaction. By allowing the tragedy of the commons to play itself out, the government automatically favored the rich over the poor. The rich—whether larger fishing operators with more catching power, or local businessmen dependent on the fishery—could more effectively meet the challenge. Most diversified their interests, moving capital into or out of fishing as opportunity afforded. Others simply fished more and harder. In any case, the poor were much more vulnerable to any setback. It is almost inevitable that, in a conflict over a declining resource base, the strong displaces the weak. Allowing a tragedy of the commons can be seen as a policy of favoring the rich without appearing to do so. More explicit was the use of the fisheries conflict as a pretext to extend networks and structures of governmental control to the villages. The cooperatives and the involvement of the marine police were seen as desirable channels of political power in villages often famous for their independence.

The main thrust of the governments actions in Malaysia in the early 1970s was avoid effective intervention in the fishery's problems. Such a tragedy of the commons may be explained with a model of how intervention fails. I have prepared such a model based on findings on the psychology of individual intervention (Piliavin *et al.* 1981). This model can be summarized as a flow chart (Fig. 16.1).

In this model "to duck" means to define the problem as trivial. "To derogate" means to blame the victims and to say that they are not worthy of help. In the Kampong Mee fishery the main participants were poor and Chinese, and thus the lowest in the government's scale of priorities of groups to help. "To diffuse" means either to scatter authority among many weakly involved polities or to say that other interested parties are really better placed to intervene, or at least should do so along with the decider. In the Kampong Mee case, the government did all of these at once (belying the strict flow-chart nature of the model). I have schematically indicated this by the dotted lines in the figure.

The four alternatives are normally considered in the order indi-

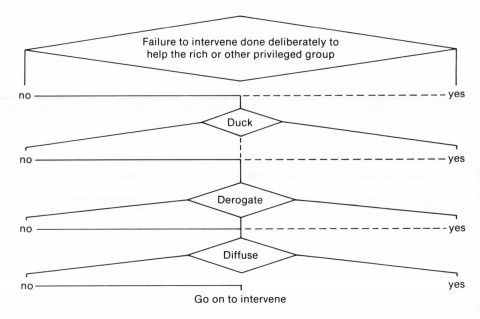

FIG. 16.1. *Flow chart of mental evasion techniques from the psychology of individual intervention.*

cated, but all of them provide excuses for inadequate coping. Piliavin *et al.* (1981) integrated the scheme in a cost-benefit model of intervention, in which the benefits may be merely the good feeling of having helped, and the costs the bad feelings of having helped incompetently. In the Malaysian fishery, both the benefits and the costs were more tangible and obvious. The government, with limited funds and policing abilities, was locked in a fight with political opposition groups, especially the "ultras," right-wing Malay groups who demanded a higher share for Malays in the economy and polity. The moderate group that dominated government in 1970–71 could not afford to seem to support such a radical Chinese population as the fishermen. Neglect of the fishery in 1971 can thus be understood as part of a wider question. If control had remained with local units, this subsumption would not have occurred.

Ultimately, all answers to conservation problems can be reduced to one principle: make the users pay the costs. Passing on costs as "externalities," to downstream users or to a diffuse public, must be prevented (Murphy 1967; Anderson 1972). In the Penang-Perak fishery, the sufferers were the fishermen themselves; they had passed on the costs to their own future enterprises. But the public as a whole also suffered by losing affordable and high-quality protein.

A government that tries to specify the commons by determining that the producers should pay the costs of production (and pass these costs along to the consumers when they can) faces some problems. The producers, and often the consumers, actively oppose this. The interests of those who would normally support the specifying process are often diffuse. Since a small, pointed interest tends more to political activism than does a large but diffuse one, the politics of specifying a commons become very problematic (Murphy 1967; Anderson 1972). Moreover, producers seem to oppose and flagrantly to violate any outside restriction on their practices, *even when they would almost certainly regulate themselves* if left in control (see McCay, Taylor, and Pinkerton, this volume; Anderson and Anderson 1978). The psychology of this seems quite understandable, although unfortunate and rather irrational from an economic point of view. People want to assert what control they can. If the government removes the possibility of sensible control, people will prefer miscontrol or the "illusion of control" to complete passivity. I have elsewhere elaborated in detail on the extreme and explicit problems and tensions caused in Kampong Mee by the felt loss of control (Anderson and Anderson 1978; Anderson 1983; see also Schulz 1977).

The only reasonable solution is for a government or polity to act as a disputing ground or judicial authority and leave control and initiation to the directly affected parties: producers and consumers, including all those who would be hurt by destruction of the resource base. Higher government levels may have to enforce restraint, however. The appropriate locus of control, in terms of the level at which action is initiated and also the level at which adjudication is performed, will vary according to the resource, ranging from worldwide (as in the case of whales) to local. A tradition that goes back to the Chinese sage Sheng Pu-Hai (Creel 1972) and his contemporaries, and that is embodied today in systems theory, focuses on exactly this problem as it applies to general administration.

342 THE STATE AND THE COMMONS

Another way to look at this is that control is most effectively exerted on a resource at the point of maximal information, that is, at the point at which one knows most about the level of resource. For salmon, this would be the actual entry of the spawning river, where one can count the fish as they pass; traditional Native American systems of salmon management took this into account and could ensure adequate escapement (Swezey and Heizer 1977). In Malaysia the problem of locating such a point would have been more difficult, but careful study of mangrove swamps and nearby shallows where many or most of the marine organisms spawned would have been critical.

Ultimately, tragedies of the commons can be prevented only by invoking a mixed system. It is possible to separate three ways of specifying the commons:

1. Privatization
2. Community control, territories, controlled access, and refuges (I view all these as aspects of one type of specification, perhaps best called "localization")
3. Public control at the most general level—normally by legal limits (bag limits, quotas, antipollution laws, and the like)

Unfortunately, the prognosis for the world looks poor. The ratio of human population to resources is worsening rapidly as populations increase and resources are drawn down. Furthermore, increasing affluence and increasingly wasteful resource use (even by the nonaffluent) is adding to the pressure on the resource base. More significant, perhaps, is a trend toward unstable, authoritarian governments. A government that is trying to consolidate control by suppressing local polities is least apt to exercise that control effectively. A more stable, secure government can both use its power effectively and also give up a good deal of that power to local communities without feeling threatened.

Culture can be seen in large measure as a storehouse of strategies for solving personal and general problems, and of means to persuade people to use those strategies. The breakdown of traditional cultures and systems in the modern world thus leads to a failure of problem-solving algorithms, which leads in turn to loss of control and to violent means of resolving questions. Natural-resource depletion may be seen in part as an aspect of the same pattern.

᪇

NOTES

Research on which this chapter is based was supported by the National Science Foundation. I am grateful also to Ch'ng Teng Liang, Ooi Sang Kuang, and the University of California, Riverside; to my former wife Marja Anderson; to the people of Kampong Mee and other fishing towns of Malaysia; and to the many government officials, who must remain anonymous here, who provided information. I thank Evelyn Pinkerton and Kimberly Martin for help with the writing.

1. I know only the Penang Hokkien names of these fish. They were so depleted by 1970 that I never saw one or found a marine biologist who knew what they were.

2. The term *bumiputra,* now used in place of the older "Malay," was not yet used in 1970–71, and I have decided to be consistently anachronistic and use the "ethnographic present" term.

17 Intercepting the State

DRAMATIC PROCESSES IN THE ASSERTION OF LOCAL COMANAGEMENT RIGHTS

Evelyn Pinkerton

BRITISH COLUMBIA FISHERMEN, hearing of the University of British Columbia study of the fishing industry, would frequently comment: "You're too late. The horse has already left the barn." Sometimes the "horse" referred simply to the health of the industry, seen as on an irreversible path of decline. At other times the "horse" represented the ability of fishermen or other citizens to influence management decisions by the Canadian Department of Fisheries and Oceans, the centralized federal agency that is the information gatherer, license administrator, international negotiator, and regulator of commercial fishing and fishermen on the British Columbia coast.

Actions of the Canadian state, especially through this bureaucracy, have played a key role in the decline of the salmon fishery in British Columbia by both inciting and exacerbating problems that in the classic bioeconomic paradigm are attributed solely to the common-property nature of the resource. After discussing the relationship of state actions to problems surrounding the decline of the fishery, I examine a case in which an Indian community, deeply disturbed about its diminishing local fishery, brought about a confrontation with the state and the eventual protection of this local fishery. The tragedy-of-the-commons model presupposes that members of a community cause problems with respect to the resources they hold in common, and it is the role of government to keep this from happening. In this case it is the state that permits and even creates the resource problem; it is the community, including local fishermen, that holds the problem in check.

This case is analyzed with reference to the anthropological lit-

344

erature on informal property rights held by communities in industrialized countries over the fishing territories on which they depend. For purposes of this chapter, I consider informal property rights to be the ability or power of communities to exercise their collective will in resource management, an ability unrecognized by law. Such informal rights are exercised in contravention of the legal definition of the fishery as an open-access, common-property resource from which no one with a fishing license can be excluded. As Guppy (1984) notes, the limiting of access by licensing does not in itself alter the common-property, open-access nature of fish harvesting, because even a limited number of entrants may still compete to capture a mobile and limited resources.

The literature shows that informal property rights are manifested in a variety of ways by which communities control access to fishing privileges (licensing), control access to local fishing territories, control degree of effort applied to stocks within local territories, and curtail the rights of noncommunity members to fish local grounds or intercept local stocks. For example, Maine lobstermen (Acheson 1975) informally limit access to fishing privileges (the equivalent of licensing) by territorial exclusion, and in so doing can limit the degree of effort. New Jersey whiting fishermen (McCay 1980) do not control territories but informally control access, effort, and catch distribution. A Cornwall oystering municipality (Cove 1973) legally limits access, but the fishermen informally limit effort. In some cases, local communities may succeed in obtaining legal sanction and government enforcement for local management (see Langdon 1984b). The ability of communities to exercise these kinds of controls might best be conceived as a bundle of informal rights (Martin 1984). Theoretically, a community that retains complete control over its fishery holds all four of the rights mentioned above. Langdon (1984b) documents a case in which an Aleut community in Alaska controls not only access to territories within its local lagoon fishery (which also translates into control of degree of effort), but also has made the state limit fishing effort in adjacent territories where the local stocks might be intercepted by outsiders. This community might be thought of as possessing the second, third, and fourth rights, and not disadvantaged by the state's control of the first right, access to fishing licenses.

The first three of the four property rights may be useless,

however, if the fourth right (control of interception of migratory resources by outsiders) does not exist. Anthropologists in New-foundland (McCay 1979; Faris 1982; Barrett and Davis 1984) have shown that interception by offshore fleets can threaten local cod stocks such that stocks conserved by local management of access and effort may be harvested by fisherman outside the scope of local control. In this case, a tragedy of the commons may still occur, despite local property rights, whether formal or informal.

In such conflicts of local versus nonlocal interests, the role of the state as a regulator is normally the deciding factor. In this case I focus on the critical role of the state in regulating an interception salmon fishery in British Columbia and demonstrate the way in which a community can exert a degree of informal control over the interception of local stocks on which it depends, even in the absence of formal legal rights to do so. When it became apparent that local stocks were threatened, the local community, rather than contributing to the demise of the local fishery, confronted the state in a demand for proper management and put into effect its own emergency management regime.

In this case the state could have acted to diminish the problems of overinvestment, overfishing, and interception as it has, for example, in Alaska. There, the potential tragedy of the commons has been constrained on two fronts. On the one hand, the state has limited the size of vessels, has forbidden the use of hydraulic drums on seiners, has offered more limited financing, and has issued limited-entry permits specific to areas and fisheries (Rearden 1983; Langdon 1984a). On the other hand, it has also allowed a community to control the fishery in its area (Langdon 1984b). In British Columbia the state has not only exercised less control over the increase in investment and catching power of the fleet, but it has also allowed local communities almost no control over their local fisheries. The case at hand is rather exceptional as an example of a community's demand for control over interception of its threatened local stocks.

THE INTERCEPTION PROBLEM

At first glance, the salmon of British Columbia seem an extreme example of a recalcitrant resource unamenable to any form of local

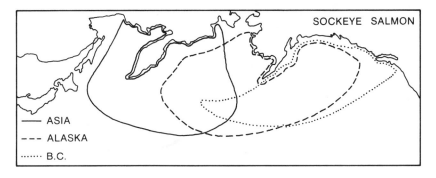

FIG. 17.1. *Sockeye salmon migrations patterns.*

control or comanagement.[1] The salmon are anadromous: they travel hundreds of miles on the high seas during their life cycle and, in the process of returning to their riverine spawning grounds, pass through U.S. waters and along many miles of Canadian coastline before reaching their "home" territory. Sockeye salmon range the most widely of the five Pacific salmon species, often crossing the international dateline (180 degrees west latitude) and returning through the Gulf of Alaska after about four years at sea (Fletcher 1983). The most important sockeye stocks originate in the Fraser River in southern British Columbia and often also pass through several B.C. fisheries and through U.S. waters off Washington State before entering the Fraser (Fig. 17.1).

In aboriginal times, interception was usually not a problem. With the exception of reef nets at Sook on the southwestern coast of Vancouver Island and in Puget Sound, salmon were usually captured in weirs or nets only after they had entered their spawning territories or the major river systems. Ceremonial life and conscious management by Indian groups dictated periods of abstention from fishing so that adequate escapement of salmon to their spawning grounds up the rivers and to other upriver groups was ensured (Rogers 1979; Cove 1982; Swezey and Heizer 1977).

The evolution of commercial salmon fishing in the twentieth century saw the capture technology move progressively seaward and become more mobile and adept at intercepting the fish before they reached the home spawning rivers (Hayward 1981b). The most dramatic development in this direction in the past fifteen years has been the rapid increase in the catching power of the purse-seine fleet, whose mobility, capture technology, and holding capacity far outweighs that of the smaller gillnet and troll vessels.

A 1969 fleet-rationalization program limiting the number of licenses resulted in enormous investment being made during the 1970s in large, five-man, purse-seine vessels at the expense of many smaller, one-man, gillnet and troll vessels that had previously kept some 6,225 vessel operators employed (Pearse and Wilen 1979). Investments in larger boats were encouraged by a combination of boat-construction subsidies, tax-credit and write-off allowances, the new Indian Fishermen's Assistance Program, and the newly upgraded Fishermen's Improvement Loan Act, which during this period made increasing amounts of capital available to fishermen for new vessel construction and acquisition of more sophisticated gear (McKay and Ouellette 1978; McKay and Healey 1981; Pearse 1982; McMullan 1984). Banks took a greater interest in supporting license and vessel purchase when the license became a limited but still transferable commodity, a quasi property right, and thus took over much of the financing traditionally performed by processing companies.

Whereas the gillnetters (especially Indian gillnetters) had focused on local areas, the seiners built since 1972 (about 36 percent of the seine fleet [Canada, Department of Fisheries and Oceans, 1982]) were larger, more costly vessels that usually required the salmon stocks of several areas to justify their investment and operating expenses. In the late 1970s and early 1980s, a large seine fleet (increased from 388 vessels in 1967 to some 532 vessels in 1981) with enormously increased capacity roamed the entire British Columbia coast to compete with smaller, local fleets for the salmon. Between 1968 and 1977, average net tonnage increased in the seine fleet by 2.9 tons, compared to an average increase of 1.2 tons by the troll and gillnet fleet (Hayward 1981a). The ratio of mobile to stationary (fishing only two or three areas) seiners went steadily from 5:1 in 1973 to 12:1 in 1976 (Hilborn and Ledbetter 1979).

One can argue, with the forgers of the bioeconomic model of common-property-driven overinvestment, that these investment decisions were individuals' rational responses to incentives. However, many of the incentives were provided directly by the government, whose mandate is presumably to provide safeguards *against* such individual rationality but collective irrationality in redundant investments. In Alaska the government was able to protect the collective interest by limiting vessel size, technology, and mobility. The result is that Alaska's limited-entry program has not attracted nearly the degree of redundant capital investment that occurred in British Columbia (see Langdon 1984a).

Fishermen acting in collective irrationality may be in the minority and need not be viewed as uncontrollable. (Two-thirds of the fleet did not make the enormous investments described.) Many seasoned fishermen correctly viewed the high salmon and herring prices of the 1970s as a brief phenomenon produced and later eradicated by fluctuations in world supplies. Since local salmon supplies had not increased, they responded cautiously. Figure 17.2 shows that the average value of seiners increased at a faster and higher rate than was true of other gear types when measured in constant 1971 dollars (with the exception of freezer trollers).[2] In addition, seiners took an increasingly greater share of the catch, as

FIG. 17.2. *Average value of salmon vessels by gear type in constant 1971 dollars (compiled from Department of Fisheries and Oceans files).*

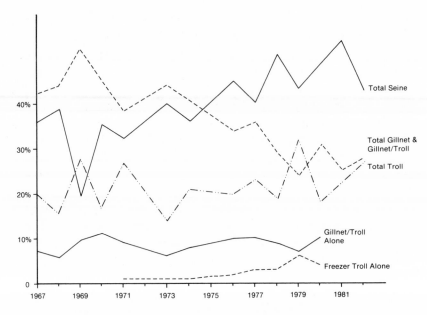

FIG. 17.3. *Percentage of total salmon catch for each gear type
by weight, 1967–82 (1972 and 1975 omitted).
Compiled from Department of Fisheries and
Oceans license files.*

shown in Figure 17.3. The modest increases in investment by
gillnetters and combination gillnet-trollers did not increase their
share of the catch: instead, their share declined.

The greatly increased investment in the mobile seine fleet appears to have had two effects. First, seine skippers who had assumed greater debts were responding to the predictions that
salmon enhancement, the two-hundred-mile limit, and the bonanza herring industry would provide unprecedented returns.
When these expectations were not borne out and fishermen ended
up heavily indebted (McMullan 1984), they had no choice but to
fish harder (see Cone 1973 and Langdon 1982).

A second effect of increased investment in seines was greater
political pressure applied to the Fisheries Department to open
areas to fishing. Department officials (Anonymous, pers. comm.)
report that large processing companies, which owned at least a
quarter of the seine fleet in addition to their joint-venture interests

in other seiners, could often use political pressure to allow fishing on stocks against the better judgment of conservative fisheries biologists who recommended closures of fishing areas.[3] As a result, many of the smaller stocks had been severely stressed and some were eliminated by the late 1970s. This was particularly true in more isolated areas such as the Queen Charlotte Islands, where the average escapement (adult salmon who escape capture and return to the river to spawn) for the 1948–52 period of 11.5 million adults had fallen to 3.4 million in the 1978–82 period. At the same time in this area at least 29 salmon stream populations have become extinct since 1947. (A salmon population is considered extinct if it has not appeared for ten consecutive years.) The rate of extinction has increased every year since 1958, so that by 1983 the average rate of extinction reached four populations per year (Shirvell and Charbonneau 1984). The Department of Fisheries and Oceans was also forced to close some formerly productive fishing grounds for a number of years (for example, Rivers Inlet, once the third largest fishery in British Columbia) to allow the stocks to recover, and to reduce the number of days of allowable fishing in many areas. Although the erosion of stocks was not new in the 1970s, and government efforts to constrain effort had suffered previous breakdowns in the 1940s and 1950s, it is important to note that the decline worsened in the 1970s, and that by the 1980s fishermen were able to link it clearly to government programs.

Efforts to rectify the problem of stock loss by "salmon enhancement," a hatchery-release aquaculture program that became large-scale by 1977, were in general successful but often at the expense of the smaller river systems. This happened partly because there was insufficient funding to enhance all the streams simultaneously in the capital-intensive style selected by the Department of Fisheries. As a result, when the larger, more economically important stocks were enhanced by large hatcheries, and later captured with the smaller unenhanced stocks, the latter were further weakened because they were taken in proportionately larger numbers. The two major river systems, the Fraser at Vancouver, and the Skeena at Prince Rupert, increased their overall salmon productivity due to hatcheries, enhancement, spawning channels, and (in the case of the Fraser River) international requirements for careful management. As the emphasis on overall productivity rose during the

1970s, research and development of smaller river systems received little attention and their importance was generally not recognized.

International factors also played a key role in salmon management. An important consideration in the harvest of sockeye and pink salmon stocks in isolated areas was a Canada-U.S. treaty requiring a division of the Fraser River stocks with the U.S. if the fish were caught in the designated "convention waters" in the southern areas of British Columbia (Fig. 17.4). In order to maximize the Canadian catch of Fraser stocks, therefore, the Fisheries Department at times sacrificed other management considerations by increasing the fishing effort on Fraser sockeye (and other local stocks) in the approach waters of more northerly areas. The desire to intercept Fraser-bound fish that passed through U.S. waters had been at earlier times also an incentive to increase the Cana-

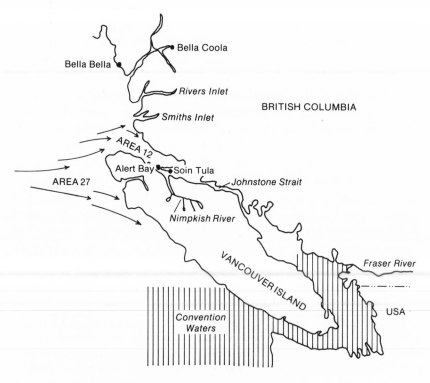

FIG. 17.4. *Migration route of Nimpkish and Fraser River sockeye through Areas 27 and 12.*

dian seine fleet. James Sinclair, Minister of Fisheries in the 1950s, imported seventy-to-eighty-foot sardine seiners from California in order to fish Fraser pink salmon stocks vigorously enough to force inclusion of pink stocks in the sockeye division treaty. These seiners were encouraged to fish seven days a week at the time, although after the treaty was achieved, their time had to be greatly reduced. A similar set of events took place with the salmon-trolling fleet, which stressed Canadian chinook stocks in an effort to intercept U.S.-bound chinook. In this manner, dependencies, fleet investment, and overfishing based on short-term political goals were encouraged at the expense of long-term control of fishing effort. Thus the state in both direct and indirect ways incited both overcapitalization and interception.

I have documented the impact of overall fleet overcapitalization and interception on the local gillnet fleet in Bella Coola elsewhere (Pinkerton, 1983). This fleet had not engaged in redundant capital investment during the 1970s and continued to take a large percentage of its catch in the immediate area. In 1982 the Bella Coola Indian fleet alone (about half of the local fleet; data are unavailable for the non-Indian fleet) took 66 percent of its catch in the immediate local area and 83 prcent in the immediate and adjacent areas, within roughly a sixty-mile radius. Yet their catch comprised only about 15 percent of the entire catch in the local area and less in the adjacent areas. This percentage would be more than twice as high if figures were available for non-Indian local residents, but these data still show the high decree of non-local fishing effort in the area, and the reason only short openings were permitted in Bella Coola by the 1980s, eventually forcing some of the local fleet to become more mobile and capitalized to survive. Interception of local stocks before they reached the local area also played an important role.

As an isolated area to which other vessels had to travel, however, the Bella Coola fleet enjoyed certain locational advantages, and the Bella Coola local of the United Fishermen and Allied Workers Union lobbied for the institution of area licensing, which would permit only a limited number of vessels into one area (Miller 1978). Because fish are legally the common property of all the licensed fishermen of any particular gear type, the Fisheries and Oceans Department cannot open an area to only a few vessels of any one gear type. Instead, the Department has to hope that few vessels will find it worthwhile to travel to Bella Coola to fish for one day a week.

Efforts by the Fisheries and Oceans Department at fine-grained, local management programs to prevent the overfishing of local stocks show how the state has reduced overfishing in an area, despite its legal definition as open access. Beginning in the late 1920s, the Department designated special gillnet areas (closed to seiners) along several parts of the coast. The Bella Coola Gillnet Area was instrumental in permitting the local small-boat fleet to survive on a local fishery longer than would have been possible otherwise. Such areas restricted to particular gear types, along with special openings and closures specific to particular gear types, are exceptions to the legal common-property access of all licensed fishermen. In 1984 an association representing seine-vessel owners used a court injunction to prevent the Department from declaring special day-long openings for gillnetters (in this case on the Skeena River and in Johnstone Straits). The basis for the injunction was that the Department was mandated to practice conservation but not to manage fishermen through allocations of fishing time to different gear types. The decision has been appealed by the Department, on the grounds that proper management would be impossible without such regulation, and, as of 1986, the issue has not been resolved.

Another system of limiting effort collapsed under comparable political pressure. This was the "transfer system," so called because it established purse-seine areas and required vessels to check in with the Fisheries Department officer when they entered an area and when they left. It reduced the number of days of fishing by the number of vessels permitted in the inlet that surpassed its estimated carrying capacity. This system, which began around 1929, broke down in the late 1950s because of the increased mobility of the seine fleet. In Bella Coola the result was that more fish were intercepted before they entered the protected local area reserved for gillnets. The absence of effective ways of limiting interception was one of the forces pushing some of the Bella Coola gillnetters to invest in more mobile vessels to fish other areas of the coast along with the rest of the overcapitalized fleet.

Other isolated areas of the coast took a similar proportion of their fish locally and suffered a similar reduction in local stocks.

Under the license-limitation program, their small gillnet and troll fleets suffered a similar decline (Fig. 17.5). Although fishermen in urban areas also suffered a decline in licenses, these fishermen had other job opportunities in the 1970s. Such was not the case in isolated villages, whether Indian or non-Indian. For them, loss of fishing jobs had particularly severe consequences. Before license limitation, licenses cost a nominal fee and most families had access to at least one small vessel; after the limitation program began, these communities entered a situation in which "fishing has become a rich man's game."

A comparison of the range of fishing incomes in the Bella Bella area (including Bella Coola) in 1969, at the onset of license limitation, with those of later years demonstrates the effect of the elimination of low-income fishermen from the fleet (Table 17.1). One of the goals of "fleet rationalization" was elimination of "marginal" fishermen. The effect was to eliminate the low-income fishermen. However, the economic marginality of these fishermen is questionable if one recognizes that their income-to-investment ratio can be as high as that of high-income fishermen, given the lower costs of the former (Pinkerton 1983, in press). Table 17.1 also shows the progressive concentration of fishing income into fewer hands. In 1969 the difference between the earnings of the bottom and top quartile of Bella Bella fishermen was $6,060; by 1976 it was $25,119.

The process of concentrating licenses and promoting greater investments in one sector of the Indian fleet was given particular impetus by the Indian Fishermen's Assistance Program. The program was available only to those who could afford a 15 percent down payment. It tended to encourage a few Indian skippers to invest in larger vessels and to circulate licenses from the Indian gillnet fleet into the Indian seine fleet. It contributed to the further decline of the Indian small-boat fleet and the build-up of a seine fleet in areas such as Alert Bay (West Coast Information and Research, 1980; Goldthorpe 1980; McKay and Healey 1981; James 1984). One might speculate that if government assistance had been made available for greater investment in labor (e.g., capital made available for paying deckhands' wages, training programs, etc.) instead of capital equipment, less investment in greater fishing power would have occurred and more skippers would have

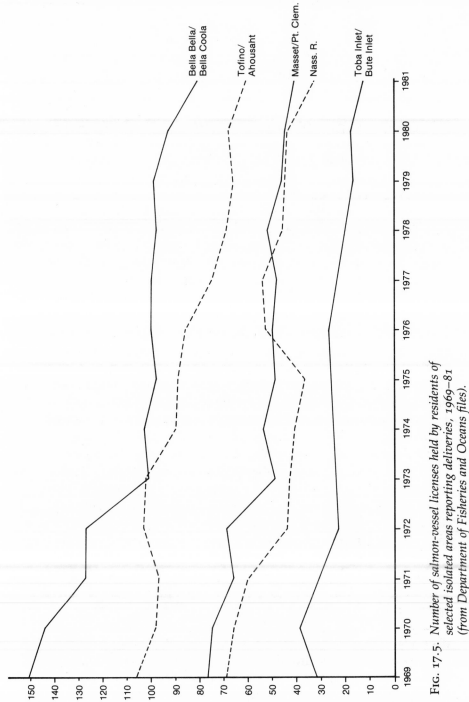

Fig. 17.5. *Number of salmon-vessel licenses held by residents of selected isolated areas reporting deliveries, 1969–81 (from Department of Fisheries and Oceans files).*

TABLE 17.1

Locally Held Salmon Licenses and Range of Incomes from Salmon Fishing for Selected Years, 1969–1981, in Bella Bella

YEAR	ALL SALMON LICENSES	B-CATEGORY LICENSES[a]	RANGE ($)	MEDIAN ($)	AVERAGE BOTTOM QUARTILE ($)	AVERAGE TOP QUARTILE ($)	DIFFERENCE BETWEEN TOP AND BOTTOM ($)
1969	53	21	17–11,515	3,019	818	6,878	6,060
1970	51	5	477–34,784	5,864	2,121	14,911	12,790
1972	31	3	730–38,624	7,017	3,535	19,993	16,458
1976	25	1	70–56,253	12,794	6,360	31,479	25,119
1979	26	2	666–67,866	18,204	4,822	41,572	36,750
1980	25	2	560–29,888	15,923	4,305	26,128	21,823
1981	19	0	5,966–23,770	12,009	7,906	22,112	14,206

SOURCE: Department of Fisheries and Oceans sales slips
[a]Delivered less than $2,500 worth of salmon

continued the more labor-intensive small-boat fishery. It is not surprising that when capital is made available for greater investment in vessels, fishermen respond by enlarging their vessels.

In sum, a number of government actions such as license limitation, fishermen's loan programs, vessel-construction subsidies, tax incentives, as well as the regulation of fishing effort, acquaculture, and interception, contributed to a situation in which the character of isolated maritime communities dependent on fishing appeared to be radically altered. Far fewer people had fishing licenses, many more people were unemployed or on welfare, and those employed had far higher investments, incomes, and often indebtedness than formerly.

The presumed increase in stratification within the community, as well as the increasing pressure on fishermen with high investments to conduct themselves in purely "businesslike" ways (Sewid 1969), could lead to the prediction that community members would be less able to exert control over local fishermen. It is not clear how much the increased economic stratification in the Kwakiutl community to be described affected community solidarity and control, since traditional Kwakiutl society was highly stratified. However, in the traditional system and that which lasted into the 1950s and longer, everyone worked and participated in some way, whatever his or her status. The "food fishery" that plays a large part in the social drama to be discussed was important not only as a source of food for most households but also because it enabled even impoverished, low-status families to participate in some way. The unprecedented fact of the middle to late twentieth century was that large numbers of people lost access to jobs and began to drop out of social participation as well, with concurrent demoralization and social problems.

Much of the literature on community and ethnic enclaves suggests that egalitarian communities, more than stratified ones, are likely to exert social control successfully within their ranks and to act in a united fashion against outside interests (Orans 1969). The following case study demonstrates how, even in a case of stratification and economic dissolution, a community can discipline its most "businesslike" members as well as its most impoverished citizens to act in a unified fashion to protect its collective and long-term interests.

THE AREA 27 CONTROVERSY:
A SOCIAL DRAMA

"Social dramas" are occurrences that do not need to be frequent to reveal (and perhaps to transform) underlying structural relationships (Turner 1974; Moore and Myerhoff 1975). A social drama took place in 1977 in Alert Bay, a Kwakiutl Indian community of about six hundred people on the northeast coast of Vancouver Island (see Fig. 17.4), that had lost most of its gillnet fleet and had, by 1977, approximately 35 seiners. (Six hundred non-Indians in Alert Bay operated 15 seiners.) The Indian community, particularly the Nimpkish Band, responded to imminent loss of a local salmon run in a political and social process that I conceive of as a social drama, one that included the development of a stronger sense of *communitas* (Turner 1974) against the reality of highly divergent interests in the economically stratified community. This in turn made possible concerted political action in "intercepting the state" and protecting the Nimpkish River sockeye salmon stocks.

The inhabitants of longest standing in Alert Bay were the Nimpkish Band, who had originally lived at the mouth of the Nimpkish

River, the largest river system on Vancouver Island and the spawning ground of sockeye salmon stocks critical to the Alert Bay food fishery and important to the local commercial fishery. In the mid-1800s, when a saltery and a mission were established on Cormorant Island, the Nimpkish were persuaded to relocate across the straits from the Nimpkish River to their present site on Cormorant Island because the Nimpkish River estuary was unsuitable for boat moorage. The saltery, which became a cannery in 1881, used Kwakiutl labor and exploited the sockeye salmon stocks of the Nimpkish River, where the company obtained a drag-seine license (Gillis and McKay 1980; Department of Fisheries and Oceans files). After the cannery closed in 1931, the population of Alert Bay and the surrounding island villages, most of which eventually amalgamated into the town of Alert Bay, became dependent almost exclusively on fishing.

During the 1950s and 1960s residents of Alert Bay and the many Kwakiutl communities on surrounding islands were chiefly gillnetters. The saying was, "Every household had at least one boat," and the fishery was almost entirely local (see Rohner 1967: 45). The major Kwakiutl villages involved in fishing were Gilford Island, Village Island, New Vancouver, Kingcome Inlet, Turnour Island, and Alert Bay. Most villages had more than twenty gillnets (Basil Ambers, pers. comm.). Some of these boats may have been rented from, and later repossessed by, processors who held mortgages on them (see Rohner 1967).

Historical records of the numbers of "deliveries" (boatloads of salmon delivered to processors at the end of a fishing trip) in the Alert Bay area, known as Area 12 within the state's management system, suggests that in the 1950s and 1960s the overall gillnet effort in the area was far greater than seine effort (Table 17.2). In the 1970s, seine deliveries began to equal or exceed gillnet deliveries. This may be partially due to the fact that only a few local gillnet boats remained by the late 1970s because most of the local fishermen had converted to seiners. Some fishermen indicate that they converted to seiners because of the government incentives described above. The more marginal fishermen did not have sufficient catches in 1967 and 1968 (the qualifying years) to qualify for licenses,[4] or sold their licenses under the 1971 government buyback program and abandoned their vessels. Some sold older vessels because they could not afford to repair them; others sold out

TABLE 17.2

Number of Deliveries in Area 12 by Seiners and Gillnetters per Year (Selected Years Between 1954 and 1980)

			SEVEN-YEAR AVERAGE	
YEAR	SEINE	GILLNET	SEINE	GILLNET
1954	355	431		
1955	656	1586	503	1473
1956	302	1263		
1957	502	1429		
1958	578	2034		
1959	711	2075		
1960	419	1496		
1966	481	1314		
1967	829	1674	628	1370
1968	529	1570		
1969	440	1179		
1970	625	1883		
1971	572	828		
1972	922	1148		
1973	125	377		
1974	482	447	481	537
1975	441	517		
1976	577	673		
1978	551	848		
1979	697	479		
1980	497	419		

SOURCE: Department of Fisheries and Oceans files.

later because they could not afford to upgrade the vessels under a new inspection program (see also McKay and Healey 1981).

Five-year average fishing effort on all sockeye stocks (Nimpkish, Fraser, and others) in Area 12 increased, beginning in the 1956–60 period, the most notable increase occurring in the periods 1966–70 and 1976–80 (Table 17.3). The fluctuation in sockeye catches over these periods appears to co-vary positively with the migration of Fraser River sockeye through Area 12 (instead of around the west coast of Vancouver Island and through Juan de Fuca Strait, which occurred in years of lower water temperature). Fishing effort in Area 12 was increased to capture the sockeye before they entered convention waters and had to be divided with the U.S. (Nimpkish

TABLE 17.3

Five-Year Average Commercial Salmon Catch in Area 12 (× 1000)

YEARS	SOCKEYE	COHO	PINKS	CHUM	CHINOOK
1946–50[a]	310.6	483.8	2,000.8	1,176.8	50.2
1951–55[b]	241.6	392.2	2,032.2	749.4	31.6
1956–60	624.4	365.0	1,442.6	377.4	40.6
1961–65	235.8	317.2	1,002.6	108.1	40.2
1966–70	686.0	473.6	2,392.4	462.0	47.4
1976–80	892.4	180.4	1,822.0	436.0	61.0

SOURCE: Nimpkish Band Council 1982 and Department of Fisheries and Oceans files
[a]Data from Area 11 and 12 combined
[b]1951–53 data for Areas 11 and 12 combined

Band Council 1982). When Fraser sockeye migrated chiefly down the west coast of Vancouver Island, the major fishery occurred by U.S. and Candian seiners in Juan de Fuca Strait and Puget Sound, and most of the Fraser sockeye was divided evenly between the two countries, according to a 1940s treaty. It appears that the increasing fishing effort on sockeye in Area 12 was thus a result not only of the build-up of the seine fleet, but also of the government's attempt to maximize the Canadian catch before the sockeye entered waters covered by the treaty.

Maximizing the Fraser River sockeye catch of all Canadian fishermen entailed a cost for the Nimpkish River sockeye, which were taken in proportionately greater numbers during the heavy mixed-stock fishery in Area 12. Notable declines in Nimpkish sockeye escapements from their early 1950s level of 100,000 began in the mid-1950s, but the first estimates of fewer than 50,000 returning spawners did not appear until 1965. From 1975 to 1980, all sockeye escapements were less than 50,000, with returning spawners hitting an all-time low in 1978 of 8,500 (Nimpkish Band Council 1982; see Table 17.4). Escapements did not improve until 1981, when a return of 60,000 occurred (chiefly because of the successful efforts of the community, detailed below). It is in the context of these declining escapements that the social drama of 1977 must be viewed.

Nimpkish Band officials learned in March 1977 that a regional Department of Fisheries study conducted in 1976 had concluded that the Nimpkish River sockeye stocks were in grave danger and should not be fished in 1977. In 1973 a gill disease (*Dermocystidium*)

TABLE 17.4

Nimpkish River Escapement Estimates, 1949–83

Year	Sockeye	Coho	Pink	Chum	Chinook
1949	100,000+	15,000	7,500	100,000+	3,000
1950	100,000+	1,500	15,000	100,000+	7,500
1951	100,000+	15,000	7,500	100,000+	15,000
1952	100,000+	15,000	15,000	100,000+	15,000
1953	100,000+	15,000	3,000	100,000+	15,000
1954	80,000	7,500	3,000	35,000	15,000
1955	80,000	15,000	1,500	75,000	15,000
1956	80,000	15,000	3,000	35,000	7,500
1957	100,000+	15,000	1,500	35,000	1,500
1958	80,000	7,500	3,000	35,000	7,500
1959	80,000	7,500	3,000	15,000	7,500
1960	80,000	7,500	3,000	35,000	7,500
1961	80,000	15,000	3,000	35,000	7,500
1962	100,000+	35,000	3,000	15,000	15,000
1963	100,000+	35,000	1,500	15,000	7,500
1964	80,000	15,000	3,000	15,000	7,500
1965	40,000	35,000	400	15,000	3,000
1966	120,000+	15,000	7,500	35,000	1,500
1967	120,000+	3,000	400	15,000	1,500
1968	40,000	7,500	15,000	75,000	7,500
1969	100,000+	1,500	400	7,500	400
1970	40,000	35,000	3,000	15,000	7,500
1971	80,000	15,000	3,000	7,500	750
1972	80,000	7,500	15,000	35,000	7,500
1973	100,000+	15,000	N.O.	25,000	10,000
1974	150,000	8,000	12,000	5,000	5,000
1975	40,000	2,000	600	8,000	1,100
1976	35,000	7,500	400	6,000	7,000
1977	15,000	1,500	75	15,000	750
1978	8,500	2,500	1,700	16,500	1,300
1979	20,000	500	N.O.	6,000	500
1980	24,000	600	7,500	13,500	300
1981	60,000	2,500	UNK	10,000	700
1982	60,000	UNK	1,500	55,000	700
1983	70,000	100	1,500	75,000	1,000

SOURCE: Nimpkish Band Council 1982 and Department of Fisheries and Oceans files

had killed a large percentage of the spawners, and the 1977 return run from this brood year (this species has a four-to-five-year life cycle) was thus considerably weakened. As a protective conservation measure, the regional fisheries biologists who had conducted the study felt it was imperative to prohibit fishing during the month of July in Area 27 (on the west coast of Vancouver Island, where the stocks first approached land) and in the northern half of Area 12, where the Nimpkish stocks passed on their way to the river.

From an overall Canadian perspective, both Area 27 and Area 12 were considered important interception areas for Fraser sockeye stocks before they entered convention waters and had to be divided with the Americans. It was thus considered highly desirable to concentrate as much Canadian effort as possible on these stocks. A July seine fishery had been introduced in Area 27 in 1975 and 1976, representing a major increase in fishing effort: in 1973 there were 2 seine and 89 gillnet deliveries in Area 27; in 1976, 80 seine and 1,389 gillnet deliveries. Any effort to close the area would thus represent the precedence of conservation concerns in one area over allocation of fish to Canadians over Americans and to the rest of the fleet, which had suffered under increased closures elsewhere on the coast. However, the regional biologists estimated that only 20 percent of the fish passing through Area 27 in mid-July were Fraser stocks; the rest were Nimpkish and Smith's Inlet stocks. Fearing an unbearable pressure on the Nimpkish stocks, their recommendation was "to eliminate the July net fishery in Area 27. If, however, it is politically desirable to fish Fraser River sockeye, an opening after July 20th would give non-Fraser stocks adequate protection." (Department of Fisheries Memorandum, quoted in Nimpkish Band "Area 27 Fact Sheet").

Nimpkish sockeye stocks provided the major food fishery upon which most Nimpkish households depended, as well as being an important contributor to the local commercially fished stocks in Area 12. When a few individuals in the Nimpkish Band mysteriously obtained possession of the study and began circulating the information in the community, alarm became to build. Many citizens began to favor demanding a closure, on the grounds that it would be cutting their own throats to threaten the major Nimpkish Band food fishery.

At first about 50 percent of the local fishermen stated at public meetings that they would definitely fish the area. (The Alert Bay fleet was almost exclusively a seine fleet by this time, and an increasing percentage of this fleet was becoming more highly mobile.) At this point the predictable expressions of different interest groups might have prevented united action. Commercial fishermen with large payments to make on their boats might not be expected to bow to the interests of the community at large in the food fishery. However, as information about the stocks was disseminated and as community opinion in favor of a closure strengthened, the resolve of the commercial fishermen gradually wavered. As the drama of the episode built, the spirit of *communitas* (Turner 1974), expressed most narrowly as the Nimpkish interest in their food fishery (both for immediate use and as a resource over which they claimed exclusive ownership under aboriginal title) and most broadly as local community interest in local stocks, held sway over individual interests. The Land Claims Committee and the Band Council (on which influential fishermen sat) took the position that the area should be closed, and their leadership eventually prevailed.

Over a three-month period the Nimpkish Band held meetings attended by representatives from Bella Bella and Bella Coola (who depended on Smith's Inlet stocks, which would also be passing through Area 27 at the same time) and Sointula (adjacent to Alert Bay). They circulated information and demanded a closure. The Department of Fisheries in Vancouver and Ottawa responded that Area 27 in July contained 80 percent Fraser stocks (the opposite of the regional biologist's report) and must therefore remain open (Miller 1978). Apparently at this point the Department was using the interception issue to justify its fishing plan, which included important allocations to the already hard-pressed, highly-capitalized, mobile seine fleet.

The two trade-union fishing organizations (the United Fishermen and Allied Workers Union and the Native Brotherhood of British Columbia) at first opposed the closure of Area 27, because their (primarily net-fishing) membership desperately needed the fishing time. However, as they became involved with the conservation issue through their locals in these communities, they eventually supported the closure. As support solidified around the issue, the Nimpkish began to lobby Ottawa and to circulate the embarrassing studies more widely. They continued to declare that they would close their Nimpkish River food fishery voluntarily and that they would blockade part of Area 12 where the Nimpkish stocks approached the river. They were able to make this declaration by obtaining a commitment from their seine-boat skippers to supply the food fish during the closure. The community thus disciplined its members in three important ways: it required them to support the Area 27 closure; it required them to abstain from fishing the Nimpkish River; it required the seine-boat owners to supply food fish to the rest of the community.

Finally, a few weeks before the July fishery, the community succeeded in getting the Department of Fisheries and Oceans to close Area 27 during the first three weeks of July. The test fishery and scale analysis during the closure established that Area 27 sockeye in this part of July were made up of 10 percent Fraser stocks and 90 percent Nimpkish and Smith's stocks. (The second two are indistinguishable from each other.) This resulted in a more cautious management of stocks in Area 12 as well, and a closure of part of that area until the Nimpkish stocks had passed in July. As of 1986, Area 27 has not been opened since to a net fishery in July or even in the first few days of August.

Overall policy appears to have been affected as well. In 1978 the Advisory Council to the head of the Fisheries Department's Vancouver office decided to work toward closing net fishing in areas where stocks could not be separated. Although they decided to postpone action on this objective in order to "rectify imbalances between gear types and to take more Fraser stocks," there was a clear recognition of the problem, a recognition to which the social drama of Area 27 had contributed. An improved program of scale sampling in later years to monitor the Nimpkish component of the Area 12 sockeye catch has made more appropriate management possible (Nimpkish Band Council 1982).

On the Nimpkish side, several recognitions have emerged. Clearly the food-fishery closure was both inconvenient and expensive to local community members as well as to fishermen and was undertaken only because it was evident to local people that only *they* could and would protect the fish stocks. Apparently their efforts were rewarded, because sockeye salmon that were hatched in 1977 returned in improved abundance in 1981 and 1982. Band members lobbied for finer-grained management of the Nimpkish salmon stocks for several years following the 1977 incident, but they recognized the social drama of Area 27 as a response to a crisis that reinforced the political will essential to their lobbying efforts.

In the longer term, the Nimpkish are concerned that little recognition has been given to the value of the individual and collective knowledge of Nimpkish elders and fishermen to the decision makers. Indeed, according to a long-term local Department of Fisheries manager, it would be impossible for him to manage the area without the contributions of these individuals. First, over the years the older fishermen have spent many hours explaining the movement patterns of the fish to him, so that he could acquire an understanding of the complex migration routes, timing, cycles, and variability of various runs among the maze of islands, inlets, and currents. Second, during the season the fishermen provide to the local manager daily information on the timing and conditions of all the runs, based on observation and on their catches. Applying their quite sophisticated and detailed understanding of the area, they recommend closures or short fisheries in specific local areas where their catches show a weak return. The local Department office of course receives other information from the head office in Vancouver as well, and explains to local fishermen in detail all the information on which local closures are based. Over the years a trust and a *de facto* comanagement system have been established. The existence of this system may explain how the Nimpkish Band acquired the information on the threat to their stocks in the first place.

However, this use of Nimpkish expertise works only informally and is limited by the personality and intentions of the local manager as well as by the number and nature of decisions made in the centralized office in Vancouver or even at headquarters in Ottawa. It is partly because they recognize the preponderance of centralized decision making and its role in the creation of the decline of the fishery that the Nimpkish were moved to challenge the Vancouver and Ottawa office of the Department.

CONSEQUENCES OF THE AREA 27 CLOSURE

Confrontations over several of these issues have continued. In 1984, for example, militance about the increasing importance given by the Department to the local sport fishery was evident. The social drama described above revealed the structure of power and rights in salmon fishery management, including the ability of local communities—with great effort—to do something about resource management. The drama focused on the question of the legitimacy of the Department's role and the state's role in management. The Alert Bay community has become more insistent in its demand for a recognized comanagement position with more power than the advisory committee role[5] permitted by the Department. Their insistence parallels a province-wide crisis in legitimacy, although it is seldom expressed so forcefully on the local level. In 1982 the Western Fishermen's Federation, an ad hoc group assembled from many fishermen's organizations in response to the final report of a commission on Canadian Pacific fisheries policy, demanded comanagement rights.

In this incident over the closure of Area 27, the principles of community welfare and long-term stock management were successfully affirmed as having precedence over the short-term allocation needs of the fleet at large, including local fishermen. The local community could be said to have comanaged the Nimpkish stocks on both a regional and local level by exercising its informal right to prevent interception that would threaten a local stock of fish. In so doing, the community may not have altered significantly the framework of authority and decision making that played a large role in creating the problem. However, it contributed to the development of better management, and in the long run this and other instances may alter the framework itself.

Ironically, these informal property rights over resource management were asserted when fishermen and fishing communities had the least amount of political power and the smallest base from which to launch their demands because of their diminished numbers. Yet it was also a time when fishermen and maritime communities in British Columbia were most threatened, most desperate, and most aware of the role of the state in bringing about the increased fishing effort and interception.

This discussion has emphasized the role of the state in creating the extremes of redundant capital investment, interception of local stocks, and increased fishing pressure on stocks. Although I have not claimed that a common-property situation as conceived by the economists and biologists is completely absent or irrelevant, I have shown that problems often ascribed to the common-property nature of the resource can be created and exacerbated by state policies. The Alaska example to which I have contrasted the British Columbia case suggests that state policies can be used to reduce rather than increase common-property problems if they include area-specific licensing, limits on vessel size and technology as well as licenses, formal prevention of interception of local stocks, and the operation of informal controls.

NOTES

Research for this chapter was supported by a grant from the Social Science and Humanities Research Council of Canada to the University of British Columbia, Department of Anthropology and Sociology's "Fish and Ships" Research Project. I am particularly grateful to E. N. Anderson, Jr., Neil Guppy, Brian Hayward, and Brian Martin for critical comments on earlier drafts.

1. The term *comanagement* has been used in government-sponsored studies of management regimes worked out in Washington State and in Quebec (see Harper 1982), as well as in the submissions of Indian groups in British Columbia (Gitksan-Carrier Tribal Council 1981).

2. Some of the increase in investment in seiners relative to the smaller vessels is explained by the fact that seiners used their vessels directly for herring fishing, whereas the smaller vessels bought punts (very small boats) for herring. The herring investments of the smaller vessels do not appear in these statistics, which apply only to vessels used also for salmon.

   The development of a roe-herring fishery cannot completely explain the buildup of the salmon seine fleet because only 43 percent of the seine vessels that fished for salmon also fished for roe herring (Canada, Department of Fisheries and Oceans, 1982).

3. It is not clear whether this pressure resulted chiefly from a desire to obtain a greater volume of fish or a desire to realize profits from vessel ownership. In either case, the result was the same. A Department of Fisheries and Oceans official (pers. comm.) reports that pressure for

openings from the processors decreased in the 1980s. At this time some processors were attempting to disinvest in the seine fleet, whose debt load had become burdensome. Simultaneously, processors were importing cheap raw salmon from the bonanza runs in Alaska to supply their canning needs.

4. Rohner (1967) notes that in 1962 the average annual income for Gilford Island gillnetters was $2,300. To qualify for the "A" salmon license, a fisherman had to have delivered at least $2,500 worth of salmon in 1967 and 1968.

5. Alert Bay fishermen were represented on the Johnstone Straits Advisory Committee, set up in the late 1970s, which made recommendations on the management of Areas 12 and 13. Province-wide fishermen's organizations were represented on an advisory committee to the Minister of Fisheries in Ottawa. Most fishermen felt that these committees had little impact.

18 The Grass Roots and the State

RESOURCE MANAGEMENT IN ICELANDIC FISHING

E. Paul Durrenberger and Gislí Pálsson

PEOPLE OFTEN SEE THEIR PARTICULAR FORMS OF PROPERTY as part of the natural order rather than the socially constituted order; for example, numerous commentators on common property see it as a "natural" regime for fisheries, wildlife, and other resources. However, property rights define differential access to resources and productive technology. Thus, they embody and enforce the social relations entailed in production.

As a socially meaningful category, common property must always enter into some *system* of property relationships. Lisu swidden cultivators of northern Thailand, for example, who have no such system, can all clear swiddens wherever there is forest to clear. The lands are neither owned in common nor owned in other form of property. They are simply a productive resource that does not enter any system of ownership, collective or private (see Durrenberger 1976). Karen, in contrast, claim collective ownership of forests surrounding their irrigated fields. A major difference is that Karen have irrigated fields that can be owned whereas traditionally Lisu had none. Karen use the nearby hillsides to supplement their irrigated rice harvests and consider the tracts of forest as the common property of the village. Lisu, with no similar category of private ownership in land, have no opposed category of common property.

If common property exists as part of a system of property relationships, it follows that there are other concepts of property whose function is to limit access to productive resources to certain groups or individuals, as ownership of irrigated fields does among Karen. It follows that common property is a characteristic of stratified societies since it demarcates one kind of access to resources as

370

opposed to others. In truly egalitarian societies, by Fried's (1967) definition those in which access to critical resources is equal, common property has no meaning.

For common property to be defined, it must be problematic. There must have been claims that the resource was neither simply a resource freely available to all, nor a common resource available to all members of a specific group. There must have been claims that access to it should be limited. This is likely to happen only under the pressure of overuse of the resource, which is the beginning of the tragedy of the commons. Such overuse is a function of trying to produce more from the resource than it can yield over the long term. The conditions for such overproduction are found when production is organized for exchange rather than for use, a phenomenon of stratified societies.

One of the characteristics of egalitarian societies, and household production in general, is production for use rather than exchange. Such forms of production do not provide the pressure necessary to define a resource as common property because there are limits on any household's production, as both Chayanov (1966) and Sahlins (1972) argue. Rather, such pressure develops when there is production for exchange, which has no such limits on production. Concepts of property are, then, responsive to particular forms of production.

Common property sets the framework for a contradiction between individual and group interests. The very concept of the individual and of individual interests is a consequence of certain forms of production. As Marx points out in *Capital*, the ideology of the free individual with rights is a necessary condition of a labor market in which free individuals must sell their labor. If there were no concept of the individual, there would be no free agents to sell labor, and a wage system would not be possible.[1] The contradiction between individual and group interests is most apparent in modern societies. One recalls the Socialist slogan of World War I that a bayonet is a weapon with a working man at each end.

When regulation enters a discussion of common property, we can be certain that the social unit is organized as a state. Where there are forms of regulation to safeguard what some have defined as common interests—interests presumably shared by all members of the group—there must be law and enforcement, the social machinery of governments. The regulation of common property is therefore a phenomenon of stratified societies organized as states. The common good becomes the responsibility of agents of the state and is focused on them. Instead of each individual's recognizing a conflict between common and individual good and coming to some terms with it, the common good is the preserve of certain well-defined and identifiable individuals and institutions. This externalization of the common good makes it possible for individuals to resist it and try to outwit it by resisting and outwitting the authorities who attempt to enforce it (J. Gatewood, personal communication; see also Maril 1983).

The social forms and forms of production in which a tragedy of the commons can develop are societies organized as states. The problem, once common property has been specified, is how to manage the common domain.

COMMON-PROPERTY FISHERIES IN ICELAND

Iceland is a small country with a population of 230,000 people. The general assembly of Icelanders (*Althing*) was established about A.D. 930. Then followed the golden age of the Icelandic commonwealth so vividly and controversially told of in the sagas. This period ended at about 1220 with the onset of the period of civil strife known as the Sturlung age, during which power was concentrated in the hands of six powerful, competing families. In 1262 Iceland was incorporated into the kingdom of Norway. Later, Norway fell under Danish rule, and Iceland remained a Danish colony until it achieved home rule in 1918 and full independence in 1944.

The national economy is heavily dependent on fishing. About 75 percent of Iceland's exports are fish and fish products, and fish is an important item for domestic consumption. Therefore, any discussion of the Icelandic economy must be a discussion of the fishing industry, and any discussion of national economic policy must consider the industry. The history of fisheries management in Iceland is a history of a number of balancing acts among different interest groups with somewhat different stakes in the fishing industry. But one of the differences between Iceland and some other countries is that ultimately everyone has an interest in the fishing industry. Accordingly, "grassroots politics" plays a particularly central role in the management of common property resources by the state.

From the time of its settlement in the ninth century, Iceland was a stratified society. Icelanders early developed a complex set of laws and legal institutions culminating with the formation of the national assembly, or *Althing,* in 930. Social relations were therefore quite explicitly formulated. Looking over the sweep of Icelandic history, we see clearly that any aspects of the fishing industry that represent a tragedy of the commons are consequences not of population growth but rather of the rapid development of capitalist production in the fisheries.

As social relations of production change, so do rules of access to resources or property laws. In Iceland we can isolate three phases in the development of fishing: the peasant, the expansive, and the consolidated capitalistic. Each had a distinct set of relations of production and a distinct cognitive framework. In the peasant phase, from settlement until the turn of the twentieth century, there were ceilings on production imposed by technology and markets. Fishing was part of the subsistence economy of households. It retained the same status for much of the following Norwegian and Danish colonial period. Fish were caught from small rowboats with limited ranges, so overfishing was not a problem.

Property Rights

The history of Iceland begins with common property in the oppositional sense we have discussed, since Iceland began as a stratified society. It evolved from highly specified notions of common property in relation to private property to the modern conception of open-access common property within the boundaries of a nation-state.

The Old Law

Much of our discussion is based on "the old law," ratified in the twelfth century and recorded in the several manuscripts called *Grágás* ("Grey Goose").[2] There are no simple clauses that apply to the resources of the sea. Property rights—largely rights of access—appear to have depended upon a range of factors, such as the occupation of coastal areas, the type of resource exploited, and the method of extraction. What follows is a necessarily brief treatment of complex historical issues, the complete understanding of which would require a detailed analysis of the politics and institutions of early Iceland.

Old Icelandic law stated that particular areas both on land and at sea were open to all (*almenningar*). The sea and its resources were not ownable. In our terms, they were not common property. But the resources of the beach belonged to the owner of the land as did the resources of "net areas" (*netlög*). Net areas were defined according to the depth at which a net with twenty meshes could be located. Beyond that, the rule of capture applied. Each man owned his prey if it was caught farther out and brought ashore by boat. In general, at sea the area open to all began where a flattened cod could no longer be seen from land, which was the criterion used to define "fishing limits" (*fiskhelgi*) accorded to owners of fishing stations (see Pálsson 1982: 271–73).

The commons included a number of usufruct rights concerning grazing, fishing, hunting birds and seals, and the use of driftwood. The exercise of such rights was as varied as the resources to which they applied, but the clauses concerning the commons applied only to the collective right to use particular resources and not to their absolute ownership. A look at the etymology of Icelandic concepts of property relations suggests that the Icelandic verb *eiga* (to "own" or "have") was applied in the old law not to direct ownership, but only to limited usufruct rights. Such rights are similar to the Kachins' rights to "make use of and enjoy for the time being" (Leach 1954: 141). Collective rights to use particular resources sometimes applied to the exploitation of territories permanently occupied by other people. If the sagas are to be believed, access to such "common" resources was settled by force quite irrespective of law.

Although most of the seas were conceived of as not ownable, in early Icelandic history access to the sea was often controlled by ownership of landing sites in the bays. Landing a rowboat on the coast was risky, especially during the winter season, and access to the ocean therefore depended upon the availability of good landing sites. Access to the fishing grounds was largely controlled by inhibiting others from gaining access to landing sites.

Peasant Cognition of
Man-Resource Relationships

During the peasant phase the folk analysis was that the catch was supplied by nature and was beyond human control. Godly design determined the fate of the fishermen. Rituals associated with fishing solicited supernatural help for the fishermen and did not imply that the people thought they had any control over the fish (see also Carrier, this volume). Fishing trips were organized by foremen who directed activities on the rowboats. A foreman's decisions were important for the safety of the boat and crew, but he was not held responsible for fishing success or failure. The foreman, in the folk analysis, contributed no more than anyone else to production.

Even though the extent of the fishing grounds was fairly limited, peasant fishermen had neither the motivation nor the technology to explore more distant grounds. The fishing grounds were seen to be a closed and stable natural domain, access to which was controlled by particular persons through their ownership of landing sites. The "natural" coding of the grounds by application of names for landmarks to individual spots reflected the idea that the fishing spots were permanent.

Social Transformations

During the peasant phase and into the twentieth century and the expansive and consolidated capitalistic phases of Iceland's fisheries, changes occurred in the social relations of production, property rights, and the cognitive framework of fishermen. During the colonial era the Danish king and the church sometimes owned landing sites. Later, Icelandic merchants gained control of some of the bays and improved them with wharves. With the abolition of the Danish trade monopoly in 1787, home rule in 1918, and the development of foreign markets for fish, the economic constraints on fishing were changed and much larger catches were both possible and useful. The technological constraint was changed late in the nineteenth century with the introduction of sailing smacks that extended the range of fishing. As the Danish trade monopoly was lifted, Icelandic merchants could trade in fish for the first time. This change in Danish colonial policy allowed local capital accumulation.

By the turn of the century, trawlers and motorboats began replacing sailing boats. The motorboats could bring their catches back to shore for icing or fresh sales daily and also enabled the individual producer to participate in capitalist fishing. Sailcraft represented large capital investments beyond the means of most peasant households. Small producers continued to use rowboats until the availability of motors. At the same time motorboats extended the range of exploitation of the fisheries resources, they also intensified competition among fishermen.

In 1944 Iceland gained full independence from Denmark. The first independent government of Iceland was committed to a policy of economic development and concentrated on the fishing industry as a means to that end. Fishing for exchange rather than household use had already begun and had intensified in the 1920s. Fishing was rapidly becoming the livelihood of Icelanders and the focus of government development policies.

All around the coast, communes (municipalities) purchased bays and improvements for general use. In the 1950s the government offered aid to municipalities to improve landing facilities if they were owned by the communes. As a result, all major harbors became public property, and access to them became open to any Icelander. The control exerted by landowners who also controlled access to landing sites in the past was reduced. To improve landing sites, it was in the general interest for the harbors to be owned by municipalities. The improvement of harbors led to dramatic increases in fishing operations and the number of fishing boats.

Cognitive Model of the Expansive Phase

The expansive phase brought a new conceptual model that was more secular and individualistic and was related to a change from dependence on nature to dependence on commodities and the fact that fishing developed into a separate economic endeavor with an elaborate role structure of its own. Modern notions of luck and chance entered the vocabulary of fishing. Instead of relying on the idea of godly design beyond comprehension and control, the expansive model introduced the ideas of the randomness of nature and of calculable risk.

The title of "skipper" instead of foreman is central to the model. "Skipper" is an honorific in Iceland. The skipper receives a much larger share of the catch than the foreman did. The skipper operates a specialized means of production that demands expertise and institutional training. Modern fishing requires a high degree of cooperation among crewmen, and the skipper is considered central to the operation. In the folk model his expertise is critical for his success relative to others—the "skipper effect" (Pálsson and Durrenberger 1982, 1983). Fish, instead of being offered to humans by some mysterious system of rationing, became something actively pursued by humans and extracted from an indifferent sea. The skipper became a frontiersman. Skippers had to compete for crews, financial resources, and access to shore facilities.

When access became free to everyone and the exploitable range increased, the ocean was seen to be "opened up." In the skippers' maps are uncharted spaces to be explored and unknown spots to be discovered. Even though the major fishing areas are associated with natural features, the names used for spots are highly transient and arbitrary. There is no concensus and the names change frequently. In most cases they are just names or their reference is only known or intelligible to a few people.

The Tragedy of the Commons

The process described above led to a classic open-access, common-property tragedy. Free competition among fishing boats led quickly to a shortage of space and to imminent overexploitation of the fish. As freezing facilities developed and frozen bait could be stored, long lines replaced hand lines. More and more boats exploited the same fishing grounds with ever longer lines (up to twelve miles of lines per boat). Fishermen expanded into new grounds and intensified their exploitation of fish stocks.

In addition, foreign fishing fleets, taking advantage of the narrow boundaries of national "territorial seas" and the "freedom of the seas" beyond them recognized in international law, joined the competition for cod, herring, and other species off the coast of Iceland. Overexploitation of fish resulted. The opportunistic exploitation of fishing stocks by freely competing skippers who tried to get what they could from the sea while stocks lasted led to sharply diminished returns. Between 1970 and 1972 the cod catch, the most important, fell 26 percent while fishing effort increased. The "natural" limit to overexploitation, "maximum sustainable yield," had been exceeded.

MANAGEMENT PROCESSES

Grass-roots Management: Rowing Times

Early management efforts focused on conflicts between groups of fishermen as their ranges and technology expanded. They show the ability of fishermen to translate common interest into common rules sanctioned and enforced by the state. Much of this discussion focuses on the fishermen of Sandgeroi and other communities in one of the major fishing areas off the southwest coast of Iceland.

When boats from Sandgeroi began to intrude into fishing areas traditionally exploited by fishermen from nearby Grindavik, conflicts broke out. Grindavik fishermen were still using very small boats because their harbor offered little shelter for larger boats. They complained about the invasion from the expanding fleet at Sandgeroi and are said to have stolen fish from their lines as late as the early 1950s. These were individual responses, however, and the cases were few. The problem seems to have disappeared when the fishermen of Grindavik increased their own competitive ability.

With the increase in competition even within fishing communities, fishermen agreed that a collective response was necessary. Regulations concerning the timing of the departure (rowing time, *rorantimi*) were, it seems, laid down by common agreement in the 1930s to prevent chaos in the fishing grounds off Reykjanes. The lines of each boat could stretch several miles, and when different boats left the harbor at different times, competing for similar locations, lines got chopped and intermingled, especially in strong currents. No one benefited.

The fishermen agreed to fix a certain time for departure for each month. The precise times were debated for years, but most fishermen favored some regulations. Because the lines were taken ashore for baiting after each trip, it was impossible for anyone to control a particular path. The fishermen's regulations were ratified by law in 1945, but the details have been changed several times. The laws in use in the 1980s were enacted in 1973.

In this episode, we see recognition of a common problem and a collective but informal solution that later attained the status of law. Given the new rules of the game, individuals still attempted to maximize their individual chances in various ways—for example, by increasing their engine power, adopting novel fishing tactics, or cheating on the rules.

With established rowing times fishermen could race for desirable locations and all could have an equal chance of attracting fish without the previous confusion and conflicts. Those with larger engines clearly had an advantage in the race, but there is no significant correlation between the horsepower of the engines and the catch if one controls for the size of the boat, the number of trips, or both (see Pálsson 1982: 254–55). Those with smaller engines were as successful as the larger ones, but they had to exploit other areas or compensate by using different fishing tactics, such as reducing the length of lines and not losing as many fish as were lost with longer lines.

Even so, skippers attempted to obtain larger engines. From 1943 to 1952 the increase in horsepower was 114 percent, much greater than the increase in boat size (68 percent). It is clear that the engine's potential was used to the utmost. Boats gathered together at particular points and, when the "sign" was given, they raced to the "best" spots. In 1953 the local Boat Owner's Association complained that during the winter season the engines were run too fast. The Skippers' and Mates' Association responded by saying that nothing could be done about this as long as the points of departure remained the same, but by changing these it would be possible to shorten the distance that boats sailed at full speed.

Cheating is not unknown. The boats leave the harbor and proceed to a starting line to await the signal for rowing time. Since they leave at night, if a skipper cuts the boat lights, he can gain a head start on the others. But during the periods of most intense competition, the boats are closely spaced along the starting line and undetected cheating is difficult. People discovered cheating may be scolded on the radio, have their lines cut, or be subjected to other informal sanctions by fellow skippers, but such cases are not usually taken to the authorities.

Grass Roots, the Cod Wars, and the International Law of the Sea

Another example of a collective response to the problem of competition for fishing space is the establishment of international fishing boundaries to exclude foreigners. The historic standard was a three-mile limit from the national shore. During the Danish colonial period, the Danes had the responsibility for enforcing this limit with their one patrol boat, which was, of course, ineffective at excluding the British trawlers from Icelandic waters. Fishermen wrote letters of complaint to the authorities to demand better coastal protection. In addition to competing for the fish, the British trawlers posed a threat to the safety of small boats, damaged breeding grounds, and often destroyed fishing gear. In one community, fishermen purchased their own patrol boats in 1920 (*Icelandic Fisheries Yearbook* 1981: 32).

The problem was apparent in the catch statistics. Since early in this century increasing fishing effort has resulted in periodic declines in catches. The cod catch from Icelandic fishing grounds was 518,000 tons in 1933. It then declined in spite of increased effort. The stock only recovered during World War II. When foreign fishing declined during the war, the Icelandic fleet expanded. The consequences of allowing foreign fishing were indisputable after the World War II. Just after the war the statistics showed a clear pattern of cod stock restoration. Foreign fleets then resumed fishing. In 1954, cod catches came to 546,000 tons. In the following years, catches declined again (see *Statistical Abstract of Iceland* 1974).

Responding to recognition of this tragedy and the pressures of fishermen, the Icelandic government took the risky international move of trying to expand its jurisdiction and exclude foreign fishing vessels from waters around Iceland. It drew Great Britain into "cod wars" that resulted in the exclusion of British trawlers from Icelandic fishing grounds in December 1976 and helped trigger the worldwide restructuring of the law of the sea during the late 1970s in a series of United Nations Law of the Sea Conferences. The commons out to two hundred nautical miles was specified as the property of Iceland alone.

Both the fixing of rowing times and the extension of the national fishing boundaries were results of a long cumulative process of recognition of a management problem, individual and informal responses, larger responses by communities, and finally a national response. But whereas the rowing time represented a collective response to resource competition that was costly for everyone, the cod wars were a contest between different social groups whose interests were seen to be mutually exclusive. The common property resource was defined as common to Icelanders only.

Technological Development and National Resource Management: Herring and Capelin

The task of restoring depleted stocks and preventing future tragedies remained. It resulted in increased use of scientific models and policies for fishery management within Iceland's domain. Iceland's fishermen were forced to accept constraints on their activities. Skippers are no longer allowed to take as much fish as technically possible. Whereas technical, economic, and social factors put a ceiling on production in earlier phases, in the 1980s political processes limit the catch. The skipper is no longer a frontiersman. Owners of capital can no longer expand. They can only diversify. This phase is one of consolidated capitalism.

The history of problems and management responses in herring fishing off Iceland provides another example of the recognition, somewhat belated, of the necessity for national resource management and diversification. This case also shows how technological innovation can be both a response to and a cause of resource problems.

The Norwegians introduced herring fishing late in the nineteenth century. They established processing plants in the eastern fjords and began drift-net fishing. Herring became an important fishing resource until the late 1960s, when the catches declined dramatically, probably due to overfishing. In addition to drift-nets, there have been three major ways of fishing for herring with purse-seine or ring-net: the two-dory method, the one-dory method, and the power block. The two-dory method was used mainly in inshore waters until 1944, when the fishery moved offshore. In about 1945 the migration and behavior pattern of herring off the north coast of Iceland changed. The fishery almost collapsed because the herring no longer entered inshore waters and good schools were seldom at hand close to the coast. Low catches encouraged skippers to experiment with a more flexible one-dory system. By 1962, all boats used ring-nets (*Aegir* 1962: 327). The one-dory system increased the speed of the casting operation, which was much easier than manual pursing. Finally, the one-dory system required smaller crews—ten instead of eighteen. The speed of casting allowed experimentation with sonar-guided casting (see Gíslason 1971).

The change to the one-dory system and sonar-guided shooting required larger and more flexible boats. The power block was introduced in 1959. The hauling was done with an engine and the net was taken aboard the main vessel, making the dory unnecessary. At the same time, the seines could be enlarged to fish at greater depths. This was very important during the last years of the herring boom of the mid-1960s, when the Norwegian-Icelandic herring went deeper by almost twenty meters per year (see Þorsteinsson 1980: 148). However, keeping the larger seines aboard and hauling increased weight with the power block required larger boats.

Since there was only a twelve-mile offshore limit at this time, and herring fishing was partly beyond the limit, Norwegians shared in the herring boom. The herring fishery collapsed in 1968 because of overexploitation and recruitment failure. In the early 1970s Iceland closed the herring fishery. In 1975 the stock had recovered sufficiently to allow limited fishing to resume under tight regulation. Iceland has tried to allow the stock to recover so that it can be exploited again. This required short-term sacrifices in favor of long-term goals.

To minimize the effects of closing the herring fishery, Icelanders concentrated on capelin fishing beginning in the early 1970s. Capelin replaced herring as the major source of fishmeal and oil. In 1978 Iceland's output of fishmeal reached 200,000 tons; in 1979, 206,000. In 1980 the Ministry of Fisheries imposed capelin quotas, and the output of meal decreased to 170,000 tons. The fishing quota can be revised during the season in response to the condition of the stock. In 1981 the marine biologists found the condition of capelin stock to be low, so they revised the quota downward.

Debates on capelin management parallel the earlier debates concerning management of herring. In spite of the findings of marine biologists, the fishermen claimed that the stock must still be strong since there were capelin to be caught in the sea. In the winter of 1982 it was clear that the next capelin season would yield relatively little. The question was what to do with the fishing and processing capacity that had developed especially for capelin exploitation. Part of the capelin fleet was converted for cod fishing. Since there is a limit on the total take of cod, this means more competition for those already fishing cod and threatens increased pressure on the stock.

The Complexity of the Management Process

The histories of Iceland's herring and capelin fisheries are dramatic examples of how technological developments, which initially represent a response to resource problems, may later require a collective regulatory response to the problem of fishery management. This does not mean, however, that individual fishermen, or even segments of the industry, see each management move as being in their best interest. The mechanisms for making management decisions must therefore be quite complex in order to strike a balance between long-term interests, short-term goals, and the different sectors of the fishing industry.

Since governmental decisions influence all sectors of the fishing industry, those involved organize to affect government policy in their favor. Some of these organizations are formal and permanent associations, such as associations of fishermen and boat owners, the various groups of processors, and the various departments of the semigovernmental Fisheries Association (*Fiskifélag Islands*), which embraces most of the interest groups involved. Boat owners and skippers also organize informally as technical coalitions to lobby for particular fishing gear in particular areas. All of these groups take part in a complicated political process, the results of which change from one season to another.

Administrative regulations are made within the framework of a general body of legislation passed by Parliament in 1976 to regulate fishing within the Icelandic waters to two hundred miles from the coast. These regulations are changed in response to the condition of the stocks and the demands of various contending groups. Some of these regulations respond only to the demands of local fishermen, whereas others meet the recommendations of the biologists of the Marine Research Institute. These regulations are the results of a series of compromises among local branches of the fisheries association and coalitions of trawler and net-boat skippers.

Formal Rules and Informal Adjustments

Management goes beyond attempts to conserve or restore fish stocks. If the stocks are constant, or at least not diminishing, one concern is how best to exploit them. The 1984 policy is to improve the quality of fish. One way to ensure high quality is to make regulations requiring the fish to be brought to processing plants with less delay. For net fishermen, this means laws that require fewer nets. The more nets a skipper sets, the less frequently he draws them, and the lower the quality of his catch.

As fishermen confront a problem and devise informal means of coping with it, the informal rules become complex and entangling, sometimes gaining the force of law and a complex administrative code. At some point those who conceived the rules for their own benefit begin to try to outwit their own rules. One skipper commented on the restrictions concerning the number of nets by saying, "The revolution eats its own children."

Net fishermen make an art of concealing the precise number of nets they use. It is impossible to pay a secret visit to most of Iceland's small fishing villages. Outsiders are immediately noticed and commented upon. News travels quickly via informal networks so that it is quite easy for skippers to be prepared for inspection by officials of the Ministry of Fisheries. Cheating at rules seems to be more likely when the rules are enforced primarily by government officials rather than through local community sanctions (see also Taylor, this volume).

When local sanctions do not work, the matter is taken to the respective government bureau. The fishing areas for various types of gear (line, net, trawl, Danish seine) are mapped by a complex process. During the negotiation, parties to the disagreement may state their case by provoking conflict on the water and attempting to obtain help from the government. Sometimes nets and lines conflict with trawls in the same areas. Since the trawl would destroy the stationary nets or lines in its path, the two technologies are usually used in different areas. In one area off Reykjanes in March of 1982, trawler fishermen claimed that net boats had invaded their traditional areas. At meetings were heard statements such as "We have been able to trawl in peace in small spots, but now it isn't possible to remain there, as the net fishermen have invaded our areas. We are caught if we invade their areas, but nothing is done if they invade our traditional spots." The trawlermen claimed that "traditionally" they had access to certain areas that net boats were encroaching upon. The skippers exchanged insults on the radio, and a coast-guard vessel was sent to ensure that the conflict did not escalate to gear destruction or a more intensive confrontation on the sea. The trawlermen requested a meeting to work out explicit rules of who can fish what areas. Such conflicts are likely to influence the administrative decisions that map out areas for fishing.

Limited Goods and Equal Access

The threat of overfishing has usually been met with measures that do not discriminate between groups of fishermen. Thus the government has tried to put a ceiling on the total catch of cod by deciding upon the length of the winter season, and when the herring stock failed, no one was allowed to fish for herring. Such measures affect all fishermen in a similar way. Indeed, there seems to have been general agreement among fishermen that no one should be denied access to the fish. If the supply suffers as a consequence, the solutions have tended to be ones that guarantee that the benefits and the costs are spread among all the fishermen rather than concentrated among a few, even though the latter choice might be simpler to design, administer, and enforce and might ensure a more coherent management policy.

There are exceptions. In the shrimp and lobster fisheries fishermen have favored a tight licensing policy. But generally fishermen have seen the policy of licensing as a threat that undermines the previously held assumptions about equal access.

The following is a case in point. In 1981 the Parliament passed a bill proposed by the Minister of Fisheries concerning the legalization of fishing with Danish seines in Faxafloi. The bill allowed a restricted number of boats to use this gear to fish for plaice. The use of the Danish seine in the bay has been debated for decades. It was banned in 1971 because it killed young fish and damaged breeding grounds, but a few years later several boats were allowed to experiment with it under the supervision of the Marine Research Institute. The scientists claimed that the plaice stock was underexploited and that 1,500 tons could be caught annually without endangering stocks of plaice or other species.

Among fishermen, however, heated discussions took place about the legalization of the Danish seine. Fishermen's unions issued statements against the bill, and a public meeting was organized by owners of small boats. The fishermen argued that, in the past, declining catches had shown that the Danish seine threatened some stocks, particularly haddock, and that this could happen again. The scientists argued, on the other hand, that modifications had made the seine harmless to the bottom and that its meshes were larger than before, which would minimize its catching of small haddock. To illustrate these points, they showed underwater photographs of actual catching operations. At the meeting, the owners of the larger boats who had been experimenting with the seine added that the opponents of the bill were "romantic sport fishermen full of rubbishy ideas about fish protection." "We live," one of them said, "not from protecting fish, but from fishing."

Although the conservation of fishing stocks was central to the discussion, what was at issue was whether access was open and how selection should be made for licenses. The owners of small boats argued that the scientists and the Ministry of Fisheries had been influenced by the propaganda of the owners of four to six boats who were hoping to get the licenses to fish plaice. These few would be allowed to fish at the expense of the majority—approximately three hundred boats. The debate reopened consideration of the meaning of Icelandic property in fisheries and gave voice to the position, seemingly that of the majority, that access should be open to all. As one of them said at a public meeting, "The Danish seine should not be the privilege of a few giants; either everyone should have the right to use it—the small ones as well as the big ones—or no one."

Late in 1983 it became clear that the traditional fishing policy needed to be changed. In 1983 the total cod catch was even less than the amount recommended by fisheries biologists, and the forecast for 1984 was bleak. The government decided to reduce the cod quota for 1984 to 220 thousand tons, from an estimated catch of around 290,000 tons. At the annual conference of the Fisheries Association, most interest groups were rather unexpectedly in favor of a boat-quota system that would divide this reduced catch within the industry itself. The precise allocation of quotas was debated, but each boat was to be allocated an annual quota on the basis of its average catch over the past three years (see, for example, *News from Iceland*, January 1984). This means that the more successful ships during this period would get higher quotas than the rest of the fleet, a fundamental departure from traditional policy.

This policy was being reevaluated late in 1984. The individual quota system was recommended by the fishing industry and administered by the Ministry of Fisheries. The Ministry maintains rich and detailed data on each boat in the fleet and attempts to be impartial in its assignment of quotas, thus continuing, in a different form, the ideology of equal access to a common resource.

THE PROBLEM OF RATIONALIZATION

Numerous harvesting proposals have been discussed. In the future, access will be even more restricted, and a new level and form of socioeconomic differentiation is likely to result. Fishermen have become increasingly dominated by technoscientific knowledge and the agencies of the State. Thus one observer complains that the mathematical models of the experts are lacking in "common sense" (Björnsson 1979: 32). The skippers' rationality is likely to persist as long as the sociological constraints of competition for prestige prevail, but it is also likely to be confined to the narrowest context of fishing as it is being replaced on the public level by the more "plausible" rationality of the scientists.

Over the years proposals put forward by the marine biologists have been met with distrust and emotional reaction among fishermen. During the last cod wars, the fishermen tended to regard internal limitations of access with some skepticism, arguing that if they did not catch the fish, the British and Germans would any-way. Once the common enemy disappeared, conflict between fishermen and biologists increased. Each has angrily accused the other of following an "irrational" policy.

Fishermen frequently complain that "nowadays everything is being banned." Although the biologists are usually the target of fishermens' criticism, one should not forget the role of political decision makers. Marine biologists in Iceland act as a buffer be-tween fishermen and political figures. However, politicians are often dependent upon local support in the rural fishing villages and cannot afford to be strictly conservative in their management proposals. As a result, they have tended to argue that the social costs of a conservative management policy are much too high. Although it has been possible in some cases—in the herring fish-ery, for example—to set the catch within "reasonable limits," the decision makers have been incapable of coping with the problem of management in the case of cod fishery because of immense con-flicts in interest.

The politicians in power need the scientific arguments of the biologists, but they tend to regard them with suspicion. Former Ministers of Fisheries have argued that if the scientists had been right in their estimates and predictions, the fisheries would have collapsed. Contrary to the "Black Report" predictions of 1975, a report of the Marine Research Institute that was influential in the cod wars, the cod stock remained fairly stable until a sharp decline in catches in 1982. One former Minister has referred to the "re-ligion of the biologists" (Anonymous 1980: 17). Another former Minister of Fisheries points out that "in the biologists' own cal-culations, the size of the 1976 year class of cod keeps increasing" (Anonymous 1980: 17). It is understandable that skippers, aware of the discrepancy between reality and the "pessimistic" forecasts of the past, fail to be impressed with the rhetoric of the scientists. As one skipper commented, "They always knew about all this fish. They only used the 'Black Report' to scare the British away." An official of the Ministry of Fisheries commented that marine bi-ology is the kind of science that can tell you what you should have done three or four years ago.

As power has shifted in favor of the scientists, they sometimes forget that no theory, ecological or economic, can tell what is a "rational" policy. What is *socially* optimal will always depend on social context (Godelier 1972). Theory can only be used to arrive at policy decisions if value goals are specified beforehand. The skippers' strategies of maximizing immediate returns are not irrational, though the result is the tragedy of the commons (Hardin 1968). On the contrary, as McCay paraphrases the theory (1981a: 4), it is "irrational" for the actor who does not own the resource he exploits to limit his efforts, "because the benefits of his restraint cannot be reserved for himself."

But rationalization is not only relative to social values. Due to the complex feedback loops in modern fishing and the nature of decision making, technocratic reationalization is pointless beyond a certain limit. Smith and McKelvey (1983) argue that fishery scientists and managers tend to assume that fishermen are a homogeneous population whereas in reality different groups of fishermen exhibit different behaviors. Similarly, Jentoft (1982) has developed the argument that local fleets have systemic properties in the sense that they are not simply sums of boats. Fishery management too often ignores the fact that a local fleet is composed of different kinds of production units that mutually affect each other. The consequence is that it is probably impossible to rationalize skippers' decisions about where to fish in order to increase catches, save time and fuel, and meet other economizing objectives (Durrenberger and Pálsson 1986).

INDIVIDUAL AND SOCIETAL INTERESTS IN BALANCE

Löfgren (1982) observes that when the herring fishery collapsed in Sweden the number of fishermen and boats declined by half and boats went begging for buyers. This was not the response in Iceland. There were short-term dislocations in many communities as fishing plants laid off workers during the summer season. The response was not to abandon fishing but to intensify the exploitation of cod and develop alternative summer fisheries such as capelin.

One does not have to look far to find the reasons for this difference in response. When there are many alternatives one selects the most advantageous one. If an endeavor becomes unprofitable, one develops another. In Iceland there are few alternatives to living from the sea. This ecological fact seems to make Iceland somewhat different from most of its Nordic neighbors. Perhaps for this reason, one official response has been not to attempt to limit access to fishing by licensing, but to ensure fair and equal access through quotas. Economic decisions are not always made according to a strictly economic calculus. The commitment to full employment and equal access has resulted in "overcapitalization" of the Icelandic fleet by strictly economic calculations. This poses a certain threat to the long-term availability of marine resources, as the experiences with herring, capelin, and cod indicate. In this sense the Icelandic fleet may be too modernized.

If it is continued, the new quota system may favor some forms of boat ownership over others. As of late 1984, the system had been in effect for less than a year and was being reevaluated by all parties. The point, however, is that apparently neutral "scientific" management decisions may have important effects on the structure of the fishing industry by changing the possibilities and alternatives with respect to access to the fish. The contemporary shape of the Icelandic fishing fleet is in large part a response to such policies of the past.

In the beginning of this chapter we argued that concepts of property encode concepts of differential access to resources. When there is competition among classes or other groups for access to the same resources, some may be defined as common property in contrast to private property. From the beginning there has been debate, discussion, and various codifications of what is properly common property and what is properly private property in Iceland. This debate continues in some contexts, though maritime resources have been defined as common property in recent times. The issue of property rights in the 1980s is largely a consequence of the policies of the Icelandic government for economic development.

The contemporary problem is how to manage the common domain once it has been defined. A small country, Iceland can afford a degree of complexity in this manner to ensure social goals that have been indisputable. The values of equal access, fairness, and equitability have dominated the rhetoric of common-resource management. Perhaps as a consequence of the scale of Icelandic politics, the management process has remained open and flexible so that there is a dynamic balance of tensions among various components of the fishing industry, each attempting to ensure or improve its position: the fishermen and processors, the scientific community, the politicians, and the government bureaucracy.

Sometimes there has been agreement among all sectors, as evidenced in the securing of the two-hundred-mile limit for Icelandic fishing. Sometimes the pressure for regulation has come from the fishermen themselves, as in the example of the establishment of rowing times. Sometimes the government or the scientific experts have moderated between different components of the fishing industry such as between trawlers and line and net boats or between proponents and opponents of the use of certain types of gear in certain places. Sometimes the scientific community has set the framework for negotiation among sectors as in the herring, capelin, and cod fisheries. All of these episodes represent the tension between the motivation to profit as much and as quickly from the common resource as possible and the necessity to preserve the resource for long-term use. Production for exchange rather than use, a consequence of Iceland's economic and political history, is the basis of the first motive. The second motive follows from the fact that the nation as a whole relies on the fisheries for its livelihood and prosperity and will into the foreseeable future.

NOTES

1. But see Dumont (1972) on hierarchical cultures in which individuals may be defined simply as aspects of their social groups, so that the contradiction between individual good and common good cannot arise.

2. The details of the law were apparently variable from place to place and time to time, and often the application of the law was less than

straightforward to the modern mind. During some periods, such as the Sturlung period of civil strife from 1220 to 1262, the status of the law was extremely dubious. In addition it is difficult to generalize about this law since new clauses were added from time to time.

Bibliography

Acheson, J. M.
   1972   The Territories of the Lobstermen. *Natural History* 81: 60–69.
   1975   The Lobster Fiefs: Economic and Ecological Effects of Territoriality in the Maine Lobster Industry. *Human Ecology* 3 (3): 183–207.
   1979   Variations in Traditional Inshore Fishing Rights in Maine Lobstering Communities. In *North Atlantic Maritime Cultures*, R. Andersen, ed., pp. 253–76. The Hague: Mouton.
   1980   Factors Influencing Productivity of Metal and Wooden Lobster Traps. *Maine Sea Grant Technical Report 63*. University of Maine Sea Grant Program, Orono, Maine.
   1981a   Cultural and Technical Factors Influencing Fishing Effectiveness in the Maine Lobster Industry: An Assessment by Fishermen and Biologists. In *Social and Cultural Aspects of New England Fisheries: Implications for Management*, J. M. Acheson, ed., pp. 643–716. Final Report to the National Science Foundation of the University of Rhode Island, University of Maine Study of Social and Cultural Aspects of Fisheries Management in New England Under Extended Jurisdiction.
   1981b   Patterns of Gear Changes in the Northern New England Fishing Industry. In *Social and Cultural Aspects of New England Fisheries: Implications for Management.* J. M. Acheson, ed., pp. 451–499. Final Report to the National Science Foundation of the University of Rhode Island, University of Maine Study of Social and Cultural Aspects of Fisheries Management in New England Under Extended Jurisdiction.
Acheson, J. M., A. W. Acheson, J. Bort, and J. Lello
   1980   *Fishing Ports of Maine and New Hampshire: 1978.* Orono, Maine: Maine Sea Grant Publications.
Aegir
   1962   (Journal of the Icelandic Fisheries Association) Reykjavík.
Agnello, R. J., and L. P. Donnelley
   1975   Property Rights and Efficiency in the Oyster Industry. *Land Economics* 18: 521–33.
Allan, C.
   1957   *Customary Land Tenure in the British Solomon Islands Protectorate.* Honiara: Western Pacific High Commission.
Anderson, R.
   1979   Public and Private Access Management in Newfoundland

Fishing. In *North Atlantic Maritime Cultures*, R. Anderson, ed., pp. 299–336. The Hague: Mouton.

Anderson, E. N., Jr.

1972 The Life and Culture of Ecotopia. In *Reinventing Anthropology*, D. Hymes, ed., pp. 264–83. New York: Random House.

1973 Chinese Fishermen in Hong Kong and Malaysia. In *Maritime Adaptations of the Pacific*, R. Casteel and G. Quimby, eds., pp. 231–46. The Hague: Mouton.

Anderson, E. N., Jr., and M. L. Anderson

1978 *Fishing in Troubled Waters.* Taipei: Orient Cultural Service.

Anderson, L. G.

1977 *The Economics of Fisheries Management.* Baltimore: Johns Hopkins University Press.

Anderson, T. L., and P. J. Hill

1977 From Free Grass to Fences: Transforming the Commons of the American West. In *Managing the Commons*, G. Hardin and J. Baden, eds., pp. 200–216. San Francisco: W. H. Freeman.

Anes, G.

1977 *Historia de Asturias: El Regimen.* Salinas. Ayalga.

Ardi, I.

1982 Informasi Aspek Non Harga Komuditi Peternakan Itik de Kabupaten Hulu Sungai Utara; Diskusi Proyek Pengembangan Sistim Informasi Pasar Priode I, Tahun Anggara 1981/1983. Paper presented at Marketing Seminar, Amuntai, October 11, 1982.

Arensberg, C.

1968 [1937] *The Irish Countryman.* Reprint. New York: Natural History Press.

Arnhem, K.

1976 Fishing and Hunting Among the Makana. *Arseryck (Annals):* 22–47. Goteberg, Sweden.

Asada, Y., Y. Hirasawa, and F. Nagasaki

1983 Fishery Management in Japan. *FAO Fisheries Technical Paper No. 238.* Rome: Food and Agriculture Organization (United Nations).

Aspelin, L.

1975 External Articulation and Domestic Production. Latin American Studies Dissertation Series, No. 58. Cornell University.

Atlantic States Marine Fisheries Commission

1953 *Twelfth Annual Report.* Washington, D. C.

Axelrod, R., and W. D. Hamilton

1981 The Evolution of Cooperation. *Science* 211: 1390–96.

Bacqueville de la Potherie, C. C. L. R.

1931 *Letters of La Potherie: Documents Relating to the Early History of Hudson Bay.* J. B. Tyrrell, ed. Toronto: The Champlain Society.

Bailey, C. R.

1982 Cattle Husbandry in the Communal Areas of Eastern Botswana. Ph.D. dissertation, Cornell University.

Bailey, F. G.
  1969   *Strategems and Spoils: A Social Anthropology of Politics.* Oxford:
  Basil Blackwell.
Baird, S. F.
  1873   Report on the Condition of the Sea Fisheries of the South Coast
  of New England in 1871 and 1872. In *Report of the U.S. Commission of
  Fish and Fisheries for 1871*, pp. 1–274. Washington, D. C.: U.S. Gov-
  ernment Printing Office.
Baksh, M.
  In press   Faunal Food as a "Limiting Factor" on Amazonian Cultural
  Behavior: A Machiguenga Example. *Research in Economic Anthropology*
  7.
Barrett, G., and A. Davis
  1984   Floundering in Troubled Waters: The Political Economy of the
  Atlantic Fishery and the Task Force on Atlantic Fisheries. *Journal of
  Canadian Studies* 19(1): 125–37.
Bates, R. H.
  1983a   *Essays on the Political Economy of Rural Africa.* Cambridge:
  Cambridge University Press.
  1983b   Some Conventional Orthodoxies in the Study of Agrarian
  Change. *Social Science Working Paper 458.* Division of the Humanities
  and Social Sciences, California Institute of Technology, Pasadena.
Bauer, D. F.
  1973   Land, Leadership, and Legitimacy Among the Inderta Tigray of
  Ethiopia. Ph.D. dissertation, University of Rochester.
  1975   For Want of an Ox . . .: Land, Capital, and Social Stratification
  in Tigre. In *Proceedings of the First United States Conferences on Ethiopian
  Studies, 1973*, H. Marcus and J. Hinnant eds., pp. 235–48. East Lansing: African Studies Center, Michigan State University.
  1977   *Household and Society in Ethiopia.* East Lansing: African Studies
  Center, Michigan State University.
  1985   *Household and Society in Ethiopia*, rev. ed. East Lansing: African
  Studies Center, Michigan State University.
Beckerman, S.
  1983   Carpe Diem. In *Adaptive Responses of Native Amazonians*, R.
  Hames and W. Vickers, eds., pp. 269–97. New York: Academic Press.
Behar, R.
  1983   The Presence of the Past: A Historical Ethnography of a Leonese
  Village. Ph.D. dissertation, Princeton University.
Behnke, R. H., Jr.
  1985   Open-range Management and Property Rights in Pastoral Af-
  rica: A Case of Spontaneous Range Enclosure in South Darfur,
  Sudan. Pastoral Development Network, Overseas Development Institute, Paper 20f.
Beinart, W.
  1980   Production and the Material Basis of Chieftainship: Pondoland

c. 1830–1880. In *Economy and Society in Pre-Industrial Southern Africa,* S. Marks and A. Atmore, eds., pp. 120–47. London: Longmans.

Bell, F. L. S.

1947 The Place of Food in the Social Life of the Tanga. . . . *Oceania* 17: 310–26.

Belshaw, C.

1951 Recent History of Mekeo Society. *Oceania* 22: 1–23.

Benveniste, E.

1966 *Problèmes du linguistique generale.* Paris: Gallimard.

Bergman, R.

1980 *Amazon Economics: The Simplicity of Shipibo Indian Wealth.* Ann Arbor: University Microfilms International.

Berkes, F.

1977 Fishery Resource Management in a Subarctic Indian Community. *Human Ecology* 5: 289–307.

1979 An Investigation of Cree Indian Domestic Fisheries in Northern Quebec. *Arctic* 32: 46–70.

1981 Fisheries of the James Bay Area and Northern Quebec: A Case Study in Resource Management. In *Renewable Resources and the Economy of the North,* M. M. R. Freeman, ed., pp. 143–60. Ottawa: Association of Canadian Universities for Northern Research/Man and the Biosphere.

1982a Preliminary Impacts of the James Bay Hydroelectric Project, Quebec, an Estuarine Fish and Fisheries. *Arctic* 35: 525–30.

1982b Waterfowl Management and Northern Native Peoples with Reference to Cree Hunters of James Bay. *Musk-Ox* 30: 23–35.

1983 Quantifying the Harvest of Native Subsistence Fisheries. In *Resources and Dynamics of the Boreal Zone,* R. W. Wein, R. R. Riewe, and I. R. Methven, eds., pp. 346–63. Ottawa: Association of Canadian Universities for Northern Research.

1985 Fishermen and the "Tragedy of the Commons." *Environmental Conservation* 12: 199–206.

Berkes, F., and T. Gonenc

1982 A Mathematical Model on the Exploitation of Northern Lake Whitefish with Gillnets. *North American Journal of Fisheries Management* 2: 176–83.

Binswanger, H. P., and V. W. Ruttan

1978 Induced Innovation: Technology, Institutions, and Development. Baltimore: Johns Hopkins University Press.

Birdsell, J.

1968 Some Predictions for the Pleistocene Based on Equilibrium Systems Among Recent Hunter-Gatherers. In *Man the Hunter,* R. Lee and I. DeVore, eds., pp. 229–40. Chicago: Aldine.

Biro Pusat Statistik

1979 *Statistik Indonesia.* Jakarta.

1980 *Penduduk Kalimantan dan Sulawesi Menurut Propinsi dan Ka-*

bupaten/Kotamadya; Hasil Pencacahan Lengkap Sensus Penduduk 1980. Jakarta.

Bishop, C.
1970 The Emergence of Hunting Territories Among the Northern Ojibwa. *Ethnology* 9(1): 1–15.
1974 *The Northern Ojibwa and the Fur Trade.* Toronto: Holt, Rinehart and Winston.
1981 Northeastern Indian Concepts of Conservation and the Fur Trade: A Critique of Calvin Martin's Thesis. In *Indians, Animals, and the Fur Trade,* S. Krech, ed., pp. 39–58. Athens: University of Georgia Press.
1984 The First Century: Adaptive Changes Among the Western James Bay Cree Between the Early Seventeenth and Early Eighteenth Centuries. In *The Subarctic Fur Trade: Native Social and Economic Adaptations,* S. Krech, ed., pp. 21–53. Vancouver: University of British Columbia.

Björnsson, O.
1979 Akvarðanir í sjávarútvegi. In *Ráðstefna um áhrif sérfraeðinga á ákvarðanir stjórnvalda.* Reykjavík: BHM.

Bloch, M.
1930 La Lutte pour l'individualism agraire dans la France de XVIIIe siècle. *Annales d'histoire economique et sociale* 11: 329–83, 511–56.

Blomquist, W., and E. Ostrom
1986 Institutional Capacity and the Resolution of a Commons Dilemma. *Policy Studies Review* 5(2): 383–93.

Bohannan, P.
1963 Land, "Tenure," and Land Tenure. In *African Agrarian Systems,* Daniel Biebuyk, ed., pp. 101–15. Oxford: Oxford University Press for IAI.

Braudel, F.
1980 *On History.* Chicago: University of Chicago Press.
1981 *The Structures of Everyday Life: The Limits of the Possible,* vol. I. S. Reynolds, trans. New York: Harper and Row.

Bromley, D. W.
1982 Land and Water Problems in an Institutional Perspective. *American Journal of Agricultural Economics* 64: 834–44.

Brotherston, G.
1979 *Images of the New World.* London: Thames and Hudson.

Brown, J.
1964 The Evolution of Diversity in Avian Territorial Systems. *Wilson Bulletin* 6:160–69.

Buchanan, J., and G. Tullock
1962 *The Calculus of Consent.* Ann Arbor: University of Michigan Press.

Bulmer, R.
1982 Traditional Conservation Practices in Papua New Guinea. In

Traditional Conservation in Papua New Guinea: Implications for Today, L. Morauta, J. Pernetta, and W. Heaney, eds., pp. 59–77. Boroko, PNG: Institute of Applied Social and Economic Research.

Burgesse, J. A.
1945 Property Concepts of the Lac St. Jean Montagnais. *Primitive Man* 16: 44–48.

Butt-Colson, A.
1973 Inter-tribal Trade in the Guiana Highlands. *Anthropologica* 34: 1–70.

Byrne, F. J.
1967 Early Irish Society. In *The Course of Irish History,* T. W. Moody and F. X. Martin, eds., pp. 126–65. Cork: Mercier.

Calabresi, G., and P. Bobbitt
1978 *Tragic Choices.* New York: Norton.

Campbell, J.
1964 *Honor, Family and Patronage.* London: Oxford University Press.

Canada, Department of Fisheries and Oceans
1982 *Fleet Rationalization Committee Report.* Vancouver, B.C.

Carkhuff, R., and B. G. Berenson
1977 *Beyond Counseling and Therapy* (2nd ed.). New York: Holt, Rinehart and Winston.

Carl Bro International
1982 *An Evaluation of Livestock Management and Production in Botswana: Main Report.* Gaborone and Brussels.

Carrier, J.
1980 Knowledge and Its Use: Constraints Upon the Application of New Knowledge in Ponam Society. *Papua New Guinea Journal of Education* 16: 102–26.
1981 Ownership of Productive Resources on Ponam Island, Manus Province. *Journal de la Société des Océanistes* 37: 205–17.
1982 Fishing Practices on Ponam Island (Manus Province, Papua New Guinea). *Anthropos* 77: 904–15.
n.d. The Ponam Fish Freezer: A Small-scale Development Project in Manus Province. Manuscript.

Carrier, J., and A. Carrier
1983 Profitless Property: Marine Ownership and Access to Wealth on Ponam Island, Manus Province. *Ethnology* 22: 133–51.

Carroll, T. M., D. H. Ciscil, and R. K. Chisholm
1979 The Market as a Commons: An Unconventional View of Property Rights. *Journal of Economic Issues* 8(2): 605–27.

Carruthers, I., and R. Stoner
1981 *Economic Aspects and Policy Issues in Groundwater Development.* World Bank Staff Working Paper No. 496. Washington, D. C.: The World Bank.

Cass, R. C., and J. J. Edney
1978 The Commons Dilemma: A Simulation Testing the Effects of Resource Visibility and Territorial Division. *Human Ecology* 6: 371–86.

Castanon, L.
1970   Andecha. *La Gran Enciclopedia Asturiana*, vol. 1: 226–27, 326.
Chagnon, N., and R. Hames
1979   Protein Deficiency and Tribal Warfare in Amazonia: New Data. *Science* 203: 910–13.
Chapman, M.
1985   Environmental Influences on the Development of Traditional Conservation in the South Pacific Region. *Environmental Conservation* 12(3): 217–30.
Charnov, E.
1973   Optimal Foraging: Some Theoretical Explorations. Ph.D. Dissertation, University of Washington.
1976a   Optimal Foraging: The Marginal Value Theorem. *Theoretical Population Biology* 9: 129–36.
1976b   Optimal Foraging: The Attack Strategy of a Mantid. *American Naturalist* 109:343–52.
Charnov, E., G. Hyatt, and G. Orians
1976   Ecological Implications of Resource Depression. *American Naturalist* 110: 247–59.
Charnov, E., and G. Orians
1973   Optimal Foraging: Some Theoretical Explorations, Department of Biology, Salt Lake City: University of Utah.
Chayanov, A. V.
1966   In *The Theory of Peasant Economy*, D. Thorner, B. Kerblay, and R. E. F. Smith, eds. Homewood, Ill.: American Economic Association.
Cheung, S. N. S.
1970   The Structure of a Contract and the Theory of a Non-exclusive Resource. *Journal of Law and Economics* 13(1): 45–70.
Christy, F. T.
1973   Fishermen Quotas: A Tentative Suggestion for Domestic Management. *Occasional Paper 19*, Law of the Sea Institute, University of Rhode Island, Kingston.
Christy, F. T., and A. Scott
1965   *The Common-Wealth in Ocean Fisheries*. Baltimore: Johns Hopkins University Press.
Ciriacy-Wantrup, S. V., and R. C. Bishop
1975   "Common Property" as a Concept in Natural Resources Policy. *Natural Resources Journal* 15(4): 713–27.
Clark, C. W.
1973   The Economics of Over-exploitation. *Science* 181: 630–34.
1976   *Mathematical Bioeconomics: The Optimal Management of Renewable Resources*. New York: Wiley.
Clark, M., and S. Fiske, eds.
1982   *Affect and Cognition*. Hillsdale, Nova Scotia: Lawrence Erlbaum Associates.
Coase, R. H.
1960   The Problem of Social Cost. *Journal of Law and Economics* 3:1–44.

Colclough, C., and S. McCarthy
   1980   *The Political Economy of Botswana.* Oxford: Oxford University Press.
Cole, J. W., and E. R. Wolf
   1974   *The Hidden Frontier: Ecology and Ethnicity in an Alpine Valley.* New York: Academic Press.
Colson, E.
   1971   The Impact of the Colonial Period on the Definition of Land Rights. In *Colonialism in Africa 1870–1960,* vol. 3. V. Turner, ed., pp. 193–215. Cambridge: Cambridge University Press.
Comaroff, J.
   1985   *Body of Power, Spirit of Resistance: The Culture and History of a South African People.* Chicago: University of Chicago Press.
Consumers' Association of Penang
   1976   *Pollution: Kuala Juru's Fight for Survival.* Penang.
Cooper, J. M.
   1939   Is the Algonquian Family Hunting Ground Systems Pre-Columbian? *American Anthropologist* 41: 66–90.
Costa, J.
   1902   *Derecho consuetudinario y economía popular en España.* 2 vols. Barcelona: Manuel Soler.
   1915   *Colectivismo agrario en España: Partes I y II, Doctrinas y hechas.* Madrid: Biblioteca Costa.
Cove, J.
   1973   Hunters, Trappers, and Gatherers of the Sea: A Comparative Study of Fishing Strategies. *Journal of the Fisheries Research Board of Canada* 30: 249–59.
   1982   The Gitksan Traditional Concept of Land Ownership. *Anthropologica* 24(1): 3–17.
Cox, S. J. B.
   1985   No Tragedy on the Common. *Environmental Ethics* 7:49–61.
Creel, H. G.
   1972   *Shen Pu-Hai.* Chicago: University of Chicago Press.
Crocombe, R.
   1971   The Pattern of Change in Pacific Land Tenure. In *Land Tenure in the Pacific,* R. Crocombe, ed., pp. 1–24. London: Oxford University Press.
Crocombe, R., ed.
   1971   *Land Tenure in the Pacific.* London: Oxford University Press.
Crocombe, R., and G. R. Hogbin
   1963   Land, Work and Productivity at Inonda. *New Guinea Research Bulletin 2.* Canberra: Australian National University Press.
Cronon, W.
   1983   *Changes in the Land: Indians, Colonists, and the Ecology of New England.* New York: Hill and Wang.
Crowe, B. L.
   1977   The Tragedy of the Commons Revisited. In *Managing the Com-*

mons, G. Hardin and J. Baden, eds., pp. 53–65. San Francisco: W. H. Freeman.

Crush, J.
  1985 Landlords, Tenants and Colonial Social Engineers: The Farm Labour Question in Early Colonial Swaziland. *Journal of Southern African Studies* 11(2): 235–37.

Crutchfield, J. A.
  1964 The Marine Fisheries: A Problem in International Cooperation. *American Economic Review Proceedings* 54: 207–18.
  1973 Resources from the Sea. In *Ocean Resources and Public Policy*, T. S. English, ed., pp. 105–33. Seattle: University of Washington Press.
  1979 Economic and Social Implications of the Main Policy Alternatives for Controlling Fishing Effort. *Journal of the Fisheries Research Board of Canada* 36: 742–52.

Crutchfield, J. A., and G. Pontecorvo
  1969 *The Pacific Salmon Fisheries: A Study of Irrational Conservation*. Baltimore: Johns Hopkins University Press.

Crutchfield, J. A., and A. Zellner
  1962 *Economic Aspects of the Pacific Halibut Fishery*. Washington, D. C.: U.S. Government Printing Office.

Dachs, A.
  1972 Missionary Imperialism—the Case of Bechuanaland. *Journal of African History* 13(4): 647–58.

Davidson, D. S.
  1926 The Family Hunting Territories of the Grand Lake Victoria Indians. *Proceedings of the International Congress of Americanists* 22: 69–95.

Davis, L. E., and D. C. North
  1971 *Institutional Change and American Economic Growth*. Cambridge: Cambridge University Press.

Dawes, R. M.
  1980 Social Dilemmas. *Annual Review of Psychology* 31: 169–93.

DeWolf, G.
  1974 The Lobster Fishery of the Maritime Provinces: Economic Effects of Regulations. *Bulletin 187*. Ottawa: Fisheries Research Board of Canada.

DeGregori, T. R.
  1974 Caveat Emptor: A Critique of the Emerging Paradigm of Public Choice. *Administration and Society* 6(2): 205–28.

Demsetz, H.
  1967 Toward a Theory of Property Rights. *American Economic Review* 62(2): 347–59.

Denevan, W. M., ed.
  1976 *The Native Population of the Americas in 1492*. Madison: University of Wisconsin Press.

Diaz-Nosty, B.
  1975 *La Comuna asturiana*. Bilbao: Zero.

Dinas Peternakan Kalimantan Selatan
1981   *Laporan Tahunan 1980/1981.* Banjarbaru.
Dobbs, A.
1744   *An Account of the Countries Adjoining to Hudson's Bay.* London: J.
Robinson.
Dobyns, H. E.
1966   Estimating Aboriginal American Population: An Appraisal of
Techniques with a New Hemispheric Estimate. *Current Anthropology*
7: 396–416.
Dowling, J. H.
1975   Property Relations and Productive Strategies in Pastoral So-
cieties. *American Ethnologist* 2(3): 419–26.
Drage, T. S.
1968   [1748–49]   *An Account of a Voyage for the Discovery of a Northwest
Passage . . .* 2 vols. Reprint. New York: S and R Publishers.
Drucker, C. B.
1977   To Inherit the Land: Descent and Decision in Northern Luzon.
Ethnology 16: 1–20.
Dumont, L.
1972   *Homo Hierarchicus: The Caste System and Its Implications.* London:
Paladin.
Dunbar, M. J.
1973   Stability and Fragility in Arctic Ecosystems. *Arctic* 26: 179–85.
Dunn, J.
1845   *The Oregon Territory.* Philadelphia: G. B. Zieber.
Durham, W.
1978   Toward a Coevolutionary Theory of Human Biology and
Culture. In *The Sociology Debate,* A. L. Caplan, ed., pp. 428–48. New
York: Harper and Row.
1981   Overview: Optimal Foraging Analysis in Human Ecology. In
Hunter-Gatherer Foraging Strategies, B. Winterhalder and E. A. Smith,
eds., pp. 218–31. Chicago: University of Chicago Press.
Durrenberger, E. P.
1976   The Economy of a Lisu Village. *American Ethnologist* 3: 633–44.
Durrenberger, E. P., and G. Pálsson
1985   Peasants, Entrepreneurs, and Companies: The Evolution of Icelandic Fishing. *Ethnos* 1–2: 103–22.
1986   Finding Fish: The Tactics of Icelandic Skippers. *American Ethnologist* 13(2): 213–29.
Dyson-Hudson, R., and E. A. Smith
1978   Human Territoriality: An Ecological Reassessment. *American
Anthropologist* 80: 21–41.
Ebenreck, S.
1984   Stopping the Raid on Soil: Ethical Reflections on "Sodbusting"
Legislation. *Agriculture and Human Values* 1(3): 3–9.

Edney, J. J.
1981 Paradoxes on the Commons: Scarcity and the Problem of Inequality. *Journal of Community Psychology* 9: 3–34.
Ellen, R.
1982 *Environment, Subsistence, and System.* New York: Cambridge
University Press.
Ellis, H.
1967 [1748] *A Voyage to Hudson's Bay by the Dobbs Galley and California
in the Years 1746 and 1747.* New York: Johnson Reprint Co.
Emerson, D. K.
1980 *Rethinking Artisanal Fisheries Development: Western Concepts,
Asian Experiences.* World Bank Staff Working Paper No. 423, Washington, D.C.: The World Bank.
Evans, E. E.
1939 Some Survivals of the Irish Open Field System. *Geography* 24:
24–36.
1942 *Irish Heritage.* Dundalk: The Dundalgan Press.
1964 Ireland and Atlantic Europe. *Geographische Zeitschrift* 52 Jahr, 3
Heft, August.
Evans-Pritchard, E. E.
1940 *The Nuer.* Oxford: Oxford University Press.
Faris, J.
1982 Modernization in Traditional Fishing Communities: The Example of Cat Harbour. In *Modernization and Marine Fisheries Policy,* J.
Maiolo and M. Orbach, eds., pp. 177–202. Ann Arbor: Ann Arbor
Science.
Feeny, D.
1982 *The Political Economy of Productivity.* Vancouver: University of
British Columbia Press.
Feit, H. A.
1973 The Ethno-Ecology of the Waswanipi Cree; or, How Hunters
Can Manage Their Resources. In *Cultural Ecology,* B. Cox, ed., pp.
115–25. Toronto: McClelland and Stewart.
Feuilletau de Bruyn, W. K. H.
1920 Schouten-ed Padaido-Eilanden. Meded Bureau Bestuurszaken
Encycloped Bureau 21.
1933 Bijdrage tot de kennis van de Afdeeling Hoeloe Soengei. In
Overdruk vit Kolonial Studien, Jaarg 17, no. 1, XXI 4302: 53–93.
Fife, D.
1977 Killing the Goose. In *Managing the Commons,* G. Hardin and J.
Baden, eds., pp. 76–81. San Francisco: W. H. Freeman (reprinted
from *Environment* 13(3): 20–27, 1971).
Fittkau, E.
1970 Role of Caimans in the Nutrient Regime of North Lakes Afflu-
ents. *Biotropica* 2: 138–42.

1973   Crocodiles and the "Nutrient" Metabolism of Amazon Waters. *Amazonia* 4: 104–33.

Flannery, K.
1972   The Cultural Ecology of Civilizations. *Annual Review of Ecology and Systematics* 3: 399–425.

Fleming, R. H., ed.
1940   *Minutes of Council, Northern Department of Rupert's Land, 1821–1831.* London: Hudson's Bay Record Society.

Fletcher, H.
1983   Salmon Interception: Problems and Prospects. Department of Fisheries and Oceans, Vancouver. Manuscript.

Fortune, R.
1935   *Manus Religion.* Philadelphia: American Philosophical Society.

Fox, R.
1979   *The Tory Islanders.* Cambridge: Cambridge University Press.

Franke, R. W., and B. H. Chasin
1980   *Seeds of Famine: Ecological Destruction and the Development Dilemma in the West African Sahel.* Montclair, N.J.: Allenheld, Osmun.

Freeman, S. T.
1972   *Neighbors.* Chicago: University of Chicago Press.

Fried, M.
1967   *The Evolution of Political Society.* New York: Random House.

Friedman, J.
1974   Marxism, Structuralism, and Vulgar Materialism. *Man* 9: 444–69.
1975   Tribes, States, and Transformations. In *Marxist Analyses and Social Anthropology,* Maurice Bloch, ed., pp. 161–202. New York: J. Wiley.

Friedrich, P.
1979   The Relative Non-Arbitrariness of the Linguistic Sign. In *Language, Context, and the Imagination,* A. S. Dil, ed., pp. 1–61. Stanford: Stanford University Press.

Furubotn, E. H., and S. Pejovich
1972   Property Rights and Economic Theory: A Survey of Recent Literature. *Journal of Economic Literature* 10: 1137–62.

Gadacz, R.
1975   Montagnais Hunting Dynamics in Historicoecological Perspective. *Anthropologica* 17: 149–68.

Gaigo, B.
1982   Past and Present Fishing Practices Among the People of Tatana Village, Port Moresby. In *Traditional Conservation in Papua New Guinea: Implications for Today,* L. Morauta, J. Pernetta, and W. Heaney, eds., pp. 301–02. Boroko, PNG: Institute of Applied Social and Economic Research.

Galis, K. W.
1955   *Papua's van de Humboldt-Baai.* The Hague: Voerhoeve.

1970 Land Tenure in the Biak-Numfor Area. *New Guinea Research Bulletin* 38: 1–12.

García Fernández, J.
1976 *Sociedad y organización tradicional del espacio en Asturias.* Oviedo: Instituto des Estudios Asturianos.

Geertz, C.
1963 *Agricultural Involution: The Processes of Ecological Change in Indonesia.* Berkeley: University of California Press.

Gersuny, C., and J. J. Poggie, Jr.
1974 Luddites and Fishermen: A Note on Response to Technological Change. *Maritime Studies and Management* 2: 38–47.

Gilles, J. L., and K. Jamtgaard
1981 Overgrazing in Pastoral Areas: The Commons Reconsidereed. *Sociologica Ruralus* 21 (September): 129–41. Reprinted in *Nomadic Peoples* 10: 1–10, 1982.

Gillis, D. J., and W. McKay
1980 Economic Development Planning for the Kwakiutl District. Report Prepared for the Kwakiutl District Council, P. O. Box 2940, Port Hardy, B.C.

Gilmore, D.
1980 *People of the Plain: Class and Community in Lower Andalucia.* New York: Columbia University Press.

Gíslason, T.
1971 The Icelandic Technique of Sonar Guided Purse Seining. In *Modern Fishing Gear of the World*, vol. 3, J. Kristjánsson, ed., pp. 206–17. London: Fishing News.

Gitksan-Carrier Tribal Council
1981 Submission to the Commission on Pacific Fisheries Policy, Hazelton, British Columbia.

Godelier, M.
1972 *Rationality and Irrationality in Economics.* London: New Left Books.

Godwin, R. K., and W. B. Shepard
1979 Forcing Squares, Triangles and Ellipses into a Circular Paradigm: The Use of the Commons Dilemma in Examining the Allocation of Common Resources. *Western Political Quarterly* 32(3): 265–77.

Goldthorpe, W. G.
1980 Report to the Minister on Indian Health and Health Care, Alert Bay, B. C. Testimony of Basil Ambers, March 4, 1980, pp. 116–40.

Gordon, H. S.
1954 The Economic Theory of a Common Property Resource: The Fishery. *Journal of Political Economy* 62: 124–42.

Graham, A.
1969 [1767–91] *Andrew Graham's Observations on Hudson Bay.* G. Williams, ed. Reprint. London: Hudson Bay Record Society.

Grant, S.
   1980   Reduced Almost to Nothing? Chieftaincy and the Traditional
   Town. The Case of Linchwe II Kgafela and Mochudi. *Botswana Notes
   and Records* 12: 89–100.
Gray, H.
   1915   *English Field Systems.* Reproduction edition, 1981. New York:
   Kelley.
Gregory, C. A.
   1982   *Gifts and Commodities.* London: Academic Press.
Gross, D.
   1975   Protein Capture and Cultural Development in the Amazon
   Basin. *American Anthropologist* 77: 526–49.
   1983   Village Movement in Relation to Resources in Amazonia. In
   Adaptive Responses of Native Amazonians, R. Hames and W. Vickers,
   eds., pp. 429–50. New York: Academic Press.
Grotius, H.
   1609   *Mare Liberum.* Excerpted in *The Law of the Sea: Cases, Documents,
   and Readings* (1976), H. Gary Knight, comp. Washington, D.C.: Nau-
   tilus Press.
Guillet, D.
   1981   Land Tenure, Ecological Zone, and Agricultural Regime in the
   Central Andes. *American Ethnologist* 8(1): 139–56.
Gulbrandsen, O.
   1980   *Agro-Pastoral Production and Communal Land Use: A Socio-Eco-
   nomic Study of the Bangwaketse.* Gaborone: Ministry of Agriculture.
Gulland, J. A.
   1974   *The Management of Marine Fisheries.* Bristol: Scientechnica.
Guppy, N.
   1984   Property Rights and Changing Class Formation in the Social
   Organization of the B.C. Commercial Fishing Industry. Paper presented at the Western Regional Association of Sociology and Anthropology, Regina, Saskatchewan.
Haines, A. K.
   1982   Traditional Concepts and Practices and Inland Fisheries Management. In *Traditional Conservation in Papua New Guinea: Implications
   for Today,* Monograph 16, L. Morauta, J. Pernetta, and W. Heaney,
   eds., pp. 279–92. Boroko, PNG: Institute of Applied Social and Economic Research.
Halewijn, M.
   1838   Borneo, Eenige Rizen in Binnenlanden van dit Eiland, Door
   Eenen Ambtenaar van het Gouvernement, In het Jahr 1824, *Tijdschrift
   voor Nederland's Indie,* le Jaargang, vol. 2, pp. 193ff. Cited in *Hikajat
   Bandjar: A Study in Malay Historiography,* J. J. Ras, 1968, p. 626. The
   Hague: Martinus Nijhoff.
Hall, A.
   1894   Notes on the Oyster Industry of New Jersey. In *Report of the*

U.S. Commission of Fish and Fisheries for the Year Ending June 30, 1892, pp. 463–528. Washington, D.C.: U.S. Govermment Printing Office.

Hallowell, A. I.
1955 *Culture and Experience*. Philadelphia: University of Pennsylvania Press.

Hames, R.
1979 A Comparison of the Efficiencies of the Shotgun and the Bow in Neotropical Forest Hunting. *Human Ecology* 7: 219–52.
1980 Game Depletion and Hunting Zone Rotation Among the Ye'kwana and Yanomamo of Amazonas, Venezuela. In *Studies of Hunting and Fishing in the Neotropics*, R. Hames, ed., *Working Papers on South American Indians*, vol. 2. Bennington, Vt.: Bennington College.
1983 The Settlement Pattern of a Yanomamo Population Bloc. In *Adaptive Responses of Native Amazonians*, R. Hames and W. Vickers, eds., pp. 393–427. New York: Academic Press.
n.d. Time, Utility, and Fitness in the Amazonian Protein Quest. Department of Anthropology, University of Nebraska, Lincoln. Manuscript.

Hames, R., and W. Vickers
1983 Optimal Foraging Theory as a Model to Explain Variability in Amazonian Hunting. *American Ethnologist* 9: 379–91.

Hamlisch, R., ed.
1962 *Economic Effects of Fishery Regulation*. FAO Fisheries Report No. 5. Rome: Food and Agriculture Organization (United Nations).

Hammond, K. R., J. Rohrbaugh, J. Mumpower, and L. Adelman
1977 Social Judgment Theory: Applications in Policy Formation. In *Human Judgment and Decision Processes in Applied Settings*. M. Kaplan and S. Schwartz, eds., pp. 1–27. New York: Academic Press.

Hanks, L. M.
1972 *Rice and Man: Agricultural Ecology in Southeast Asia*. Chicago: Aldine.

Hannesson, R.
1978 *The Economics of Fisheries*. Oslo: Universitetsforlaget.

Hardin, G.
1968 The Tragedy of the Commons. *Science* 162: 1243–48.
1977a What Marx Missed. In *Managing the Commons*, G. Hardin and J. Baden, eds., pp. 3–7. San Francisco: W. H. Freeman.
1977b Denial and Disguise. In *Managing the Commons*, G. Hardin and J. Baden, eds., pp. 45–52. San Francisco: W. H. Freeman.

Hardin, G., and J. Baden, eds.
1977 *Managing the Commons*. San Francisco: W. H. Freeman

Harmon, D.
1905 [1821] *A Journal of Voyages and Travels in the Interior of North America*. Reprint. New York: Allerton.

Harper, J.
   1982   Indian Fisheries Management in the State of Washington. Indian and Northern Affairs, Vancouver, B.C. Manuscript.
Harris, M.
   1966   The Cultural Ecology of India's Sacred Cattle. *Current Anthropology* 7: 51–60.
   1974   *Cows, Pigs, Wars, and Witches: The Riddles of Culture.* New York: Random House.
Hasslof, O.
   1984   Customs, Laws and Organization in Nordic Fishing. In *The Fishing Cultures of the World*, vol. 1, B. Gunda, ed., pp. 223–28. Budapest: Akadémiai Kiado.
Hawkes, K., K. Hill, and J. O'Connell
   1983   Why Hunters Gather: Optimal Foraging and the Ache of Eastern Paraguay. *American Ethnologist* 9:379–91.
Hayami, Y., and M. Kikuchi
   1982   *Asian Village Economy at the Crossroads: An Economic Approach to Institutional Change.* Baltimore: Johns Hopkins University Press.
Hayward, B.
   1981a   The B.C. Salmon Fishery: A Consideration of the Effects of Licencing. *B.C. Studies*, No. 50.
   1981b   The Development of Relations of Production in the British Columbia Salmon Fishery. M.A. thesis, University of British Columbia.
Hearn, W.
   1977   High Fertility in a Peruvian Amazon Indian Village. *Human Ecology* 5: 355–68.
Hearne, S.
   1958 [1795]   *A Journey from Prince of Wales Fort in Hudson's Bay to the Northern Ocean in the Years 1769, 1770, 1771, and 1772.* R. Glover, ed. Reprint. Toronto: Macmillan.
Heinsohn, G. E., J. Wake, H. Marsh, and A. V. Spain
   1977   The Dugong (*Dugong dugon* [Muller]) in the Seagrass System. *Aquaculture* 12: 235–48.
Hennemuth, R.
   1979   Man as a Predator. In *Contemporary Quantitative Ecology and Related Econometrics*, G. P. Patil and M. L. Rosenzweig, eds., pp. 507–32. Fairland, Mo.: International Cooperative Publishing House.
Hickerson, H.
   1967   Land Tenure of the Rainy Lake Chippewa at the Beginning of the Nineteenth Century. *Smithsonian Contributions to Anthropology* 2(4): 42–63.
   1973   Fur Trade Colonialism and the North American Indian. *Journal of Ethnic Studies* 1: 15–44.
Hilborn, R., and M. Ledbetter
   1979   An Analysis of the British Columbia Purse-Seine Fleet: The Dy-

namics of Movement. *Journal of the Fisheries Research Board of Canada* 36(4): 384–91.

Hitchcock, R. K.
1980 Tradition, Social Justice and Land Reform in Central Botswana. *Journal of African Law* 24(1): 1–34.

Hobbes, T.
1950 *Leviathan.* New York: E. P. Dutton and Co., Inc. Originally published in 1651.

Hoben, A.
1973 *Land Tenure Among the Amhara of Ethiopia: The Dynamics of Cognatic Descent.* Chicago: University of Chicago Press.

Hockett, C. F.
1973 *Man's Place in Nature.* New York: McGraw-Hill.

Hoebel, E. A.
1954 *The Law of Primitive Man.* Cambridge, Mass.: Harvard University Press.

Hoskins, W. G., and L. D. Stamp
1963 *The Common Lands of England and Wales.* London: Collins.

Howkins, A.
1979 Economic Crime and Class Law: Poaching and the Game Laws, 1840–1880. In *The Imposition of Law,* Sandra B. Burman and Barbara E. Harrell-Bond, eds., pp. 273–87. New York: Academic Press.

Hudson's Bay Company Archives, Provincial Archives of Manitoba
1794–95 [Remarks Going Up the Churchill River Also During the Winter 1795] Manuscript B/83/a.
1802–3 [Nelson House Post Journal] Manuscript B141/a/1.
1805–6 [Indian Lake Journal] Manuscript B91/a/1.
1815 [District Report, Nelson House and Deer Lake] Manuscript B141/e/1.
1821–36 [District Fur Returns, Nelson River] Manuscript B239/H/1.
1825–26 [District Report, Nelson House] Manuscript B141/e/2.

Hull, H., comp.
1924 *Oke's Fishery Laws,* 4th ed. London: Butterworth and Co.

Icelandic Fisheries Yearbook
1981 Reykjavík: Icelandic Review.

Inland Fisheries Commission (Ireland)
1975 *Report.* Dublin: Stationary Press.

Innis, H. A.
1970 *The Fur Trade in Canada.* New Haven: Yale University Press.

Isham, J.
1949 [1743–49] *James Isham's Observations of Hudson's Bay, 1743–1749.* Reprint. London: Hudson Bay Record Society.

Ivens, W.
1930 *The Island Builders of the Pacific.* London: Seeley, Service.

Jaffee, L. R.
    1974   The Public Trust Doctrine Is Alive and Kicking in New Jersey
    Tidalwaters: *Neptune City v. Avon-by-the-Sea*—A Case of Happy
    Atavism? *Natural Resources Journal* 14: 309–35.
James, M.
    1984   Native Claims, Data Collection and Impact Assessment. De-
    partment of Fisheries and Oceans, Vancouver. Manuscript.
Jenkins, W.
    1939   Notes on the Hunting Economy of the Abitibi Indians. *Catholic
    University of America Anthropological Series* 9: 1–31.
Jentoft, S.
    1981   *Organisasjon og ansvar: Lokale koordineringsproblemer i fisker-
    naeringen*. Tromsö, Norway: Universitetsforlaget.
    1982   *Sysselsettingsystemer i fisket*. Projektnotat nr. 4. Institutt for
    Fiskerifag, Tromsö University, Tromsö.
Jette, J.
    1907   On the Medicine Men of the Ten'a. *Journal of the Royal An-
    thropological Institute of Great Britain and Ireland* 37: 157–86.
Jochim, M.
    1981   *Strategies for Survival*. New York: Academic Press.
Johannes, R. E.
    1977   Traditional Law of the Sea in Micronesia. *Micronesia* 13: 121–
    27.
    1978   Traditional Marine Conservation Methods in Oceania and Their
    Demise. *Annual Review of Ecology and Systematics* 9:349–64.
    1981   *Worlds of the Lagoon: Fishing and Marine Lore in the Palau District of
    Micronesia*. Berkeley: University of California Press.
    1982   Implications of Traditional Marine Resource Use for Coastal
    Fisheries Development in Papua New Guinea. In *Traditional Conser-
    vation in Papua New Guinea: Implications for Today*, L. Morauta, J. Per-
    netta, and W. Heaney, eds., pp. 239–49. Boroko, PNG: Institute of
    Applied Social and Economic Research.
Johnson, A.
    1982   Reductionism in Cultural Ecology: The Amazonian Case. *Cur-
    rent Anthropology:* 23:413–28.
Johnson, L.
    1976   Ecology of Arctic Populations of Lake Whitefish, *Coregonus
    Clupeaformis*, Arctic Char, *S. alpinus*, and Associated Species in Unex-
    ploited Lakes of the Canadian Northwest Territories. *Journal of the
    Fisheries Research Board of Canada* 33:2459–88.
Johnson, R. N., and G. D. Libecap
    1980   Agency Costs and the Assignment of Property Rights: The
    Case of Southwestern Indian Reservations. *Southern Economic Journal*
    47: 332–47.
Johnston, B. F., and P. Kilby
    1975   *Agriculture and Structural Transformation*. New York: Oxford
    University Press.

Jovellanos, G. M.
    1753 *Informe sobre la ley agraria.* Madrid: Sociedad Económica.
Kabupaten Dati II, Hulu Sungai Utara
    1980 *Rencana Umum Kota Amuntai Kompilasi Data Buku I.* Amuntai.
Kecamatan Amuntai Selatan, Kantor Camat
    1982 *Registrasi Penduduk,* Juli 1982. Telaga Silaba.
Keesing, R.
    1981 Theories of Culture. In *Language, Culture, and Cognition,* R. Casson, ed. pp. 42–66. New York: Macmillan.
Kensinger, K., and W. Kracke, eds.
    1981 Food Taboos in Lowland South America. *Working Papers on South American Indians,* No. 3. Bennington, Vt.: Bennington College.
Kiltie, R.
    1980 More on Amazonian Cultural Ecology. *Cultural Anthropology:* 23:541–44.
Kimber, R.
    1981 Collective Action and the Fallacy of the Liberal Fallacy. *World Politics* 1981: 178–96.
Klee, G., ed.
    1980 *World Systems of Traditional Resource Management.* London: Edward Arnold and V. H. Winston & Sons.
Knight, H. G., comp.
    1976 *The Law of the Sea: Cases, Documents, and Readings.* Washington, D.C.: Nautilus Press.
Krauss, C.
    1983 The Elusive Process of Citizen Activism. *Social Policy,* Fall 1983: 50–55.
Krebs, J.
    1978 Optimal Foraging: Decision Rules for Predators. In *Behavioural Ecology: An Evolutionary Approach,* J. Krebs and N. Davies, eds., pp. 23–63. Oxford: Blackwell Scientific Publications.
Krebs, J., and N. Davies, eds.
    1978 *Behavioural Ecology: An Evolutionary Approach.* Oxford: Blackwell Scientific Publications.
Krech, S.
    1981 Throwing Bad Medicine. In *Indians, Animals, and the Fur Trade,* S. Krech, ed., pp. 73–108. Athens: University of Georgia Press.
Krouse, J. S.
    1973 Maturity, Sex Ratio, and Size Composition of the Natural Population of American Lobster, *Homarus americanus,* Along the Maine Coast. *Fishery Bulletin* 71: 165–73.
Ladurie, E. L. R.
    1974 *The Peasants of Languedoc.* J. Day, trans. Urbana: University of Illinois Press.
Lahontan, L. A.
    1905 [1703] *New Voyages to North America.* R. G. Thwaites, ed. 2 vols. Reprint. Chicago: A. C. McClurg.

Landes, R.
   1937   Ojibwa Sociology. *Columbia University Contributions to An-thropology No. 31.*
Langdon, S.
   1982   Managing Modernization: A Critique of Formalist Approaches to the Pacific Salmon Fisheries. In *Modernization and Marine Fisheries Policy,* J. Maiolo and M. Orbach, eds., pp. 95–114. Ann Arbor: Ann Arbor Science.
   1984a   Commercial Fisheries in Western Alaska: Implications of and for State Fisheries Policy. Paper presented at the Western Regional Science Association Meetings, Monterey, Calif.
   1984b   The Perception of Equity: Social Management of Access in an Aleut Fishing Village. Paper presented at the Society for Applied Anthropology, Toronto, March 1984.
LaPointe, J.
   1970   Residential Patterns and Wayana Social Organization. Ph.D. Dissertation, Columbia University.
Larkin, P. A.
   1977   An Epitaph for the Concept of Maximum Sustained Yield. *Transactions of the American Fisheries Society* 106: 1–11.
Lawry, S. W.
   1984   Botswana's Tribal Grazing Land Policy. In *Land Tenure and Livestock Development in Sub-Saharan Africa,* J. W. Bennett, S. W. Lawry, and J. C. Riddell, eds., pp. 73–111. Madison: Land Tenure Center.
Leach, E.
   1954   *Political Systems of Highland Burma.* London: Bell.
   1972   Anthropological Perspectives: Conclusions. In *Population and Pollution,* P. Cox and J. Peel, eds., pp. 37–40. London: Academic Press.
Leacock, E.
   1954   The Montagnais "Hunting Territory" and the Fur Trade. *American Anthropological Association Memoir no. 78,* vol. 56(5), pt. 2: 1–59.
LeClercq, C.
   1881 [1691]   *First Establishment of the Faith in New France.* 2 vols. Reprint. New York: John G. Shea.
Ledoux, G., and A. Lepage
   1973   Les conditions d'adoption d'une technique de pêche côtière sur la Côte-Nord du Golfe Saint-Laurent (Québec) à la fin du XIXe siècle. Paper presented at the International Congress of Anthropological and Ethnological Sciences, Chicago, September 1973.
Leiserson, M., S. Bose, C. Chandrasekaran, D. Chernichovsky, R. Key, O. A. Meesook, and P. Suebsaeng
   1980   *Employment and Income Distribution in Indonesia.* Washington, D.C.: The World Bank.
LeJeune, P.
   1897   *Relation of What Occurred in New France in the Year 1635. The Jesuit*

Relations and Allied Documents. R. G. Thwaites, ed., vol. 8. Cleveland: Burrows Brothers.

Lev, D. S.
1972 Judicial Institutions and Legal Culture in Indonesia. In *Culture and Politics in Indonesia,* C. Holt, ed., pp. 246–318. Ithaca: Cornell University Press.

Lévi-Strauss, C.
1973 Stucturalism and Ecology. *Social Science Information* 12(1): 7–23.

Lewis, H. T.
1982 Fire Technology and Resource Management in Aboriginal North America and Australia. In *Resource Managers: North American and Australian Hunter-Gatherers,* E. Hunn and N. Williams, eds., pp. 45–67. Boulder: Westview Press.

Libecap, G. D.
1981 *Locking Up the Range.* Cambridge, Mass.: Ballinger.

Lindblom, C. E.
1959 The Science of "Muddling Through." *Public Administration Review* 19: 79–88.

Lips, J.
1947 Naskapi Law. *Transactions of the American Philosophical Society* 37(4): 397–492.

Livingston, J. A.
1981 *The Fallacy of Wildlife Conservation.* Toronto: McClelland and Stewart.

Livingstone, I.
1977 Economic Irrationality Among Pastoral Peoples: Myth or Reality? *Development and Change* 8: 209–30.

Lloyd, W. F.
1968 [1837] Lectures on Population, Value, Poor-Laws, and Rent, Delivered in the University of Oxford during the Years 1832, 1833, 1834, 1835, & 1836. Reprint. New York: Augustus M. Kelley.
1977 [1833] On the Checks to Population. Reprinted in *Managing the Commons,* G. Hardin and J. Baden, eds., pp. 8–15. San Francisco: W. H. Freeman.

Locke, J.
1939 [1690] An Essay Concerning the True Original Extent and End of Civil Government. In *The English Philosophers from Bacon to Mill,* E. A. Burtt, ed., pp. 403–503. New York: Modern Library.

Löfgren, O.
1979 Marine Ecotypes in Preindustrial Sweden: A Comparative Discussion of Swedish Peasant Fishermen. In *North Atlantic Maritime Cultures,* R. Andersen, ed., pp. 83–110. The Hague: Mouton.
1982 From Peasant Fishing to Industrial Trawling: A Comparative Study of Modernization Processes in Some North Atlantic Regions. In *Modernization and Marine Fisheries Policy,* J. R. Maoilo and M. K. Orbach, eds., pp. 151–76. Ann Arbor: Ann Arbor Science.

Lund, T. A.
    1980   *American Wildlife Law.* Berkeley: University of California Press.
Maine, H.
    1884   *Ancient Law.* 10th ed. New York: Henry Holt.
Malinowski, B.
    1918   Fishing in the Trobriand Islands. *Man* 18: 87–92.
    1926   *Crime and Custom in Savage Society.* London: Kegan Paul, Trench and Trubner.
Maril, R. L.
    1983   *Texas Shrimpers: Community, Capitalism, and the Sea.* College Park: Texas A & M University Press.
Marks, S.
    1978   Natal, the Zulu Royal Family and the Ideology of Segregation. *Journal of Southern African Studies* 4(2): 172–94.
Marks, S., and A. Atmore, eds.
    1980   *Economy and Society in Pre-Industrial South Africa.* London: Longmans.
Martin, B.
    1984   The Application of Territorial Property Rights to British Columbia Salmon Fisheries: Prospects and Problems. Manuscript.
Martin, C.
    1978   *Keepers of the Game.* Berkeley: University of California Press.
Martin, K. O.
    1979   Play by the Rules or Don't Play at All: Space Division and Resource Allocation in a Rural Newfoundland Community. In *North Atlantic Maritime Cultures*, R. Andersen, ed., pp. 276–98. The Hague: Mouton.
Marx, K.
    1967   *Capital: A Critique of Political Economy, Vol. 1: The Process of Capitalist Production.* Trans. from the 3rd German Ed. by S. Moore and E. Aveling. F. Engels, ed. New York: International Publishers. Orig. Publ. in 1867 as Das Kapital. . . . Der Produktionsprocess des Kapitals.
McCay, B. J.
    1978   Systems Ecology, People Ecology and the Anthropology of Fishing Communities. *Human Ecology* 6: 397–422.
    1979   "Fish is Scarce": Fisheries Modernization on Fogo Island, Newfoundland. In *North Atlantic Maritime Cultures*, R. Andersen, ed., pp. 155–88. The Hague: Mouton.
    1980   A Fishermen's Cooperative *Limited:* Indigenous Resource Management in a Complex Society. *Anthropological Quarterly* 53: 29–38.
    1981a   Development Issues in Fisheries as Agrarian Systems. *Culture and Agriculture* 11: 1–8.
    1981b   Optimal Foragers or Political Actors? Ecological Analyses of a New Jersey Fishery. *American Ethnologist* 8(2): 356–82.

1984   The Pirates of Piscary: Ethnohistory of Illegal Fishing in New Jersey. *Ethnohistory* 31(1): 17–37.

McCloskey, D. N.
1975   The Peristence of English Common Fields. In *European Peasants and Their Markets: Essays in Agrarian Economic History,* W. Parker and E. Jones, eds., pp. 73–122. Princeton: Princeton University Press.

McCourt, D.
1954   Infield and Outfield in Ireland. *Economic History Review* 7: 369–76.
1971   The Dynamic Quality of Irish Rural Settlement. In *Man and His Environment,* R. H. Buchanan, E., Jones, and D. McCourt, eds., pp. 43–61. New York: Barnes and Noble.

McDonald, D.
1977   Food Taboos: A Primitive Environmental Protection Agency (South America). *Anthropos* 72: 734–48.

McGuire, R., and R. Netting
1982   Leveling Peasants? The Maintenance of Equality in a Swiss Alpine Community. *American Ethnologist* 9: 269–90.

McKay, W., and K. Oullette
1978   *A Review of the British Columbia Indian Fishermen's Assistance Program 1968/69–1977/78.* Vancouver: Will McKay Consultants Ltd.

McKay, W., and J. Healey
1981   Analysis of Attrition from the Indian-Owned Salmon Fleet, 1977 to 1979. Report Prepared for the Native Brotherhood of British Columbia and the Department of Fisheries and Oceans. Manuscript.

McKean, M. A.
1984   Management of Traditional Common Lands (iriachi) in Japan. Paper Prepared for the Fall 1984 Workshops on Common Property and Environmental Management, Duke University, Sponsored by the Board on Science and Technology for International Development of the National Research Council, National Academy of Sciences.

McMullan, J.
1984   State, Capital, and Debt in the British Columbia Fishing Fleet from 1970 to 1982. *Journal of Canadian Studies* 19(1): 65–88.

Meade, J. E.
1952   External Economies and Diseconomies in a Competitive Situation. *Economic Journal* 62: 54–67.

Miller, P.
1978   A British Columbia Fishing Village. Ph.D. Dissertation, University of British Columbia.

Milner, A. C.
1982   *Kerajaan: Malay Political Culture on the Eve of Colonial Rule.* Tucson: University of Arizona Press.

Moerman, M.
1968   *Agricultural Change and Peasant Choice in a Thai Village.* Berkeley: University of California Press.

Moloney, D. G., and P. H. Pearse
   1979   Quantitative Rights as an Instrument for Regulating Commercial Fisheries. *Journal of the Fisheries Research Board of Canada* 36: 859–
   66.
Moore, S. F., and B. Myerhoff, eds.
   1975   *Symbol and Politics in Communal Ideology.* Ithaca: Cornell University Press.
Morantz, T.
   1983   An Ethnohistoric Study of Eastern James Bay Cree Social Organization. *Canadian Ethnology Service Paper 88.* Ottawa: National
   Museum of Man Mercury Series.
Morauta, L., J. Pernetta and W. Heaney, eds.
   1982   *Traditional Conservation in Papua New Guinea: Implications for Today,* Monograph 16. Boroko, PNG: Institute of Applied Social and
   Economic Research.
Morse, W. W.
   1978   Biological and Fisheries Data on Scup, *Stenotomus chrysops* (Lin-
   naeus). National Marine Fisheries Service, Northeast Fisheries Center,
   Sandy Hook Laboratory Technical Series Report No. 12. Fort Hancock, N.J.
Murphy, E.
   1967   *Governing Nature.* Chicago: Quadrangle Books.
Murtisari, T.
   1983   Interview. Ciawi, Indonesia: Centre for Animal Research and
   Development.
Neher, P. A.
   1978   The Pure Theory of the Muggery. *American Economic Review* 68:
   437–45.
Nelson, L.
   n.d.   Untitled manuscript. B. J. McCay's files.
Nelson, R.
   1979   Athabaskan Subsistence Adaptation in Alaska. In *Alaska Native
   Cultures and History,* Senri Ethnological Studies No. 4, Y. Kotani and M.
   Workman, eds., pp. 38–54. Osaka: National Museum of Ethnology.
   1982   A Conservation Ethic and Environment: The Koyukon of Alaska. In *Resource Managers: North American and Australian Hunter-
   Gatherers,* N. Williams and E. Hunn, eds., pp. 218–32. Boulder: Westview Press.
Netboy, A.
   1968   *The Atlantic Salmon: A Vanishing Species?* Boston: Houghton
   Mifflin.
   1974   *The Salmon: Their Fight for Survival.* Boston: Houghton Mifflin.
Netting, R.
   1972   Of Men and Meadows: Strategies of Alpine Land Use. *Anthropological Quarterly* 45(3): 132–44.
   1974   Agrarian Ecology. *Annual Review of Anthropology* 3: 21–56.
   1976   What Alpine Peasants Have in Common: Observations on
   Communal Tenure in a Swiss Village. *Human Ecology* 4(2): 135–46.

1981   *Balancing on an Alp: Ecological Change and Continuity in a Swiss Mountain Community.* Cambridge: Cambridge University Press.
1982   Territory, Property, and Tenure. In *Behavioral and Social Science Research: A National Resource,* R. M. Adams, N. J. Smelser, and D. J. Trieman, eds., pp. 446–502. Washington, D.C.: National Academy Press.

New Jersey Commissioners of Fish and Game
1897   *Annual Report.* Trenton, N.J.

News from Iceland
Jan. 1984   Reykjavík, January.

Nimpkish Band Council
1982   Submission to the Royal Commission on Pacific Fisheries Policy, Vancouver. Manuscript.

Nisbett, R., and L. Ross
1980   *Human Inference.* Englewood Cliffs, N.J.: Prentice-Hall.

O'Riordan, T.
1976   *Environmentalism.* London: Pion.

Oakerson, R. J.
1978   The Erosion of Public Highways: A Policy Analysis of the Eastern Kentucky Coal-Haul Road Problem. Ph.D. Dissertation, Indiana University.

Odell, M. L., and M. J. Odell
1980   The Evolution of a Strategy for Livestock Development in the Communal Areas of Botswana. *Overseas Development Institute Pastoral Network Paper 106,* London.

Olewale, E., and D. Sedu
1982   Momoro (the Dugong) in the Western Province. In *Traditional Conservation in Papua New Guinea: Implications for Today,* L. Morauta, J. Pernetta, and W. Heaney, eds., pp. 251–55. Boroko, PNG: Institute of Applied Social and Economic Research.

Olson, M.
1965   *The Logic of Collective Action.* Cambridge, Mass.: Harvard University Press.

Ooi, S. K.
1970   A Study of the Fishing Industry on Penang. B.A. Thesis, University of Malaysia.

Orans, M.
1969   Caste and Race Conflict in Cross-Cultural Perspective. In *Race, Change, and Urban Society: Urban Affairs Annual Review,* P. Orleans and W. R. Ellis, Jr., eds., pp. 83–150. Beverly Hills: Sage Publications.

Ostrom, E.
1977   Collective Action and the Tragedy of the Commons. In *Managing the Commons,* G. Hardin and J. Baden, eds., pp. 173–81. San Francisco: W. H. Freeman.
1985a   The Origins of Institutions for Collective Action in Common-pool Resource Situations. *Working Paper 14,* Workshop in Political Theory and Policy Analysis, Indiana University, Bloomington.

1985b The Rudiments of a Revised Theory of the Origins, Survival, and Performance of Institutions for Collective Action. *Working Paper 32*, Workshop in Political Theory and Policy Analysis, Indiana University, Bloomington.

1986 An Agenda for the Study of Institutions. Presidential Address, Public Choice Society Meetings, Phoenix, Ariz., March 29–31.

Ostrom, V., and E. Ostrom

1977 A Theory for Institutional Analysis of Common Pool Problems. In *Managing the Commons*, G. Hardin and J. Baden, eds., pp. 165–172. San Francisco: W. H. Freeman.

Paine, R.

1973 Animals as Capital. In *Cultural Ecology*, B. Cox, ed., pp. 301–14. Toronto: Carleton.

Pálsson, G.

1982 Representations and Reality: Cognitive Models and Social Relations Among the Fishermen of Sandgerði, Iceland, Ph.D. dissertation, University of Manchester.

Pálsson, G., and E. P. Durrenberger

1982 To Dream of Fish: The Causes of Icelandic Skippers' Fishing Success. *Journal of Anthropological Research* 38: 227–42.

1983 Icelandic Foremen and Skippers: The Structure and Evolution of a Folk Model. *American Ethnologist* 10(3): 511–28.

Panayotou, T.

1982 Management Concepts for Small-Scale Fisheries: Economic and Social Aspects. *FAO Technical Paper No. 228*. Rome: Food and Agriculture Organization (United Nations).

1983 Territorial Use Rights in Fisheries. *FAO Fisheries Report* No. 289, Supplement 2. Rome: Food and Agriculture Organization (United Nations).

Panoff, M.

1970 Land Tenure Among the Maenge. *Oceania* 40: 177–94.

Pastor, R.

1980 *Resistencias y luchas campesinas en la época del crecimiento y consolidación de la formación feudal Castilla y León, siglos X–XIII*. Madrid: Siglo Veinteuno.

Paulus, J.

1917 *Encyclopaedia van Nederlandsche-Indie*, p. 47. Eerste Deel; A-G. S'Gravenhage: Martinus Nighoff.

Pearse, P.

1982 *Turning the Tide: A New Policy for Canada's Pacific Fisheries*. Vancouver: Commission of Pacific Fisheries Policy.

Pearse, P., and J. Wilen

1979 Impact of Canada's Salmon Fleet Control Program. *Journal of the Fisheries Research Board of Canda* 36(7): 764–69.

Peters, P. E.

1983 Cattlemen, Borehole Syndicates and Privatization in the Kgatleng District of Botswana: An Anthropological History of the

Transformation of the Commons. Ph.D. Dissertation, Boston University.

1984 Struggles Over Water, Struggles Over Meaning: Cattle, Water, and the State in Botswana. *Africa* 54(3): 29–49.

In press The Ideology and Practice of Tswana Borehole Syndicates: Co-operative or Corporation? in *Cooperatives and Rural Development*, D. W. Attwood and B. F. Baviskar, eds. New York: Oxford University Press.

Picardi, A. C., and W. W. Seifert

1977 A Tragedy of the Commons in the Sahel. *Ekistics* 43(258): 297–304.

Piliavin, J., J. Davidio, S. Gaertner, and R. Clark

1981 *Emergency Intervention.* New York: Academic Press.

Pinkerton, E.

1983 Undercapitalization in a Local B.C. Salmon Fleet: The Case for Area Management. Paper presented at the International Congress of the Anthropological and Ethnological Sciences, Vancouver.

In Press Depending Communities. In *Uncommon Property*, P. Marchak, N. Guppy, and J. McMullan, eds. London: Methuen.

Polanyi, K.

1968 *Primitive, Archaic and Modern Economies.* New York: Andover.

Pollnac, R. B.

1984 Investigating Territorial Use Rights Among Fishermen. In *Maritime Institutions in the Western Pacific*, Senri Ethnological Studies No. 17, K. Ruddle and T. Akimichi, eds., pp. 285–300. Osaka: National Museum of Ethnology.

Polunin, N.

1984 Do Traditional Marine "Reserves" Conserve? A View of Indonesian and New Guinean Evidence. In *Maritime Institutions in the Western Pacific*, Senri Ethnological Studies No. 17, K. Ruddle and T. Akimichi, eds., pp. 267–83. Osaka: National Museum of Ethnology.

Pompanio, A.

1983 Namor's Odyssey: Education and Development on Mandok Island, Papua New Guinea. Ph.D. dissertation, Bryn Mawr College.

Pontecorvo, G.

1962 Regulation of the North American Lobster Fishery. In *Economic Effects of Fishery Regulation*, R. Hamlisch, ed., pp. 240–67. F.A.O. Fisheries Report No. 5. Rome: Food and Agriculture Organization (United Nations).

1967. Optimization and taxation in an open-access resource: the fishery. In *Extractive Resources and Taxation*, ed. M. Gaffney, pp. 57–167. Madison: University of Wisconsin Press.

Pontecorvo, G., and K. Vartdal, Jr.

1967 Optimizing Resource Use: The Norwegian Winter Herring Fishery. *Statsokonomisk Tidsskrift* 2: 65–87.

Power, G.

1978 Fish Population Structure in Arctic Lakes. *Journal of the Fisheries Research Board of Canada* 35: 53–59.

Prieto Bances, R.
  1976   *Obras escritas*. 2 vols. Oviedo: University of Oviedo.
Pyke, G., R. Pulliam, and E. Charnov
  1976   Optimal Foraging: A Selective Review of Theories and Tests. *Quarterly Review of Biology* 52: 137–54.
Radisson, P. E.
  1943 [1853]   *Voyages of Peter Esprit Radisson*. G. Scull, ed. Reprint. New York: Peter Smith.
Ramatlabama Ranch Management Centre
  1981   *The Management of Communal Grazing in Botswana*. Evaluation Unit, Ramatlabama Ranch Management Centre, Botswana.
Randall, R.
  1977   Change and Variation in Samal Fishing: "Making Plans to Make a Living" in the Southern Philippines. Ph.D. dissertation, University of California, Berkeley.
Rappaport, R. A.
  1967   *Pigs for the Ancestors: Ritual in the Ecology of a New Guinea People*. New Haven: Yale University Press.
Rappoport, L., and D. Summers, eds.
  1973   *Human Judgment and Social Interaction*. New York: Holt, Rinehart and Winston.
Rapport, D. J., and J. E. Turner
  1977   Economic Models in Ecology. *Science* 195: 367–73.
Ras, J. J.
  1968   *Hikajat Bandjar: A Study in Malay Historiography*. The Hague: Martinus Nijhoff.
Ray, A. J.
  1974   *Indians in the Fur Trade*. Toronto: University of Toronto Press.
  1975   Some Conservation Schemes of the Hudson's Bay Company, 1821–1850. *Journal of Historical Geography* 1(1): 49–68.
  1978   Conservation and Competition in the Early Subarctic Fur Trade. *Ethnohistory* 25(4): 347–57.
Ray, A. J., and D. Freeman
  1978   *Give Us Good Measure*. Toronto: University of Toronto Press.
Rearden, J., ed.
  1983   Alaska's Salmon Fisheries, [Special issue] *Alaska Geographic*, 10 (3).
Republic of Botswana
  1975   *National Policy on Tribal Grazing Land*. Government Paper No. 2 of 1975. Gaborone: Government Printer.
Rich, E. E.
  1960   Trade Habits and Economic Motivation Among the Indians in North America. *Canadian Journal of Economics and Political Science* 26: 35–53.
Ridington, R.
  1982   Technology, World View, and Adaptive Strategy in a Northern

Hunting Society. *Canadian Review of Sociology and Anthropology* 19(4): 469–81.

Robson, J.
1965 [1752] *An Account of Six Years Residence in Hudson's Bay from 1733 to 1736 and 1744 to 1747.* Toronto: Johnson Reprint.

Rogers, E.
1963 The Hunting Group-Hunting Territory Complex Among the Mistassini Indians. *National Museums of Canada Bulletin 195, Anthropological Series No. 63.* Ottawa: National Museums of Canada.

Rogers, E., and M. Black
1976 Subsistence Strategies in the Fish and Hare Period, Northern Ontario: The Weagamow Ojibwa, 1880–1920. *Journal of Anthropological Research* 32(1): 1–43.

Rogers, G. W.
1979 Alaska's Limited Entry Program: Another View. *Journal of the Fisheries Research Board of Canada* 36(7): 783–88.

Rohner, R. P.
1967 The People of Gilford: A Contemporary Kwakiutl Village. *National Museums of Canada Bulletin 225.* Ottawa: National Museums of Canada.

Roosevelt, A.
1980 *Parmana: Prehistoric Maize and Manioc Subsistence Along the Amazon and Orinoco.* New York: Academic Press.

Ross, E.
1978 Food Taboos, Diet, and Hunting Strategy: The Adaptation to Animals in Amazonian Culture Ecology. *Current Anthropology* 19: 1–36.
1980 Reply. *Current Anthropology* 21: 544–46.

Ruddle, K., and T. Akimichi, eds.
1984 *Maritime Institutions in the Western Pacific.* Senri Ethnological Studies No. 17. Osaka: National Museum of Ethnology.

Ruddle, K., and R. E. Johannes, eds.
1985 *The Traditional Knowledge and Management of Coastal Systems in Asia and the Pacific.* Jakarta: Regional Office for Science and Technology for Southeast Asia, UNESCO.

Rudé, G.
1980 *Ideology and Popular Protest.* New York: Pantheon Books.

Ruiz de la Peña, J. I.
1981 Fueros agrarios asturianas del siglo XIII. *Asturiensia Medievalia* 4: 131–96.

Runge, C. F.
1981 Common Property Externalities: Isolation, Assurance and Resource Depletion in a Traditional Grazing Context. *American Journal of Agricultural Economics* 63: 595–606.
1983 Common Property and Collective Action in Economic Development. Paper Prepared for the Board on Science and Technology for

International Development, Office of International Affairs, National Research Council.

Saffirio, J., and R. Hames
   1983   The Forest and the Highway. In *The Impact of Contact*, K. Kensinger, ed. Joint Publication of *Cultural Survival*, Report #11, and *Working Papers on South American Indians*, vol. 6, pp. 4–39, Cambridge, Mass.

Sahlins, M.
   1968   Notes on the Original Affluent Society. In *Man the Hunter*, R. Lee and I. DeVore, eds., pp. 85–89. Chicago: Aldine.
   1972   *Stone Age Economics*. Chicago: Aldine.
   1981   *Historical Metaphors and Mythical Realities*. Ann Arbor: University of Michigan Press.

Saleh, M. I.
   1981   *Agrarian Radicalism in the Movements of the Native Insurrection of the 19th Century in South Kalimantan 1858–1864*. Proyek Pengembangan Pusat Dokumentasi dan Informasin Bidang Ilmu-Ilmu Sosial dan Kemanusian. Jakarta: LIPI.
   1982   Interview. Banjarbaru: Museum of South Kalimantan.

Saleh, M. I., B. Jamal, A. Korach, and D. Yustain
   1978   *Sejarah Daerah Tematis: Zaman Kembangkitan 1900–1942 di Kalimantan Selatan*. Banjarmasin: Pusat Informasi Tehnick Pembangunan. Direktorat Jenderal Cipta Karya, Departemen Perkerjaan Umum.

San Miguel, L. G.
   1956   Un estudio sociológico-jurídico de la derrota. *Boletín del Instituto de Estudios Asturianos* 55: 436.

Sandford, S.
   1980   Keeping an Eye on TGLP. Gaborone: National Institute of Development, *Working Paper No. 31*.
   1983   *Management of Pastoral Development in the Third World*. Chichester: John Wiley and Sons with Overseas Development Institute.

Sansom, B.
   1974   Traditional Rulers and Their Realms. In *The Bantu-Speaking Peoples of Southern Africa*, W. Hammond-Tooke, ed., pp. 246–83. London: Routledge and Kegan Paul.

Saussure, F. de
   1966   *Course in General Linguistics*. New York: McGraw Hill.

Schaefer, M. B.
   1957   Some Considerations of Population Dynamics and Economics in Relation to the Management of Commercial Marine Fisheries. *Journal of the Fisheries Research Board of Canada* 14: 669–81.

Schapera, I.
   1943   *Native Land Tenure in the Bechuanaland Protectorate*. Alice: Lovedale.
   1956   *Government and Politics in Tribal Societies*. London: Watts.

Schelling, T. C.
1978 *Micromotives and Macrobehavior.* New York: W. W. Norton.
Schoener, T.
1971 Theory of Feeding Strategies. *Annual Review of Ecology and Systematics* 11: 365–404.
Schulz, R.
1977 Some Life and Death Consequences of Perceived Control. In *Cognition and Social Behavior*, J. S. Carroll and J. W. Payne, eds., pp. 135–53. New York: Academic Press.
Schwartz, T.
1963 Systems of Areal Integration: Some Considerations Based on the Admiralty Islands of Northern Melanesia. *Anthropological Forum* 1: 56–97.
Scott, A.
1955 The Fishery: The Objectives of Sole Ownership. *Journal of Political Economy* 63: 116–24.
1979 Development of the Economic Theory on Fisheries Regulation. *Journal of the Fisheries Research Board of Canada* 36: 725–41.
Sharp, H. S.
1979 Chipewyan Marriage. *Canadian Ethnology Service Paper 58*. Ottawa: National Museum of Man Mercury Series.
Shirvell, C. S., and C. Charbonneau
1984 *Can Stream Indexing Improve Salmon Escapement Estimates?* Prince Rupert, B.C.: Fisheries Research Branch.
Silitshena, R.
1979 Chiefly Authority and the Organization of Space in Botswana: Towards an Explanation of Nucleated Settlements Among the Tswana. *Botswana Notes and Records* 11: 55–68.
Simpson, G.
1931 *Fur Trade and Empire: George Simpson's Journal.* F. Merk, ed. Cambridge, Mass.: Harvard University Press.
Smith, C. L., and R. McKelvey
1983 Specialist and Generalist Participation in Fisheries. Paper presented at the XIth International Congress of Anthropological and Ethnological Sciences, Quebec City, August 14–17, 1983.
Smith, E. A.
1983 Anthropological Applications of Optimal Foraging Theory: A Critical Review. *Current Anthropology* 24(5): 625–50.
Smith, J. G. E.
1975 Preliminary Notes on the Rocky Cree of Reindeer Lake. In *Contributions to Canadian Ethnology, 1975*, D. B. Carlisle, ed. *Canadian Ethnology Service Paper 31*. Ottawa: National Museum of Man Mercury Series.
Smith, M. E.
1984 The Triage of the Commons. Paper presented at the Annual

Meeting of the Society for Applied Anthropology, March 14–18, 1984, Toronto.

Smith, N. J. H.
1981   Caimans, Capybaras, Otters, Manatees and Man in Amazonia. *Biological Conservation* 19(3): 177–87.

Speck, F. G.
1915   The Family Hunting Band as the Basis of Algonkian Social Organization. *American Anthropologist* 17(2): 289–305.
1935   *Naskapi*. Norman: University of Oklahoma Press.

Spradley, J., ed.
1969   *Guests Never Leave Hungry: The Autobiography of James Sewid, a Kwakiutl Indian*. New Haven: Yale University Press.

Sproule-Jones, M.
1982   Public Choice Theory and Natural Resources: Methodological Explication and Critique. *American Political Science Review* 76: 790–804.

Stainsby, W.
1902   *The Oyster Industry: A Historical Sketch*. Monographs on New Jersey's Industries from the 25th Annual Report of the Bureau of Statistics of New Jersey. Trenton, N.J.

Statistical Abstracts of Iceland, 1974
1974   Reykjavík: Hagsatofa Íslands.

Steward, J. H.
1955   Theory of Cultural Change. Urbana: University of Illinois Press.

Stillman, P. G.
1975   The Tragedy of the Commons: A Re-analysis. *Alternatives* 4(2): 12–15.

Stjornun fiskveioa
1980   Sjavarfrettir 1980 (12). Reykjavik.

Stocks, A.
1983a   Cocamilla Fishing: Patch Modification and Environmental Buffering in the Amazon Varzea. In *Adaptive Responses of Native Amazonians*, R. Hames and W. Vickers, eds., pp. 239–68. New York: Academic Press.
1983b   Native Enclaves in the Upper Amazon: A Case of Regional Non-Integration. *Ethnohistory* 30(2): 77–92.

Strong, W. D.
1929   Cross Cousin Marriage and the Culture of the Northeastern Algonkian. *American Anthropologist* 31(2): 277–88.

Sturgess, N. H., and H. Wijaya
1983   Rice Harvesting: A View from the Theory of Common Property. *Bulletin of Indonesian Studies* 19(2): 27–45.

Sweet, D. G.
1974   A Rich Realm of Nature Destroyed: The Middle Amazon Valley 1640–1750. Ph.D. Dissertation, University of Wisconsin. Ann Arbor: University Microfilms.

Swezey, S. L., and R. Heizer
1977 Ritual Management of Salmonid Fish Resources in California. *Journal of California Anthropology* 4(1): 6–29.
Talbot, L. M.
1980 The World's Conservation Strategy. *Environmental Conservation* 7: 259–68.
Taylor, K.
1981 Knowledge and Praxis in Sanuma Food Prohibitions. In *Food Taboos in Lowland South America*, K. Kensinger and W. Kracke, eds. *Working Papers on South American Indians No. 3*, pp. 24–54. Bennington, Vt.: Bennington College.
Taylor, L.
1980 Colonialism and Community Structure in Western Ireland. *Ethnohistory* 27 (2): 169–81.
1981 Man the Fisher: Salmon Fishing and the Expression of Community in a Rural Irish Settlement. *American Ethnologist* 8: 774–88.
1983 *Dutchmen on the Bay: The Ethnohistory of a Contractual Community*. Philadelphia: University of Pennsylvania Press.
1985 The Priest and the Agent: Social Drama and Class Consciousness in the West of Ireland. *Comparative Studies in Society and History* 27(4): 696–712.
Thomas, J.
1973 An Analysis of the Commercial Lobster, *Homarus americanus*, Fishery Along the Coast of Maine, August 1966 through December 1970. *National Oceanic and Atmospheric Administration Technical Report*. Washington, D. C.: National Marine Fisheries Service.
Thomas, R. P., and R. N. Bean
1974 The Fishers of Men: The Profits of the Slave Trade. *Journal of Economic History* 34: 885–914.
Thompson, D.
1962 [1784–1812] *David Thompson's Narrative*. R. Glover, ed. Reprint. Toronto: The Champlain Society.
Thompson, E. P.
1971 The Moral Economy of the English Crowd in the Eighteenth Century. *Past and Present* 50: 76–135.
1975 *Whigs and Hunters*. London: Allen Lane.
1976 The Grid of Inheritance: A Comment. In *Family and Inheritance*, J. Good, J. Thirsk, and E. P. Thompson, eds., pp. 328–60. Cambridge: Cambridge University Press.
Thomson, D.
1980 Conflict Within the Fishing Industry. *International Center for Living Aquatic Resource Management Newsletter* 3: 3–4.
Thorsteinsson, G.
1980 *Veiðar og veiðarfaeri*. Reykjavík: Almenna bókafélagið.

Townsend, R., and H. Briggs
1982 *Maine's Marine Fisheries: Annual Data 1947–1981.* Orono: University of Maine Sea Grant.
True, F. W.
1887 The Pound-Net Fisheries of the Atlantic States. In *The Fisheries and Fishery Industries of the United States,* sec. V, vol. 1, George B. Goode, ed., pp. 597–610. Washington, D. C.: U.S. Government Printing Office.
Tuero Beltrand, F.
1976 *Instituciones tradicionales en Asturais.* Salinas: Ayalga.
Turner, Victor
1974 *Dramas, Fields, and Metaphors: Symbolic Action in Human Society.* Ithaca: Cornell University Press.
Turvey, R.
1964 Optimization and Suboptimization in Fishery Regulation. *American Economic Review* 54: 64–76.
Umfreville, E.
1954 [1790] *The Present State of Hudson's Bay.* W. S. Wallace, ed. Reprint. Toronto: Ryerson Press.
van der Sande, G. A. J.
1907 Ethnography and Anthropology. *Nova Guinea* 3, 390 pp.
Vayda, A. P.
1986 Actions and Consequences as Objects of Explanation in Human Ecology. Paper Presented at the Second International Conference of the Society for Human Ecology, Bar Harbor, Maine.
Vayda, A. P., and B. J. McCay
1975 New Directions in Ecology and Ecological Anthropology. *Annual Review of Anthropology* 4: 293–306.
Veblen, T.
1919 *The Place of Science in Modern Civilization.* New York: Heubsch.
Vecsey, C.
1980 American Indian Environmental Religions. In *American Indian Environments,* C. Vecsey, ed., pp. 1–37. Syracuse: Syracuse University Press.
Vickers, W.
1980 An Analysis of Amazonian Hunting Yields as a Function of Settlement Age. In *Studies of Hunting and Fishing in the Neotropics,* R. Hames, ed., *Working Papers on South American Indians,* vol. 2, pp. 7–29. Bennington, Vt.: Bennington College.
Vondal, P. J.
1984 Entrepreneurship in an Indonesian Duck Egg Industry: A Case of Successful Rural Development. Ph.D. Dissertation, Rutgers University, New Brunswick.
Wagner, H.
1943 *Gaelige Theilinn.* Dublin: Government Printing Office.

Waiko, J., and K. Jiregari
  1982 Conservation in Papua New Guinea: Custom and Tradition. In
  Traditional Conservation in Papua New Guinea: Implications for Today, L.
  Morauta, J. Pernetta, and W. Heaney, eds., pp. 21–38. Boroko, PNG:
  Institute of Applied Social and Economic Research.
Weiner, A.
  1980 Reproduction: A Replacement for Reciprocity. *American Ethnologist* 7(11): 71–85.
Welch, W. P.
  1983 The Political Feasibility of Full Ownership Property Rights: The
  Cases of Pollution and Fisheries. *Policy Sciences* 16(2): 165–80.
Werbner, R. P.
  1980 Introduction. *Journal of African Law* 24(1): i–xvi.
Werlich, D. P.
  1968 The Conquest and Settlement of the Peruvian Montana. Ph.D.
  dissertation, University of Minnesota.
West Coast Information and Research
  1980 *Native People and Fishing: the Struggle for Survival.* Report prepared for the Nuu-chah-Nulth Tribal Council, Port Alberni, B.C.
Williams, G.
  1966 *Adaptation and Natural Selection.* Princeton: Princeton University
  Press.
Wilson, J.A.
  1977 The Tragedy of the Commons: A Test. In *Managing the Commons,* G. Hardin and J. Baden, eds., pp. 96–110. San Francisco: W. H.
  Freeman.
  1980 Adaptation to Uncertainty and Small Numbers Exchange: The
  New England Fresh Fish Market. *Bell Journal of Economics* 11(2): 491–
  504.
  1982 The Economical Management of Multispecies Fisheries. *Land
  Economics* 58: 417–34.
Wilson, J. A., and J. M. Acheson
  1981 A Model of Adaptive Behavior in the New England Fishing Industry. *Report to the National Science Foundation,* vol. 3 of the University
  of Rhode Island, University of Maine Study of Social and Cultural
  Aspects of Fisheries Management in New England Under Extended
  Jurisdiction.
Winter, S. G.
  1975 Optimization and Evolution in the Theory of the Firm. In *Adap-
  tive Economic Models,* R. Day and T. Groves, eds., pp. 73–118. New
  York: Academic Press.
Winterhalder, B.
  1981 Foraging Strategies in the Boreal Forest: An Analysis of Cree
  Hunting and Gathering. In *Hunter-Gatherer Foraging Strategies,* B.
  Winterhalder and E. A. Smith, eds., pp. 66–98. Chicago: University
  of Chicago Press.

1983   Opportunity-cost Foraging Models for Stationary and Mobile Predators. *American Naturalist* 122: 73–84.

Winterhalder, B., and E. A. Smith, eds.
1981   *Hunter-Gatherer Foraging Strategies: Ethnographic and Archaeological Analyses*. Chicago: University of Chicago Press.

Wolf, E.
1957   Closed Corporate Peasant Communities in Mesoamerica and Central Java. *Southwestern Journal of Anthropology* 13(1): 1–18.

Woodburn, J.
1972   Ecology, Nomadic Movement and the Composition of the Local Group Among Hunters and Gatherers: An East African Example and Its Implications. In *Man, Settlement and Urbanism*, P. J. Ucko, R. Tringham, and G. Dimbleby, eds., pp. 48–67. London: Duckworth.

Yengoyan, A. A.
1971   The Effects of Cash Cropping on Mandaya Land Tenure. In *Land Tenure in the Pacific*, R. Crocombe, ed., pp. 362–74. London: Oxford University Press.

Yost, J., and P. Kelley
1983   Shotguns, Blowguns, and Spears: The Analysis of Technological Efficiency. In *Adaptive Responses of Native Amazonians*, R. Hames and W. Vickers, eds., pp. 189–223. New York: Academic Press.

Young, O. R.
1982   *Resource Regimes: Natural Resources and Social Institutions*. Berkeley: University of California Press.

Zajonc, R.
1980   Feeling and Thinking: Preferences Need No Inference. *American Psychologist* 35(2): 151–75.

Index

Access, 13, 87, 171, 200, 202, 236, 302; controlling, 8, 11, 14, 39–40, 126, 208, 255, 342, 345; to fisheries, 147, 295, 385; lobster fishing, 40, 44–45, 375, 385–86; and ownership, 161–62; to resources, 202, 204, 226, 390; rights of, 17, 258. *See also* Open access

Africa, 19, 171, 181. *See also* Botswana

African Advisory Council (Bechuanaland), 180, 182

Agrarian individualism, 266–68, 270

Agriculture, 269, 280, 282; communal, 18, 217; cooperative activity and, 274, 278–79; shifts in, 282; wet rice, 21, 231–32, 235, 249

Agronomist movement, 266

Alaska, 345–46, 349

Alert Bay, 358; fisheries management in, 359, 367, 369n

Algonquian Indians, 11, 14, 121, 123, 126, 130–31, 141n

Aller (Asturias), 271

Allocation, 292; of fishing rights, 198, 216, 354; and land use, 251, 260, 304; of pastures, 84, 189–90; and private property, 250, 261n

Allotment: of land, 220, 223

Amazon, 11, 93, 103, 108, 109; conservation in, 102, 105; hunting in, 93, 98, 100, 104; resource depletion in, 96–97; resource use in, 12–13

Amigos de Aller, 272

Amigos de la Escanda, 272

Andalusia: commons loss, 268–69

Andecha, 278, 281–82, 284

Animal husbandry. *See* Grazing; Pasturage

Arnold v. Mundy, 202

Asociación de Vecinos de El Carmín de Felechosa, 271

Asturias, 266, 270, 285; commons in, 20, 267, 283–84, 286–87; commons loss, 268–69; community in, 274–75;

cooperative activities in, 273; cooperative institutions in, 24, 273, 275–82; municipal organizations in, 271–72

Authority, 9, 26, 253, 295; community and, 276, 305, 307; cooperatives, 292, 303–4; and use, 181, 188, 253–54, 257, 302; use conflicts, 242, 245

Autonomy, 184, 274

Banjarese, 234–35, 243

Barbasco, 115

Beaver trapping, 70–72, 83, 123–24, 133, 139

Bechuanaland Protectorate, 179, 180–82, 184. *See also* Botswana

Bella Coola Gillnet Area, 354

Bella Coola Indians: salmon fishing by, 353–55

Biology: and fisheries management, 311–12, 351–52; territoriality, 52, 54–55

Black Report, 388

Blackstone, William, 202

Borneo, 21; agriculture in, 232, 235, 239, 249n; common property in, 231; duck-egg industry in, 233–34, 236–37; fishing in, 238, 240, 242–43; land use in, 231, 238, 241; swampland use in, 246–48

Botswana, 17–18; government policies in, 180, 183; grazing in, 172–74, 179, 191, 194n; rangeland in, 185–87; water rights in, 189–90

Boundaries, 11, 135, 239; of communal land, 255, 258; defending, 44, 46–49, 58; delineating, 40–42; of grazing land, 187–88, 229; international, 380–81; of marine resources, 147, 203, 211, 380

British Columbia, 31, 350; fisheries management, 344, 346–49, 351–55, 358–59, 361–67

Buy-back programs: fisheries, 320

429

Maximum sustainable yield (MSY), 4, 86, 315–17, 326n

Melanesia, 143, 158, 160; land tenure in, 146–47. *See also* Ponam Islanders

Menhaden, 213–14

MEY. *See* Maximum economic yield

Migration: in Asturias, 270; in Borneo, 234; fur trade and, 133; and grazing practices, 189; in Japan, 260; in Switzerland, 260; Tigray, 229, 230n

Mobility: and animal husbandry, 188; land use and, 184; water sources and, 188–89. *See also* Migration

Models of reality: spiritual, 14–15

Montagnais: game depletion by, 124

Mountains: as commons, 270, 272–73

MSY. *See* Maximum sustainable yield

Municipal organizations: in Asturias, 271–72

Native Advisory Council (Bechuanaland), 180

Native Communities law (Peru), 118

Native Community status (Peru), 114, 116

Natural resources: access to, 202; common property and, 19; and ideology, 106; management of, 89, 93; ownership of, 17, 146; responsible use of, 9; stability of, 14

Neighborhood associations: and conservation, 271

Neighborhoods: organization of, 292

New England, 204, 227; fisheries management in, 205, 216

Newfoundland: fisheries control in, 346; fishing in, 204; fishing regulations in, 216n

New Jersey: fisheries in, 205, 210–12, 214–16n, 345; oystering in, 208–9

New York, 213

Nimpkish Indians, 31, 358–59

Nobility: land claims and, 269

Norway, 197, 199

Nutrition: protein and, 104–5, 106n

Oceania: marine resources in, 88, 143–44

October Revolution (Spain), 275

Ojibwa Indians: conservation by, 132, 134

Old law: in Iceland, 373–74, 391–92n

Old World, 196, 200; fisheries in, 198–99; laws and rights in, 197; poaching in, 200–201

Open access, 4, 7–8, 11–13, 19, 29, 175, 187, 195, 207, 214, 251, 311; and competition, 203; conflicts of, 241; defined, 326n; to fisheries, 198, 211, 213, 238, 313, 316–17, 377–78; in Iceland, 374; marine resources and, 62–63, 214; and resource use, 232, 312; to swamplands, 235, 240

Optimal-foraging management, 111, 113; by Cocamilla, 112, 114

Optimal foraging theory, 12, 13, 94, 104

Ottawa Indians: beaver trapping by, 123

Out-migration: community stability and, 112–13

Overcapitalization, 4; of fisheries, 313, 353, 390

Overfishing, 154–55, 206, 311; in Borneo, 242; in Iceland, 381–82, 385; in Malaysia, 329; technology of, 330

Overgrazing, 3–4, 174, 177, 257

Overhunting, 124, 132; in Canada, 125; by Cree Indians, 129–30; religious practices and, 138; trade goods and, 127

Overpopulation, 2, 6; and poverty, 3

Ownership, 7–8, 11, 234; access and, 161–62; colonial, 375; communal, 218–21, 224–27, 229, 251, 256, 260–61, 302, 370; concepts of, 305–6; and cooperation, 301; Cree Indian concept of, 71; of fisheries, 143, 215, 295; of fishing equipment, 216n; and fishing rights, 48, 73; of fishing technique, 156–59; full, 252; hereditary, 222–25, 227–29; and land use, 191; lobster fishing and, 42, 44–45; of marine resources, 146, 149; of natural resources, 11; Ponam Islanders and, 163; private, 179–80, 259; range management and, 183; and resource management, 164, 312; seasonality of, 247; and sovereignty, 181; trans-

Schaefer-Gordon model, 326n; and
fisheries management, 313–17
Schaefer, M. B., 313
Scotland, 197; fisheries management
in, 198–99
Seasonality: fishing, 242, 244–45; and
land use, 236, 238–39, 244;
ownership, 247
Sea turtles: conservation of, 153–54
Seigneurial land, 269, 270
Seigneurial protection, 280
Settlement patterns: hunting and, 96,
98, 103–5, 141n; in Ireland, 292–93;
swampland use and, 238; Tigray,
219–20, 224; of Tswana, 184
Sextaferia, 275, 276–77, 280, 282, 284,
288
Siona-Secoya: hunting by, 95–96, 98–
99, 103
Smith, Adam, 283
Snails, 237, 241; harvesting of, 238,
242
Social dramas, 358
Social judgment theory, 338
Social organization, 176; in Desa Satu,
231; grazing policies and, 188; in Japan, 257–59; land use and, 187, 191;
of Ponam Islanders, 145–46; water
rights and, 190
Social stratification: duck-egg industry
and, 246, 248; in Iceland, 373; Tigray, 226–28
Spain, 16, 20, 24, 195, 197; commons
in, 266, 268, 274, 287; fishing rights
in, 198–99; government programs
in, 272; property rights in, 288n. See
also Asturias
Spanish Civil War, 197
Spelt wheat: cultivation of, 272–73;
harvesting of, 278–79
Sports fishing, 199
Starvation, 124–25
Status, 248; and fishing rights, 163–64,
197–98; ownership and, 161, 163,
189; Ponam Islanders and, 159–60;
Tigray, 226
Subarctic, 11, 68; conservation in, 11,
12; ethnology of, 121; fish population, 74–77; fishing in the, 13–14,
76, 85

Subsistence: in Amazon, 108–9; cereal
crops and, 217; fishing, 73–74; on
Ponam Island, 145; and religion, 140
Supply and demand: in Borneo, 243;
fish, 245; fur trade, 127–28
Sustainable yield, 84–85, 111, 143, 250,
262, 316
Swamplands, 239–40, 243, 246; as
common property, 235–36; common
rights to, 21–22; conflicts in, 241–42,
244–45, 247; use of, 237–38
Swaziland, 181
Sweden, 197
Switzerland, 16, 261; communal tenure
in, 23, 254, 256–57; land use in, 259,
260–61; use regulations in, 255, 262;
use-rights in, 262
Syndicates, 186, 192; and land use,
190–91
Systems theory: control, 338

Taboos: food, 117, 118; hunting, 92–94,
100–102, 106–7n, 118
Taxation: of duck industry, 233; land
tenure and, 235
Technology: fishing, 64n, 85, 145, 147,
149, 204–5, 210–11, 213, 240, 295–
97, 319, 328, 347–48, 353–54, 359,
375–76, 379, 381–83; and fur trade,
126, 128–29, 133; and hunting practices, 101, 141n; limiting, 386; and
overfishing, 328, 330; ownership of,
156–58; territoriality and, 46–47
Teelin, 290, 295, 299, 304, 306
Tenancy: in Ireland, 292–93, 302–3;
use-rights and, 307n
Tenure, 22; changes in, 227; communal, 21, 253–59; conservation and,
134; of marine resources, 18–19, 88,
143, 146–47, 156, 165n, 209, 214. See
also Land tenure; Territoriality
Territoriality, 11, 15; benefits of, 52,
54–58; in Botswana, 17–18; conservation and, 51, 105, 135; defining,
342; economics of, 48; fishing and,
13, 72, 242, 345; of grazing land,
174, 187; hunting, 71–72; knowledge
of, 87; of lobster fishing, 13, 27, 37,
39–45, 58–59, 61, 63, 65n; in management, 59; Ponam Islanders and,

About the Editors

BONNIE J. MCCAY, associate professor of Anthropology and Ecology at Cook College, Rutgers University, received her Ph.D. from Columbia University in 1974. Her field research and writing have focused on the social, economic, and ecological relations of the fisheries of Newfoundland, New Jersey, and the Caribbean. Since 1979 she has been a member of the Scientific and Statistical Committee of the Mid-Atlantic Fishery Management Council.

JAMES M. ACHESON, professor of Anthropology and Marine Studies at the University of Maine, has done fieldwork in Mexico and in Maine. His research interests include economic anthropology and maritime anthropology. In 1975–76 he served as Social Anthropologist for the National Marine Fisheries Service. He has written numerous scholarly articles. He received his doctorate from the University of Rochester in 1970.